THE GUIDEBOOK TO
SOCIOLINGUISTICS

PRAISE FOR *THE GUIDEBOOK TO SOCIOLINGUISTICS*

"No one sees and synthesizes the theoretical connections between diverse strands of sociolinguistic research better than Allan Bell. His *Guidebook to Sociolinguistics* is comprehensive, up-to-date, and especially rich in fresh examples and perspectives."

John R. Rickford, Stanford University

"*The Guidebook to Sociolinguistics* offers ... integrated exercises derived from Bell's extensive research background and allows readers to experience both the operational details of primary analysis and the theoretical constructs that underlie the field of sociolinguistics. It's the perfect introduction!"

Walt Wolfram, North Carolina State University

"Allan Bell brings his great wealth of experience as researcher, teacher and editor of the *Journal of Sociolinguistics* to tell us not just what sociolinguistics is but how sociolinguistics is done. Best of all, he shows how we can do sociolinguistics ourselves."

Jenny Cheshire, Queen Mary, University of London

"Bell has provided a detailed and authoritative road map to sociolinguistics. Carefully structured, clearly written, lively and accessible throughout, the *Guidebook* introduces all the major traditions of sociolinguistics, pin-pointing the most important sources and perspectives, supported by a wealth of practical examples and exercises."

Nikolas Coupland, Copenhagen University
and University of Technology Sydney

THE GUIDEBOOK TO SOCIOLINGUISTICS

Allan Bell

WILEY Blackwell

This edition first published 2014

Registered Office
John Wiley & Sons, Ltd, The Atrium, Southern Gate, Chichester, West Sussex, PO19 8SQ, UK

Editorial Offices
350 Main Street, Malden, MA 02148-5020, USA
9600 Garsington Road, Oxford, OX4 2DQ, UK
The Atrium, Southern Gate, Chichester, West Sussex, PO19 8SQ, UK

For details of our global editorial offices, for customer services, and for information about how to apply for permission to reuse the copyright material in this book please see our website at www.wiley.com/wiley-blackwell.

Library of Congress Cataloging-in-Publication Data

Bell, Allan
  The guidebook to sociolinguistics / Allan Bell. – First Edition.
       pages ; cm
  Includes bibliographical references and index.
  ISBN 978-0-631-22865-3 (cloth : alk. paper) – ISBN 978-0-631-22866-0 (pbk. : alk. paper)
  1. Sociolinguistics.   I. Title.
  P40.B349 2013
  306.44–dc23
                                                          2013006625

A catalogue record for this book is available from the British Library.

Cover image: © nadla/Istock Photo
Cover design by Nicki Averill

Set in 10/12.5pt Minion by SPi Publisher Services, Pondicherry, India

1   2014

For K.

Contents

FIGURES

TABLES

PREFACE

Writing this text has been an odyssey through the field that has benefited my own understanding considerably. I have read more, more deeply and more widely in the discipline than ever before. And although I have been in sociolinguistics for decades, I have learnt a great deal that I had only been peripherally aware of in those strands of the discipline that I haven't practised directly. The historical review has been complemented by the up-to-the-minute reading required as Editor of the *Journal of Sociolinguistics*, at the rate of about three papers a week over many years. In that time I have also done a wide range of research of my own, which I have been able to make use of in many chapters, giving a hands-on flavour that I hope will benefit the text.

I have made my own task much harder in writing this textbook by taking an inordinately long time to deliver on it. At the time the book was signed, each of the chapters covered what was probably a major enough area of sociolinguistics to be served by its own textbook. By the time of finishing, each section within a chapter, and often subsections of those sections, has produced its own text. The field has grown exponentially in these years, increasing the challenge – and the fascination – of attempting to understand and corral the essence inside a single book.

Any textbook has to be selective, and I have omitted from this book some areas which I would like to have covered – most especially discourse analysis, which overlaps significantly now with much sociolinguistics. Discourse analysis does surface in several chapters, but I would have liked to give it its own chapter.

There are three areas of partiality within this text, which I hope will prove to be advantages. First, at times I break into the first person and use my own research practice, projects and publications as examples. I have always used hands-on examples from my own practice in teaching at all levels. Doing this puts students in touch with how research happens as well as what it finds. This occurs in many of the chapters: over 40 years in sociolinguistics my work has covered a good range of what the field does. The first person concentrates towards the end of the book where I tackle issues of language style and ideology, a primary research focus of mine.

Second, I refer to many studies that have been published in the *Journal of Sociolinguistics*, which I co-founded and edit. This is one of the two leading general journals in the field, and I am necessarily better acquainted with its contents than with *Language in Society*. I have read all the articles before publication, and interacted with their authors, across the past 15 and more years.

Third, the book offers what may look like a disproportion of New Zealand examples. My apologia for this is that while the country is small, it has been one of the most active sociolinguistic research sites on earth for the past 20–30 years, and much of that work earns its place in any international text. Our positioning in the world lends a perspective that is I hope beneficial to an international text. We are both periphery and centre – geographically and often socioculturally on the rim despite the internet, but at the same time part of the advantaged West, implicated as an active player in globalization. This dual perspective informs the book. I have been deliberately internationalist in the range of examples drawn on, as far as the available research permits.

Two themes arch over this book and are made explicit in the opening and closing chapters. One is a delight in the profusion that is language in all its variety. The other is a commitment to voices that are marginal in the world, to a sociolinguistics of equity. My hope is that students will be sparked by both of these.

One distinctive of my approach is that, as well as covering the content of sociolinguistics, the book is committed to acquainting students with how sociolinguistics is done. That is achieved by expecting students to conduct research themselves. This may be as small a project as a group undertaking conducted entirely in class, for example using internet data. Or it may be as major as a sole-authored thesis which takes many months under supervision. The experience of doing research is invaluable in flavouring the field for students, showing how findings are reached, and in encouraging them with the knowledge that they too can do research. In my experience, very few fail to rise to this challenge. The research activities in Chapters 3, 7 and 10 outline how to undertake a project.

The students in a sociolinguistics class are the most valuable of resources for information and data. In New Zealand my classes are usually marked by having a majority of bilinguals and multilinguals, but a class that is largely monolingual also has wide experience of linguistic variety that can feed into the content of the course. Many of the exercises invite this kind of involvement and reflection on students' own situations.

I have ordered the sequence of topics within the book on the pattern that I have found best in my own classes. I start with the macro – multilingualism at large in society – and move towards the increasingly micro specifics of particular varieties. A main reason for this is that in my experience, many students come to a sociolinguistics course with very little linguistic training behind them. Rather than overwhelm them with new terms on both the social and linguistic fronts, I introduce the linguistics gradually as the book moves towards the variationist material that requires the most skills. Teachers with students who have little linguistic background can skip the exercises that require too much technical competence. Some of these begin in Chapter 4 on language birth and death, then Chapter 5 on code switching, where some parts require knowledge of morphosyntax. From Chapter 7, more particular phonological capability is needed. In all cases I have tried to make the terminology as transparent as possible. Where help is needed, refer students to a dictionary such as the latest edition of Crystal, *A Dictionary of Linguistics and Phonetics*. My aim has been that the writing should be accessible to students of all university levels, drawing on my long-term experience as a science journalist in trying to make the difficult understandable. More advanced students will be able to use the book in more depth, for instance the exercises.

For most levels of students, teachers will want to select within the contents I have provided here, so let me offer some guidance on specific chapters. The case studies in each chapter can often stand alone or be omitted depending on the class's needs. Chapter 2.1–3 covers the basics on traditional approaches to multilingualism. Chapter 3.1 on language contact is essential background to the following couple of chapters. In Chapter 4, the teacher could choose to cover either language birth (4.1–3) or death (4.4–5), rather than both. Chapter 5.4–5 form a section on code switching that could be taught as a unit. Chapter 6.3–4 on speakers and audiences, 6.5 on speech acts and politeness, and 6.6–7 on interaction can be treated as separate topics. In introducing variationism, Chapter 7.2 on class, 7.3–4 on ethnicity and 7.5 on gender (plus 6.7) can each be the basis of a whole lesson to suit the emphasis of a course (see references under further reading in Chapter 7). Chapter 8.1–5 forms very much of a unit on language change, but the three frameworks in Chapter 8.6 can be treated separately. In Chapter 9 the content on language and tourism, language and globalization and linguistic landscape can be selected and expanded to focus on these themes. Chapter 10.2 on language attitudes can be treated independently. Chapter 11.1–4 is much of a unity.

There are nearly a hundred exercises in the book, and many tables, figures and examples also have a question or two attached to them. This will enable teachers to be selective in choosing those that suit their classes. They can also select within exercises: although questions are sequenced through an exercise, some can be skipped to serve the purposes of the class. Some exercises are explicitly set up for in-class work, others for solo or group attention.

For quick acquaintance with the contents of a chapter, the summaries in the second-to-last section of each of the core chapters are bulleted to match the sections and subsections in the body of the chapter.

There are some internet links given directly in the text (valid at the time of going to press). Some exercises make explicit use of the affordances of the internet and for many others, internet data can be sought.

One interesting fact I discovered during the back-reading for this book was that some often-cited studies did not actually do or find what the secondary literature at large commonly reports them to have done or found. Or that the thing a publication is cited for was marginal to what the study was aiming to do. Or that the study on which a particular received fact is based actually provided a very slight foundation for that finding. I have tried to represent what I read in the primary sources rather than what subsequent derivations have presented.

Since this book draws on a long time in sociolinguistics, I am hard put to call up all my indebtedness to mentors and colleagues over that time. I have made an unusual career for an academic. Having for decades worked as an editor and journalist as well as a freelance researcher, I came late to teaching – and discovered that I both enjoyed and was effective in it.

Thanks to institutions and colleagues who have hosted me during periods of writing on this book: the Research Center for World Englishes at the University of Regensburg and its Director, Edgar Schneider; the retreat centre of Schloss Mittersill in the Austrian Tyrol; and not least Catalina Café, Hobsonville Point, Auckland, where much of my reading occurs over a cappuccino. Also to colleagues, collaborators and mentors over several decades, especially Janet Holmes, Walt Wolfram and Donna Starks. I pay special tribute to the hundreds of scholar-colleagues whose work I have read and cited in this text, many of whom I know personally but many I don't: I hope you will find I have done you justice.

To my colleagues at Auckland University of Technology I am indebted for the most constant academic support, especially in the Institute of Culture, Discourse and Communication: Philippa Smith, Andy Gibson, Sharon Harvey, Jennie Billot. Alwin Aguirre has provided invaluable assistance with practical aspects of the book, and I am very indebted to his efficiency and reliability. And thanks to Trish Brothers for her meticulous proofreading skills, and to Thi Hang Nguyen for her assistance.

The students I have taught these past couple of decades from many countries have been especially central to this textbook. Some provided material which has informed the book, but in particular, our in-class interactions have shaped my approach although I have radically remoulded content covered in our courses.

My colleagues present and past on the *Journal of Sociolinguistics* have been my daily network in the field, and I have used the work of most of them in the book: Nik Coupland, Monica Heller, Adam Jaworski, David Britain, Lionel Wee, Devyani Sharma, Bonnie McElhinny, Rakesh Bhatt.

I am grateful to Philip Carpenter who commissioned this book so long ago he has probably forgotten, and to the current staff at Wiley-Blackwell, Danielle Descoteaux and Julia Kirk. My appreciation to Anna Oxbury for her high-quality copy editing.

Lastly to my whanau, for their support and sociolinguistic enthusiasm and expertise: my wife Karen, a Canadian Kiwi with her own track record in sociolinguistics, and Hester and Willem. I am proud of you and your different genius. And to Bonzer, a faithful companion who was named as an emblem of earlier New Zealand English and whose lifespan almost covered the length of the book's preparation.

1

WHAT ARE SOCIOLINGUISTICS?

Sociolinguists are professional eavesdroppers – not on what people say, but on how they are saying it:

> I am on a train heading out of London and I can overhear a young family of four sitting a few rows ahead. When I heard them boarding the train, I thought they were speaking French, but now I am sure I hear German, and then English.
>
> It turns out the father is speaking mostly English to his partner and their two young boys. He is obviously a native English speaker, but occasionally he switches into – fluent – French, and he uses some German to the older boy. The mother is speaking mainly French to her partner and especially to the younger boy. But she is also using a good deal of German, and a little English, although with a non-native accent. The older boy talks to his father largely in English but with a lot of German, and rather less French. His English accent has audible traces from both his father and mother.
>
> Then, to keep the children amused, the parents begin a song, the round Frère Jacques. But the next verse is Bruder Jakob, and finally Brother John. The trilingual switching is remarkable to me, the overhearer, partly because it seems utterly ordinary to the participants themselves.

This book is about the profusion of voices in society. It is about language as social fact and as identity bearer; language as interaction, as communication, as a bridge between self and other; language as expresser; language as delight. We are immersed in languages, dialects, varieties, genres, accents, jargons, styles, codes, speech acts. They eddy and swirl round us in an always-changing current of linguistic reproduction and creation. Each voice has its time and its place, its desire to be heard, its timbre. This is the linguistic profusion of Babel, that ancient story that I believe champions rather than condemns language diversity (see Chapter 12 for a re-reading).

The Guidebook to Sociolinguistics, First Edition. Allan Bell.
© 2014 Allan Bell. Published 2014 by Blackwell Publishing Ltd.

Language is also implicated in the shape of society. As well as a truth-teller, language can be a deceiver. Social inequities produce linguistic inequities, and language reproduces inequity in many areas of society: structures, demographics, power, gender, ethnicity, interaction, globalization. Not all voices are equally or easily heard. The founding theorist of sociolinguistics, Dell Hymes (1974: 195), distinguished three ways in which sociolinguistics may view the relationship between the social and the linguistic:

1   **the social as well as the linguistic**: addressing social issues which have a language component
2   **socially realistic linguistics**: basing linguistic investigation on real-society data
3   **socially constituted linguistics**: affirming that language is inherently social and society is inherently linguistic.

In opting for a socially constituted linguistics Hymes emphasized a concern for equity and how that is evidenced and substantiated in the voices of society – who speaks, who is listened to, who is valued, who is disregarded. 'One way to think of the society in which one would like to live is to think of the kinds of voices it would have', he wrote (1996: 64). In such a Sociolinguistics of Voice, linguistic equity is something that is not a given but needs to be achieved in society. It invites engagement. These are the two core ideas which run through this book: the profusion that is language, and the drive to a sociolinguistics of equity. I will return particularly to the second of these issues in the book's concluding chapter.

1.1   WHAT IS LANGUAGE?

Sociolinguists probably don't spend enough time pondering this most basic question. Sociolinguistics began in a time and place when most linguists treated language as if it occurred in a vacuum. In American linguistics of the 1960s the transformational-generative theory of Noam Chomsky was in the ascendant. This reduced language competence to an abstract ability to judge whether sentences were grammatical, and sidelined all other aspects of language behaviour as mere 'performance'. The focus on 'an ideal speaker-listener, in a completely homogeneous speech-community' (Chomsky 1965: 3) was at odds with any kind of interest in examining how language was actually used when people talked.

In this intellectual climate that was inhospitable to bringing the social into linguistics, Hymes became the leading early advocate of sociolinguistics. He took over Chomsky's narrow notion of linguistic competence and broadened it to encompass much of what Chomsky had treated as performance, coining the term **communicative competence**. Hymes's focus on 'the competence that enables members of a community to conduct and interpret speech' (1972: 52) shifts the interest away from the purely grammatical and on to native speakers' ability to use language in a range of social situations. Any learner of a second language knows that even if you can speak totally grammatically, unless you also know the right ways to use those grammatical sentences, you will sound nothing like a native speaker. Worse, you may offend or insult those who are native speakers. You have to know when and how to use the language as well as what language to produce.

Communicative competence involves not just linguistic knowledge, but cultural knowledge and interactional skills. How speakers and hearers function linguistically with each other in social context is a central concern of sociolinguistics.

I offer four characteristics of what language is to a sociolinguist. They follow one from the other:

1 Language is social

The stuff – the matter – of language is to be found not in mental judgements on sentences but in the **utterance** – the minimal unit in which speakers say things. And beyond that, in the **discourses** and **conversations** in which utterances gather. Language is situated, it has a context. There are speakers and hearers, a time and a place, a topic and a purpose.

Some of the best statements about this sociolinguistic view of language come from non-sociolinguists, although the terms they use may be different such as 'speech', 'discourse', 'message' or even 'the word'. The French philosopher Paul Ricoeur argued against the view that language was a disembodied, de-social matter. The social life of speech and discourse does not bracket out the profusion of language in order to get at the formality of the code:

> Whereas structural linguistics simply places speech and use in parentheses, the theory of discourse removes the parentheses. (Ricoeur 1981: 133)

2 Language is dialogue

Language happens between people and is shaped by them. It involves listeners as well as speakers, with all the consequent messiness of verbal interaction, where turn follows turn with interruptions, overlaps, utterances completed by someone else. Such real-world complexity is both the delight and the challenge of the sociolinguist. We are interested in hearers, in the audience. We should no more conceive of language without hearers than of a language that has no speakers. Language is co-created, in the words of another non-sociolinguist:

> *Word is a two-sided act*. It is determined equally by *whose* word it is and *for whom* it is meant. As word, it is precisely *the product of the reciprocal relationship between speaker and listener, addresser and addressee*. Each and every word expresses the 'one' in relation to the 'other' … A word is a bridge thrown between myself and another. If one end of the bridge depends on me, then the other depends on my addressee. A word is territory shared by both addresser and addressee, by the speaker and his interlocutor. (Voloshinov 1973: 86)

3 Language is profusion

The fruit of dialogue is **heteroglossia** – linguistic variety. Language cannot be tamed to an idealized standard. It is always and everywhere variegated, according to a collaborator of Voloshinov:

> At any given moment of its historical existence, language is heteroglot from top to bottom: it represents the co-existence of socio-ideological contradictions between the present and the past, between differing epochs of the past, between different socio-ideological groups in the present, between tendencies, schools, circles and so forth, all given a bodily form. (Bakhtin 1981: 291)

> ## Exercise 1.1   Language myths
>
> The book *Language Myths*, edited by Laurie Bauer and Peter Trudgill (1998), deals with 21 frequently expressed folk ideologies about language. Here are some of the chapter titles:
>
> French is a logical language
> Some languages have no grammar
> Italian is beautiful, German is ugly
> They speak really bad English down south and in New York City
> Aborigines speak a primitive language
> Black children are verbally deprived
>
> 1   These are language ideologies. Examine one or more of them. What sort of linguistic arguments can be advanced as evidence for it? How much do these justify the myth?
> 2   Are there linguistic counter-arguments to the myth? Specify them.
> 3   What are the social foundations of the myth? For example, what are the perceived characteristics of the people with whom a named language or variety is associated? How have these perceptions come about?
> 4   Where did the myth come from? Is there any truth in it?

4 Language is ideology

Language is not only – perhaps not even primarily – about communication of content. Rather it is about social meaning. That is, all language use 'indexes' social meanings, evokes places, periods, groups, classes, genders. It carries ideology, it serves power. Language 'tastes' of its former uses. Our hearers place us against the backdrop of all their prior experience of language. We cannot talk without giving ourselves away socially, ethnically, geographically. The indexing of social meaning is deeply embedded in language and its use. As George Bernard Shaw wrote in the preface to *Pygmalion*, words later paraphrased into one of the songs of *My Fair Lady*:

> An Englishman's way of speaking absolutely classifies him,
> The moment he talks he makes some other Englishman despise him.

Exercise 1.1 debates some other language myths.

1.2   WHAT IS A LANGUAGE?

When I begin teaching a class in sociolinguistics, during the first session I will ask the members of the class what languages they speak. A typical list – for a New Zealand university graduate-level class – will include English, Mandarin, Cantonese and Japanese. Often also German, French, Bahasa Malaysia, Afrikaans or Korean. Sometimes there is Khmer, Samoan, Māori, Italian, Spanish or Russian. Most students in the class will be speakers of two languages, several speak three or four. Occasionally someone claims to speak five or more languages – and usually there are one or two monolingual English speakers, from various dialect backgrounds. One student claims a language that is not spoken. New Zealand Sign Language is the native language of several thousand deaf New Zealanders. It was legislated as an official language in 2006. Sign languages have been recognized as full languages in a number of countries, but still struggle for recognition in many parts of the world.

This multilingualism offers a rich ground to examine and illustrate the social workings of language. A class with a dozen languages is a gift, because many of the topics and issues in the course are manifested in the experiences of the class itself.

Naming languages

But these acts of language naming are more problematic than they look. China regards Mandarin and Cantonese as dialects of the same national language, although many linguistic criteria – including mutual intelligibility – would differentiate them as distinct languages rather than 'Chinese'. The cluster of Romance languages (French, Spanish, Portuguese, Italian and so on) is arguably less linguistically diverse than 'Chinese'. The character system in which the language is written does not represent pronunciation so it enables the fiction of a single Chinese language.

We have the puzzle, then, that there are in the world languages that have different names but are linguistically very similar – Hindi/Urdu, Swedish/Danish/Norwegian, Serbian/Croatian. And there are other sets of codes that are linguistically very diverse but bear a single name such as Arabic or English. In addition, such definitions may run in one direction but not the other: Bulgarians may see Macedonian as a dialect of Bulgarian, but Macedonians do not regard Bulgarian as a dialect of Macedonian. Languages can also be qualified by various adjectives. What does it mean to call Tamil a 'minor' language when it has 70 million speakers? And Piedmontese a 'failed' language because it has never been adequately standardized (Tosco 2008)?

Naming a language, then, is a very social, very political matter. This is not surprising. The linguistic anthropologist Susan Gal writes (2006: 14):

> It may seem odd to say so, but 'language' was invented in Europe. Speaking is a universal feature of our species, but 'language' … is not equivalent to the capacity to speak … Languages in this limited sense are assumed to be nameable (English, Hungarian, Greek), countable property (one can 'have' several), bounded and differing from each other.

The notion of a language, and its identification with a nation, is an eighteenth-century European construct – but one that was imposed on the rest of the world through European colonization, which enthusiastically distinguished, defined and named 'languages' wherever it went. To avoid such judgements, sociolinguists may choose to use the more neutral term **code**. And they may prefer **variety** over **dialect** to avoid the latter's baggage of implied inadequacy and marginalization.

1.3 WHAT THEN *ARE* SOCIOLINGUISTICS?

The easiest way to begin grasping a field is to visualize it. Figure 1.1 tries to map the components, traditions, strands that have gone to make up sociolinguistics, and Table 1.1 schematizes some detail on the main elements. The large oval in Figure 1.1 represents the notion of what sociolinguistics encompasses. The three mid-sized ovals show the main approaches as they have developed from the mid-twentieth century. Most of the

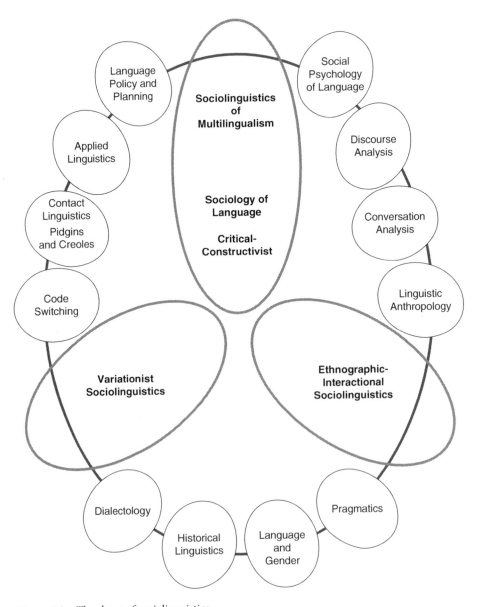

Figure 1.1 The shape of sociolinguistics

Table 1.1 Strands of sociolinguistics

	Sociolinguistics of Multilingualism		Ethnographic-Interactional Sociolinguistics	Variationist Sociolinguistics
	Sociology of Language	Critical-Constructivist		
Focus	How languages operate in a society	How language operates as social practice	How individuals and small groups use language	How linguistic features vary with social factors
Orientation	Towards society	Language, society, politics	Both society and language	Towards language
Discipline	Sociology	Anthropology, education, linguistics	Sociology, linguistics, anthropology	Linguistics
Premises	Empiricist	Constructivist	Interpretive	Empiricist
Scale	Macro	Macro and micro	Micro	Micro
Founders/leaders	Joshua Fishman	Monica Heller, Peter Auer	Dell Hymes, John Gumperz	William Labov
Typical research question	What language is used?	What linguistic resources are drawn on?	What language is used in particular situations?	What variety of a language is used?
Typical method	Survey	Discourse analysis	Participant observation	Recorded interviews
Typical findings	Language shift: from one language to another by different age groups	Language mix: multiple codes in globalized situations	Language use: different language codes used to different interlocutors	Language change: different linguistic features used by different age groups
Example study	Paraguay Joan Rubin	Corsica Alexandra Jaffe	British/Indian Englishes John Gumperz	New York City William Labov

areas of these three main ovals lie within the sociolinguistic circumference, but part is shown as beyond. The small ovals represent other areas which have varying levels of commonality with sociolinguistics but also have more or less purchase in other fields. The diagram comes with due warning: this kind of display has to be a severe idealization. It draws hard lines to show boundaries that are ragged, fuzzy and porous. It cannot show the subtleties of fields and sub-fields (that both columns 2 and 4 in Table 1.1, for example, may deal with multilingualism, though at different scales). But such idealizations will help me to map the terrain for this book.

We turn to what I categorize as the three main approaches in sociolinguistics: multilingualism, ethnographic–interactional and variationist. Table 1.1 lists some characteristics of each of these (which are of course subject to the same warning about reductionism as the diagram). The sociolinguistics of multilingualism divides into two. While historically the study of multilingualism was dominated by the sociology of language (column 2), that has shifted in the past couple of decades. Now more recent critical–constructivist takes (column 3) are increasingly important. Columns 2, 4 and 5 of Table 1.1 represent the three historical strands of sociolinguistics as it originated from the 1960s, while the second column shows what multilingualism research is becoming in the twenty-first century.

Sociology of language

The sociology of language arose in the 1950/60s and its interests were those of the American structuralist sociology of that time. Its orientation is to the large scale – it is sometimes called 'macro-sociolinguistics'. It concerns itself with whole languages and their distribution and usage within society and not, for example, with language features or structures or with more micro-social processes. Typically the focus is on the use of languages by particular groups. The usual research method is a survey asking who speaks what language – including that mega-survey of social information, the national census, which routinely includes a language question. The focus has often been on what languages a particular ethnic group speak, especially if their language preference is changing. Example 1.1 gives the flavour of a typical early study.

The sociology of language was founded by Joshua Fishman, its longtime chief advocate and theorist, and especially influential as an editor. He started the *International Journal of the Sociology of Language* and embarked on an editing and publishing programme. His *Readings in the Sociology of Language* (1968) and *Advances in the Sociology of Language* (1971, 1972) remain indispensable sources of early sociolinguistic work which ranged widely across the field. Fishman wanted to corral as much of sociolinguistics as possible into the sociology of language, and these early publications were very broad. But as work developed the label came to denote the specifically sociological strand. This approach still retains a role, as research instruments such as the survey remain arguably the best way to get rapid baseline information about languages in society. Chapters 2 and 3 major on this strand. With Chapter 4 on contact languages, they make up the first section of this book.

Example 1.1

Sociology of language
Choosing languages in Paraguay

Paraguay has two national languages – Spanish, as in many other Latin American countries, but also the indigenous Guaraní. So which language do people use and when? In the 1960s the American sociologist of language, Joan Rubin, conducted a survey asking what language speakers would use with a whole range of different people – their spouse, servant, godmother, boss.

Guaraní proved to be the language of intimacy, while Spanish is for acquaintances. Guaraní is the language of the country, Spanish is more likely in town. So what language do you speak with a barefoot woman? – Guaraní, of course. 'With your sweetheart making love'? – surprisingly, Spanish. With 'an unknown man wearing a suit' – Spanish. And with 'a woman wearing a long skirt and smoking a big black cigar'? – 89 out of 91 people said Guaraní (Rubin 1968: 519). Spanish was also used always and everywhere with a schoolteacher. In the capital Asunción more Spanish was used, and more Guaraní in the country. Spanish was favoured for formal occasions, but Guaraní for non-serious discourse.

It would be interesting to know whether and how these patterns have shifted over the intervening 50 years.

Critical-constructivist sociolinguistics

As sociolinguistics has been increasingly influenced by shifts in social theory, research into multilingualism has changed radically. Language has come to be seen as a social practice, with speakers drawing on all kinds of linguistic resources for their own purposes. Such research still focuses on macro issues of language in society – including the most macro of all, globalization. It may look at how minority languages are commodified and take on commercial value in the linguistic 'marketplace' of the nation. The work of scholars such as Jan Blommaert and Monica Heller has taken a leading role over two decades in reshaping the way in which we see languages as constructing society as well as being constructed in society (e.g. Heller 2011). Example 1.2 shows the sociopolitical nuances of one language situation.

To some extent the critical-constructivist stream has overtaken the sociology of language and increasingly predominates in the conduct and theorization of multilingual research. It offers both new questions, and new answers to old questions. The shift is well illustrated in the differences between the available handbooks of bi- and multilingualism. Where Bhatia and Ritchie's 2004 volume reflects the original paradigm, the handbook edited by Martin-Jones, Blackledge and Creese (2012) intentionally represents more recent critical and constructivist work. While some of the critical-constructivist work surfaces in my Chapters 2 and 3, it is more influential in Chapters 5, 6, 8, 9 and especially 10.

Example 1.2

> ## Critical-constructivist sociolinguistics
> ## Language politics on Corsica
>
> Philippe owns *U Carminu* 'The Fireplace', a tiny shop in the town of Bastia on the Mediterranean island of Corsica. He specializes in traditional Corsican products.
>
> But Corsica is part of France, and Corsican is a minority language in retreat as the community shifts to the dominant language, French. Philippe speaks fluent Corsican and identifies deeply with the language. He won a prize in a recent Corsican-language short story competition. He filled out the researcher's questionnaire about the language with enthusiastic detail.
>
> Philippe has also been in prison for nationalistic activity. His public identification with Corsican excludes Frenchness. He spoke only Corsican till he was 4 or 5, and still speaks it both naturally and intentionally.
>
> But his personal life does not match his ideology, linguistic anthropologist Alexandra Jaffe found in the course of a year's participant observation (1999: 13). His wife comes from Tunisia and can speak no Corsican. His children bear French names and are growing up not just in a French-dominated society but in a home where French in fact also predominates. Philippe keeps the languages separate in public but cannot do so in private. Although speaking Corsican is closely bound to his linguistic and nationalistic identity, this is in unresolved conflict with his home life.

Ethnographic-interactional sociolinguistics

Ethnography is an approach to social research which concentrates on how individuals and small groups behave and interact (Table 1.1). It has a strongly anthropological character, combined with the skills of linguistic analysis. The founding figures were John Gumperz and Dell Hymes, whose names are closely linked through their editing of one of the foundational collections of sociolinguistic articles (1972). Hymes's research concerned Native American languages and cultures, and in the 1960s he was the lead advocate for and theorist of emergent sociolinguistics, especially the 'ethnography of speaking'. In 1972 he founded the original sociolinguistics journal, *Language in Society*, which he edited for 20 years, exercising an enormous influence on the shape of the field. Hymes (1974) is a key collection of his writings.

Gumperz's and Hymes's approaches were broadly consonant with each other, but with very different working scales and methods. The 'interactional sociolinguistics' that Gumperz founded emphasizes research on the minutiae of language code choice in specific interactions. His fieldwork covered several countries. Two 1982 books bring together his own approach and contributions by his students. Example 1.3 is drawn from Gumperz's research.

Example 1.3

Interactional-ethnographic sociolinguistics
Interethnic miscommunication

Mr A is a fluent speaker of Indian English, a teacher of mathematics who has not been able to get a permanent job in England because he 'lacks communication skills'. He has been referred for an interview with Ms B at a centre which deals with interethnic communication problems in British industry.

The interview does not go well, running for a full hour on parallel tracks which never converge into understanding (Gumperz 1982a: 185). What has gone wrong? Early in the interview the teacher requests an introduction from the interviewer. She takes this to mean an exchange of names, and gives hers. The teacher responds: 'Would it be enough introduction'? (How odd!) As the interview progresses, he says 'I want to waive that condition.' (What condition and why?) Gumperz teases apart the tissue of pauses, intonations, false starts and interruptions to reach an interpretation of what the communicative trouble is.

The teacher's problem remains unclear even in Gumperz's exposition. Mr A tries to explain himself in the course of a half-hour narrative, which the interviewer punctuates with attempts to divert him to the point of the interview as **she** sees it – to identify what training he still needs. The exchanges are thick with misunderstandings of fact and misreadings of intent. The two speakers fail utterly to find common ground or to agree what is at issue. Although both parties' language is grammatical English, their different sociocultural conventions affect their speech production and interpretation at all levels, resulting in comprehensive and sustained miscommunication.

The turn to the critical-constructivist that has radically changed multilingualism research has come very naturally to ethnographic-interactional sociolinguistics, and there is a lot of commonality now between the approaches in columns 3 and 4 of Table 1.1. The second section of this book, Chapters 5–6, majors on ethnographic-interactional approaches.

Variationist sociolinguistics

This is the dominant paradigm in the United States, whose academy tends to set the trend for the rest of the West, but it is also widely adopted elsewhere. Its focus is on linguistic issues and its founder, William Labov, originally opposed the concept and label of 'sociolinguistics' because he believed this approach should be seen as the best way just to do linguistics. Variationism has focused on researching how particular linguistic features vary with different social factors such as age or gender.

Variationism works at the micro level linguistically, although its social dimension has been derived from traditional sociology. Most of the analysis is of the phonology of the

Example 1.4

Variationist sociolinguistics: the deviant case of Nathan B.

Nathan B. was a middle-aged man of the Upper Middle Class recorded by Labov in his study of New York English. He held a PhD in political science and had published several books.

But he pronounced his /th/ and /dh/ sounds with stops not fricatives: *dese* for 'these', *dose* for 'those'. His pronunciations were consistent with those of the lower class, not his own (Labov 2006: 158).

He had captained a debating team at university, but another student delivered the speech he wrote. He had been advised to take remedial speech lessons so he could get an academic appointment, but refused: there was no job, and he worked freelance. Even when striving to produce fricatives when reading aloud, he could not do so.

Nathan B.'s pronunciation difficulty was paralleled in perception. To a question about the operation of *fate* in people's lives, he responded: 'I'm very proud of my Judaic heritage, and when you mentioned the word *fate*, to me this means Judaism.' A non plussed Labov eventually caught on when Nathan B. spelled out: F-A-I-T-H. Labov counter-spelled: F-A-T-E, and the interview came back on track.

language, looking at where different speakers use different vowel or consonant pronunciations. The field has been dominated by Labov, whose interest has been more in language change than in sociolinguistic variation itself. His major work is contained in the three volumes of *Principles of Linguistic Change*, produced across 20 years. More recently, critical-constructivist approaches have become increasingly influential here also, as variation research deepens and diversifies.

The founding study was Labov's *Social Stratification of English in New York City* – see Example 1.4. Labov followed this with a project on the language of adolescent gangs, and the fruits of both studies were collected in two 1972 books, *Sociolinguistic Patterns* and *Language in the Inner City*. With colleagues, Labov founded the journal *Language Variation and Change*. Variationism has its own North American conference (NWAV), which has met annually for over 40 years. Chapters 7–9 of this book deal with language variation and change.

1.4 NEIGHBOURING AND OVERLAPPING FIELDS

So much for the major strands of the field of sociolinguistics. The dozen areas graphed in the small ovals in Figure 1.1 are a diverse set which more or less overlap with sociolinguistics. Some of each neighbouring field's interests are sociolinguistic, other interests fall elsewhere. I sketch these briefly, moving anti-clockwise round the largest oval, especially indicating those areas which I have been able to cover in this book and those which I have decided to omit.

Language policy and planning grew out of the sociology of language, with an interest in the configuration of languages within and beyond nations, and an applied outworking in policies for areas such as language education, maintenance and standardization. Here, I will not deal with policy and planning as such, but aspects of it surface in Chapter 3 on language maintenance, and Chapter 10, language ideologies.

Applied linguistics is a huge field in its own right with many links into and overlaps with sociolinguistics. Traditional applied linguistics is concerned with language teaching and learning, but 'linguistics applied' can cover many things that have a strong social emphasis, such as language and the law. I regard the social applicability of knowledge as important, particularly in its impact on equity. So, although I will not attempt to deal with specific topics, I return to principles of the applications of sociolinguistics briefly in the concluding Chapter 12.

Contact linguistics is mainly focused on the study of pidgins and creoles, languages that have resulted from contact. Much of the research takes account of the social context of these languages: their histories involve radical social injustice which their present situations still reflect. Chapter 3 introduces contact linguistics, and Chapter 4 both new-born languages and language death.

Code switching is when multilingual speakers mix their languages as they talk. Some code switching research involves a purely formal linguistic description of the ways in which the two languages intertwine structurally. However most approaches take the social context and shaping into account (Chapter 5).

Dialectology is a direct ancestor of sociolinguistics. Its traditional focus since the nineteenth century was on rural dialects, but Labov took it into urban areas and revolutionized its methods. Dialectology has been reconfigured and revived through its crossing with sociolinguistics (Chapter 9).

Historical linguistics studies how languages have changed in the past, often with little regard for the society in which the changes took place. Labov devised methods to investigate and explain language change in the present and in its social context (Chapter 8).

Language and gender interact throughout society. With the rise of twentieth-century feminism, gender discrimination through language became a target for both research and activism. Some of the most innovative work in sociolinguistics has focused on gender/language issues and made them central to much sociolinguistic theorizing. See Chapters 6, 7, 8, 10 and 11.

Pragmatics examines language use in its immediate interactional context. It can involve just formalistic descriptions, but usually there is a necessary social dimension. Pragmatic research overlaps a good deal with sociolinguistic accounts of syntactic and discourse variation (Chapter 6).

Linguistic Anthropology (or anthropological linguistics) also overlaps significantly with sociolinguistics, involving particular methods rather than different subject matter. Early sociolinguistics was partly nurtured under the wing of anthropology in both the United States and the United Kingdom. Anthropological approaches have always been influential on both sociolinguistic theory and method, starting with Hymes and Gumperz and continuing today through the critical–constructivist turn. Most of the book's chapters touch on linguistic anthropological matters, but see especially 5, 6 and 10.

Conversation Analysis (CA) is interested in the detailed investigation of verbal interaction, the rules by which conversation operates, and the way in which the participants understand what is going on between them. Traditionally it sidelines social forces and motivations and operates as a formalistic description of language use. Although it is increasingly open to the role of the social in conversation, Conversation Analysis will not be covered in this book.

Discourse Analysis is a field closely linked to sociolinguistics by its interest in the social and political significance of language. For Critical Discourse Analysis, this lies particularly in the implication of language in social inequity. Many sociolinguists work with discourse data, for example in language ideology research, and there are major sociolinguistic implications in discourse patterns. Although discourse surfaces especially in Chapters 6 and 8–11, discourse analysis is the overlapping field that I most regret lacking space or time to include in this book.

The **social psychology of language** studies language attitudes, the role of language in group behaviour and relations, and language and ethnicity. Its interests overlap considerably with sociolinguistics, to which it brings a different disciplinary take and methodology that can feel either alien or stimulating to the sociolinguist. It appears in Chapters 2, 3 and 10.

1.5   A GUIDE TO THE GUIDEBOOK

The book's trajectory

Twin principles of linguistic profusion and social engagement underlie this book. On this basis the book aims to attune you to the sociolinguistic life that is about you, to:

- give you a sense of the shape of sociolinguistics, its content, concepts and terms
- give you an understanding of sociolinguistic research – its goals, its methods, its findings
- introduce you to the methods and skills of doing sociolinguistic research, and offer hands-on experience of doing it
- present you with the opportunity to reflect on your own sociolinguistic situation – the profusion of languages and voices which are part of your life
- offer you the chance to engage with how language affects and constitutes society, in particular where that produces inequity.

The book proceeds from the macro to the micro – the order in which I have expounded the strands of sociolinguistics in this chapter. This enables me to ease the narrative towards those areas of sociolinguistics that demand more linguistic terminology and skills rather than beginning with them. The core chapters of the book (2–11) effectively fall into four parts of two or three chapters each. The first three of these parts deal with the historical strands of sociolinguistics as shown in columns 2, 4 and 5 of Table 1.1. I begin with languages and their configuration in society at large, so Chapters 2–4 cover largely multilingualism and its issues. The second section moves on to the more micro choices that speakers make in using language on the ground, in Chapters 5 and 6 – the ethnographic-interactional strand. Refining the linguistic focus further, Chapters 7–9 cover language variation, change and contact between dialects. Finally, the book rounds up with two chapters which bring together many of its underlying themes and interests: language ideology (10) and style and identity (11). The critical-constructivist strand surfaces as a major trend in all chapters from 5 onwards.

Each chapter offers some 15–20 exercises, examples, tables and figures (the Preface provides notes on these for teachers). And all of the core chapters end with a standard sequence of the following four sections:

- Case study: a particular issue, person or piece of research, which is addressed in some depth. These range from recent work to classic studies of 50 years ago, from theoretical issues to practice, from Brazil to Vanuatu, from Marlene Dietrich to M. M. Bakhtin.
- Research activity: a range of tasks, methods and issues which complement the exposition throughout the book. These deal with areas such as bilingual surveys, linguistic landscape, internet language, ethnography. In particular three of the activities teach the conduct of a sociolinguistic project, of any scale, in nine steps. These are spelled out in the activity sections of Chapters 3, 7 and 10.
- Summary: a list of bullet points which précis the sections of the chapter.
- Further reading: guidance on articles, books, readers and journals which offer more detail on the matter of the chapter.

General reading

While the further reading at the end of each chapter recommends references specific to that chapter's topics, there are general publications which encompass a wide swathe of sociolinguistics. These are the readers, handbooks, multi-volume collections and journals (and of course, other introductory textbooks …). Some of these I have found invaluable aids in my own research for this book. Here are my recommendations:

- **Handbooks**: The Cambridge (Mesthrie 2011), Sage (Wodak, Johnstone and Kerswill 2011) and Oxford (Bayley, Cameron and Lucas 2013) *Handbooks of Sociolinguistics* contain newly commissioned articles, with some excellent content. They are major publications and with remarkably different strengths. There are also handbooks in specific areas (such as language policy, Spolsky 2012) or in overlapping fields (e.g. linguistic anthropology, Duranti 2004).
- **Readers**: Two readers – collections of existing articles – are Coupland and Jaworski (2009b) and Meyerhoff and Schleef (2010), although the latter makes a lot of cuts within articles.
- **Collections**: Routledge publishes a wonderful series of collections, each between four and six volumes, which bring together up to a hundred of the key contributions – historical and recent – to a part of the field. For this textbook I have found these a great resource on areas of sociolinguistics that I have not known so well. They are also an ideal place to find hard-to-locate articles – including many cited in this book's references – on *Sociolinguistics* (edited by Coupland and Jaworski 2009a), *Anthropological Linguistics* (Schieffelin and Garrett 2011), *Language and Gender* (Ehrlich 2008), *Bilingualism and Multilingualism* (Li Wei 2010), *Contact Languages* (Holm and Michaelis 2009) and *World Englishes* (Bolton and Kachru 2006).
- **Journals**: *Language in Society* and the *Journal of Sociolinguistics* are the field's general journals, the former with a 40-year-plus history. The *International Journal of the*

Sociology of Language carries mainly theme issues on languages or regions. *Language, Language & Communication, Journal of Linguistic Anthropology* and *American Speech* all publish quite widely across sociolinguistics. More specialist – in accord with their titles – are *Language Variation and Change, English World-Wide, Journal of Pragmatics, Journal of Multilingual and Multicultural Development* and *Journal of Language and Social Psychology*.

Doing sociolinguistics

My belief is that the best way to learn sociolinguistics – including at the most introductory level – is to **do** sociolinguistics. So in this book I talk about how sociolinguists do their work as well as what they have found. And I anticipate that – regardless of whether you are a first-

---

Exercise 1.2   The Guidebook Quiz

Sociolinguistics abounds in the eccentric stuff of human nature and endeavour. You will find the answers to the following questions (and many more …) in this book. In my class the first student to come back with all the answers – *and* the number of the page where they found them – will be rewarded with a chocolate fish.

1   What national language is named after an aphrodisiac?

2   Why was the sociolinguist looking for the fourth floor?

3   Who said this, and about whom?
     If she had nothing more than her voice she could break your heart with it.

4   What language classifies 'women, fire and dangerous things' together?

5   The American from another state thought the man from Michigan said:
     Belle's body just caught the fit gnat.
     But what had the Michigander really said?

6   What sociolinguistic theorist smoked away the last remaining copy of one of his own book manuscripts, and why?

7   Where will you find a shop called *No socks, no panties*?

8   Who said this, where and why?
     High tide on the sound side, last night the water fire, tonight the moon shine. No fish. What do you suppose the matter, Uncle Woods?

9   Who was James Murray and how many languages did he know?

10   One man complimented another: *I like that shirt on you.*
     The other responded: *Thanks, I like your face.*
     Why?

11   Who wears dark eyeliner, tight jeans, fringed rawhide boots – and tense front vowels?

12   Who spent the last five years of the nineteenth century cycling round France interviewing 700 people, and why?

13   And why a chocolate fish?!

year or a postgraduate – you, the student, will do research. The nature and the level of research will differ widely, ranging from a limited, joint, in-class undertaking to significant months-long individual projects which you design and carry out yourself under guidance. I also expect that you will find this prospect daunting – but it is my experience that nearly every student who is challenged to undertake a piece of research in this way will bring it off. The research activity in Chapter 3.6 will introduce you to how to start a project.

The next chapter begins our discussion of multilingualism. But before you begin that, test yourself on the Guidebook Quiz on quirky facts in sociolinguistics (Exercise 1.2). Then as you move through the book, return to the unanswered questions until you complete it.

REFERENCES

Bakhtin, M.M., 1981 [1935]. 'Discourse in the novel'. In M.M. Bakhtin, *The Dialogic Imagination*. Austin, TX: University of Texas Press. 259–422.

Bauer, Laurie and Peter Trudgill (eds), 1998. *Language Myths*. Harmondsworth: Penguin.

Bayley, Robert, Richard Cameron and Ceil Lucas (eds), 2013. *The Oxford Handbook of Socio-linguistics*. New York: Oxford.

Bhatia, Tej K. and William C. Ritchie (eds), 2004. *The Handbook of Bilingualism*. Malden, MA: Blackwell Publishing.

Bolton, Kingsley and Braj B. Kachru (eds), 2006. *World Englishes (Critical Concepts in Linguistics)*, 6 vols. London: Routledge.

Chomsky, Noam, 1965. *Aspects of the Theory of Syntax*. Cambridge, MA: MIT Press.

Coupland, Nikolas and Adam Jaworski (eds), 2009a. *Sociolinguistics (Critical Concepts in Linguistics)*, 6 vols. London: Routledge.

Coupland, Nikolas and Adam Jaworski (eds), 2009b. *The New Sociolinguistics Reader* (2nd edn). Basingstoke, UK: Palgrave Macmillan.

Duranti, Alessandro (ed.), 2004. *A Companion to Linguistic Anthropology*. Malden, MA: Blackwell.

Ehrlich, Susan (ed.), 2008. *Language and Gender* (4 vols). London: Routledge.

Fishman, Joshua A. (ed.), 1968. *Readings in the Sociology of Language*. The Hague: Mouton.

Fishman, Joshua A. (ed.), 1971. *Advances in the Sociology of Language*, vol. 1: *Basic Concepts, Theorys and Problems – Alternative Approaches*. The Hague: Mouton.

Fishman, Joshua A. (ed.), 1972. *Advances in the Sociology of Language*, vol. 2: *Selected Studies and Applications*. The Hague: Mouton.

Gal, Susan, 2006. 'Migration, minorities and multilingualism: language ideologies in Europe'. In Clare Mar-Molinero and Patrick Stevenson (eds), *Language Ideologies, Policies and Practices: Language and the Future of Europe*. Basingstoke, UK: Palgrave Macmillan. 13–27.

Giles, Howard, Richard Y. Bourhis and Donald M. Taylor, 1977. 'Towards a theory of language in ethnic group relations'. In Howard Giles (ed.), *Language, Ethnicity and Intergroup Relations*. London: Academic Press. 307–48.

Gumperz, John J., 1982a. *Discourse Strategies*. Cambridge: Cambridge University Press.

Gumperz, John J. and Dell Hymes (eds), 1972. *Directions in Sociolinguistics*. New York: Holt, Rinehart & Winston.

Heller, Monica, 2011. *Paths to Post-nationalism: A Critical Ethnography of Language and Identity*. New York: Oxford University Press.

Holm, John and Susanne Michaelis (eds), 2009. *Contact Languages (Critical Concepts in Language Studies)*, 5 vols. London: Routledge.

Hymes, Dell, 1972. 'Models of the interaction of language and social life'. In John J. Gumperz and Dell Hymes (eds), *Directions in Sociolinguistics*. New York: Holt, Rinehart & Winston. 35–71.

Hymes, Dell, 1974. *Foundations in Sociolinguistics: An Ethnographic Approach*. Philadelphia, PA: University of Pennsylvania Press.

Hymes, Dell, 1996. *Ethnography, Linguistics, Narrative Inequality: Toward an Understanding of Voice*. London: Taylor & Francis.

Jaffe, Alexandra, 1999. *Ideologies in Action: Language Politics on Corsica*. Berlin: Mouton de Gruyter.

Labov, William, 1972a. *Language in the Inner City: Studies in the Black English Vernacular*. Philadelphia, PA: University of Pennsylvania Press.

Labov, William, 1972b. *Sociolinguistic Patterns*. Philadelphia, PA: University of Pennsylvania Press.

Labov, William, 2006. *The Social Stratification of English in New York City* (2nd edn). Cambridge: Cambridge University Press.

Li Wei (ed.), 2010. *Bilingualism and Multilingualism: Critical Concepts in Linguistics* (4 vols). London: Routledge.

Martin-Jones, Marilyn, Adrian Blackledge and Angela Creese (eds), 2012. *The Routledge Handbook of Multilingualism*. London: Routledge.

Mesthrie, Rajend (ed.), 2011. *The Cambridge Handbook of Sociolinguistics*. Cambridge: Cambridge University Press.

Meyerhoff, Miriam and Erik Schleef (eds), 2010. *The Routledge Sociolinguistics Reader*. London: Routledge.

Ricoeur, Paul, 1981. *Paul Ricoeur: Hermeneutics and the Human Sciences – Essays on Language, Action and Interpretation* (ed. and trans. John B. Thompson). Cambridge: Cambridge University Press; and Paris, France: Éditions de la Maison des Sciences de l'Homme.

Rubin, Joan, 1968. 'Bilingual usage in Paraguay'. In Joshua A. Fishman (ed.), *Readings in the Sociology of Language*. The Hague: Mouton. 512–30.

Schieffelin, Bambi B. and Paul B. Garrett (eds), 2011. *Anthropological Linguistics (Critical Concepts in Language Studies)*, 5 vols. London: Routledge.

Spolsky, Bernard (ed.), 2012. *The Cambridge Handbook of Language Policy*. Cambridge: Cambridge University Press.

Tosco, Mauro, 2008. 'Introduction: *Ausbau* is everywhere!' *International Journal of the Sociology of Language* 191: 1–16.

Voloshinov, V.N., 1973 [1929]. *Marxism and the Philosophy of Language*. New York: Seminar Press.

Wodak, Ruth, Barbara Johnstone and Paul Kerswill (eds), 2011. *The Sage Handbook of Sociolinguistics*. London: Sage.

2

A PROFUSION OF LANGUAGES

Chapters 2 to 4 of this book deal with multilingualism, mainly from a large-scale social perspective. In these three chapters we focus on how languages operate and are distributed in societies, and how they are researched. We look at contact between languages, how that can lead to language shift and loss, and at efforts to maintain endangered languages (Chapter 3). We examine the death and the birth of languages, both of which can occur as a result of contact (Chapter 4).

2.1 BEING MULTILINGUAL

Here is a case of significant, if specialist, multilingualism:

> I have to state that Philology, both Comparative and special, has been my favourite pursuit during the whole of my life, and that I possess a general acquaintance with the languages & literature of the Aryan and Syro-Arabic classes – not indeed to say that I am familiar with all or nearly all of these, but that I possess that general lexical & structural knowledge which makes the intimate knowledge only a matter of a little application. With several I have a more intimate acquaintance as with the Romance tongues, Italian, French, Catalan, Spanish, Latin & in a less degree Portuguese, Vaudois, Provençal & various dialects. In the Teutonic branch, I am tolerably familiar with Dutch (having at my place of business correspondence to read in Dutch, German, French & occasionally other languages) Flemish, German and Danish. In Anglo-Saxon and Moeso-Gothic my studies have been much closer, I having prepared some works for publication upon these languages. I know a little of the Celtic, and am at present engaged with the Sclavonic, having obtained a useful knowledge of Russian. In the Persian, Achaemenian Cuneiform, & Sanscrit branches, I know for the purposes of Comparative Philology. I have sufficient knowledge of Hebrew & Syriac to read at sight the O.[ld] T.[estament] and Peshito; to

The Guidebook to Sociolinguistics, First Edition. Allan Bell.
© 2014 Allan Bell. Published 2014 by Blackwell Publishing Ltd.

a less degree I know Aramaic Arabic, Coptic and Phenician to the point where it was left by Gesenius.

The text comes from a draft of a letter of application for a position at the British Museum Library, written by James Murray and dated 20 November 1866 (cited in Murray 1977: 70). He later became founder-editor of the Oxford English Dictionary. This application was unsuccessful.

- *How many languages is Murray claiming?*

Most of the world is bilingual – knowing more than one language – or multilingual, knowing more than two. Yet monolingualism is often regarded as somehow natural, and multilingualism as a deviation. This view has its roots in the development of the Western European nation-state, which presented 'one nation – one language' as the political ideal. Other languages that existed within the borders of the pioneer nation-states were marginalized and diminished through policies and practices ranging from passive neglect to active banning.

The monolingualism of the early western nations was always only partial, a construct which ignored facts that did not fit. The Celtic fringe languages such as Welsh in Britain and Breton in France were stubborn in their persistence. Neither German nor Italian were – or are – unified languages. Both encompass dialects so linguistically different that they merit classification as separate languages. Speakers of German dialects on the northwest border with the Netherlands may understand Dutch more easily than they do dialects of Austrian German from the southeast. At the same time, the eastern European empires with their sprawling multilingualisms also made a clear nonsense of the myth of the monolingual state.

In the second half of the twentieth century, the recently achieved 'monolingualisms' of the European states faced another challenge from post-war immigration, which across 50 years brought in sizeable minorities who did not share the majority language of their new nation. Speakers of Urdu and Jamaican Creole settled in the United Kingdom, Turkish and Slovenian in Germany, Arabic and various creoles in France. These immigrations are one side of the sociolinguistics of postcolonialism, feeding into the globalization processes that have also brought increasing numbers of Spanish speakers into the United States. Another side was the independence of the former colonies which led to a felt need for new nations to have a national language. The legacy of these political moves and movements is that in the world of nation-states multilingualism is rife although monolingualism may be treated as the goal. In this discourse, a shift towards monolingualism may be framed as an evolution-like progression, part of the wider socioeconomic development of emerging, postcolonial states. But scholars like Heller (2007b) and Auer and Li Wei (2007b) argue there is an ideological bias towards monolingualism in much practice and thinking about language.

In this chapter I prefer the open-ended term 'multilingualism' to cover use of more than a single language, but in fact most of the research has been on just two languages and therefore strictly speaking is about bilingualism. Much of what we know about bilingualism 'multiplies up' to apply to multilingualism. Switzerland is often cited as the

---

Exercise 2.1 English only

In 2004 the director of a company in Auckland, New Zealand, sent this memo to his workers:

> It has come to my attention that staff are communicating with one another in a language other than English.
>
> The only language to be spoken in this organisation is ENGLISH.
>
> This is an official warning that other languages will not be tolerated. I will have no hesitation in dismissing anyone who persists in this matter.
>
> Be warned.

Maurice Clist said the warning was needed 'for safety reasons' (*New Zealand Herald*, 29 June 2004). Some of the workers had objected to other (Indian) workers using their own language in the lunchroom. Mr Clist told the *Herald*:

> The lunchroom was a place for staff to relax during their breaks and when a foreign language, particularly the one the Indians used, was spoken it could create a 'trying' atmosphere, not a relaxing one.
>
> 'They don't want jabberwocky or gobbledegook going full bore. It [the Indians' language] is like machine-gun fire. It is a staccato-type speech.'

- Debate in class the case for and against Mr Clist's memo, each side laying out their arguments for or against his action.
- Then consider these questions:
    1 What views of language, monolingualism and multilingualism are embedded in the report? And what views about other groups?
    2 How would you address those views from a sociolinguistic viewpoint?

---

archetypal long-established multilingual nation, and in many ways so it is, with its four official languages (French, German, Italian, Romansch). But in practice it operates more like an amalgam of monolingualisms. In any given area of the country most of the interactions are carried out in just one of the languages. Out of the 26 cantons in Switzerland, 22 are officially monolingual, and many individuals are practically monolingual in just one of the languages.

For radically multilingual situations and individual repertoires we must go to remote tribal areas of some countries. The Hua people of the Papua New Guinea highlands practised exogamy, with women marrying members of other language communities and going to live in the husband's village. A survey by Haiman (1979) found that people were commonly fluent in four or five languages. Only 2 out of the 359 people surveyed claimed that they were monolingual, and only 11 were merely bilingual. Areas such as these are the home base for most of the world's estimated 6,000-plus languages. The highest numbers of languages are found in some of the poorest countries – 830 in Papua New Guinea,

722 in Indonesia, 521 in Nigeria – or among poor sectors of countries such as Australia (207 languages), Mexico (297) or Brazil (193), according to the sixteenth edition of *Ethnologue*, the compendium of the world's languages (Lewis 2009). By contrast, there are estimates that half of humankind speak just 10 major languages, and 90 per cent speak 100 languages (Romaine 2004).

Who is bilingual?

Defining what it means to know a language is a fraught business for monolinguals let alone for bilinguals. Does it require equal competence in both languages? The founding American linguist Leonard Bloomfield thought so, describing bilingualism as 'the native-like control of two languages' (1933: 56). The term 'balanced bilingual' is often used to describe such speakers, but in reality most bilinguals are differently competent in their two languages. They may, for example, write easily in one but not the other.

At the other end of the capability scale, John Edwards maintains, not entirely tongue-in-cheek:

> Everyone is bilingual. That is, there is no one in the world (no adult, anyway) who does not know at least a few words in languages other than the maternal variety. If, as an English speaker, you can say *c'est la vie* or *gracias* or *guten Tag* or *tovarisch* – or even if you only understand them – you clearly have some 'command' of a foreign tongue. (Edwards 2004: 7)

Obviously, to be described as bilingual implies some level of knowledge of both languages and the capacity to operate in them. This leaves uncommitted **what** level of knowledge or operation is enough to qualify.

The issue of defining who is bilingual is further complicated because fluent bilinguals may shift rapidly between their two languages. Sometimes they borrow words wholesale, or undertake frequent 'code switching' – mix their two languages in the same conversation, often within the same sentence. Code switching may involve rampant linguistic mixing which makes it difficult to distinguish where one language stops and the other starts. Such behaviour is common but is often condemned as indicating an inability to speak either language properly. Code switching is a sensitive area for bilinguals and a complex research topic, which we will deal with in Chapter 5.

How multilingualism arises

For the individual, multilingualism originates most obviously in growing up in a multilingual environment, or through the formal learning of additional languages later in life. For a society, increased bilingualism is often the result of the historical shifting of people through immigration. The immigration may be voluntary, in search of a better life, or enforced on refugees or slaves. People may shift between language areas for reasons of trade or conquest or religion (either to escape persecution, or as missionaries to spread their own religion). Large-scale immigration may lead to a reconfigured sociolinguistic

Exercise 2.2   Class language profile

1 Survey the language repertoires of class members using these three questions:
   - What do they consider their first language (L1)?
   - What other languages do they speak fluently (L2 fluent)?
   - What other languages do they know to some degree (L2 other)?

2 Log the answers in a grid on the board (languages by fluency level by number of speakers) to construct a sociolinguistic profile of the class.

3 Then have class members describe one linguistic feature about their first language(s) that they think is unusual – e.g. it may have a lot of noun cases, or none at all, or an unusual word order, or a rare consonant.

4 And then describe one notable sociolinguistic characteristic of the language(s) – perhaps it has a complicated system of choices among pronouns based on respect, or very different usages by men compared with women, or a distinctive variety spoken by one ethnic group.

- Doing this brief informal 'survey' at the start of a course gives both students and teacher an idea of the diversity of languages that are available in the class as a resource of experience and examples for discussing the sociolinguistic issues to come. Because the survey is done face to face, contested terms such as 'fluent' and 'first language' can be debated. Even the apparently straightforward exercise of naming one's language(s) involves choices which remind us how fluid languages and multilingualism may be for participants. Is your language Chinese or Hokkien? French or Cajun? Serbian or Croatian?

- If the class is largely monolingual but with differing dialects, apply the exercise to dialects rather than languages.

distribution in a country, for instance in the substantial replacement of native languages in South America by Spanish or Portuguese. Even minority immigration may impose a new language, as by the British in India.

Social multilingualism may also result from the shifting not of peoples but of the political borders that divide or unite them. A bilingual political entity can be created by annexation, federation or unification, for example of French and Dutch speakers to create Belgium in the nineteenth century. The sociolinguistic map of central and eastern Europe has been rewritten as well as the political map since the breakup of the Soviet empire (Pavlenko 2008; see Exercise 2.3). The linguistic composition of the states changed, and over time the language repercussions of these changes permeated to local and individual levels as a new or different nation required a different language for education or government. Even relatively stable border regions typically host the same languages on both sides of a border. Often a language will be in a majority on one side and a minority on the other – for example, the presence of Hungarian in states neighbouring Hungary. Where political borders have been drawn arbitrarily with little regard for local realities, as in parts of colonial Africa, we can expect cross-border linguistic commonalities (see Omoniyi 2004 for a Nigerian case).

Exercise 2.3   Shifting sociolinguistic boundaries

Have there been changes in your area – e.g. city or nation – in the past 25 years which have affected its sociolinguistic character?

1   Has there been immigration from other countries? Have people moved from the country to the city, or to different cities? Have people moved to different parts of the city?
2   What have been the sociolinguistic effects of these changes? Are languages (or dialects) now spoken in areas where they were not previously?

The map of central and eastern Europe has been radically redrawn since the late twentieth century:

3   Identify regions where national boundaries have shifted.
4   Choose one of the new nations (e.g. Serbia) and consider what have been the repercussions of the border changes for its sociolinguistic profile.

The values of multilingualism

Bilinguals' languages have identity value for their speakers. Bilinguals represent one part of themselves rather than another through their choice of language (Pavlenko 2006). One of the most thorough studies of what their two languages mean to bilinguals is research by Michele Koven on young Portuguese women who live in France (2007). The study combined overt discussion of how the women feel in and about the different languages, with telling stories of personal experience in both French and Portuguese, and their reactions to recordings of other participants. The speakers were clearly perceived as 'not quite the same person' when they told the same stories in the two different languages.

Another value of multilingualism is its relationship to cognitive capability. One view has been that being bilingual retards brain development. This has been adopted by many teachers, concerned many parents, and affected the lives of many children. Although such a view has been widespread popularly, the weight of 50 years of research on bilingual children's mental development shows the opposite. Beginning with a study by Peal and Lambert in 1962, the evidence is that bilinguals experience cognitive advantages over monolinguals rather than disadvantages.

In contrast to monolingual folk views of the disadvantage of multilingualism, radically multilingual communities seem to place high value on their members' multilingual capacities. Control of several languages allows for presentation of multiple identities, and multilingual skills are seen as a sign of superiority. The Tewa people of Arizona are proud of their ability in other languages as a form of cultural capital (Kroskrity 1993). In the Papua New Guinea highlands the Emmenyo people reportedly cultivated the learning of other languages from speakers who came their way and performed songs in languages that they claimed not to understand. The extended linguistic knowledge was seen as prestigious in its own right regardless of the utility of the language (Salisbury

---

Exercise 2.4   Multilingualism in your area

If a range of languages operate in the area where you live, make your own observations of the multilingualism around you.

- Note down how many different languages you hear spoken in the course of a single day, and how often you hear them.
- What languages are present in the 'linguistic landscape' of your area (see e.g. Gorter 2006 for this concept)? Is there multilingual signage in street names or on signposts? What languages do you see in shop windows and on packaging of merchandise? Or on posters and billboards?
- What languages are used in the media, for example in the press or on radio?
- Summarize your findings in a short multilingual profile of your area.
- Evaluate the particular kinds of information you have collected and what it says about multilingualism in your area. How reliable are your information sources? Is the information narrowly based or quite comprehensive?
- You could extend the project by comparing the results from your immediate area with what you find in a neighbouring town or suburb.

Sociolinguists have often used the concept of 'speech community' for the kind of geographical area you are examining. We deal with this term in detail in Chapter 5.2, but without pre-empting that, do you think your area could be described as a speech community in whatever way you want to define that at this point? What characteristics indicate that?

1962), displaying the speakers as sophisticated and cosmopolitan. The valuing of language and languages will be a recurring motif through this book, and is the focus of Chapter 10.

2.2   SIX DIMENSIONS OF BILINGUALISM

A first approach to thinking about bilingualism is through a number of dichotomies. Like most such distinctions, these actually often represent tendencies rather than opposites, but they make a useful tool for beginning to examine the nature of bilingualism.

1: Individual versus social

We can distinguish between individual bilingualism and collective, social or societal bilingualism. If people who know two languages are bilinguals, a society consisting mostly of such individuals could be also considered bilingual. Much of the southern United States bordering Mexico is bilingual in English and Spanish, because many people can operate in both languages. However, many others cannot, and that makes such a description contestable.

An aggregate of bilingual individuals is not the only – or even the usual – way that a bilingual social unit comes about. A grouping of people of any size may be described as bilingual even if the two languages are spoken by different individuals, who are more or less monolingual but in the different languages. A nation like Belgium may turn out to have overlapping monolingualisms (in French and Flemish) rather than individual bilingualism. A city such as Melbourne is home to many languages spoken by significant numbers of people, but most of its population are still English monolinguals. There are minorities of bilinguals who speak their community's language as well as English, and small numbers who are monolingual in languages such as Greek, Arabic, German or Vietnamese (Clyne and Kipp 2006).

Historically, an acute case of social bilingualism as overlapping monolingualisms occurred in European society in the eighteenth and nineteenth centuries. The ruling classes in some countries were largely monolingual in the elite language, French, while the ruled were monolingual in the local language such as Russian or German. At the other end of the scale from such multilingualisms, a country like Japan may be described as overwhelmingly monolingual because of the massive preponderance of the Japanese language and people who can speak only Japanese.

2: Productive versus receptive

Bilinguals' competence in their languages often differs widely for different language skills. In formal language learning, receptive capability routinely outstrips production, but even bilinguals who have learnt their languages from the home will commonly have differential abilities across speaking, listening, writing and reading in the two languages. Some may have largely 'passive' capability in one of their languages: they can speak one language fluently but not the other, although they understand most things in it.

Adult children of migrant families often lose productive competence in their original language. They can still understand their grandparents even though they have difficulty responding to them in the same language. But there are many nuances to what may seem like 'limited' productive capacity in a language. Nancy Dorian's classic study of language death in a Scottish Gaelic community (1981) found that there was a class of 'semi-speakers' who were still able to participate fully in conversation because they understood everything and knew how to make the appropriate contributions with their limited Gaelic. We look more closely at this case in Chapter 4.6.

3: Primary versus secondary

Primary bilingualism is where both languages are acquired 'naturally' in a social context, while in secondary bilingualism one of the languages is learned later through formal instruction. These two may of course mesh into each other. Immigrants will often be taking formal courses in the language of their new host country at the same time as being immersed in that language every day. Theories in applied linguistics acknowledge the immense importance for language learning of the social context of the learning and of the social motivations and attitudes of the learner.

There may be a good deal of difference in the sociolinguistic significance and out-comes of the primary versus the secondary path to bilingualism. A heartland rural Welsh speaker who has grown up with that language as an everyday environment – that is a 'primary bilingual' – may have a very different competence and experience of Welsh from the Cardiff city teenager who has learned it 'secondarily' at school, even if that learning has involved some immersion. Both may be counted as fluent bilinguals by measures such as the census but their daily experience of Welsh will be quite different (Coupland and Aldridge 2009).

4: Additive versus subtractive

When bilingualism is transitional – that is, if a person or group is learning a second language – the acquisition of the second language can be seen as adding to or subtracting from their linguistic repertoire. In additive bilingualism, the person retains their full capability in their original language and to that adds capability (to some level) in another, new language. Generally an adult who emigrates does not lose much competence in their original language in the process of gaining a new one.

Subtractive bilingualism, on the other hand, is where learning a new language occurs at the gradual expense of the original language. The classic case is that of the immigrant child, say 6 years of age, who was fully competent in her original language when she emigrated, but whose learning of the dominant language in the new country submerges productive command of her former language, often quite rapidly.

5: Stable versus dynamic

Bilingualism may be stable or changing. Change can occur for individuals, particularly adults learning a new language and moving through successive levels of capability in it. Language capability also varies with people's changing circumstances across their lifetime. Bilinguals who have acquired one of their languages after immigrating to a country as young adults may lose some of that capability again after they retire from the workforce. This happens where the 'public' language is different from a commu-nity's ingroup language and its use diminishes if a person becomes less involved in public life.

The situation of the individual who adds or loses a language is mirrored in shifts in the distribution of bilingualism in a society at large. When the configuration of languages remains largely unchanged over time in a society, we call it 'language maintenance', with neither language advancing or receding. More commonly, and largely through migration, the social configuration of languages in a nation undergoes continual change. New languages enter or spread, monolinguals become gradually bilingual. This is the typical development after minority migration to countries such as the United States, Singapore or France. These newly minted bilinguals learn the dominant language and usually retain their original language, and so diversify the sociolinguistic character of the new country. But their children, or at least their grandchildren, will probably lose their heritage language and become monolingual under the pressure of the dominant language of the host country. Chapter 3 focuses on the nature of language shift and maintenance in different societies.

6: Indigenous versus immigrant

In a dynamic sociolinguistic situation, when two languages meet through migration, there will always be a majority and a minority language (although this can re-weight over time). The minority language will tend to be either indigenous or immigrant.

Indigenous languages which were once the majority (or even sole) language of their space are pressured and in due course may be overwhelmed by one or more immigrant languages, as the indigenous populations are themselves overtaken by the newcomers. In Canada, the First Nation ('Indian') languages have regressed in the face of both English and French. The native Polynesian language of Easter Island (Rapa Nui) in the south-eastern Pacific Ocean is under threat from the Spanish of Chile, to which the island belongs politically (Makihara 2005). The many languages of the ethnic minorities on the northern and western margins of China are under pressure from the majority Han Chinese language (Bradley 2005).

New immigrants, on the other hand, usually remain a disadvantaged minority along-side the established majority. Typically such groups will lose their original language to the majority language within three generations. As Edwards has noted, 'In many immigrant contexts ... bilingualism has been a generational way-station on the road between two monolingualisms' (2007: 458).

Exercise 2.5   Interviewing a bilingual

Interview a bilingual you know. Ask about their bilingual usage and capability in terms of the six distinctions used in this section:

1 Is most of their community individually bilingual, or do people tend in practice to be monolingual in one of the languages?
2 Is there a difference in their productive and their receptive capability in the different languages? And between the different skills of speaking, listening, writing and reading?
3 Is one of their languages primary and the other secondary? – that is, in the way they learned it.
4 Has their bilingualism been additive or subtractive? Has their capability in one language reduced as they have learned the other? Has one language tended to replace the other?
5 Is their bilingualism stable or dynamic? Has it changed during their life? Is it still changing?
6 Has their bilingualism come about as a result of their own or their family's immigration, or because they belong to an indigenous minority, or from some other circumstance?

2.3 APPROACHES TO MULTILINGUALISM

I will distinguish three main approaches to the sociolinguistic study of bi- and multilingualism here. Each comes with quite different disciplinary assumptions, interests, theorizing, methods and priorities. There are also commonalities between them, particularly between the first and second approaches. But, on the other hand, not all the research fits neatly into these categories. The first two predate the third, and are in some degree being superseded by it.

The sociology of language

The study of bilingualism grew in the 1950s, led by Uriel Weinreich's *Languages in Contact* (1953) – a deceptively slim book that became enormously influential. From the 1960s multilingualism research was nurtured under the American functionalist sociology of the time. The sociology of language is a broad-brush approach, dealing with the situation of whole languages in societies. It focuses on how languages operate in a society, their standing, functions and social distribution. Its interest is in the place of entire languages, which can be defined as named entities such as 'Hindi' or 'Catalan' or 'Kiswahili'. It takes those languages as wholes rather than micro-analysing their structures and features. It tends to deal in macro social factors, for instance looking at which age or ethnic groups in a society use which languages. Its typical method is the survey questionnaire. The sociology of language is a study of society rather than of language, and many practitioners tend to see themselves as doing sociology rather than doing linguistics.

The sociology of language examines not what individuals, or even small groups, do so much as the linguistic behaviour of whole nations or their major constituent groups (particularly ethnicities). The question asked is: what is the sociolinguistic profile of India or Spain or Tanzania, rather than how do individual speakers in those countries use their languages. This emphasis includes the study of how bilingualism and multilingualism operate in society, and how different languages relate within a nation or ethnic group. Not surprisingly, this focus often reflects the multilingual origins of the scholars involved, including those of the founder of the sociology of language, Joshua Fishman. Although his main personal focus was on the 'macro' level of language–society interaction, he was keen in the early years for 'micro' sociolinguistics to also be corralled under a sociology-of-language umbrella. While his own empirical research concentrated on statistical analyses of the place of languages in societies and nations, his early activity as an editor encompassed a lot of work with a more 'micro' focus (see the further reading section at the end of this chapter).

The sociological survey approach continues today to provide basic information about bilingual communities around the world. In Miami, high numbers of immigrant Cubans make for a strong presence of Spanish alongside English. A statistical study by Jorgen Porcel (2006) found that shift away from Spanish among these immigrants was influenced by factors like being born or educated in the US and contact with English speakers.

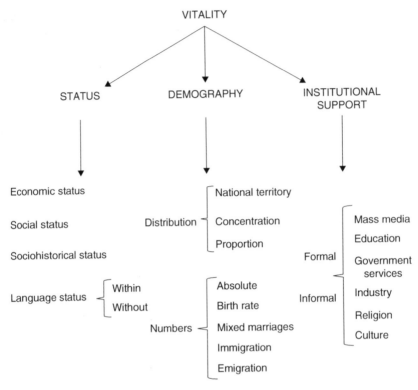

Figure 2.1   A taxonomy of the structural variables affecting ethnolinguistic vitality
Source: Giles, Bourhis and Taylor (1977: 309)

Ethnolinguistic vitality

The concept of ethnolinguistic vitality was developed in the 1970s to explain the relationship between ethnicity and language, in particular the place of social and cultural factors
in accounting for groups' language behaviour and attitudes. Central in developing this
approach was Howard Giles, a British social psychologist now in California, who specialized in the role of language in social relations. Working with a range of collaborators,
Giles initiated an approach to multilingualism based in the insights of social psychology
(compared with the sociological origins of Fishman's work). In their original proposal of
this approach, Giles, Bourhis and Taylor (1977: 308) write: 'The vitality of an ethnolinguistic group is that which makes a group likely to behave as a distinct and active collective entity in intergroup situations.' They suggest that three kinds of structural variables
affect vitality (Figure 2.1), and detail their characteristics:

1 **Status** derives from the prestige of the speakers of a language. In general, the more
   status a linguistic group has, the more vitality it will possess.
2 **Demography** is the basic numerical shape of the group, including its birth and
   immigration rate. The more favourable the group's numbers and geographical distribution, the more vital it is likely to be.

3 **Institutional support** is the extent to which a group's language is used and supported by social institutions. The more institutional support a language enjoys, the
   more vitality it will have.

The demographic aspect of this is similar to the sociological approach, but the
difference comes with a focus on the subjective element in bilingualism. Giles and
collaborators suggested making a distinction between objective and subjective
ethnolinguistic vitality. Objective vitality involves the factors laid out above, such as
number of speakers. Subjective vitality covers group members' perceptions of the
standing of their group and its language, which may not necessarily directly reflect the
'objective' reality. Different interested groups may perceive the same conditions
differently.

Like the sociologists of language, social psychologists use questionnaires to research
group members' attitudes, for example in Allard and Landry's study (1986) of Moncton,
a French–English bilingual city in New Brunswick, Canada. These researchers argue
(Landry and Allard 1994) that a group can possess four different kinds of 'capital' –
demographic, political, economic and cultural. A study of the vitality of the Welsh
language in a diaspora community in Patagonia (Johnson 2010) used focus groups as
a method rather than a pre-set questionnaire. There, Welsh serves as a heritage language for display to tourists and appears superficially robust, but is rather weak in
actual everyday community usage. The value of Welsh as linguistic capital in this local
economy is hard to explain through normal vitality measures.

Much of the current research on bilingualism continues to build on the concept of
ethnolinguistic vitality, although it may modify the methods and conclusions. Yagmur
and Ehala's overview (2011) acknowledges that while there have been an increasing
number of studies using ethnolinguistic vitality, there has been little development in the
theory since it was first put forward.

Critical/constructivist approaches

With the development of critical and constructivist thinking on society and on language,
the twenty-first century has seen challenges to the traditional sociological and social
psychological approaches to bilingualism research. These question the ways we do such
research, how we think of bilingualism in both the individual and society, and even how
we talk about languages as distinct from each other. The term 'bilingualism' itself
becomes problematic. 'Multilingualism' is less of a problem, but 'monolingualism' more
so (Exercise 2.6). Increasingly the critical/constructivist approach is redefining the way
in which multilingualism is thought about, how it is researched, what questions are
asked and what findings are significant.

The German sociolinguist Peter Auer has specialized in researching code
switching – those occasions where bilingual speakers mix their languages together
(see Chapter 5). He argues that research into code switching demands that we begin
not with identifying the two languages but with the overall linguistic practices of the
speakers. What language they are speaking may not be the important question –
may not even be answerable. Italian 'guestworkers' in Germany often blend their two

Exercise 2.6 Bias to monolingualism

Auer and Li Wei introduce their handbook of multilingualism with this manifesto:

> Why should multilingualism be a problem? We estimate that most of the human lan-
> guage users in the world speak more than one language, i.e. they are at least bilingual.
> In quantitative terms, then, monolingualism may be the exception and multilingualism
> the norm. Would it not make more sense to look at monolingualism as a problem that is
> real and consequential, but which can be 'cured'? … Aren't we turning something into a
> problem which is the most natural thing in the world? (2007b: 1)

Debate this view:

1 Do you agree that there is a bias towards monolingualism in your society?
   Or internationally? Or in your linguistics courses? Or in this textbook?
2 If so, how does the bias show in these different spheres?

languages together in ways that make it unclear which language a particular item belongs to – it may be either or both (Auer 2007). And speakers can intentionally manipulate this ambiguity for their own communicative ends. This is a very basic challenge to how we think about and research bilingualism, when the nature of the object to be researched is put in doubt.

Language is a social practice, a range of resources on which speakers draw rather than a set of linguistic 'codes', according to Monica Heller, a Canadian francophone and bilingual. Such an approach follows closely from developments in social anthropology, and it typically uses qualitative research methods such as ethnography, analysing the specifics of particular bilingual interactions and discourses rather than conducting questionnaire surveys. Heller (2007b) argues against regarding languages as entities that can serve as the objects of research. Actual multilingual usage shows how permeable the edges of languages may be.

Jaffe's study of the minority language movement in the French island of Corsica is an example of this kind of work, which addresses:

> … the extent to which bilingualism is practised or imagined as two separate monolingual-
> isms (linked to two separate identities), vs. as a potentially uneven mixture of codes, prac-
> tices and competencies distributed across different individuals and different moments and
> domains of social action. (Jaffe 2007b: 51)

Minority languages such as Corsican and their associated bilingualisms are emerging as marketable commodities in a globalizing economy and as valuable assets under political shifts such as European regionalization. Tourism is just one sector where local languages can become emblems of their particular region in a global world. Labelling a souvenir from Lapland in an indigenous Sámi language validates its claim to local authenticity, while English may be used alongside it as a means of wider communication (Pietikäinen and Kelly-Holmes 2011).

Example 2.1

Hindi and English in India

India is a sociolinguistic giant of a nation. With a population now well over 1 billion, it has 22 legally 'Scheduled' languages plus hundreds of others. Hindi is by far the largest and has been promoted as a national lingua franca. Examining census data as in a sociology-of-language approach might lead to a conclusion about the spread of Hindi, but critical/qualitative work points to a more ambiguous situation.

The social elite of the capital, Delhi, have spoken English rather than Hindi for generations. Vineeta Chand interviewed members of this elite and recorded comments like these from Sonal, a 60-year-old woman:

> We all speak in English together. We all – I mean, I don't think there's hardly anyone who speaks in, much in Hindi and who's very fluent in Hindi. They [family] do speak Hindi, but it's not a very – you know, like a fluent Hindi. Maybe we make mistakes, grammatical mistakes here and there. But if I have to speak to the help, domestic help, it has to be Hindi, or if I speak to somebody who doesn't know English, my neighbors, for example, then it has to be Hindi. But that is a language in which I'm – English – in which I have grown up in, written. I speak … in English. And letters and everything, whatever, essays, whatever I do, it's only in English. (Chand 2011: 23)

- From the quote, what different uses do these elite speakers make of Hindi and of English, and why?

The critical/constructivist approach is closely interwoven with an attention to ideologies of language, which we will return to late in the book in Chapter 10. Ideologies are central to how languages are positioned relative to each other in society. These approaches offer the chance to reconsider many things that have been taken for granted in earlier approaches to multilingualism. They recognize that we can no longer sideline the amount of untidy flux and multiplicity that insists on our attention in real multilingual situations. Martin-Jones, Blackledge and Creese's reader (2012) provides a state-of-the-art overview of the burgeoning research following this approach to multilingualism.

2.4   LANGUAGE SURVEYS AND CENSUSES

Despite the fuller picture that qualitative methods give, the survey remains the basic method for investigating the language profile of a society or group. Two of the exercises earlier in this chapter are in effect small-scale sociolinguistic surveys (2.2 and 2.5). A much bigger enterprise, which took about a year to design and another year to carry out, was a study that I and colleagues conducted into Pasifika languages in New Zealand (see e.g. Taumoefolau et al. 2002). Manukau is in the south of the city of Auckland, and is home to a third of the country's Polynesian population, who come mainly from the south Pacific islands of Samoa, Tonga, Niue and the Cook Islands. We interviewed 120 people, using a questionnaire that was developed first in English in consultation with the project's bilingual advisors, then translated into the four languages. It blended a mix of sociological and social psychological questions, and – in the terms of ethnolinguistic vitality – the objective and subjective issues. The finished product had six sections:

1   demographic information, including residence history and education
2   childhood, upbringing and family history, including language history
3   language fluency
4   language usage – at home, with family and relatives, at church, at work, etc.
5   language attitudes – identity, expressing feelings, future of the language
6   language maintenance – at home, by government, in education.

At 27 pages long this was a typical large-scale survey questionnaire (available on http://www.aut.ac.nz/research/research-institutes/icdc/projects/pasifika-languages-of-manukau/project-details).

The biggest social survey of all is the census which most countries conduct every five or ten years. Many censuses ask language questions, and since the 1950s sociolinguists have used the resulting data to profile the distribution of languages in a nation. Their analyses have often focused on comparing data from successive censuses to identify shifts as – for example – new immigrant groups bring new languages into the country.

Different nations ask different language questions. Some ask about home language, others about fluency, still others about mother tongue. These different questions make comparison across countries problematic. The Australian census asks what languages are used in the home. Clyne and Kipp (2006), the leading analysts, comment that targeting home usage will underestimate the total number of a language's users. For example, someone in Australia may use a language such as Greek at a community function even though there is now no one else in their own household to speak it to. New Zealand asks: 'In what language(s) could you have a conversation about a lot of everyday things?' The question aims to gauge the linguistic capabilities of New Zealanders rather than their actual behaviour (Starks, Harlow and Bell 2005). An elderly former immigrant may remain fully fluent in the Dutch or Gujerati that they learned back home, but may never have the chance to use that language nowadays. Lastly, Canada has concentrated on 'mother tongue' in its census, as we see in the next section.

2.5   THE CASE OF CANADA

Each of the core chapters in this book includes a case study. These take a specific piece of sociolinguistic research, and present and interpret it as an example of the chapter's theme. The case study for this chapter deals with the language findings of the Canadian census.

Controversy over questions

Bilingual research from Canada has already had several mentions in this chapter, and that is no accident. The country has been the site of a great deal of research which reflects the sharp social and political issues involved in the relationship between French and English, the two official languages. Language therefore bulks large in the five-yearly Canadian

census. The main question asked has been about mother tongue, but its changing definition over time raises an issue. Until 1941 the definition was 'the language first learned and
still spoken' (Edwards 2007). From then until 1976, it was 'the language first spoken and
still understood', switching the emphasis from active production to comprehension. Since
1981 it has been 'the language first learned and still understood'. When definitions change
like this from census to census, it becomes difficult to be sure the answers mean the same
thing across time and therefore to make comparisons or identify trends.

For the 2011 census, the language questions themselves became a political issue.
The Canadian government had decided to make it voluntary for people to answer the
40-page long-form census questionnaire, which contained most of the language questions. Francophone activist groups believed this would disadvantage their language
and took the government to court. The government bowed to the pressure and agreed
to include the questions on home language and fluency as well as on mother tongue
in the short-form questionnaire which everyone had to answer. As a result, three out
of the ten questions in the full 2011 census deal with language, and the census gives
information on fluency, home language and mother tongue.

It takes years to process census data, so the latest results available at the time of writing
come from the 2006 census. The findings are summarized in Statistics Canada's report
on the 'evolving linguistic portrait' of Canada, principally authored by Corbeil and
Blaser (2007). The census analysts concentrate on the mother-tongue findings.

Comparing French and English

Table 2.1 summarizes the language results for the whole of Canada drawn from Corbeil
and Blaser and other tables on Statistics Canada's website:

- 22 per cent of the population are 'Francophones' – have French as their mother
  tongue – while 58 per cent are 'Anglophones'.
- One-fifth speak mostly French at home, two-thirds mostly English.
- Nearly a third say they know French, and five-sixths know English.
- One-eighth claim to know only French, and two-thirds only English.

Table 2.1   The standing of the French and English languages in Canada, 2006 census

	French		English	
	Millions	*Percent*	*Millions*	*Percent*
Mother tongue	6.9	22	18.1	58
Home language	6.7	21	20.8	67
Know	9.5	30	26.5	85
Know only	4.1	13	21.1	68
Total population	31.2			

Source: Derived from Corbeil and Blaser (2007), tables A3–A6, together with tables on Detailed
Mother Tongue × Knowledge of Official Languages at http://www12.statcan.gc.ca/census-
recensement/2006/dp-pd/tbt/Index-eng.cfm accessed 11 April 2011

We have here several measures of the standing of these two official languages in Canadian society. Probably the least favourable statistics for French are those that show bilingual capability tends to be differentially distributed between the two mother-tongue communities. While 42% of Francophones are bilingual in English, 9% of Anglophones are bilingual in French. And while just 13% know only French, five times that number of Anglophones know only English. On the other hand, more Anglophones say they know French than at the previous census.

Language transfer

Another measure of the French–English relationship is what the census reporters call 'language transfer' – the current home use of a language that was not the person's mother tongue. We can see transfer operating by comparing the first and second rows in the English columns of Table 2.1. There are 2.7 million more Canadians who say English is their home

---

Exercise 2.7   Census mis-reporting?

The 2006 figure of 42 per cent for Francophone bilingualism (i.e. mother-tongue French speakers who know English as well as French) gave the census reporters an intriguing interpretive puzzle: it had gone down from earlier censuses. Until 2006 the trend had been for Francophone bilingualism in English to rise. The census interpreters note that this trend reversal is difficult to account for, but suggest the following:

A plausible explanation

About one month before the Census, an anonymous e-mail written in French was circulating on the Internet. It contained false information and urged bilingual Francophones not to report, at the Census of Population, on May 16, 2006, that they knew both official languages, purportedly to ensure that the federal government would not cut services to Francophones. Francophones were encouraged to say that they knew French but not English. The e-mail spread across the country. A note was posted on Statistics Canada's website alerting Canadians to the e-mail's erroneous contents and asking them to answer the questions accurately. (Corbeil and Blaser 2007: 29)

That is, the census interpreters believe the apparent change was not a genuine reversal of a trend, but the result of intentional, tactical misreporting by some Francophones.

1   Do you agree that this email campaign could be a 'plausible explanation' of the reversed trend? Can you suggest any other reasons?
2   The above explanation (originally retrieved in 2009) no longer appears on Statistics Canada's website at the time of writing. Can you suggest why?
3   Locate the equivalent finding for the 2011 census on Statistics Canada's website. Has Francophone bilingualism risen or fallen again? What might be the explanation?

Table 2.2   The standing of French and English in Québec
compared to the rest of Canada, 2006 census, in percentages

	Québec (%)	Rest of Canada (%)
Mother tongue French	80	4
Home language French	82	3
Know French	95	10
Know only French	54	1
Mother tongue English	8	73
Home language English	11	84
Know English	45	98
Know only English	4	88
Total population	7.4 million	23.8 million

Source: Derived from Corbeil and Blaser (2007), tables A3–A6,
together with tables on Detailed Mother Tongue × Knowledge of
Official Languages at http://www12.statcan.gc.ca/census-
recensement/2006/dp-pd/tbt/Index-eng.cfm accessed 11 April 2011

language (20.8 m) than say it was their mother tongue (18.1 m). This means these people have 'transferred' from French to English. By contrast, there are 0.2 million fewer people who speak French at home (6.7 m) than claim it as a mother tongue (6.9 m), also meaning they have transferred to using English. The census reporters' interpretation is:

> Although it has no direct impact on the size and growth of Francophone minorities outside Québec, language transfer of Francophones to English is often a harbinger of future change. The language spoken most often at home is generally the language transmitted to the children as their mother tongue. (Corbeil and Blaser 2007: 17)

They conclude that outside Québec fewer and fewer children of Francophone women are learning French, and more and more younger Francophones are speaking English. So the Francophone population is ageing faster than the Anglophone, and French outside Québec is experiencing reduced takeup in the next generation.

The place of Québec

Although there are large French-speaking minorities in other provinces, Québec is where French is the majority language, reversing the situation that holds for English in the rest of Canada (Table 2.2). In Québec, 80% of people have French as mother tongue, 82% mostly use French at home, and 95% can converse in French. In contrast the rest of Canada has very low percentages of French (top rows of right column). Outside Québec less than 1% of people claim to be monolingual in French, compared with 88% who are monolingual in English. But in Québec, one of the most interesting trends supporting French is that more immigrants there are now speaking French at home rather than English. Montreal is attracting immigrant speakers of Italian,

Spanish, French-based Creoles, Portuguese and Romanian. The census reporters suggest that the linguistic similarity of these Romance languages to French may have helped bring their speakers to Montreal.

The uses of censuses

Surveys and censuses provide invaluable macro language information that is hard to win in any other way. But they are relatively blunt research instruments, and there are challenges and pitfalls to dealing with census and survey data about languages, including:

- Deciding what measure/s will serve as the best indicators of language distribution in a society
- Settling the best wordings for questions and the best frame for answers
- Defining terms such as 'mother tongue' and 'speaking a language'

Exercise 2.8   Censuses in Canada and elsewhere

Look across all the data presented in this section concerning French and English in Canada in 2006, and scan the Statistics Canada website for further relevant data.

1 Re-examine Tables 2.1 and 2.2 for more clues to the relationship of the two languages in 2006. There are, for example, patterns in Table 2.2 that point to further differences between them.
2 On the basis of this data set, how would you assess the standing of French in Canada relative to English in 2006?

Canada's 2011 census was conducted in May 2011, and the initial report on language results was published in October 2012 (http://www12.statcan.gc.ca/census-recensement/2011/as-sa/index-eng.cfm). Many of the tables make comparisons with 2006 (and earlier).

3 Compare the 2006 and 2011 findings on the website (note the caution that the reporters offer about comparability).
4 What are the changes, what are the similarities? In particular, what are the trends in the relationship between French and English?
5 What projection would you make for the futures of French and English in Canada?

Note that because the 2006 data I have presented in this section have been combined from a number of tables, they may not directly match numbers in any one table on the website.

For your own country or another nation that interests you, scan the language findings from the most recent census.

6 Interpret them in the kind of way we have done for Canada.
7 What questions were asked, and what are the results?
8 What sociolinguistic profile do they give of the nation?

- Understanding the factors that can sway how individuals and communities may answer a survey question – the politics of language in a society may derail the apparently objective, factual surface of a survey such as a census
- Deciding what to count and how to count it is always an issue, and the bigger the survey, the bigger the challenge.

Analysing and interpreting a data set as massive and complicated as a census is fraught with compromises and many opportunities to get it wrong. This applies to my own extracting and adapting of numbers from the census, despite all care being taken. Interpreting major trends needs to be equally careful. For example, the aggregated figures for all of Canada in Table 2.1 are misleading without taking into account the regional breakdown (Table 2.2). This shows the extent to which French and English are territorially in complementary distribution between Québec and the rest of the country.

Despite all these caveats, there is worthwhile and interesting sociolinguistic information to be gained through censuses and other surveys, especially if the survey is complemented by more qualitative, situational information of the kind we will deal with in later chapters.

2.6   RESEARCH ACTIVITY: A BILINGUAL SURVEY

Exercise 2.9 contains a short questionnaire on bilingual language usage which I use with my students in class. The activity serves as a microcosm of a survey project. It gives students a taste of interviewing – and being interviewed – in a supportive environment. It also requires them to analyse the information they have been given through the questionnaire answers, interpret it and present it to others.

This questionnaire was designed to cater mainly for international students, who are usually a majority in the classes I teach, but it can be easily adapted for other bilinguals. The interviews can be done in pairs during class. The interviewer puts the questions to the informant and enters the answer on the sheet. The questionnaire should be spaced out over two pages to give enough room for entering answers. The activity needs to be conducted in accordance with the institution's ethical guidelines.

If half the class is bilingual, the monolinguals can interview the bilinguals. If more than half the students are bilingual, then for at least some pairs, the interviews can go in both directions. If there are not enough bilinguals in the class, interviewing can be shared by pairs of monolinguals. Alternatively, this can be used as an out-of-class activity, with students interviewing a bilingual person they have ready access to. Ensure that these are conducted in line with the institution's ethical procedures.

These interviews take about 10 minutes each. The interviewer then quickly summarizes the bilingual profile of the informant, and reports back to the class as a whole on the findings. The informant can then comment on whether she or he finds the interviewer has given a fair report on their usage.

Once the interviewing and reporting is completed, students can evaluate the questionnaire itself:

- Were some questions redundant or inappropriate for some kinds of informants?
- Was anything important missing from the questionnaire?

- Could some wordings be improved? Were any unclear?
- Did students find themselves deviating from the wordings, adding follow-up questions, or expanding on terms? How would they modify the questionnaire to suit?

Exercise 2.9　Bilingual language use questionnaire

The interviewer should ask the bilingual informant the questions below and enter the information on to the sheet. Not all questions will be applicable to all informants. Informants are free to not answer particular questions if they do not want to.

A　Social and linguistic background

1　What language did you first learn to speak?
2　Do you still use that language frequently?
3　Can you carry on a casual conversation in that language?
4　Can you discuss university work in that language?
5　What other languages are you fluent in?
6　Do you ever 'code switch' between your languages (use words from both languages in the same sentence)?
7　How long have you lived in this country?
8　What country did you come from?
9　What country do your family live in?
10　Do you live permanently in this country? If not, are you going to return to the country you came from after you finish your studies?
11　What language do your parents speak?

B　Interlocutors: Which language do you use with:

1　grandparents
2　parents
3　aunts/uncles
4　sisters/brothers
5　friends in this country whose first language is the same as yours
6　friends in this country whose first language is different from yours
7　university lecturers
8　university or government officials

C　Domains: Which language do you use in these situations:

1　at home in the country you came from/in this country
2　in a shop in the country you came from/in this country
3　in a religious service in the country you came from/in this country
4　in a class at university
5　sitting in the university café
6　discussing your studies with other students/with a lecturer
7　in any particular group you belong to in this country (e.g. sports or other club) – specify
8　at an ethnic community centre

2.7   SUMMARY

- Multilingualism in three or more languages is a daily fact of life in countries such as Switzerland and Papua New Guinea. It is valued for the cognitive advantages that research has shown it offers, for its identity importance, and for its potential to display linguistic skills. Historically multilingualism usually arises through inheritance, immigration or the shifting of borders. There is a bias towards monolingualism as a national norm despite widespread multilingualism even in West European nations.
- We can approach bilingualism through a number of dichotomies:
  - ➤ Bilingualism may be social or individual. Social bilingualism may result from overlapping individual monolingualisms.
  - ➤ A bilingual usually has different levels of skills in their different languages, often being receptive in both languages but productive in only one.
  - ➤ In primary bilingualism both languages are learned 'naturally', in secondary bilingualism one is learned through formal instruction.
  - ➤ In additive bilingualism the speaker fully retains their existing language as they acquire another, while under subtractive bilingualism the former language diminishes.
  - ➤ Bilingualism can be stable, or it can be dynamic – undergoing change.
  - ➤ Bilingualism often involves a majority group and one or more minorities, either indigenous or immigrant.
- I distinguish three main approaches to the study of multilingualism. The sociology of language flourished from the 1960s and typically uses a survey questionnaire to gather data. Its focus is on the languages of whole nations or groups and their distribution.
- A second approach is ethnolinguistic vitality, which developed in the 1970s from social psychology. The vitality of a minority language is affected by its demography, status and institutional support. Subjective ethnolinguistic vitality focuses on a group's perceptions of its standing.
- Lastly there are more recent critical/constructivist approaches, which deconstruct the very notion of distinct languages and see multilingualism in terms of a suite of resources on which speakers draw. This approach raises basic challenges to many of the premises underlying the first two approaches.
- Questionnaire surveys are the standard methodology of the sociology of language and ethnolinguistic vitality research. Many national censuses ask language questions, and sociolinguists have used the resulting data to profile the linguistic shape of their nation. Censuses usually ask questions about one of three things: home language, fluency, or mother tongue.
- A detailed case study of the 2006 Canadian census concentrates on the relation of French and English. It shows that 22 per cent of the population are Francophones, with French as their mother tongue, while 58 per cent are Anglophones. Overall nearly a third say they know French, and five-sixths English. However, in Québec, the positions of French and English are roughly reversed.
- Surveys and censuses provide invaluable macro language information that is hard to win in any other way. They are relatively blunt research instruments, and can

have problems such as question wording and defining terms. But there is worthwhile and interesting sociolinguistic information to be gained, especially if surveys are complemented by more qualitative information.

2.8   FURTHER READING

Several journals are devoted specifically to bi- and multilingualism – the *International Journal of Bilingualism, Journal of Bilingualism and Bilingual Education, Multilingua* and the *International Journal of Multilingualism*. Ethnolinguistic vitality work has often appeared in the *Journal of Multilingual and Multicultural Development* and *Journal of Language and Social Psychology*. *Ethnologue* (Lewis 2009) is the updating compendium of information on the world's languages from the Summer Institute of Linguistics. The current edition can be searched on line. The Mercator Centre runs a very comprehensive website on multilingualism especially in Europe at www.mercator-research.eu/home.

From the late 1960s Joshua Fishman undertook an editing and publishing programme aimed at defining and establishing the sociology of language as a field. In a succession of important 'readers', Fishman (1968, 1971, 1972, 1978) collected articles that had been scattered in often inaccessible places. Fishman's collections – together with others edited especially by Hymes (e.g. 1964; Gumperz and Hymes 1972) – were influential in beginning to define the embryonic field of sociolinguistics, and he would continue to publish voluminously into the twenty-first century. Perhaps Fishman's biggest editorial contribution was his founding of the *International Journal of the Sociology of Language* in 1974. This journal appears in six issues totalling nearly 1,000 pages a year. Most issues cover a specific theme, often the sociolinguistics of a particular language or region.

There are several good readers – collections of key papers and chapters – on multilingualism from the 1960s onwards. More recent volumes include Li Wei's *Bilingualism Reader* (2000), which carries some of the earlier classic articles that I cite in these opening chapters. Auer and Li Wei's *Handbook of Multilingualism and Multilingual Communication* (2007a) contains commissioned chapters on various facets of multilingualism. The compendious *Handbook of Bilingualism* by Bhatia and Ritchie (2004) covers psychological and neurological dimensions as well as the sociolinguistic. It concludes with a useful series of survey articles of bilingualism in major world regions such as Central Asia and southern Africa. Volume 4 of the six-volume Coupland and Jaworski (2009a) assemblage of leading papers covers 'the sociolinguistics of multilingualism'. There is also the four-volume *Bilingualism and Multilingualism* compilation in the same series (Li Wei 2010). Ralph Fasold's 1984 text *The Sociolinguistics of Society* is now a generation old but offers a lot of detail on macrosociolinguistic studies up to that time. An intentionally different thrust comes in Martin-Jones, Blackledge and Creese's *Routledge Handbook of Multilingualism* (2012), which showcases more recent critical and constructivist work.

Howard Giles's 1977 *Language, Ethnicity and Intergroup Relations* is the foundation collection of ethnolinguistic vitality research. A special issue of the *Journal of Multilingual and Multicultural Development* edited by Ehala and Yagmur (2011) brings together some more recent studies and their introduction (Yagmur and Ehala 2011) presents a good overview of ethnolinguistic vitality. Heller's *Bilingualism: A Social Approach* (2007a) offers a good range of chapters which bring a critical perspective to bear on multilingual issues.

There is a long tradition of sociolinguistic analysis of census data. Fishman (e.g. 1971) worked on US census data over many years, as did Clyne in Australia (Clyne and Kipp 2006). There are early studies in Canada by Lieberson (1972), and more recent analysis of the Welsh census by Aitchison and Carter (2004). Websites are now the best way to access census data on language, although most government statistics agencies provide only rudimentary analyses.

Canadian research on bilingualism focuses particularly on French in relation to English and is found in work by scholars such as Lambert (e.g. 1967), Edwards (2004, 2007), Bourhis (Bourhis, Giles and Rosenthal 1981) and Heller (1988, 2007a). Statistics Canada's website carries reports, tables and other information on the language findings of the Canadian censuses.

REFERENCES

Aitchison, John and Harold Carter, 2004. *Spreading the Word: The Welsh Language 2001*. Talybont, UK: Y Lolfa.

Allard, Réal and Rodrigue Landry, 1986. 'Subjective ethnolinguistic vitality viewed as a belief system'. *Journal of Multilingual and Multicultural Development* 7: 1–12.

Auer, Peter, 2007. 'The monolingual bias in bilingualism research, or: why bilingual talk is (still) a challenge for linguistics'. In Monica Heller (ed.), *Bilingualism: A Social Approach*. Basingstoke, UK: Palgrave Macmillan. 319–39.

Auer, Peter and Li Wei, 2007b. 'Introduction: multilingualism as a problem? Monolingualism as a problem?' In Peter Auer and Li Wei (eds), *Handbook of Multilingualism and Multilingual Communication*. Berlin: Mouton de Gruyter. 1–12.

Bloomfield, Leonard, 1933. *Language*. New York: Henry Holt & Co.

Bourhis, Richard Y., Howard Giles and Doreen Rosenthal, 1981. 'Notes on the construction of a "Subjective Vitality Questionnaire" for ethnolinguistic groups'. *Journal of Multilingual and Multicultural Development* 2: 145–55.

Bradley, David, 2005. 'Introduction: language policy and language endangerment in China'. *International Journal of the Sociology of Language* 173: 1–21.

Chand, Vineeta, 2011. 'Elite positionings towards Hindi: language policies, political stances and language competence in India'. *Journal of Sociolinguistics* 15: 6–35.

Clyne, Michael and Sandra Kipp, 2006. 'Australia's community languages'. *International Journal of the Sociology of Language* 180: 7–21.

Corbeil, Jean-Pierre and Christine Blaser, 2007. *The Evolving Linguistic Portrait, 2006 Census*. Ottawa: Statistics Canada (http://www12.statcan.gc.ca/census-recensement/2006/rt-td/lng-eng.cfm; retrieved 6 April 2011).

Coupland, Nikolas and Michelle Aldridge, 2009. 'Introduction: a critical approach to the revitalisation of Welsh'. *International Journal of the Sociology of Language* 195: 5–13.

Dorian, Nancy C., 1981. *Language Death: The Life Cycle of a Scottish Gaelic Dialect*. Philadelphia, PA: University of Pennsylvania Press.

Edwards, John V., 2004. 'Foundations of bilingualism'. In Tej K. Bhatia and William C. Ritchie (eds), *The Handbook of Bilingualism*. Malden, MA: Blackwell Publishing. 7–31.

Edwards, John, 2007. 'Societal multilingualism: reality, recognition and response'. In Peter Auer and Li Wei (eds), *Handbook of Multilingualism and Multilingual Communication*. Berlin: Mouton de Gruyter. 447–67.

Ehala, Martin and Kutlay Yagmur (eds), 2011. *Ethnolinguistic Vitality*. Special issue of the *Journal of Multilingual and Multicultural Development* 32: 101–200.

Fasold, Ralph, 1984. *The Sociolinguistics of Society*. Oxford, UK: Basil Blackwell.

Fishman, Joshua A. (ed.), 1971. *Advances in the Sociology of Language*, vol. 1: *Basic Concepts, Theorys and Problems – Alternative Approaches*. The Hague: Mouton.

Giles, Howard (ed.), 1977. *Language, Ethnicity and Intergroup Relations*. London: Academic Press.

Giles, Howard, Richard Y. Bourhis and Donald M. Taylor, 1977. 'Towards a theory of language in ethnic group relations'. In Howard Giles (ed.), *Language, Ethnicity and Intergroup Relations*. London: Academic Press. 307–48.

Gorter, Durk (ed.), 2006. *Linguistic Landscape: A New Approach to Multilingualism*. Clevedon, UK: Multilingual Matters.

Haiman, John, 1979. 'Hua: a Papuan language of New Guinea'. In Timothy Shopen (ed.), *Languages and their Status*. Cambridge, MA: Winthrop Publishers. 35–89.

Heller, Monica (ed.), 1988. *Codeswitching: Anthropological and Sociological Perspectives*. Berlin: Mouton de Gruyter.

Heller, Monica (ed.), 2007a. *Bilingualism: A Social Approach*. Basingstoke, UK: Palgrave Macmillan.

Heller, Monica, 2007b. 'Bilingualism as ideology and practice'. In Monica Heller (ed.), *Bilingualism: A Social Approach*. Basingstoke, UK: Palgrave Macmillan. 1–22.

Jaffe, Alexandra, 2007b. 'Minority language movements'. In Monica Heller (ed.), *Bilingualism: A Social Approach*. Basingstoke, UK: Palgrave Macmillan. 50–70.

Johnson, Ian, 2010. 'Tourism, transnationality and ethnolinguistic vitality: the Welsh in the Chubut Province, Argentina'. *Journal of Multilingual and Multicultural Development* 31: 553–68.

Koven, Michele, 2007. *Selves in Two Languages: Bilinguals' Verbal Enactments of Identity in French and Portuguese*. Amsterdam: John Benjamins.

Kroskrity, Paul V., 1993. *Language, History, and Identity: Ethnolinguistic Studies of the Arizona Tewa*. Tucson, AZ: University of Arizona Press.

Lambert, Wallace E., 1967. 'A social psychology of bilingualism'. *Journal of Social Issues* 23: 91–109.

Landry, Rodrigue and Réal Allard, 1994. 'Diglossia, ethnolinguistic vitality, and language behavior'. *International Journal of the Sociology of Language* 108: 15–42.

Lewis, M. Paul (ed.), 2009. *Ethnologue: Languages of the World* (16th edn). Dallas, TX: SIL International (online version: http://www.ethnologue.com; (retrieved 6 April 2011).

Li Wei (ed.), 2010. *Bilingualism and Multilingualism: Critical Concepts in Linguistics* (4 vols). London: Routledge.

Lieberson, Stanley, 1972. 'Bilingualism in Montreal: a demographic analysis'. In Joshua A. Fishman (ed.), *Advances in the Sociology of Language* (vol. 2). The Hague: Mouton. 231–54.

Makihara, Miki, 2005. 'Rapa Nui ways of speaking Spanish: language shift and socialization on Easter Island'. *Language in Society* 34: 727–62.

Martin-Jones, Marilyn, Adrian Blackledge and Angela Creese (eds), 2012. *The Routledge Handbook of Multilingualism*. London: Routledge.

Murray, K.M. Elisabeth, 1977. *Caught in the Web of Words: James A. H. Murray and the Oxford English Dictionary*. New Haven, CN: Yale University Press.

Omoniyi, Tope, 2004. *The Sociolinguistics of Borderlands: Two Nations, One Community*. Trenton, NJ and Asmara, Eritrea: Africa World Press.

Pavlenko, Aneta, 2006. 'Bilingual selves'. In Aneta Pavlenko (ed.), *Bilingual Minds: Emotional Experience, Expression and Representation*. Clevedon, UK: Multilingual Matters. 1–33.

Pavlenko, Aneta (ed.), 2008. *Multilingualism in Post-Soviet Countries*. Bristol, UK: Multilingual Matters.

Peal, E. and W.E. Lambert, 1962. 'The relation of bilingualism to intelligence'. *Psychological Monographs* 76, no. 27: 1–23.

Pietikäinen, Sari and Helen Kelly-Holmes, 2011. 'The local political economy of languages in a Sámi tourism destination: authenticity and mobility in the labelling of souvenirs'. *Journal of Sociolinguistics* 15: 323–46.

Porcel, Jorgen, 2006. 'The paradox of Spanish among Miami Cubans'. *Journal of Sociolinguistics* 10: 93–110.

Romaine, Suzanne, 2004. 'The bilingual and multilingual community'. In Tej K. Bhatia and William C. Ritchie (eds), *The Handbook of Bilingualism*. Malden, MA: Blackwell Publishing. 385–405.

Salisbury, R.F., 1962. 'Notes on bilingualism and linguistic change in New Guinea'. *Anthropological Linguistics* 4/7: 1–13.

Starks, Donna, Ray Harlow and Allan Bell, 2005. 'Who speaks what language in New Zealand'. In Allan Bell, Ray Harlow and Donna Starks (eds), *Languages of New Zealand*. Wellington, New Zealand: Victoria University Press. 13–29.

Taumoefolau, Melenaite, Donna Starks, Karen Davis and Allan Bell, 2002. 'Linguists and language maintenance: Pasifika languages in Manukau, New Zealand'. *Oceanic Linguistics* 41: 15–27.

Weinreich, Uriel, 1953. *Languages in Contact: Findings and Problems*. The Hague: Mouton.

Yagmur, Kutlay and Martin Ehala, 2011. 'Tradition and innovation in the Ethnolinguistic Vitality theory'. *Journal of Multilingual and Multicultural Development* 32: 101–10.

3

LANGUAGE SHIFT
AND MAINTENANCE

When two or more languages are in contact in a society, the situation between them is often unstable, as we saw in the previous chapter. That usually shows up as language shift, when speakers move from using one language to using another. In turn, once communities become aware that language shift is occurring, they will usually make efforts to maintain their own language. This chapter introduces language contact, and then turns to deal with language shift and maintenance.

3.1 INTRODUCING LANGUAGE CONTACT

Languages come into contact when people come into contact. If these languages (or varieties of languages) are different, and if the contact is more than fleeting, there can be a range of linguistic and sociolinguistic effects. There are situations in the world where languages co-exist over a long period in a quite stable relationship – Finnish and Swedish in Finland, for example. But such stability is much less common than change. The focus of contact linguistics is on situations either of fresh contact or where the linguistic configuration begins to change in a contact situation which has appeared stable. This is happening in the northeastern United States where the German of the Old Order Amish people of Pennsylvania is shifting after apparently holding stable for centuries (Johnson-Weiner 1998).

Language contact mainly occurs as a result of mobility through which speakers of one language encounter speakers of another. The mobility may be current, recent or in the historical past – for example by the ancestors of a once-migrant group, which sets the scene for contemporary language contact. Throughout history people have had a variety of reasons for travelling, which typically produce different kinds of contacts:

The Guidebook to Sociolinguistics, First Edition. Allan Bell.
© 2014 Allan Bell. Published 2014 by Blackwell Publishing Ltd.

- exploration – especially important in European expansion from the fifteenth century
- trade, commerce, business – has always been a prime cause of contact
- conflict – waging war, taking refuge from war, military service
- migration in pursuit of a better life – e.g. rural to urban, or from one country to another, singly or in numbers
- colonization – mass migration which usually takes over the destination area
- work – migrant or slave labour
- religion – escaping persecution or undertaking missionary activity, both of which were influential components of European colonization
- education – an increasingly important reason for mobility, although dating back to at least medieval Europe
- tourism – a major contemporary source of language contact, although with several centuries of pedigree in Europe.

Certain times and places tend to concentrate the circumstances for language contact. Border areas routinely host the continual contact of two or more languages for trade, work – or conflict. Alsace between France and Germany, and the US–Mexico border, are two examples. Large cities such as New York, Shanghai or Johannesburg are also magnets for work-oriented immigration, tourism, educational opportunities, commercial enterprise and the language contact that these involve. Historically, periods of expansion, invasion or war create new or intense contact. The centuries of European expansion were characterized by almost all the contact types listed. The conquests of Alexander the Great and Ghenghis Khan, and the world wars of the twentieth century, led to widespread new contacts among disparate languages.

The different situations listed have different kinds of language outcomes. A colonizing language sometimes largely wipes out the local languages, as Latin did to create

Exercise 3.1   Occasions of language contact

Section 3.1 listed nine types of mobility leading to language contact: exploration, trade/business, conflict, migration in pursuit of a better life, colonization, work, religion, education, and tourism.

- Which of these operate or have operated in your region or nation?
- What are their linguistic effects?
- What new languages do newcomers bring with them?
- How do locals respond to that?
- What language/s are used for communication between locals and newcomers?

For example, if international education is a major industry in your area:

- What languages do the students tend to speak?
- How much interaction is there between incoming students and locals?
- What language gets used for communication with these students?

Do local people also travel to other places and have contact with other languages, e.g. for business, education or tourism? What kind of contact?

languages such as French and Portuguese. In other cases, the colonizing language yields to the local language, as French was eventually absorbed by English after the Norman Conquest. Sometimes the colonizing language remains locally significant, as does English in India, in yet other instances it is lost almost without trace, e.g. Dutch in Indonesia (Ostler 2005). In all these, the contact leads to either language maintenance or language shift. More radical are two other outcomes: the ultimate in language shift, language death; and language creation. When people who do not share a language need to communicate, they will create that means through making a new language – called a 'contact language'. These are the pidgins which arise typically in trading situations, or the creoles which result from the enslaving together of people from different language backgrounds. We deal with the birth and death of languages in Chapter 4.

Mobility is not the only way in which languages come into contact. Media have long been the other main means, from scrolls in ancient times through to newspapers from the eighteenth century and the internet in the twenty-first. Media can make a language present in a place where it is not normally encountered face to face. The sacred texts of Islam, Judaism and Christianity have for millennia put their languages – Classical Arabic, Hebrew and Greek – in contact with other languages across the world (Ostler 2005). Through most of history this has been a one-way process, with media sending a message and the public receiving it. With the interactive media of the twentieth and twenty-first century, that has changed. Beginning with the telephone there can be interchange between users of different languages. This has increased exponentially with widespread digital media so that through the internet, contact with distant languages can be a daily experience. The international portability of a cultural form such as hiphop has carried the language of rap around the world.

When languages come into contact, there are a range of linguistic and sociolinguistic repercussions. These depend on the kind and degree of the contact, and the social and linguistic relationship of the languages:

- **Language choice**. When languages make contact, speakers have to begin making choices on which language/s to use and when.
- **Language stratification**. Languages become socially stratified in relation to each other, for example through 'diglossia' (see Chapter 5.3).
- **Language change**. Languages interfere with each other linguistically in different ways and degrees – they borrow words, lose or borrow structures. These changes can be minimal or wholesale. The field of contact linguistics focuses on contact-induced change in language.
- **Language shift**. One language is adopted instead of another.
- **Endangerment**. One of the languages is threatened with the possibility of loss, **attrition** and **death** (Chapter 4).
- **Code switching**. Two languages are mixed in the same discourse or sentence (Chapter 5.4).
- **Language creation**. Pidgins and creoles are languages newly minted in a contact situation (Chapter 4).
- **Dialect creation**. As speakers shift from one language and acquire another, they may create a new variety of that language influenced by distinguishing features from their previous language (see Chapter 7.4). This may run in tandem with language loss.

Language choice, stratification, shift and maintenance, birth and death, change, attrition and code switching are all fruits of language contact. In this and following chapters, we will look at these outcomes, and in Chapter 9 at dialect contact.

3.2   LANGUAGE FUNCTIONS

The notion of 'language function' is often used in discussing language contact, maintenance and shift. It is a 'macro' concept, used to characterize the sociolinguistic profile of a nation or society: a related concept at the micro level of individual choices is 'domain', which we will deal with in Chapter 6.1. The question of what languages are used for what functions in a nation is a consistent focus of language shift and maintenance research and advocacy, with its concern over the vitality of languages. The patterning of language use in a nation therefore always has a strongly political dimension.

In a society or nation, there will be a tendency for different languages to be used for different purposes, with the usages being driven by the sociopolitical character of the nation. Language functions can be classified as broadly public or private. Private includes communication among family, friends and in community situations, and sometimes local commercial activity. In most societies there will be one – or few – widespread, majority languages, which are used in all functions, both public and private. There may also be a number of minority languages which are used in some public functions as well as in private. And there will be other minority languages with relatively few or socially marginalized speakers, and these languages will tend to be used only in private functions.

Public functions are regarded by a dominant society as prestigious, and the non-use of a particular language in public functions will be both an indicator and a reinforcement of that language's lack of social standing. Typical public social functions of a language are education, media, government, law, parliament or equivalent body, religion, and business or commerce (Exercise 3.2).

The three main language-bearing institutions in society are education, the media and government/law. These institutions are usually dominated by majority languages, or those which have standing through, for example, international utility. A minority language will generally be regarded as robust to the degree in which it is used in these public functions, as we saw under the ethnolinguistic vitality approach in Chapter 2. When a language is confined to the private sphere of the home, or the traditional ethnic functions of ceremony, it tends not to be regarded even by its own speakers as having prestige in the wider society.

Of the three functions, education is arguably the most important. It is very common for parents to want their children educated in the prestige language of their country rather than in their own community language. Often they are not aware of the advantages to children of at least starting off their schooling in their community language. The 'Ebonics' controversies in the US in the late 1990s, over the official use of African American vernacular in schools, were typical of the polarizations that can occur (Rickford 1999). Many parents believe that educational use of the vernacular language or variety will entrench their children in disadvantage because they are not being taught in the language most likely to get them a good job.

Exercise 3.2 Language function profiling

What languages are used in what functions in your society? Take the five or so most widespread languages, and record the class's assessment of their use in these functions:

- Education
- Media
- Government (administration)
- Law (writing laws, and in the courts)
- Parliament (debate in an elected assembly)
- Religion
- Business, commerce
- Family
- Friends
- Community

Log the answers in a grid (languages × functions) to construct a language function profile of the nation.

1 What does this tell you about the functional distribution of the different languages, and about their relative social standing?
2 What areas of social life will some languages **not** be heard in? Which languages, and why?

If there are class members from other nations or regions, they can do the same kind of assessment for their home territory. Compare the findings between territories, and explain similarities and differences.

Official usage in government and law is also clearly influential in a language's standing, although it may not permeate daily language behaviour much. Media provide probably the most obvious public showcase for languages, and among the media, broadcasting has had a leading place. Broadcast languages are accorded an authoritative status as disseminators of desirable culture, including prestige language (Bell 1983). Winning a presence in broadcasting has therefore frequently been a focus of minority ethnic and language rights movements, for example in Wales and the Basque country. The case study at the end of this chapter looks at the contribution of broadcasting to the revitalization of one minority language.

Official and national languages

Closely linked with the notion of the public functions of languages are the concepts of national and official language. An official language may either be designated official through legislation, or be used de facto for government business – and preferably both. The concept of official language is an instrumental one, it has to do with the practicalities of governance – what Fishman dubbed 'nationism' (1972). What languages are and are not official in different states can often be surprising. English is not a designated official language in England, the United States or New Zealand despite being the dominant – often in

Exercise 3.3   Problematizing 'language functions'

The concept of 'language function' has tended to be applied as an objective descriptive term, but is it really so neutral?

1   Does it stratify languages and their uses according to a particular view of what matters in society?
2   If so, whose view is that? What are its effects?
3   What alternative views could there be, and how would they value the languages differently?

See Chapter 10 for more in-depth consideration of the social valuing of language and its political consequences.

practice, the sole – vehicle of government business in all three nations. It is however official in India (together with Hindi), Kenya and Tanzania (with Swahili). In Ireland both Irish and English are official, although Irish is in practice the active language of only a minority of the population.

The reason why languages such as Irish are official shades across into the concept of 'national language'. This is linked not to the pragmatism of 'nationism' but to Fishman's contrasting term 'nationalism', a sense of national identity and attachment. In Ireland, Irish is a national language but not English. In Paraguay, the indigenous language Guaraní is national, but Spanish is not. National languages may be legislated, although they need not be. And some languages may be both national and official.

For newer states – particular the postcolonial nations formed in the second half of the twentieth century – there may be a conflict between the instrumental and the identity goals, between nationism and nationalism. The former colonial language (such as French, Spanish, English) most easily serves instrumental functions, but as Fasold says (1984: 5), is 'usually a terrible choice' on nationalistic grounds. For identity reasons, one or more indigenous languages are stronger candidates, such as Irish or Swahili or Hindi, but they are often identified with one particular group and not others.

Malawi

We look now at how language functions in one specific nation, Malawi in East Africa (I am grateful here to Chimwemwe Patricia Kalikokha for first-hand information). Malawi became an independent nation in 1964, inheriting a legacy of British colonial support for English in certain social functions. The country has three major local languages, Chitumbuka, Chichewa and Chiyao, spoken in the north, centre and south of the country. As with other new African states, Malawi faced a language choice at independence, most starkly as to whether they would use the ex-colonial language as their national language, or whether they would opt for one or more local languages. Malawi chose to promote Chichewa, the language of the most politically powerful group and of the country's first president, Dr Hastings Banda, who ruled for 30 years. The process of 'Chichewazation' promoted one indigenous language at the expense of the others and was largely the work of Banda himself (Kamwendo and Mooko 2006). English was promoted as the main official language, with Chichewa favoured above other local languages – in some sense, then, a de facto 'national' language.

Despite this, Chichewa is not particularly strong in public functions, as Table 3.1 shows (note that a schematization like this makes the functions easier to compare, but tends to

Table 3.1 The functions of Chichewa and English in Malawi

	Chichewa	English
Official language	–	✓
National language	(✓)	–
Education	(✓)	✓
Govt admin	(–)	✓
Law (e.g. courts)	–	✓
Parliamentary debate	–	✓
Media	(✓)	✓
Religion	✓	(–)

✓ present
(✓) limited presence
– absent
(–) largely absent

- Why is Chichewa not more prominent in public language functions in Malawi? Use the internet to locate information on the nation's history, society, politics and international relations that helps explain this.

Exercise 3.4 Languages on official websites

Choose a nation – your own or another – and examine the role of official and national languages in its public self-presentation and communication. Do this by accessing several governmental websites and noting what language/s they are written in:

1 What are the official and national language/s?
2 Are the websites only in the official language/s? Or the national language/s?
3 Is there any information in other languages, especially minority languages?
4 Are the minority languages indigenous or immigrant ones?
5 Is there information written in international languages which are not official inside the country?
6 Is there any pattern to what language is used for different functions and contents?
7 If the nation has an explicit language policy, does the language usage on these websites follow that or not?
8 Does absence of national or official languages on these websites question the reality of the languages' designation as national or official?
9 Does it challenge our definitions of what is a national or official language?

absolutize a fluid situation). English is overwhelmingly the medium of education right through secondary and tertiary levels. Chichewa is used for the first few years at primary school level, and there has been some mother tongue instruction in Chiyao and Chitumbuka, although against a good deal of local opposition. Government is conducted largely in English, and the elected legislature operates solely in English. Political candidates are required to pass an English proficiency test before they are allowed to stand for election. In the media English is dominant, although some Chichewa is also used. Religion is the only one of these public functions commonly allowed to other languages, for example in religious publications.

3.3 Shifting languages

We saw in Chapter 2 that bilingual situations may be broadly classified as either dynamic or stable. These terms are, of course, relative – even a very stable-looking bilingual situation will have some aspects that may be undergoing change. But there do exist sociolinguistic situations where the distribution of languages is obviously changing. This is termed language shift, a dynamic sociolinguistic process where people who have traditionally spoken one particular language begin to speak another.

The most common trigger for language shift is people migrating to another country or language area. Such migrations have always between part of human history since ancient times. In the twentieth century there were waves of migration in many parts of the world, especially after the Second World War and in the 1990s. All of these have had linguistic consequences. We can observe the process of language shift in dozens of immigrant groups around the world – Chinese in Australia, Indians in Mozambique, Japanese in Peru, or Polynesians in California. The eventual linguistic outcome of minority immigration has usually been subtractive bilingualism: sooner or later group members lose their heritage language as they assimilate to the language of the host country.

There is also a second migration scenario, less common but with major sociolinguistic consequences: some large historical migrations have eventually led to the immigrants becoming the majority population in the host territory, as in the classic cases of the (mostly) British settler colonies – United States, Canada, Australia, New Zealand. Relatively quickly the settlers outnumbered – or at least outgunned – the indigenous peoples. Then local languages gave way to the immigrant language, meaning that it is the indigenous populations which lose their languages rather than the incoming migrants. Now all the hundreds of indigenous languages in these four countries have become endangered, and many have already been lost altogether.

Sometimes the colonizers need not even be a majority for their language to take over. In most of Latin America, the colonizers' languages have long been dominant – Portuguese in Brazil, and mostly Spanish elsewhere. However, in a few countries, indigenous languages co-exist as significant languages alongside Spanish. In Paraguay, Guaraní has long been an official language. In Ecuador and Bolivia, Quechua is a strong lingua franca, and in Peru it has been an official language since 1975 (Grenoble and Whaley 1998). Quechua had been the language of Inca colonization and was adopted by the Spanish as a vehicle of Christianization.

A lot of factors contribute to language shift, and most are common to shift from both indigenous and immigrant minority languages. We can bring many of them together under the headings of the three 'structural variables' of ethnolinguistic vitality theory outlined in Chapter 2 – status, demography and institutional support (Giles, Bourhis and Taylor 1977).

Low status

Immigrants routinely find themselves occupying low-status positions in their new society, living in poorer areas and working at jobs far below their qualifications. Their language will also lack status compared with the established language or languages of their host country. Indigenous minorities will usually have been forced into such a lower status position anyway, having been marginalized in the country that used to be theirs – as with Native Americans or Australian Aboriginals. Such low standing will be felt keenly by the immigrant or indigenous minority, who consequently themselves take on majority group attitudes which favour them shifting to the dominant language. An immigrant language such as Polish or Tongan – which back home was used naturally across all public functions – shrinks from the public ear in the United States and becomes confined to private functions only. Often the majority community opposes even hearing minority languages spoken in public places (recall Exercise 2.1 in the previous chapter about the banning of Indian languages in a workplace lunchroom). This creates pressure on speakers not to talk their language when there are people within earshot who do not understand it.

Unfavourable demographics

The numbers, composition and location of the minority group in comparison to the existing population play a crucial part in the promotion of language shift. If immigrants

---

Exercise 3.5   Immigrant parent–child debate

It is common for immigrant parents to encourage their children to speak the language of the host country rather than their heritage language. In due course this trend, adopted with the children's best interests at heart, routinely comes back a full circle to haunt the parents. The children – who may themselves have refused to speak or even listen to their community language when growing up – often turn around a decade or two later and accuse their parents of depriving them of their community language and ethnic heritage.

Stage a debate between the once-immigrant parents and their now adult children about why the parents did not actively pass on their community language:

- Why exactly did the parents encourage the majority language and discourage the community language?
- Why do the adult children now wish they had learned their heritage language?
- What has changed?
- What can be done about it?

Pasifika language shift

The findings of a major study of Pasifika languages in Manukau, New Zealand, in 2000–2 (Taumoefolau et al. 2002) give many evidences of language shift from the Pasifika languages to English. Language use shows age grading, such as using English to younger family members. Fluency in the community languages is also age graded. While all of the older generation and most of the middle-aged are fluent, a large number of younger community members are not. Such age grading is a typical marker of intergenerational language shift away from the community language and towards the dominant language.

Many individuals offered striking comments on their perception of the shift away from the community language:

I speak Niuean to my children and they respond in English.

Children need English to get a good job. You can't get a good job if you only know Cook Islands Māori.

Learning to speak Samoan, and the culture, is important. But in New Zealand, English is also important, job-wise.

If you can't speak Tongan, then you are not Tongan. Language tells us what you are.

- Apply these statements to the minority languages where you live, and debate the dynamics and outcomes that you see.

from the same language background settle close together they may form an island or 'enclave' where their language can be used in at least some public functions. By contrast, if the immigrants are widely scattered amongst the majority population, they will have fewer opportunities to cohere as a community and speak their own language. The clustering of Chinese in Californian cities and Greeks in Australia produces the potential for a critical mass of speakers who can interact publicly in those languages. Demographic distribution is one factor which frequently places indigenous minorities in a stronger position than immigrants for resisting language shift. They will often be historically concentrated in particular areas, remote from main population centres, which readily serve as language enclaves.

Institutional opposition

The education system will almost always operate in the national language/s of the host country. The attitudes of schools to minority languages usually range from benign neglect to mockery to outright prohibition of the language at school. It is a sociolinguistic universal, illustrated by poignant stories from all over the world, for children to be punished for speaking their indigenous language in schools where the dominant language is the medium of instruction. The nineteenth-century 'Welsh Not' was probably the most notorious instance – the board that was hung round the neck of a student found speaking Welsh. It could be removed only by catching another student in the same act, and the wearer at the end of the day was punished. Other established social institutions such as government or the media tend to show little interest in a minority language unless, for example, the numbers of an immigrant group become significantly large. In some societies the extreme is reached where an indigenous language is outlawed from public use, as Kurdish was in Turkey for some time (Skutnabb-Kangas and Bucak 1994).

There are well-trodden paths by which immigrant communities shift from their own language to that of their host country. At some point, the language begins to be not fully transmitted to the next generation, often within three generations. The first or immigrant generation arrived in the country as adults, monolingual in their original language. The second generation came as children and are bilingual, though perhaps with reduced speaking skills. The third generation may not speak their parents' language much and have limited comprehension. At this stage grandparents and grandchildren may strike difficulty communicating with each other. However, individual communities vary a lot. The Dutch have proved notably adept at shifting particularly to English (Klatter-Folmer and Kroon 1997), sometimes in as few as two generations. Other communities have tended to hold on to their languages much longer– Cantonese has persisted for generations in overseas Chinese communities.

A similar process of language shift has often applied when a local indigenous minority is overwhelmed by incoming settlers. In this case language shift may take much longer and is often vigorously resisted by the community. And the linguistic stakes are much higher: whereas immigrant languages usually leave behind a secure community of speakers in the former home country, indigenous languages are often found only in their own place. If the language ceases to be spoken there, it ceases to be spoken everywhere. Language endangerment and death are a topic in Chapter 4. From this extreme point in language shift, we turn now to examine the flip side – language maintenance.

3.4   MAINTAINING AND REVITALIZING LANGUAGES

Most communities resist shift from their own language to the majority tongue. Many community members regard their language as an intrinsic part of their culture and identity and wish to retain that distinctiveness against pressure from the surrounding society. Social psychological as well as sociological forces are at play in the flux between language shift and maintenance. Attitudes, motivations, community power and relationships are all operating. Within communities, attitudes towards their language may vary widely. Some members believe you have to speak the language to be a real community member, while others embrace the alternative, majority language. Actual behaviours may also differ greatly from expressed attitudes: statements of support for the language are not the same as taking supportive decisions and actions on language issues. Parents in Ecuador, for example, declare strong commitment to the indigenous lingua franca Quechua in competition with Spanish, but they are still not passing it on to their children (Rindstedt and Aronsson 2002).

Reversing language shift

Most of the voluminous research on language shift over the past 50 years has been motivated by the desire for language maintenance. Even when the research has been conducted by academics with no direct stake in the languages or communities involved, an activist impetus has usually been part of their motivation. Joshua Fishman, the leading advocate of minority language maintenance for decades, declared that to be the prime driving force of his own academic enterprise (e.g. Fishman 1991: xi). His activism was squarely based on support for Yiddish in the United States, and on the belief that 'the destruction of a language is the destruction of a rooted identity' (Fishman 1991: 4). To promote retention of such 'identity languages', he proposed the Reversing Language Shift (RLS) model, which seeks to unravel the threads of language shift and schematize the processes of language maintenance.

At the heart of the RLS model is Fishman's 'Graded Intergenerational Disruption Scale' (GIDS), based on the premise that the key to language maintenance is continuity of transmission between generations. The disruption scale is, as Fishman says (1991: 87), the flip side of the measures of ethnolinguistic vitality, that is: low status, unfavourable demographics and institutional opposition. The distinction is that the GIDS is also an **implicational** scale. Each level of increasing strength (from the weakest at stage 8 to the strongest, stage 1) implies the previous levels. Conversely, each stage can lead on to the next stage in succession. Table 3.2 paraphrases the eight stages.

Table 3.2   Fishman's Graded Intergenerational Disruption Scale, GIDS. In this rather opaque terminology, 'Xish' refers to the minority group and their language, and 'Yish' to the majority and their language. The scale is implicational, meaning that each successive stage presupposes the presence of the preceding stages.

8	Reconstruction of Xish from residual users; teaching to adults
	▼
7	Cultural interaction in Xish, mostly among older generation
	▼
6	Intergenerational oral communication in Xish, demographically concentrated in home, family and neighbourhood – this stage is the basis of mother-tongue transmission
	▼
5	Xish literacy in home, school and community, but without extra-communal support
	▼
4b	Public schools for Xish children with some instruction through Xish, but Yish curriculum and staffing
	▼
4a	Schools that meet compulsory education requirements but with Xish curriculum and staffing
	▼
3	Xish in local and regional work sphere beyond the Xish community and involving Yish community members
	▼
2	Xish in local and regional government and media services
	▼
1	Xish in educational, occupational, governmental and media operations at national levels

Source: Adapted from Fishman (1991)

This framework is at once a description of how language maintenance has proceeded in some cases, and a practical step-by-step **prescription** for how to achieve it. The programme is based on Fishman's belief that home and family are the heart of language maintenance, and on use of the community's own resources rather than depending on the wider society or state. The difficulty of community-wide planning for a unit as decentralized as the family presents the main challenge to language maintenance. Stages 8–5 in Table 3.2 remain largely within the community's own sphere and effort. From stages 4–1, increasing levels of majority-society input are required. According to Fishman, relatively few minority language movements reach stages 2 and 1. His detailed consideration of language maintenance practices and cases assesses some of the best-known instances in the light of his framework: Irish, Basque, Frisian and Māori (to which we turn in the next section). However, he concludes that the successes are outnumbered by the failures (see Exercise 3.7).

The RLS approach has fuelled a lot of further research and activity, and some imaginative revitalization techniques have been created, such as the language-immersion retreats used with the Tlingit language in Alaska (Mitchell 2005). But there have also been criticisms (some contained in a 2001 book edited by Fishman):

1   There is an excessive essentialism about Fishman's view that solidifies languages as clearly bounded entities. As Heller (2007b) argues (see Chapter 2), languages are not as discrete as people often think.

Exercise 3.6   Applying the intergenerational scale

Are there languages in your area or nation that are targets of language maintenance measures? Apply Fishman's Graded Intergenerational Disruption Scale (Table 3.2) to assessing the situations of two minority languages, preferably one which is the subject of considerable maintenance activity and one that is not.

- What stages are the two languages at?
- Compare their relative situations in the present, and their histories.
- How effective do you think the maintenance measures are for the one language?
- How serious do you think the lack of maintenance measures is for the other language?
- What do you think are the prospects of these languages being maintained in the future?

Evaluate the scale itself in the light of the cases you have looked at:

- Did you find the scale enlightening and useful for understanding these situations?
- Did any steps not seem to apply to your communities?
- Did you think the steps of the scale are in the appropriate order for your communities?
- Do you agree that transmission within the family (6) is the crucial stage for language revitalization?
- Would you suggest modifications of the scale?

> ### Exercise 3.7   For and against language revitalization
>
> Although he is the leading advocate of language maintenance, Fishman gave this gloomy evaluation of the success rate:
>
> > Most efforts to reverse language shift are only indifferently successful, at best, and outright failures or even contra-indicated and harmful undertakings, at worst. (1991: 1).
>
> Debate the pros and cons of language maintenance and revitalization efforts, taking opposing sides and views:
>
> 1   What are the reasons for attempting to reverse language shift?
> 2   And what are the reasons for a do-nothing attitude?

2   An allied criticism is the somewhat romantic identification of language with ethnicity (Canagarajah 2008) – reflected in the title of one of Fishman's books, *In Praise of the Beloved Language* (1996). We know that groups vary in the strength of their attachment to their community language. However, to say that language and ethnicity are detachable from each other is not to overlook the considerable passions that commitment to a language may evoke from its speakers (May 2005).

3   The standing of a language largely reflects the conditions in which its speakers live. Language management measures are only likely to prosper in the context of action over the usually disadvantaged social and economic situations of the minority group (Spolsky 2004).

4   A commitment to maintenance of the minority language may limit the linguistic options of the minority group themselves. In the practical realities of their lives, they may have their own good reasons – particularly economic and educational – for wanting to move away from their community language. We can lament the wider socioeconomic forces which result in such a decision, but are not entitled to judge the on-the-spot choices of the speakers themselves.

5   The family – which is the linchpin of RLS action – cannot be treated as an autonomous unit, able to operate independently of other social forces. Rather, families are subject to the influences and limitations of the wider group and the society (Canagarajah 2008).

Linguistic human rights

Another approach which has been centrally concerned with language maintenance issues is the movement for 'linguistic human rights' (LHR). Although Fishman's work takes account of higher-level political dimensions, his focus has been on local grassroots concerns and activities. By contrast, LHR operates at a very high level of national and often international policy and politics, although it also concerns itself with the local outworkings of these. The approach arose in the 1990s in a campaign spearheaded by Tove Skutnabb-Kangas and Robert Phillipson (e.g. 1994).

Exercise 3.8 Linguistic human rights

In the introduction to their book on linguistic human rights, Skutnabb-Kangas and Phillipson argue that 'linguistic rights should be considered basic human rights' (1994: 1).

1 What in fact are linguistic rights?
2 Should they be considered basic? Why?
3 What does that mean in principle and practice?

Look online at major human rights documents such as the United Nations Charter, the Universal Declaration of Human Rights, and the 1992 European Charter for Regional or Minority Languages:

4 What do they say directly about language?
5 What linguistic rights could be inferred or derived from what they say?
6 Do they have any actual effect on languages?

Lastly, consider the situation in your own country:

7 Are linguistic rights protected in your country – for example through a constitution or bill of rights?
8 Do those rights have any practical effects or do they seem to be largely lip-service?
9 Do they benefit the country's minority languages?

LHR as a cause draws on the human rights discourses of the twentieth century, in particular the 1945 United Nations Charter and 1948 Universal Declaration of Human Rights. These and many other international conventions aim to eliminate discrimination between groups and individuals. Language is usually a minor factor in general conventions such as these, and has had little coverage overall except in education-related statements. But more recently, specific language measures within Europe have offered the possibility of support for disadvantaged languages there, especially through the 1992 European Charter for Regional or Minority Languages (Spolsky 2004).

Skutnabb-Kangas and Phillipson argue that, while speakers of majority, dominant languages tend to have access to a full range of language rights, linguistic minorities frequently do not. Majorities often regard minorities and their languages as a threat because they do not assimilate to a monolingualist state. Minorities may not be entitled to education in their own language, but receive education in a language which – at least initially – they do not even understand. They may not be allowed to use their language in court. They may even not be permitted to name themselves in their own language. The focus here, then, is less on specific actions aimed at maintaining the viability of a language and more on the standing of the language and the right to use it in a range of public functions.

LHR has had and continues to have its critics, not least because of its activist and interventionist rhetoric. The first four criticisms of RLS listed earlier have also been levelled at LHR – a tendency towards essentializing (May 2005), romanticizing, abstracting language from the immediate sociopolitical context (Donna Patrick 2007), and limiting speakers' choices. It is also worth noting that minority languages are not just of sentimental value (May 2005). They also have – or may acquire – instrumental value, for example when used for tourism purposes.

LHR reminds us that the plight of minority languages is the result of social disadvantage at best and oppression at worst, so it is not a morally neutral issue. An address to both the social and linguistic issues is possible, as evidenced in several countries over the past 20 years. Norway has given some autonomy to Sámi in the regional area of Finnmark, including in government, law and education. Similarly, in northeastern Canada, the Arctic province of Nunavik now has the local Inuit language of Inuktitut as a co-official language – although the consequences of that move appear to be equivocal (Donna Patrick 2005).

Language maintenance and shift have political dimensions that are inescapable. Language shift always involves issues of power, dominance, marginalization and discrimination which reflect the political realities of a particular place and time. And maintenance will always require language policy initiatives to make any impact on the situation of minority languages. Language policy and planning developed as a major applied sub-field of sociolingustics in the 1960s when the new ex-colonial nations were needing to make decisions about national languages and varieties. The approach – led by Fishman, Ferguson, Haugen and others – was closely tied to the perceived need for 'development'. In due course this would be challenged as simplistic, and from the 1990s approaches included centre–periphery critiques (e.g. Canagarajah 1999) and examinations of the international role of English (Pennycook 2001). See Chapter 10.5 for language standardization as policy and planning.

3.5   THE CASE FOR MĀORI

A short history of language shift

We saw earlier how colonization has impacted on indigenous languages, resulting in speakers shifting from their own to the imperial language. This has occurred for hundreds of languages in recent centuries, particularly throughout the Americas and the Pacific Ocean and its rim. One such case is *te reo Māori*, the Polynesian language spoken by the Māori people who settled Aotearoa/New Zealand some thousand years ago. Māori people now number more than half a million, about 15 per cent of New Zealand's population. However the Māori language has only a few thousand fluent speakers, and many Māori people are monolingual in English. *Te reo*'s path from being the sole language of the country before first European contact in 1769, through to endangerment two centuries later, is a sadly textbook case of language shift.

In 1840, after half a century of scattered European settlement, the British governor signed the Treaty of Waitangi with Māori tribes. This became the foundation document of the nation – and 150 years later also an important player in language revitalization moves. The shift from Māori began in the mid nineteenth century and was most conspicuous in education. Initially the mission schools usually taught in Māori, with the result that New Zealand was more literate than England – but in Māori not English. As more settlers arrived, Māori had become a minority language by the 1860s, and English was introduced as a medium of instruction in schools. A decade later, after wars between

Māori and British, downgrading of the Māori language was prevalent enough for some Māori leaders to petition that 'there should not be a word of Māori allowed to be spoken in the School'. Such internalization of stigma perhaps marks the saddest phase of language shift, when a colonized people lead the drive for the abolition of their own language. By the early twentieth century all use of Māori was banned at school, and Māori children were beaten for speaking it there.

Language shift spreads from public to private functions, including into the home. For Māori, mid-twentieth-century migration to the cities was a major factor, and by the 1970s it had not been transmitted naturally for two successive generations in most areas. The language was hovering around the two lowest stages (7 and 8) on Fishman's inter-generational scale.

With ethnic revival and minority rights movements spreading internationally, the key first actions for revitalizing Māori began in the early 1980s with the grassroots *kohanga reo* ('language nest') movement, which has become a model for other revitalization efforts, especially in the Pacific. It sought to re-establish intergenerational transmission by bringing together the grandchildren and grandparent generations in immersion pre-schools. It was followed by the establishment of official bilingual and immersion classes and schools. In 1987 Māori was made an official language of New Zealand – a legislative status that English had never received (or required) – and the Māori Language Commission, Te Taura Whiri, was established.

The Treaty, *te reo* and television

At this point the Treaty of Waitangi began to figure in *te reo*'s history. In 1985 Māori language organizations brought a legal case arguing that the Treaty required the state to actively guarantee and promote the Māori language. The Māori version of the Treaty says (in modern English translation):

> The Queen of England agrees to protect the chiefs, the subtribes and all the people of New Zealand in the unqualified exercise of their chieftainship over their lands, villages and all their treasures.

The language was argued to be a *taonga* or treasure, and this would require the state to support it through the radio and television stations it owned. Being a specialist in issues of language and broadcasting, I was called on as an expert witness to support the Māori advocacy groups which fought the legal cases. I argued that greater exposure of Māori on television could be crucial to the language's future because it would enhance the prestige of the language for its own speakers and hearers (Bell 2010).

Over the course of a decade, a series of cases made their way up the New Zealand court system. These battles were eventually all lost, but the war in fact seemed to be won because the wording of the judgments handed down required the government to take action for the language. Two of the key statements are shown in Example 3.2.

The end result was a stand-alone, publicly funded channel, Māori Television, which began broadcasting in 2004. Within a few years, it had established itself as a part of the New Zealand television sphere, although remaining a minority channel. By 2006 two-thirds of its programming was in Māori, and 70 per cent of non-Māori supported its establishment, a notable turnaround from previous attitudes.

Example 3.2

Legal statements on protecting *te reo Māori*

The word 'guarantee' [in the Treaty of Waitangi] meant more than merely leaving the Māori people unhindered in their enjoyment of language and culture. It required active steps to be taken to ensure that the Māori people have and retain the full exclusive and undisturbed possession of their language and culture. (Waitangi Tribunal 1986, confirmed by Court of Appeal 1992)

Foremost amongst [the] principles are the obligations which the Crown undertook of protecting and preserving Māori property, including the Māori language as part of taonga, in return for being recognised as the legitimate government of the whole nation by Māori. (Lord Woolf, Privy Council, 1995)

Exercise 3.9   Language as 'treasure'

The New Zealand courts endorsed the claim of the Māori language to Government support because they accepted that it is legally a *taonga* 'treasure' (see Example 3.2). However the senior American anthropologist Jane Hill argues in her introduction to a suite of articles on linguists and endangered language advocacy (2002: 120, 124) that the treasure discourse is problematic:

> The discourse of hyperbolic valorization converts endangered languages into objects more suitable for preservation in museums patronized by exceptionally discerning elites than for ordinary use in everyday life by imperfect human beings ... The entailments of expressions like 'priceless treasure' go beyond mere commodification to turn endangered languages into a special kind of symbolic capital that is exchanged within a sphere in which only certain kinds of people can participate.

Assess the implications of using a discourse of 'treasure' to advocate for an endangered language.

1 Which groups and audiences are likely to be most impacted by treating a language as a treasure?
2 What benefits does this terminology offer in seeking support for the language? To whom?
3 Are there any disadvantages? For whom?
4 How could possible negative effects of the term be counteracted?
5 What obligations do you think follow from judging a language to be a 'treasure' under the law of a nation?
6 Do you think that Hill's warning applies to the Māori case?

Mainstream television stations, however, remained opposed to carrying much Māori programming. The chief executive of Television New Zealand said:

> We are, at the end of the day, a commercial broadcaster. Let's be realistic about this – less than 4 per cent of New Zealanders speak Māori and so putting a Māori language programme in prime time ... it simply won't rate. (*NZ Herald*, 24 May 2007)

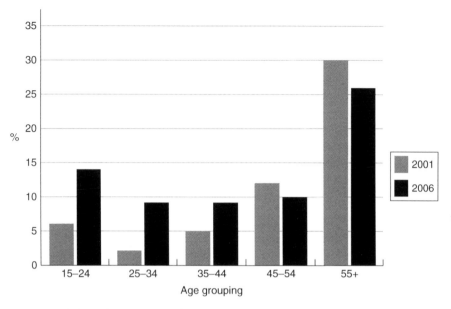

Figure 3.1 Shifts in the percentage of adults who can speak Māori well/very well, by age group, 2001–6
Source: Te Puni Kōkiri (2008a), figure 5

Māori revitalized?

Te reo Māori now has behind it 30 years of revitalization effort, spearheaded by the *kohanga reo* preschool movement, reinforced by official and institutional recognition, and most recently by the establishment of a dedicated television channel. What then is the state of the language now? There have been several surveys since the 1970s, including five-yearly census data since 1996. The results are not easy to interpret and compare, but seem to trace a continued decline through to the 2006 census.

The most recent and comprehensive research has been the 'Health of the Māori Language' surveys conducted by Te Puni Kōkiri (Ministry of Māori Development, 2008a and b). Their 2006 survey found much increased support for Māori language usage and initiatives compared to 2001, including an upturn in positive acceptance from non-Māori. Home usage with children was gauged to be increasing, although the language remains largely confined to ingroup settings. And the language health survey showed a marked rise in proficiency. Figure 3.1 displays a doubling between 2001 and 2006 of the number of people aged 15–44 who say they can speak Māori well to very well. This is a remarkable statistic, which the report attributes to educational participation as well as informal home learning.

The survey findings are indeed encouraging for the language but not, I think, for the obvious surface reason. Such a rapid rise in reported fluency invites enquiry, especially since all except the youngest of these groups (15–24 years) are too old to have been produced by the revitalization measures begun in the 1980s. These are self-report figures, and more than a rise in actual Māori speakership, they represent a rise in **claimed**

Exercise 3.10   Media and language revitalization

Fishman is scathing about the role of the media in revitalizing languages:

> There is no evidence whatsoever that the mass media can overcome or compensate
> for basic weaknesses in stage 6 [family transmission of the language, see Table 3.2].
> (1991: 175)

1   Do you agree with his opinion? Debate the place of media in language maintenance and revitalization.
2   See the quote from Television New Zealand's chief executive in section 3.5, arguing that the Māori language cannot be broadcast in prime time because too few
   people speak it. Marshall the evidence on both sides of this issue, and put the
   case for and against his view.
3   Examine the profile of minority languages in the media in your area by both scan-
   ning those media directly and surveying internet information about them.
   • How much television programming is there in these languages?
   • What about in other media such as radio and the press?
4   Using similar methods through the internet, examine the profile of some well-
   known minority languages in the media in their own nations – e.g. Irish, Welsh,
   Catalan in Spain.
5   Compare the media presence of any two or more of these languages, possibly
   including assessing the current presence of Māori. Evaluate what the comparison shows, and form an opinion of what this means for the languages involved.

speakership. Such an increased desire to register as a speaker is itself a strong sign of the
enhanced standing of the language, so the statistic is encouraging even if it overstates the
increase in actual fluency.

The survey report itself does conclude on a measured and sober note (Te Puni Kōkiri
2008a: 35):

> It must be noted that the Māori language remains at risk. Although it is the first language of
> New Zealand, it is a 'minority' language in all senses of the word. That is, the Māori lan-
> guage is spoken almost exclusively by a minority population and in total only 4% of New
> Zealanders (Māori and non-Māori combined) can speak the language. Further it is spoken
> by a minority of the Māori population … The Māori language is clearly used in a minority
> of communications by people that can speak the language. Although there is evidence of the
> re-emergence of intergenerational Māori language transmission, this is only at the initial
> budding stage, and is not the norm in Māori homes and communities.

Spolsky (2003) concludes in his overview that the revitalizing structure of Māori is not
one which will ensure 'natural' intergenerational transmission. Rather, this revitalization
provides the kind of institutional infrastructure that will enable survival, similarly to
Irish or Catalan. He does believe that, although intergenerational transmission has not
yet been restored, language loss has been checked.

This brings us back to the role of broadcasting, about which Fishman is sceptical (Exercise 3.10). As I argued earlier, the crucial thing for the language is increasing its standing, which encourages potential speakers to use it. Just such an enhancement of Māori has been reflected in this new millennium. As with Welsh, the once-despised indigenous language is now prestigious in some public language functions, including the media (Coupland and Aldridge 2009). The startup of Māori television in 2004 is the main new development in the period, and does appear to have contributed to the growing status of the language.

3.6   RESEARCH ACTIVITY
DOING A PROJECT (1) – THE SETUP

My belief is that the best way to learn sociolinguistics is by doing it. Ideally 'it' is a project that students design and carry out themselves. In this and the previous chapter students have been introduced to doing research through exercises in gathering information about multilingualism in their area, including interviewing class members about their language choices. Now it is time to look more generally at the process of doing a research project. Even in a short, early undergraduate course, there is scope for students to do a small project, perhaps in class time (such as the bilingual survey in Chapter 2.6).

There follows an outline of how to begin a project. This is the setup phase – the first three steps of what I describe as a nine-stage process (Table 3.3). The remaining steps will be covered in Chapters 7 and 10. This presentation is necessarily a quite general outline. It does not allow for all ranges of projects, but majors on questionnaire, interview and text methodologies. It assumes that students will be advised on the specifics of their projects.

The framework can serve equally for any scale of research, whether small individual projects, group projects, or a major study. The scale depends on the length of the course, level of the class, individual versus group work, etc. If it is not practical for students to

Table 3.3   Nine steps to a research project

The setup		
1	Aims and rationale	
2	Literature review	This chapter
3	Design and method	
Data collection		
4	Getting the data	
5	Processing the data	Chapter 7
Findings and reporting		
6	Coding the data	
7	Data analysis	
8	Data interpretation	Chapter 10
9	Writing up	

design their own projects, one or more pre-designed alternatives can be provided which effectively cover stages 1, 3 and possibly 2.

An excellent practical guide to doing language research, including several hundred project ideas, is Wray and Bloomer (2012). For detailed guidance on researching language variation, see Tagliamonte's textbook (2012). The Research Activity in Chapter 11 gives information and guidance for undertaking a project in performance language, such as film or comedy.

Step 1: Aims and rationale

Setting the project's aims is the important first step. In practice, some projects do not start with a research aim but, for example, with an interest in a particular piece of language data, such as a video clip. But explicit aims are needed before a project goes anywhere – otherwise it is likely to go nowhere. There are three 'simple' questions to ask of an idea for a research project:

1   Is it interesting?
2   Is it worth doing?
3   Can it be done?

This process clarifies what is the research issue or question you are addressing, what is the justification or rationale for doing this project, and what application or usefulness the findings may have. You may formulate this in a formal hypothesis, or just have a less specific hunch of what you are looking for. Crucially, point 3 addresses whether the project is feasible. There is always the temptation to bite off too much, and advice from an experienced researcher is essential to ensure this does not happen.

Step 2: Literature review

All research benefits from knowing what has gone before – the theory, the methods, the findings of prior studies.

- Read both in the general area of your project, and studies that are specifically relevant to what you are doing. If you are studying bilingualism in some part of Los Angeles, read about bilingualism in general, about Spanish/English bilingualism in the US, and anything you can find specifically on Spanish in the local area.
- Don't just list off the contents of one reading after another – synthesize common points and topics across what you have read.
- Assess the readings and critique them, don't just report what they say.
- Draw out the relevance of the readings for your own project.

For a small project, a rule of thumb is that you need at least 10 scholarly articles or their equivalent (e.g. book chapters) as the basis for a literature review. For a larger project, correspondingly more.

Step 3: Design and method

The design is how you get from your aims to your results: what is the project going to do and how? The central issue is deciding on exactly what your data is and how you are going to get it. Usually setting your aims (step 1) will give at least a general indication of what sort of data you will need, but at the design stage this has to become quite specific.

There are few limits to what may serve as sociolinguistic data. Sociolinguists occasionally get their data through experiments, but not often because their interest is mainly in studying language in actual use. More commonly they will use observation, noting down language behaviours that they see. More frequent again is research **about** language rather than **on** language, using social survey and analysis methods – for example, working with census data about language use, or surveying attitudes to languages (see Chapter 10.2). The language use questionnaire in Exercise 2.9 is this kind of instrument.

However most sociolinguistic research involves, naturally enough, gathering a sample of language itself and analysing some aspect of it. This means that the language has to be recorded in order to make it available for analysis. Recording speech is the core of sociolinguistic research – it is no accident that the birth of sociolinguistics followed the invention and accessibility of sound recording technology. The study of language variation in particular presupposes that speech has been captured for multiple re-listenings and coding. The interview is the standard technique for obtaining recorded speech, with William Labov developing thorough techniques for sociolinguistic interviewing, which we will see in Chapter 7.

But there are other kinds of ready-made recorded data. Written texts have always been available in hard copy, but the internet has opened up ready access to a vast range of written material in blogs, social network sites, online newspapers, and so on. Mega-corpora of English are now available online (see Wray and Bloomer 2012: 209 for a list). Still more usefully for sociolinguists, the internet is a treasury of recorded speech in audio and video, particularly through YouTube. If, for example, you want to research a dialect of English, already-recorded performances like these will be available:

- Lyrics or recordings of songs (in any musical genre – classical, popular, reggae, hiphop, folk, etc.)
- Excerpts from television programmes, in any dialect and any number of genres (comedy, soap opera, mystery, game show, etc.)
- Excerpts from feature films
- Excerpts from novels with representations of local speech
- Excerpts from local newspapers or magazines
- Radio talk
- Advertisements from press, radio or television

For such a project, you will select a specific strip of language that you believe contains interesting linguistic features for analysis, casts light on the dialect being performed, and carries social meanings which you can interpret.

Exercise 3.11   The ethics of sociolinguistic research

In the Manukau Pasifika languages project described in Chapter 2, the research team learned some home truths about the ethics of sociolinguistic work. Feedback from a community meeting made it quite clear that the research required much more active involvement of community members than we had allowed for. We started intensive community consultation, which redirected the design, conduct, personnel and outcomes of the project. This extended to how the project was named, with the area being referred to as 'Manukau' rather than 'South Auckland', which had accrued negative overtones. It was an object lesson – which others have learned before us (e.g. Wolfram 1998) – in the appropriate involvement of the researched in the research process, and applies also to small-scale projects.

In an excellent book, Cameron et al. (1992) distinguish three levels of relationship between the researchers and the researched:

1 research on – 'ethical research'
2 research on and for – 'advocacy research'
3 research on, for and with – 'empowering research'.

- Debate what is meant by these different conceptions of the research relationship, and how the differences might work out in practice.
- If you are working on a project, sketch three alternative designs in line with the three different approaches.
- Specify the differences between these three designs: which will you adopt and why?

Once you have decided on your project's data and how to access and gather it, you will then need to:

- Map out the steps of the project, including how you will handle and analyse your data (see Chapters 7 and 10).
- Attach a timeline to these steps, to bring it in before the deadline.
- Identify what resources you need – internet search and downloads? A digital recorder? Hard-copy questionnaires? Computer software?
- What are the ethical issues involved in the project, and how will they be addressed (Exercise 3.11)? In many countries permission from the university's ethics committee is required to begin any research with human subjects. Often there may be a general permission for students on a course to do projects under supervision.

3.7   SUMMARY

- Language contact occurs mainly through mobility, when speakers of one language encounter speakers of another. Travel may be for reasons as varied as exploration, trade, conflict, migration, colonization, work, religion, education or tourism.

Language contact prevails in certain places such as large cities and in certain periods such as invasions.

- Media have long been a second main means of contact, from scrolls in ancient times to twentieth-century broadcasting. The interactive media of the twentieth and twenty-first centuries have increased exponentially the opportunities for language contact. The linguistic and sociolinguistic repercussions of contact include language choice, stratification, shift and maintenance, birth and death, change, attrition and code switching.

- In a nation, different social 'functions' may be filled by different languages. Language functions are classified as broadly public or private. Public functions such as government, education or media are generally regarded as prestigious for a language. An official language is one used for government business, while a national language is symbolic of the nation and its identity. In the case of Malawi, English rather than Chichewa fulfils most public functions.

- Language shift is a dynamic process where people who have traditionally spoken one language begin to speak another, usually because of migration or colonization. Most immigrant minorities lose their community language and assimilate to the language of the host country, and indigenous minorities find their languages under pressure. Low status, unfavourable demographics and institutional opposition are the factors that contribute to language shift. Most communities resist shift from their own language, regarding it as an intrinsic part of their identity.

- Fishman's Reversing Language Shift model schematizes the processes of language maintenance. His 'Graded Intergenerational Disruption Scale' measures increasing language strength, focused on continuity of transmission through the family.

- A second approach to language maintenance is through 'Linguistic Human Rights'. Both these have been criticized for essentializing languages, overly romantic identification of language and ethnic identity, ignoring the general social situation of a minority community, and limiting the linguistic options of the group.

- As a case of language shift and maintenance, the Māori language of Aotearoa/New Zealand has lessening numbers of fluent speakers. The language diminished across 150 years of colonization to a low point in the 1970s.

- Māori revitalization started in the 1980s with the *kohanga reo* ('language nest') movement, followed by bilingual and immersion classes and schools. In 1987 Māori was made an official language. After court cases begun in the 1980s the Government was required to take action for the language, which resulted in the establishment of Māori Television in 2004. Subsequent surveys showed a marked rise in people claiming to speak Māori, reflecting increased status which was arguably a flow-on effect of Māori Television.

3.8 FURTHER READING

The field of contact linguistics is served by a number of introductory texts. Winford 2003 offers thorough though rather prosaic coverage across themes of shift and maintenance, borrowing, structural diffusion, code switching, pidgins and creoles. Thomason (2001) is a quirky and avowedly personal introduction, offering fascinating perspectives and a vast array of examples. It is notable for comprehensive and evaluative end-of-chapter reading guides, and a long glossary. Thomason's joint book with Kaufman (1988) synthesizes a framework for contact linguistics drawing on language maintenance and shift, historical linguistics, and pidgin/creole studies. Ostler's *Empires of the Word* (2005) is a readable compendium of information on the linguistic repercussions of imperialism from ancient times on.

A good proportion of the contents of the bi/multilingualism journals and readers listed at the end of Chapter 2 cover language shift and maintenance studies and issues. The publisher Multilingual Matters has specialized in publishing on maintenance and shift, including resources for those working to maintain languages – see their website.

Fishman's 1991 book on Reversing Language Shift is basic in language maintenance practice, together with the follow-up edited collection (2001). The foundation publication of Linguistic Human Rights is the collection edited by the field's initiators, Skutnabb-Kangas and Phillipson (1994). It combines chapters on issues in linguistic human rights, alongside case studies in specific countries. Arzoz (2008) overviews a lot of information about language diversity throughout Europe.

Bernard Spolsky's text on language policy (2004) covers the policy aspects of minority language maintenance, and evaluates Fishman's RLS approach. Ricento (2006) offers critical approaches to the theory and method of language policy, and to topical issues such as language policy and national identity. The field has its own journals (*Language Policy* and *Language Problems & Language Planning*). Spolsky's edited Handbook for Cambridge (2012) gives comprehensive coverage. The website of the Language Policy Research Network (http://www.cal.org/lpren/index.html) offers information, connections to research and a listserv for online exchange.

For information on New Zealand Māori, see the many reports held on the website of Te Puni Kōkiri, the Ministry of Māori Development (e.g. 2008a, 2008b). These include surveys and Māori language broadcasting history and policy. Bauer (2008) offers a re-analysis and critique of the surveys. See also the website of the Māori Language Commission, Te Taura Whiri. Richard Benton (e.g. 1983) and Bernard Spolsky (e.g. 2003) have both researched and published longterm on the state of Māori. Chrisp (2005) addresses the issue of intergenerational transmission. Fishman (1991) devotes a chapter to Māori as one of its case studies. Hollings (2005) and Bell (2010) cover broadcasting issues and developments.

REFERENCES

Arzoz, Xabier (ed.), 2008. *Respecting Linguistic Diversity in the European Union*. Amsterdam: John Benjamins.

Bauer, Winifred, 2008. 'Is the health of te reo Māori improving?' *Te Reo* 51: 33–73.

Bell, Allan, 1983. 'Broadcast news as a language standard'. *International Journal of the Sociology of Language* 40: 29–42.

Bell, Allan, 2010. 'Advocating for a threatened language: the case for Māori on television in Aotearoa/New Zealand'. *Te Reo* 53: 3–25.

Benton, Richard A., 1983. *The NZCER Māori Language Survey*. Wellington, New Zealand: NZ Council for Educational Research.

Cameron, Deborah, Elizabeth Frazer, Penelope Harvey, M.B.H. Rampton and Kay Richardson, 1992. *Researching Language: Issues of Power and Method*. London: Longman.

Canagarajah, A. Suresh, 1999. *Resisting Linguistic Imperialism in English Teaching*. Oxford: Oxford University Press.

Canagarajah, A. Suresh, 2008. 'Language shift and the family: questions from the Sri Lankan Tamil diaspora'. *Journal of Sociolinguistics* 12: 143–76.

Chrisp, Steven, 2005. 'Māori intergenerational language transmission'. *International Journal of the Sociology of Language* 172: 149–81.

Coupland, Nikolas and Michelle Aldridge, 2009. 'Introduction: a critical approach to the revitalisation of Welsh'. *International Journal of the Sociology of Language* 195: 5–13.

Fasold, Ralph, 1984. *The Sociolinguistics of Society*. Oxford, UK: Basil Blackwell.

Fishman, Joshua A. (ed.), 1972. *Advances in the Sociology of Language*, vol. 2: *Selected Studies and Applications*. The Hague: Mouton.

Fishman, Joshua A., 1991. *Reversing Language Shift: Theoretical and Empirical Foundations of Assistance to Threatened Languages*. Clevedon, UK: Multilingual Matters.

Fishman, Joshua A., 1996. *In Praise of the Beloved Language: A Comparative View of Positive Ethnolinguistic Consciousness*. Berlin: Mouton de Gruyter.

Fishman, Joshua A. (ed.), 2001. *Can Threatened Languages be Saved? Reversing Language Shift, Revisited: A 21st Century Perspective*. Clevedon, UK: Multilingual Matters.

Giles, Howard, Richard Y. Bourhis and Donald M. Taylor, 1977. 'Towards a theory of language in ethnic group relations'. In Howard Giles (ed.), *Language, Ethnicity and Intergroup Relations*. London: Academic Press. 307–48.

Grenoble, Lenore A. and Lindsay J. Whaley (eds), 1998. *Endangered Languages: Language Loss and Community Response*. Cambridge: Cambridge University Press.

Heller, Monica, 2007b. 'Bilingualism as ideology and practice'. In Monica Heller (ed.), *Bilingualism: A Social Approach*. Basingstoke, UK: Palgrave Macmillan. 1–22.

Hill, Jane H., 2002. '"Expert rhetorics" in advocacy for endangered languages: who is listening, and what do they hear?' *Journal of Linguistic Anthropology* 12: 119–33.

Hollings, Mike, 2005. 'Māori language broadcasting: panacea or pipedream'. In Allan Bell, Ray Harlow and Donna Starks (eds), *Languages of New Zealand*. Wellington, New Zealand: Victoria University Press. 111–30.

Johnson-Weiner, Karen M., 1998. 'Community identity and language change in North American Anabaptist communities'. *Journal of Sociolinguistics* 2: 375–94.

Kamwendo, Gregory and Theophilus Mooko, 2006. 'Language planning in Botswana and Malawi: a comparative study'. *International Journal of the Sociology of Language* 182: 117–33.

Klatter-Folmer, Jetske and Sjaale Kroon (eds), 1997. *Dutch Overseas: Studies in Maintenance and Loss of Dutch as an Immigrant Language*. Tilburg, the Netherlands: Tilburg University Press.

May, Stephen (ed.), 2005. 'Debating Language Rights'. Theme issue of *Journal of Sociolinguistics* 9/3.

Mitchell, D. Roy, IV, 2005. 'Tlingit language immersion retreats: creating new language habitat for the twenty-first century'. *International Journal of the Sociology of Language* 172: 187–95.

Ostler, Nicholas, 2005. *Empires of the Word: A Language History of the World*. London: HarperCollins Publishers.

Patrick, Donna, 2007. 'Language endangerment, language rights and indigeneity'. In Monica Heller (ed.), *Bilingualism: A Social Approach*. Basingstoke, UK: Palgrave Macmillan. 111–34.

Pennycook, Alastair, 2001. *Critical Applied Linguistics: A Critical Introduction*. Mahwah, NJ: Lawrence Erlbaum.

Ricento, Thomas (ed.), 2006. An Introduction to Language Policy: Theory and Method. Malden, MA: Blackwell Publishing.

Rickford, John R., 1999. 'The Ebonics controversy in my backyard: a sociolinguist's experiences and reflections'. *Journal of Sociolinguistics* 3: 267–75.

Rindstedt, Camilla and Karin Aronsson, 2002. 'Growing up monolingual in a bilingual community: the Quichua revitalization paradox'. *Language in Society* 31: 721–42.

Skutnabb-Kangas, Tove and Sertaç Bucak, 1994. 'Killing a mother tongue – how the Kurds are deprived of linguistic human rights'. In Tove Skutnabb-Kangas, Robert Phillipson and Mart Rannut (eds), *Linguistic Human Rights: Overcoming Linguistic Discrimination*. Berlin: Mouton de Gruyter. 347–70.

Skutnabb-Kangas, Tove and Robert Phillipson (eds), 1994. *Linguistic Human Rights: Overcoming Linguistic Discrimination*. Berlin: Mouton de Gruyter.

Spolsky, Bernard, 2003. 'Reassessing Māori regeneration'. *Language in Society* 32: 553–78.

Spolsky, Bernard, 2004. *Language Policy*. Cambridge: Cambridge University Press.

Spolsky, Bernard (ed.), 2012. *The Cambridge Handbook of Language Policy*. Cambridge: Cambridge University Press.

Tagliamonte, Sali A., 2012. *Variationist Sociolinguistics: Change, Observation, Interpretation*. Malden, MA: Wiley-Blackwell.

Taumoefolau, Melenaite, Donna Starks, Karen Davis and Allan Bell, 2002. 'Linguists and language maintenance: Pasifika languages in Manukau, New Zealand'. *Oceanic Linguistics* 41: 15–27.

Te Puni Kōkiri, 2008a. *Te Oranga o te Reo Māori 2006/The Health of the Māori Language in 2006*. Wellington, New Zealand: Te Puni Kōkiri.

Te Puni Kōkiri, 2008b. *Te Oranga o te Reo Māori i te Rāngai Pāpāho 2006/The Health of the Māori Language in the Broadcasting Sector 2006*. Wellington, New Zealand: Te Puni Kōkiri.

Thomason, Sarah G., 2001. *Language Contact: An Introduction*. Edinburgh: Edinburgh University Press.

Thomason, Sarah G. and Terrence Kaufman, 1988. *Language Contact, Creolization, and Genetic Linguistics*. Berkeley, CA: University of California Press.

Winford, Donald, 2003. *An Introduction to Contact Linguistics*. Malden, MA: Blackwell Publishing.

Wolfram, Walt, 1998. 'Scrutinizing linguistic gratuity: issues from the field'. *Journal of Sociolinguistics* 2: 271–9.

Wray, Alison and Aileen Bloomer, 2012. *Projects in Linguistics and Language Studies* (3rd edn). London: Hodder Education.

4

LANGUAGE BIRTH AND DEATH

The most radical repercussions of language contact are language birth and death. To take the second of these first: we saw in Chapter 3 how speakers may shift from the use of one language to another in situations where the other language is dominant, as in immigration or colonization. Immigration usually involves no threat to the incoming language as a whole because it leaves a viable community of speakers behind it. Even if all Greek immigrants and their descendants in Australia stopped speaking Greek, the language would remain strong in its homeland. But an indigenous language in a colonized country such as Australia will usually be spoken only in that country. If the language is lost there, it is lost everywhere. When the Aboriginal people who speak Dyirbal shift entirely to English, the Dyirbal language will die. The latter part of this chapter looks at the sociolinguistics of language death, and at what happens to the structures of languages which are in the process of dying.

But languages can be also be born. When groups of people who have no common language are thrown together, they will very quickly cobble up a rudimentary new language in order to communicate. Among the contact situations listed in Chapter 3.1, this has happened typically in situations of exploration, trade, colonization and, especially, enforced labour. The resulting language is a pidgin. In everyday speech 'pidgin' is a negative term, used to mean language or speech that someone regards as underdeveloped or corrupted. But in linguistics, pidgin is a descriptive, technical term for a contact language. Some pidgins are short lived, but if one persists, it may over time develop the characteristics of a full language. Children will start to learn it as their mother tongue, and the outcome is then termed a 'creole' (another term that in everyday usage is often negative). Linguistically these contact languages are fascinating because they enable us to see a language actually on the production line, being made as we watch.

Some sections of this chapter remain at a macro level, examining the social place of these languages. However, other parts – especially some examples, exercises and the

The Guidebook to Sociolinguistics, First Edition. Allan Bell.
© 2014 Allan Bell. Published 2014 by Blackwell Publishing Ltd.

research activity – look in micro detail at the way in which language structure is developed or lost as languages are born or die. These require some use of linguistic terminology. For any unfamiliar terms, refer to a dictionary of linguistics such as Crystal (2008).

4.1   PIDGINS AND CREOLES

Jargons

First contact between people who do not share a language creates what linguists call a 'jargon' – again a technical use different from the lay meaning. Here jargon does not mean the specialist or obscure vocabulary of a profession. It is a temporary and small-scale means of linguistic communication. It is thrown together for the immediate occasion, a set of words – a small vocabulary – that never settles down to become a broad or long-term means of communication. A jargon begins in the kind of word-exchanges that traders – or tourists – everywhere conduct with local peoples they want to deal with. It has few words and little structure, and doubtless most instances have gone unrecorded because they were so fleeting.

But with repeated contact, some jargons start to solidify beyond the immediate encounters that triggered them. So we have Chinook Jargon in the pre-European northwest of North America, which was first recorded by Captain Cook in 1778. With a core vocabulary of perhaps 500 words, it was clearly developing towards something more sophisticated. Russenorsk was another jargon, used for communication between Norwegian fishermen and Russian merchants during the nineteenth century. Typically for such codes, Russenorsk lacked the copula (verb *to be*):

tvoja		grot	rik
you	(are)	very	rich

(Broch and Jahr 1984)

South Pacific Jargon had up to 200 words and died away in much of the Pacific after whaling stopped in the 1860s. However, in the southwest Pacific its vocabulary grew and it continued to become part of something that was much bigger – Melanesian Pidgin, which now has several million speakers, and is the case study later in this chapter.

Pidgins

There is good reason to believe that pidgins will have existed through much of human history when the right contact situation existed, but usually in situations where their presence has not been recorded. The mass deportations of subject peoples by ancient empires such as Assyria (Ostler 2005) were likely triggers for pidgins. The best-known older pidgin has a Romance-language base and is called simply 'Lingua Franca'. It was used around the Mediterranean from the twelfth century, and some scholars have held that it formed the base of all subsequent pidgins and creoles. An even older pidgin has been found, dating from a thousand years ago, although the manuscript was rediscovered only in 1982. An eleventh-century Arab geographer reported what is clearly an Arabic-based pidgin from a town in north central Africa. His evaluation – 'the Blacks have mutilated our beautiful language and spoiled its eloquency with their twisted tongues' (Thomason 2001: 163) – could be the template for public commentary on pidgins ever since, including the racist overtones.

Known pidgins began to be created on a large scale with European exploration and expansion from the fifteenth through to the nineteenth centuries. Shown the way by the Portuguese down the west coast of Africa, the other colonizing nations of Europe followed suit. Spain, England, France, the Netherlands all spread out, and their expansion along the coasts of the world resulted in many trading pidgins.

Creoles

But it was trade in humans that was the main path to creating long-lasting creoles. Between the sixteenth and nineteenth centuries, an estimated 10 millions of black Africans were enslaved and transported across the Atlantic to work the plantations of the Americas, many of them in the Caribbean. Thrown together from diverse language backgrounds and with white European overseers, these communities created their own means of communication from the materials at hand. This makes the Caribbean the world's contact language nexus. The second main region for plantation economies and pidgins was the southwest Pacific in the late nineteenth century. There are over 100 pidgin and creole languages in the world, some of which bear names that witness to their origins:

Kweyòl	French-derived	St Lucia
Kreyòl	French-derived	Haiti
Creolese	English-derived	Guyana
Krio	English-derived	Sierra Leone
Kriyol	English-derived	Northern Australia

Attempting definitions

Virtually any generalization in pidgin and creole studies is controversial, as Thomason (2001) says, including some of what I have already written in this section. And it is a field peopled with larger-than-life characters who debate the issues with vigour. The differences of opinion begin with the definitions, and it seems that every scholar and every publication put forward their own. This is partly because almost any definition

Exercise 4.1   What is a pidgin or creole?

Scholars disagree about exactly how to define pidgins and creoles. Below are several of their definitions.

1   Clarify what the definitions mean and evaluate them.
2   Identify and evaluate any common points of agreement.
3   Identify and evaluate the differences. What do they mean? How important are the differences?
4   Can a distinction between pidgin and creole be maintained?
5   Create your own definition on the basis of these inputs.

- Thomason 2001

  Traditionally, a pidgin is a language that arises in a new contact situation involving more than two linguistic groups. The groups have no shared language ... They do not learn each other's languages, but instead develop a pidgin, with vocabulary drawn typically ... from one of the languages in contact. The new pidgin's grammar does not come from any one language; instead it is a kind of crosslanguage compromise of the grammars of the languages in contact, with more or less (usually more) influence from universals of second-language learning ... A creole, by contrast, is the native language of a speech community. (p. 159)

- Hymes 1971

  Pidgins arise as makeshift adaptations, reduced in structure and use, no one's first language; creoles are pidgins that become primary languages. (p. 3)

- Holm 1988

  A pidgin is a reduced language that results from extended contact between groups of people with no language in common ... A creole has a jargon or a pidgin in its ancestry; it is spoken natively by an entire speech community (pp. 4 and 6).

- Mufwene 2001

  A creole is a restructured variety of its lexifier [superstrate language]. (p. 28)

- Muysken and Smith 1995

  Pidgin languages ... represent speech-forms which do not have native speakers ... The degree of development and sophistication attained by such a pidgin depends on the type and intensity of communicative interaction among its users ... Pidgins do not have native speakers, while creoles do ... a creole language can be defined as a language that has come into existence at a point in time that can be established fairly precisely. (p. 3) ends up excluding some language which we would like to include as a pidgin or creole. But let me still attempt them:

- A **pidgin** is a language that is created when groups who lack a common language are in ongoing contact. It has a limited vocabulary, simplified structures and no native speakers who learn it as a first language.
- A **creole** is a language created when groups who lack a common language are in extensive contact. It has a full vocabulary and complex grammar, and has native speakers.

The dominant language in this mix is called the **superstrate**, and the languages of the powerless are the **substrate**. The superstrate language (such as Portuguese) usually contributes most of the vocabulary and is therefore called the **lexifier** language. The substrate languages (such as African languages) contribute more to the grammar. Many pidgins and most creoles share a common social history in the importing of enslaved or indentured workers from widely diverse ethnolinguistic backgrounds across long distances, and lumping them together under the control of small numbers of colonists. That is, as Arends, Muysken and Smith have noted (1995), creoles tend to be the result of social and linguistic violence. Different local demographic and socioeconomic conditions, such as the requirements of the particular crop being cultivated, contributed to different linguistic outcomes. Different creoles have grammars that are closer to or more distant from their superstrate, lexifier language such as English or French.

4.2 WHERE DO PIDGINS AND CREOLES COME FROM?

The central issues in contact linguistics concern where the different components of the new languages have come from and how, and what shared principles may be detected behind these processes. Why do widely scattered pidgins and creoles have so much in common linguistically? There is most agreement over the lexicon. Usually the situations in which pidgins arise involve social inequality, so the less powerful tend to defer to the more powerful and adopt their vocabulary. Most pidgins and creoles take their vocabulary largely from a single superstrate language – the lexifier. This is why speakers of the colonizing language (such as English) often have some comprehension of a derived creole (although the meanings of the words may be different in the new language), and regard it as a debased form of their own, superstrate language. Often there are also substantial lexical inputs from one other language, and some from elsewhere (Holm 1988). Because European colonists dominated in the situations where most known pidgins and creoles arose, most of their lexicons are based on English, French, Portuguese, Dutch and Spanish (in roughly descending order of frequency). Some however derive from other languages such as Bazaar Malay in southeast Asia and Hiri Motu in Papua New Guinea.

While the source of the lexicon is usually quite clear, where the grammars of pidgins and creoles come from is highly contested. Usually one language can be named as the main lexifier, but there may be many candidates for grammatical input because of the diverse input languages of the speakers. Alongside these influences there are also operating, in a largely unpredictable mix, broad principles of universal grammar and processes of second language acquisition.

Example 4.1

Making words in Sranan

Sranan is the national language and lingua franca of Suriname (Migge and Smith 2007). It is a creole that arose in the late seventeenth century, and most of the vocabulary is from English. Two processes that are frequently used to create new words in creole languages are reduplication (the repetition of an element) and compounding (which combines two or more elements). In Sranan reduplication is used to mark several meanings. The following examples come from Adamson and Smith (1995) – the accent indicates a stressed syllable.

Diminutive-pejorative

| fatu | 'fat' | fát(u)fátu | 'fattish' |

Augmentative (increasing)

| ferfri | 'to paint' | ferfiférfi | 'to paint a lot' |

Iterative (repeating)

| bow | 'to build' | bówbow | 'to build in different places' |

Sranan also uses compounding as the preferred means of extending the lexicon:

dray-ay	turn-eye	'dizziness'
dungru-oso	dark-house	'prison'
agu-meti	pig-meat	'pork'

For pidgins, the phonology generally draws on the input languages but tends to be simpler. The vocabulary is much smaller (a few hundred words at most), and morphology such as inflections is minimal or absent. In syntax, word order is the main means of structuring, and there is little subordination. By contrast, creoles have a lexicon able to serve the communicative purposes of a community. The creole's phonology tends to mix super- and substrate influences, and the syntax provides the full range of structures such as relativization and other forms of subordination.

There are however counter-examples to all of these generalizations. A pidgin does not even have to acquire native speakers to complexify to full-language status. In Papua New Guinea, Tok Pisin expanded its structure and functions before it had any native speakers, and became one of a number of 'extended pidgins' that looked little different linguistically from creoles. It may be that the crucial factor for creolization of a pidgin is the spread of its usage across a wide range of functions, which usually – but not necessarily – co-occurs with its acquiring native speakers.

Comparing theories

Creolists' attempts to come to terms with the enormously complex data of their subject have thrown up a wide range of explanations and theories, some contradictory, others shading into each other, all of them warmly contested. The differences between theories are largely focused on the relative importance that different scholars give to the superstrate, the substrate or linguistic universals, to the sociolinguistic processes they believe were involved, and to the relative importance of the social, historical and economic contexts. My listing here represents much of the range of opinion but is by no means comprehensive and does not attempt to map theories in relation to each other:

1   The **Monogenesis** theory sees all creoles as derived from a Portuguese-based West African pidgin, and perhaps ultimately from the medieval Mediterranean Lingua Franca. In its strong form this may deal neatly with similarities but does not cater for the diversity that is obvious across contact languages. However, there are modified versions involving 'relexification' – the process by which the vocabulary of an existing language is replaced by vocabulary from another language while keeping the grammar of the first language.

2   The **Language Bioprogram Hypothesis** is a universalist approach put forward by the controversial creolist Derek Bickerton (1981) and based largely on Hawai'ian Creole English. Bickerton claimed that children construct the grammar of a creole from the unstable pre-pidgin used by adults around them. They do this on the basis of universal principles in the manner of first – rather than second – language acquisition. This is an abrupt process, taking only a single generation. Although most creolists reject the hypothesis, it has had an enormous impact on debate in the field, largely because many scholars – in the process of lengthy refutations – continue to define their own positions over against it (see for example Siegel 2008; Veenstra 2008). Nevertheless, most scholars recognize that linguistic universals – such as the more ready adoption of unmarked forms – play their part in the creolization process.

3   The **Relexification Hypothesis** emphasizes the substrate role. It holds that creoles arise through combining the vocabulary of a superstrate language with the grammar of a substrate through relexification (see point 1). So in the case studied by Lefebvre (1998), Haitian Creole arose through grafting French vocabulary on to the grammar of the West African language Fon or Fongbe. Few scholars accept that the strong version of this theory can account for many creoles.

4   While the approaches in 1–3 imply a rapid or 'abrupt' creolization process, others take a **gradualist** line, stressing the continuity of transmission within a colony. Scholars such as Singler (e.g. 1996) argue from demographic evidence that creoles in the Caribbean developed over a time frame closer to a century rather than a single generation. At a particular point there was a socioeconomic watershed when a shift from smallholdings to big sugar plantations required large numbers of slaves to work them, and their presence may then have triggered rapid creolization.

5   Still other creolists prioritize the **superstrate** and a gradual process. Focusing on French-lexifier creoles in the Indian Ocean, Chaudenson (2001) believed the first slave arrivals learned dialects of French from their masters, albeit imperfectly. Each subsequent new wave of slaves learned in succession the current form of the language and in turn contributed to the shape of the next, increasingly divergent version. Eventually the outcome was different enough from French to be considered a separate, creole language. Mufwene has generalized this process to his 'Founder

Principle' (2001), which holds that the first generation of settlers had a disproportionate importance in setting the linguistic agenda for later comers.

6   Finally, some scholars (e.g. Winford 2003) stress that pidginization and creolization can to a large degree be regarded as processes of mass, serial **Second Language Acquisition**. This approach draws on the considerable body of research into how people learn second languages (Lefebvre, White and Jourdan 2006; Siegel 2008). Put in a situation where second language acquisition was required in order to communicate, the displaced slaves tried to make sense of the target language that was available to them (initially the superstrate). In the process they produced forms showing interference of their native, source language with the target, resulting in an **interlanguage** that is a cross-linguistic compromise. These are the same processes that operate in second language acquisition, where learners produce an interlanguage that shows imperfect learning of a target language influenced by their own native language. Again, the same happens when new immigrant groups learn the language of their host nation imperfectly and so create distinctive varieties of that language (see Chapter 7.4 on ethnic varieties).

There is among all these approaches none that is clearly preferred or dominant. Given the complexity of the linguistics involved, and reliance on often fragmentary evidence, there is unlikely to be a consensus on the origins of pidgins and creoles soon.

Exercise 4.2   Debating creole genesis

See the six theories or hypotheses or explanations listed in the text that have been put forward for the origins of creole languages. Remember that there are overlaps between some of these, and other theories that are not discussed here, and the summaries I have provided are very brief presentations of proposals that are often complicated.

1   Have the class divide into six groups, with each group taking one of the theories.
2   The group researches that theory, beginning with the references supplied in the text.
3   They summarize the theory, explain which languages it has been put forward for, describe some of the language and social data presented as evidence, and how these support the theory's explanation.
4   Each group briefly presents its findings on its allocated theory to the class – including evaluating the adequacy of the summary I have given in the text.
5   During the presentations the class note the common points and differences between the theories.
6   At the end, the class discusses the similarities and differences, strengths and weaknesses of the six approaches. Are there common points across the theories which seem strongly supported?
7   The class draws a conclusion on which theory (or combination or variant) it finds the most convincing.

4.3   THE CREOLE CONTINUUM

Most creoles continue to co-exist with their lexifier languages, and over time this has consequences for the shape of the creole. The lexifier language (say French) will usually have maintained its superstrate standing in comparison to the creole. It will be a standardized language with social prestige and perhaps international status. The lexifier rather than the creole will often be the target language of schooling. This puts social pressure on speakers to shift towards the standard language in some situations. So in countries like Jamaica and Guyana, the creole finds itself sharing the sociolinguistic space with standard English, and in Haiti with standard French. This may lead to 'decreolization' – the process by which the creole language converges with the lexifier language. What transpires is not a clean switch between creole and standard but a continuum. At one end is the most deeply creole speech, called the **basilect**. At the other end of the continuum is the most standard speech, the **acrolect**. In between is a gradient of forms with many successive levels, the **mesolects**.

As Peter Patrick writes, 'Between the basilect and the acrolect … lies this apparently seamless web of minimally differentiated varieties' (2008: 474). Like everything in creole studies, the continuum is contested – many scholars point out that it may take different

---

Exercise 4.3   From acrolect to basilect

The following example is adapted from Alleyne (1980: 192) and shows the range in the Jamaican Creole continuum, with several linguistic changes occurring at most of the levels. Many of these changes are typical of creole grammars.

Acrolect	1	he is eating his dinner
	2	(h)im is eatin' (h)im dinner
Mesolects	3	(h)im eatin' (h)im dina
	4	im a eat im dina
	5	im a nyam im dina
Basilect	6	ĩ a nyam ĩ dina

Specify the linguistic changes that take place at each level from acrolect to basilect, and what area of the language these are from (e.g. phonology, morphology, syntax). For example, from level 1 to 2 there are three changes:

he becomes *(h)im*	syntax (pronounced with or without /h/)
his becomes *(h)im*	syntax
eating becomes *eatin'*	phonology

- What structure is lost at level 3?
- What is the major change in the verb system in 4?
- At level 5, *nyam* is a word of West African origin.
- At 6, the nasalized /ĩ/ has no gender marking: it can mean *he, she* or *it.*

Example 4.2

Attitudes to creoles

Negative attitudes to creoles are often held by communities and even by the languages' own speakers. But contrasting sets of uses and attitudes show up between two Pacific creoles – Hawai'i Creole (HC), and the Melanesian Pidgin (MP) spoken in Vanuatu, Papua New Guinea and the Solomon Islands. Both have strong local identity value but differ in other ways, to the extent that one is seen as a dialect and the other as a distinct and national language, according to Pacific creolist Jeff Siegel (2008: 267):

> While most speakers of MP consider it to be a language separate from English, most speakers of HC think of it as an incorrect form of English – i.e. at best a non-standard dialect and at worst broken English. MP has had its own orthography for many years, and it is normally used to write the language. HC has only recently acquired its own writing system ... but it is rarely used ... MP is used in a wide variety of functions – including parliamentary debates, newspapers, radio broadcasting, and religion. HC ... is rarely used other than in informal conversation.

shapes in response to different influences. One theory of the origins of African American Vernacular English is the 'creolist' hypothesis that it is a decreolized version of an earlier creole language.

Not all creoles encompass an acrolect-to-basilect continuum. Siegel (2008) finds that the Melanesian Pidgins do not decreolize, despite being in ideal conditions to do so. They remain distinct from English. This is because a language like Tok Pisin is regarded by its speakers as separate from English, and is itself a national language of Papua New Guinea and used in a wide range of public functions. Attitudes to creoles are often very ambivalent. Overt community opinion often downgrades basilectal creole as a broken form of language compared to the acrolect, but more covert attitudes tend to value it as an emblem of local identity (see Chapter 10 on language attitudes and ideologies).

Such are the processes by which new languages can be born. Much more frequent in our era is the phenomenon of language death, to which we now turn.

4.4 LANGUAGE DANGER AND DEATH

In Chapter 2 I touched on the occurrence of 'subtractive bilingualism', where speakers such as indigenous children acquire a new dominant language at the cost of losing their former language. When there is no successful stay or reversal of such language shift, the end point will be the total loss of the language if this is its only community of speakers. To reach this stage of threatened language loss, there has to be a break in the intergenerational transmission of the language – more children grow up no longer learning their parents' language. Recall Fishman's stress (Chapter 3 earlier) on the importance of such transmission, and how its breakdown contributed to the diminution of Māori. The factors that break transmission are the continuing pressure of those factors which I listed in Chapter 3.3 as promoting the earlier phases of language shift:

- Low status and the pressure of economic disadvantage are regarded by Hale (1998) as the most compelling trigger for language death
- Unfavourable demographics, which have often included displacement or decimation of a colonized indigenous population
- Institutional neglect or opposition, especially in education

The monolingualist attitudes and practices which we noted in Chapter 2 have bred distrust of bilingualism and contempt for subordinate languages. The result has been that minority languages have been – in Nancy Dorian's memorable phrase – 'despised to death' (1998: 3), dispiriting their speakers into abandoning them. Pictish, Etruscan and Gothic were early European casualties. Celtic languages were more recent, with the last speaker of Cornish dying in 1777 and of Manx in 1974. Those Celtic languages which remain – Irish, Gaelic, Breton and Welsh – are in varying degrees of danger. Although Latin is often referred to as a 'dead' language, under this definition it is not so: it developed into Italian and the other Romance languages.

Counting languages in danger

Language endangerment is an issue which linguists have become particularly aware of over the past two decades. Individual linguists have long known of the endangerment of particular languages, or even of whole sets of languages in a particular area. But the scale of endangerment, and its significance for those whose profession is the study of languages, was highlighted by the publication in 1992 of a suite of articles by Ken Hale and others in *Language*, the leading international linguistics journal. For the first time, this set down informed – although avowedly approximate – estimations of the state of languages around the world, calculated by Michael Krauss of the Alaska Native Language Center. He drew heavily on the then current edition of the compendium of the world's languages, *Ethnologue* (Grimes 1988). Krauss grouped the world's languages into three categories:

- 'Safe' languages are those which have high numbers of speakers and/or official support.
- Endangered languages are those which children look likely to cease learning during the twenty-first century.
- Moribund languages are those already in an advanced state of decline.

Setting 100,000 speakers as a lower limit, Krauss's estimate is that perhaps 600 out of the approximately 6,000 languages in the world may be deemed safe. His conclusion (1992: 7):

Therefore, I consider it a plausible calculation that – at the rate things are going – the coming century will see either the death or the doom of 90% of mankind's languages.

Exercise 4.4   An endangered language near you

Most nations of the world have endangered languages within their borders, and some have dozens or even hundreds of them. Identify any endangered languages in your nation.

1   Who are the speakers of these languages? Where do they live? What is their standing in society?
2   Do they use their languages extensively in their homes or within their community? Do all community members speak their languages or only some? Do young people speak them as well as older people?
3   Are the languages used in any public functions? Do you hear them spoken on the street?
4   Are the languages used in religious contexts?
5   Are they used in education? Are children dissuaded from speaking them at school?
6   Do you hear or see them in the media, on the internet? Or in government documents?
7   Is there any government policy about these languages? What is it? Is the policy carried out in practice?
8   Are any steps being taken to maintain or revitalize these languages? By the community itself or by the state? Whose responsibility is it?
9   If nothing is currently being done to support these languages, should anything be done? What? Why? If not, why not?
10 What would be the effects on their speakers if the languages were lost?

These figures have continued to be the most commonly cited, and Krauss reaffirmed them in 2007. Regardless of the specifics and roughness of such calculations, clearly widespread language death is an imminent reality, and all commentators agree it is proceeding at a much faster pace than previously. For the area where figures are most reliable, North America, Krauss estimates that 149 out of 187 indigenous languages are not being learned by children, thus 80 per cent are moribund. Some 90 per cent of the 250 Australian Aboriginal languages are also moribund. It is worth noting that under Krauss's definition, Māori would be presumed a 'safe' language because it is official, although Chapter 3.5 showed its situation to be anything but secure.

Discourses of language death

We are understandably shocked by such statistics of dying languages, but it is worth reflecting on what exactly is lost when a language is lost. Linguists such as Hale identify several related losses, which are listed in Exercise 4.5. The common thread is that different languages contain dimensions that are unique to them, and that their loss is therefore irretrievable.

So what should or can linguists do about it? Some, like Hale, have committed to advocacy. Others such as Dorian have given long-term support to struggling languages. Like ecologists who study an endangered species, the commitment to help preserve a

---

Exercise 4.5 What is lost with a language?

Linguist-advocates for endangered languages have suggested these as the kinds of repercussions entailed by the loss of a language:

- Loss of culture: each language serves as a uniquely suited carrier of the culture from which it arises. In cases such as poetry or story, cultural products only exist through language.
- Loss of world view and thought patterns: each language embodies a unique way of looking at the world.
- Loss of identity: language instantiates a unique connection to a group's heritage and sense of itself.
- Loss of linguistic diversity: there is a great variety of linguistic structure present in languages that are endangered, some of it not occurring in other languages.

Unpack the specifics of these losses and assess them:

1 Do you think such losses do result if a language dies?
2 How great a loss do you think each of these four would be?
3 How would these effects impact on your nation if an endangered language within it was completely lost?

---

language you are deeply interested in as a scholar is natural. It may also be or become part of the obligation that is placed on a researcher by the community whose language it is, as England (1992) argues. In the concrete circumstances of language endangerment, it may become impossible – in principle or in practice – for a linguist to stand aside from the situations of the communities they are involved with. Such decisions may lead to heartsearching. Rob Pensalfini researched a moribund language in the Northern Territory of Australia. He begins a reflection on 'Whose linguist am I?' like this: 'I am vexed by the question of who benefits from linguistic work on moribund languages' (2004: 154). Recall the issue of conducting research on, for or with people that was examined in Exercise 3.11.

In discussing advocacy for Māori in Chapter 3.5, we saw the potentially problematic nature of the 'treasure' metaphor applied to endangered languages. Probably the most frequent discourse used in this area is to parallel language death to the loss of biological species, and understandably so. The similarities are hard to resist and draw on a tradition of language ecology stretching back decades to Einar Haugen (e.g. 1972). In such situations the discourses of species endangerment and 'linguicide' seem to come naturally to the lips (see Bell 1991c for my own use of this discourse in advocating for Māori).

Nevertheless, although bio-discourse is a serviceable, even powerful, strategy for indigenous groups asserting their entitlements, it can have a down side (Donna Patrick 2007). It associates readily with images which risk exaggeration – 'predator' languages which commit 'linguicide'. The biological parallel has limits even though it has been drawn by some of the most prominent advocates (Hale et al. 1992; Nettle and Romaine 2000). Languages, for example, do not disappear in the same way as bio-species and, in the case of Hebrew, have been famously brought back from the brink.

The other primary discourse is that of the 'health' of languages, which entails a corresponding potential for 'illness', and invites quasi-medical comparisons. The concept of language health is also the presupposition for the notion of language 'death' itself. Several of the contributors to Dorian's edited volume on 'language obsolescence' (1989) problematize the death metaphor, and prefer alternatives such as 'contraction'. Heller and Duchêne (2007) question the definability and therefore countability of languages at all. For my own part, I acknowledge the limitations, histories and ideologies involved in all these discourses and have misgivings about my own use of them (Bell 1991c). On the other hand, I know that we will always need images for speaking about such things. And I lament the potential loss of languages around the world, particularly for their speakers, and will continue to advocate for those that are at risk in my nation.

The most important consideration here must be the speakers rather than the language. In concentrating on the language, discourses of biodiversity or health can sideline the speakers themselves. Speakers are very resourceful in creating new forms to serve their needs, and these may include mixed or 'impure' linguistic structures which do not cleanly fit into the bounds of the traditional language. If social conditions make speakers or communities shift to another language, we cannot address the language loss without taking account of the social conditions that produce it.

Exercise 4.6   Discourses of endangerment

There are a range of discourses – ways of talking – about language endangerment and death. Below are the most prominent of these, along with some references where they are either advocated or addressed. The book edited by Duchêne and Heller (2007) makes a deconstructive assessment of many of these discourses and their sociopolitical positioning. See also the suite of articles that includes Hill (2002), and Austin and Sallabank's collection (2011). Search out other references, including websites devoted to endangered languages (see the further reading section at the end of this chapter).

Biodiversity	Hale et al. 1992; Nettle and Romaine 2000; Muehlmann 2007; Donna Patrick 2007
Enumeration (of endangered languages)	Krauss 1992; Nettle and Romaine 2000; Hill 2002
Universal ownership (of language diversity)	Hill 2002
Health, illness	Hamp 1989; Te Puni Kōkiri 2008a
Endangerment	Heller and Duchêne 2007; Jaffe 2007a
Death	Several articles in Dorian 1989
Linguicide	Skutnabb-Kangas and Phillipson 1994

Questions:

1 Summarize each discourse in a sentence.
2 Who uses this discourse? Who is it addressed to?
3 What implications does this way of talking have for languages and speakers?
4 What benefits does this discourse have? Who for?
5 What disadvantages does it have, and who for?
6 Do you believe this discourse should be used in advocacy for endangered languages?

Processes of language death

In an important overview of the linguistics and sociolinguistics of language death, Campbell and Muntzel (1989) distinguish four types:

1   **Sudden** language death: Languages usually die as the result of language shift, when speakers abandon their language in favour of another. But there have been cases of languages being lost because all their speakers perished in a short space of time. This could be through natural disaster: all speakers of Tamboran in what is now Indonesia died in a volcanic eruption in 1815, and their language went with them (Nettle and Romaine 2000). Humanly perpetrated disaster has been known to achieve the same effect nearly as abruptly, through massacre and/or epidemic. In 1857 the entire Yeeman tribe in Queensland, Australia, were killed by white settlers: nothing is known of their language. The Yahi people and their language in northern California were annihilated in the wake of the gold rushes there.

2   The quirkily labelled **radical** language death: This is a little less sudden than the previous category. The language's speakers survive a traumatic event but then relinquish their language. In El Salvador in 1932, the massacre of an Indian population led to the survivors' abandonment of their own languages in order to avoid being identified (Campbell and Muntzel 1989).

3   **Gradual** language death: The previous two are unusual cases. Most language death takes a slower path although it often involves less radical instances of the same factors, e.g. reduction of an indigenous population by disease. It occurs over several – perhaps many – generations, and is characterized by differential competence in the language according to age. Typically it will involve a reduction in contexts of use from public to private. These processes are clearly similar to those involved in ordinary language shift.

4   **Bottom-to-top** language death is the opposite of the foregoing. Here the language is lost from informal contexts but persists as a ritual language, rather on the pattern of church Latin or the much more ancient Vedic Sanskrit.

European imperial languages are not the only culprits contributing to the death of other languages. Small local languages are often threatened by regional or national lingua francas such as Wolof in Senegal, or Hausa in northern Nigeria – which is said to be more of a threat to local languages than is English (Igboanusi and Lothar 2004). Kore, a language once spoken in coastal Kenya, is a case of Campbell and Muntzel's radical language death (Dimmendaal 1992). It was replaced in a single generation by Somali and the regional lingua franca, Swahili, whose promotion is impacting today on many smaller east African languages.

4.5   THE MICROLINGUISTICS OF DYING LANGUAGES

As a language is lost, it changes and is subject to attrition. Structures and features drop away, its functions diminish, its range of variation reduces. When we compare this with the information about contact languages earlier in the chapter, these changes appear as broadly the opposite of what languages undergo as they are being created. This is true, but the parallels are only at the most general level, mainly because individual cases of both language birth and death differ so widely in their specifics. Speakers may also experience their own individual language 'death' even though the language itself lives on. This is known as language **attrition**, when individual speakers gradually lose their capability in a language as a result of long-term contact with another language, for example after migration (Schmid and de Bot 2004).

Campbell and Muntzel (1989) suggest some generalizations for linguistic attrition in dying languages, such as losing phonological contrasts, overgeneralizing unmarked forms, making obligatory features variable and diminishing the range of styles. The most widely shown change is a reduction in morphology. China has many minority languages that have become endangered through being ignored or oppressed under the

Example 4.3

'Women, fire and dangerous things'

The Australian language Dyirbal has been one of the most closely documented cases of a dying language. Schmidt (1985) recorded the children and grandchildren of speakers that Dixon (1972) had worked with in the 1960s. By 1982 no one under 15 could construct a sentence in Dyirbal. The changes affected all levels of the language, but differentially:

- Lexicon – a lot of vocabulary loss
- Syntax – the traditional free word order of Dyirbal shifting towards an English-style Subject-Verb-Object pattern
- Morphology – major changes in affix systems
- Phonology – only minor changes

Schmidt concluded that Dyirbal 'bears all the symptoms of a language whose death is imminent' (1985: 233). In particular, there were radical changes in the way Dyirbal classifies nouns. The system used to be based on intimate cultural knowledge:

Class I	masculine and animate nouns
Class II	feminine nouns and those to do with water, fire and fighting
Class III	edible plant food
Class IV	everything else.

Younger Dyirbal speakers are losing the knowledge needed to make the traditional classifications and are shifting to a simplified system based only on animacy (referring to persons or animals) and sex. This means that the world is losing the unique and striking system which lumped 'women, fire and dangerous things' into a single category and gave the American linguist George Lakoff the quirky title for his classic book on what linguistic categorizations reveal about the human mind (1987).

To the best of my knowledge, there has been no updating study of Dyirbal since.

immense sway of the national language, Mandarin (Bradley 2005). One of these is Oroqen, spoken by a few thousand former hunter-gatherers in a once-inaccessible area of northeastern China. Under colonization by the Han Chinese, Oroqen speakers are losing the morphological complexity of their language (Li Fengxiang 2005). One of the earliest changes has been loss of 'emphatic reduplication' in colour adjectives. This operates through copying the first syllable of the adjective to make it mean an intense hue of the particular colour:

bagdarin	'white'	bag-bagdarin	'very white, white as snow'
shingarin	'yellow'	shib-singarin	'very yellow, golden yellow'
kara	'dark, glossy'	kab-kara	'very dark, glossy black'

These subtleties are now lost to the language. Oroqen is also losing its plural marking, borrowing vocabulary and the phonology is changing. The external pressures come mostly from Mandarin, which has been aggressively promoted in recent decades. The language shifts accompany a raft of social changes such as static settlement (rather than nomadism), new resource-related occupations, intermarriage, modern communications and majority language education.

Borrowing – often large amounts of it – is seen in many language contact situations, and is common with dying languages. Thomason (2001) maintains that, in extreme cases, a language can end up borrowing virtually everything from another, dominant language. The Anglo-Romani language used by Romany ('Gypsy') people in England has English grammar and lexicon, but only a few hundred words remaining from the original Romani. Over time speakers have been known to borrow the entire grammar and lexicon of another language, so that the language dies through being transformed into the other language (as with the Finnic language, Votic).

But a dying language may not necessarily undergo this kind of attrition. In the United States, the Native American language Montana Salish has been under intense pressure from English since the nineteenth century and is seriously endangered. Nevertheless it has borrowed no structure and few words from English (Thomason 2001).

4.6   THE CASES OF GAELIC AND MELANESIAN

This chapter's case study takes two cases not one. The first is a case of language death in Scotland, and the other, language birth in the southwest Pacific Ocean.

East Sutherland Gaelic in Scotland

When the American sociolinguist Nancy Dorian first went to the East Sutherland region of northern Scotland in 1963, she found 200 speakers of Gaelic in three coastal fishing villages north of Inverness. By the time she completed her fieldwork there 15 years later, half of those had died (Dorian 1981). A further 20 years on, nearly all the fluent speakers were dead or incapacitated (Dorian 2002). These older speakers were not being replaced because children were growing up monolingual in English, making East Sutherland Gaelic a dying variety of an endangered language.

Gaelic is the Celtic language of the highlands and islands of Scotland, brought from Ireland well over a millennium ago. It has been under pressure from English for many centuries. English colonialism in the region culminated in the 'clearances' of the early nineteenth century by which the mainly absentee landowners swept their Scottish tenants off the land to make way for sheep. In East Sutherland many of these 'crofters' were resettled on the coast and formed the villages that Dorian later studied, distinguished by their fisher identity and its manifestations in dress, diet and language.

Dorian's study (1981) combines ethnographic perception and linguistic precision. As well as studying the fluent speakers, she focused on those who were not fully proficient and described the linguistic detail of their influency. She distinguished three groups of speakers graded by both age and proficiency:

- Older fluent speakers: the most conservative speakers, although showing some differences to traditional Gaelic grammar
- Younger fluent speakers: numerous but subtle grammatical differences, which go largely unnoticed
- Semi-speakers: imperfect control of the grammar (often because of incomplete acquisition) which is noticed by the community

Exercise 4.7   On semi-speakers

While most of the ESG [East Sutherland Gaelic] semi-speakers *produce* a Gaelic with very evident deficiencies, their *receptive* control of the language is outstanding. They are fully privy to all ordinary conversation in ESG; they can laugh at jokes and stories, pick up whispers, enjoy repartee, and make out messages under high-noise conditions. It is not difficult for the visiting linguist to learn to speak more correct ESG than the SSs [semi-speakers], and even to speak it more readily and connectedly than many of them. But it is unlikely that he or she will ever equal the SS's effortless and complete understanding of the rapidly spoken language. Because of their outstanding passive skills in ESG, the SSs have a strong sense of inclusion in the speech events of the community, however little they may say themselves. It even happens that a very weak speaker conceals from himself as well as from others how incomplete his productive control of the grammar is by remaining primarily a listener and making judicious use of his limited spoken Gaelic in verbal interactions. With full passive skills, a little active use of Gaelic can be made to go a long way toward adequate social interaction. (Dorian 1981: 155)

- What do you make of the strong asymmetry between the semi-speakers' speaking and listening abilities in East Sutherland Gaelic? What does it mean socially for the community, and linguistically for the language and its speakers?
- What is the relative role of grammatical competence compared to communicative capability in their conversational involvement?
- What does the performance of these semi-speakers mean for our understanding of what it means to know a language?

There is also a fourth group: 'passive bilinguals' who may understand everything and know a lot of individual words but cannot make sentences.

The semi-speakers are a sociolinguistically fascinating group (Exercise 4.7). In terms of the dimensions of bilingualism identified in Chapter 2, their receptive skills far outstrip their production. They cannot make sentences, but they can follow everything and participate highly in Gaelic interactions. They tend to be people who may have been among the youngest children of a family, had strong early attachment to an older relative like a grandparent, with heightened local allegiance through having spent time away, or just especially gregarious.

Linguistically, Dorian found a highly variable picture of what features are decaying in East Sutherland Gaelic and how much. She judged the changes were similar to those that occur during normal language change, but that the amount of change was both greater and faster. In language death it is quite unpredictable what structures will be lost or retained and by whom. No particular linguistic features or processes are sure precursors of language death – most of these changes can also occur in contact situations which do not result in death. All we can say is very general: language death does often involve simplification, and especially in the morphology.

Creoles of the Pacific

Melanesian Pidgin is a unique language: it has gone from birth to national language status in little more than a century. Its origins and development are much debated among Pacific creolists, so any scenario and timeline are open to challenges. Here I distil an account mainly informed by the work of Siegel (2008) and Tryon and Charpentier (2004).

Example 4.4

Ten Commandments in a pidgin

Below is an 1871 Queensland mission translation of the biblical Ten Commandments into pidgin, quoted in Dutton and Mühlhäusler (1984: 246). Note how close this is to the lexifier language, English, and therefore transparent to English speakers (compare with Exercise 4.8).

   I   Man take one fellow God; no more.
   II   Man like him God first time, everything else behind.
   III   Man no swear.
   IV   Man keep Sunday good fellow day belong big fellow master.
   V   Man be good fellow longa father mother belonga him.
   VI   Man no kill.
   VII   Man no take him Mary [wife/woman] belong another fellow man.
 VIII   Man no steal.
   IX   Man no tell lie bout another fellow man.
   X   Spose man see good fellow something belong another fellow man, he no want him all the time.

Melanesian Pidgin had its roots in the South Pacific Jargon of the whaling era from about 1800 and the pidgins of the Australian east coast. After the demise of whaling, a lingua franca was required to enable trade with the locals in *bêche-de-mer*, an aphrodisiac sea cucumber which would eventually give its name to the new language of Vanuatu – 'Bislama'. These lingua francas became widely used and were stabilizing by the 1860s, although still limited in structure and lexicon (Example 4.4).

What turned the jargon into a burgeoning pidgin from the 1860s was the establishment of plantations in Queensland (Australia), New Guinea, and some islands of Melanesia and Polynesia, including Fiji and Samoa (Figure 4.1). In the 40-plus years up to 1907, more than 100,000 Pacific men – speakers of hundreds of different languages – were recruited and transported, resulting in social and economic upheaval in their home islands. They came mainly from Vanuatu (New Hebrides), the Solomon Islands, Papua New Guinea and Kiribati (Gilbert Islands, pronounced 'kiribass'). They were transported by the 'blackbirders' – ships that circulated the Pacific picking up men to work in the plantations. Some recruits doubtless came voluntarily, but others were tricked, and still others were forced – effectively kidnapped and enslaved. But they were called 'indentured labourers', since slavery had been officially abolished in Britain and the Empire.

Early Melanesian Pidgin continued to establish and grow during the rest of the nineteenth century. It became quite uniform, and fairly stable in its syntax and morphology, although with vocabulary differences. In due course, the labourers' return to their home islands set the scene for its elaboration towards an 'extended pidgin'. By the early twentieth century there was a 'common Pacific Pidgin pool, with variant forms … which gradually

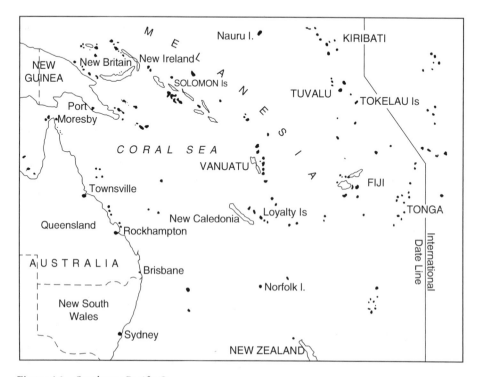

Figure 4.1   Southwest Pacific Ocean

Exercise 4.8 Konstitusin blong Ripablik blong Vanuatu

Specification of the place of language is one of the first clauses in the 1980 Vanuatu constitution. Bislama is to be the national language, English and French the languages of education. All three are official languages. Here is that clause in Bislama:

3. (1) Lanwis blong Ripablik blong Nyuhebredis, hemia Bislama. Trifala lanwis blong mekem ol wok long kantri ya, i gat Bislama mo Inglis mo Franis. Tufala big lanwis blong edukesen long kantri ya, i gat Inglis mo Franis. (reproduced in Tryon and Charpentier 2004: 487)

Saying the words aloud often makes them easier to translate into English: *wok* = 'work'.

   Contrast this modern text with Example 4.4, from Queensland a century earlier, and note the different relative distances of the two texts from English.

1 What non-English features can you see in common between this extract and the 1871 pidgin?
2 Identify the meanings of the main Bislama words.
3 Write an English translation of the Bislama.
4 Identify some of the features of Bislama grammar that you can see, for example prepositions and numbers.
5 What is the significance of the constitution being written in Bislama?

differentiated into the three sister dialects Bislama, Solomons Pijin and Tok Pisin, at the end of the recruiting period' (Tryon and Charpentier 2004: 296). This was a much slower process than many scholars believe occurred with the Atlantic creoles, which scarcely had time to pass through a pidgin stage before being spoken natively as creoles. By the mid twentieth century, the Melanesian Pidgins had entered the phase of 'the acquisition of native speakers by a language', to quote Sankoff and Laberge's striking title (1980): children were being born into the language environment and learning it as their mother tongue. The languages have now been full creoles with their own native speakers for decades, although certainly many more people speak them as second rather than first languages. They have more than 3 million speakers and serve as lingua francas for three countries where nearly 1,000 different languages are spoken – Tok Pisin in Papua New Guinea, Bislama in Vanuatu, and Solomons Pijin in the Solomon Islands. They are widely used for prestigious public functions, although English predominates in education.

4.7   RESEARCH ACTIVITY
THE MAKING OF MELANESIAN PIDGIN

It is clear that the Melanesian Pidgin languages have English as their lexifier. However, the origins of their syntax and morphology are – as with most creoles – more complicated and contested. This research activity examines several structures in these creoles, considering their origins and the different outcomes in the three varieties.

Siegel considers that some Melanesian Pidgin structures show a discernible 'substrate' effect (2008). That is, while English provided the lexicon 'from above', local languages have influenced the grammar of the new language 'from below'. The three Melanesian Pidgin varieties all derive from the same English lexical base, but aspects of their grammars differ in ways which, Siegel argues, reflect the differences in the grammars of the local, substrate languages in their respective regions. His 2008 book details and analyses a wide range of grammatical structures in making this case.

In the early pidgin shown in Example 4.4, we saw the word *fellow* appearing frequently.

1   Examine its occurrence in that example, and try to specify what kind of item it is, what it accompanies and what it means.

In the eventual creoles, *fellow* has persisted, developing into the suffix *-pela* in Tok Pisin and *-fala* in Bislama and Solomons Pijin.

2   What has happened to *fellow*, grammatically and phonologically, in the three pidgins?

These suffixes are used to create a number of syntactic categories, for example demonstrative *dispela* in Tok Pisin, and *desfala* in Solomons Pijin, obviously derived from the English *this* + *fellow*. In modern Melanesian Pidgin the same suffix attaches to numerals and attributive adjectives (immediately preceding a noun) as in these examples:

New Guinea Tok Pisin	Mi lukim	tripela	bikpela	kar
Vanuatu Bislama	Mi luk	tri(fala)	big(fala)	trak
Solomons Pijin	Mi lukem	trifala	big(fala)	ka
	'I saw	three	big	cars.'

(Siegel 2008: 184)

Notice the different words used for 'car' in the different varieties, and the different spellings when the same word is used.

3   Specify how the three varieties differ in their uptake of the *-pela/-fala* suffix. Where is *-pela/-fala* optional and where is it obligatory?

Siegel's argument is that nineteenth-century Melanesian Pidgin remained quite variable, and it was only when labourers returned to their home islands that the morphosyntax began to settle during the twentieth century. He believes that it was a form's presence within the local substrate languages underlying a particular variety that reinforced its selection from the existing pool of features for that variety of Melanesian Pidgin. Where there is no reinforcement from the substrate, the use remains variable.

A second and more complex example lies in the relativization processes of the three varieties:

Tok Pisin	Mi save wanpela meri	0	(em) i gat twenti pikinini
Bislama	Mi save wan woman	we	i gat twenti pikinini
Pijin	Mi save wan woman	0/wea	hem i garem twenti pikinini
	'I know a woman	who	has twenty children.'

(Siegel 2008: 186)

The material either side of the relative remains largely the same, but the relativizers differ a good deal. '0' means that the relative pronoun is absent, as it can be in English – *the dog 0/that I saw*. Bislama *we* is pronounced [we] phonetically, and it and Solomons Pijin *wea* both derive from English *where*.

4 Specify what the relativizer rules are in the three varieties. What is obligatory, what is optional?

Siegel again concludes that the way in which the three varieties use the relativizing particles is mainly due to differing grammatical rules in their different substrate languages. It is one of the fascinations of these new languages that they enable us to see how language is created on the production line. We also see how the linguistic processes of language birth and death can in broad terms mirror each other, especially in gaining versus losing morphology.

4.8   SUMMARY

- The most radical repercussions of language contact are language birth and death. When people who have no common language are thrown together, they strike up a rudimentary set of words in order to communicate, called a jargon. If communication continues, they create a pidgin – a language with limited vocabulary and simplified structures. If the pidgin establishes and spreads, it may develop the features of a full language and be learned by children as their mother tongue – it is now a creole.
- Pidgins were created on a large scale with European expansion, especially the Atlantic slave trade which brought together Africans from diverse language backgrounds. The 'superstrate' languages such as English usually contributed most of the vocabulary to the new languages, so are called the 'lexifiers'. The substrate, African languages contributed more to the grammar.
- Most issues in contact linguistics are contested. Theories of creole genesis include the monogenesis theory that they all derive from a single original; the Language Bioprogram Hypothesis that children construct the creole's grammar; the Relexification Hypothesis that creoles combine vocabulary from a superstrate language with grammar from a substrate; the gradualist approach that stresses the time length needed to develop a creole; an incremental approach in which each new wave of slaves learned the language then reshaped it; finally, genesis can be seen as mass, serial second language acquisition.
- Creoles usually continue to co-exist with their lexifier languages. This may lead to 'decreolization', in which the creole re-converges with its lexifier, creating a continuum from the most deeply creole speech, the basilect, to the most standard, the acrolect.
- In our time, language death is more common than language birth. Estimates are that only 10 per cent of the world's 6,000 languages are safe, the rest are endangered or moribund. Discourses of language endangerment often parallel it to the loss of biological species, or talk of a language's 'health'. These discourses can be problematic, especially by focusing on the language rather than the interests of its speakers.

- Four types of language death have been suggested: sudden, 'radical', gradual and bottom-to-top. The most common change that occurs during language death is a reduction in morphology. As a case study of a dying language, Dorian's research on East Sutherland Gaelic identified groups of 'semi-speakers', whose interactional skills were strong although their speech was limited.
- A case of a new language is Melanesian Pidgin, which has gone from birth to national language status in little more than a century. It developed on the plantations of the southwest Pacific, then differentiated into three dialects: Bislama in Vanuatu, Solomons Pijin and Tok Pisin in Papua New Guinea. By the mid twentieth century, children were learning it as their mother tongue, and it now has over 3 million speakers. Melanesian Pidgin structures show a discernible 'substrate' effect, where different local languages have resulted in different grammatical features in the three regional varieties.

4.9 FURTHER READING

Kouwenberg and Singler's *Handbook* (2008) is a large compendium of knowledge on pidgins and creoles, with chapters by many of the leading scholars. Arends, Muysken and Smith's edited collection (1995) includes readable basic introductory chapters, a section on theories of pidgin/creole genesis, a roundup of grammatical features across languages, and serviceable chapters on eight individual creole languages. Siegel (2008) and Holm (2000) offer more detailed coverage, Siegel with an emphasis on Pacific creoles.

For further information, the second volume of Holm's overview (1989) brings together short sketches of dozens of contact languages from throughout the world. Holm and Michaelis (2009) is a five-volume collection of leading papers, providing access to many otherwise unavailable publications. Each chapter is preceded by an invaluable summarizing 'headnote'. The Creole Language Library (John Benjamins) has published some 40 books on a wide range of contact language matters. There is a well-regarded *Journal of Pidgin and Creole Studies*, and a newsletter, *The Carrier Pidgin*. Articles also appear in the general sociolinguistics and bilingualism journals listed in earlier chapters. See also the website of the Society for Caribbean Linguistics.

For language endangerment and death, the Hale et al. articles (1992) are basic. Nettle and Romaine's *Vanishing Voices* (2000) is an accessible introduction with a polemical bent. For a blend of scholarship and advocacy Nancy Dorian's work is unsurpassed, including a pivotal authored book (1981) and edited collection (1989). The collections edited by Brenzinger (1992) and Grenoble and Whaley (1998) assemble more specialist information on language loss and its social embedding. Articles on language endangerment and death appear in the general bilingualism and sociolinguistics journals. See also the long-running series of articles edited by Dorian in the *International Journal of the Sociology of Language* on small languages and their communities, many of them endangered. Austin and Sallabank's (2011) is an up-to-date compendium of information on language endangerment with an eye to linguists' involvement.

The Foundation for Endangered Languages website carries a newsletter, contact information and link details to other sites. The Linguistic Society of America has a Committee on Endangered Languages and their Preservation, with information available on their website. See also the current edition of *Ethnologue* on the web (Lewis 2009). UNESCO supports much of the endangered languages work and discourse – see its website, including for the *Red Book of Languages in Danger of Disappearing* and *Interactive Atlas of the World's Languages in Danger*. The *Green Book of Language Revitalization in Practice* is edited by Hinton and Hale (2001). Duchêne and Heller's edited volume (2007) offers challengingly contrasting views on language endangerment in sociopolitical context.

REFERENCES

Adamson, Lilian and Norval Smith, 1995. 'Sranan'. In Jacques Arends, Pieter Muysken and Norval Smith (eds), *Pidgins and Creoles: An Introduction*. Amsterdam: John Benjamins. 219–32.

Alleyne, Mervyn C., 1980. *Comparative Afro-American: An Historical-Comparative Study of English-Based Afro-American Dialects of the New World*. Ann Arbor, MI: Karoma Publishers.

Arends, Jacques, Pieter Muysken and Norval Smith (eds), 1995. *Pidgins and Creoles: An Introduction*. Amsterdam: John Benjamins.

Austin, Peter K. and Julia Sallabank (eds), 2011. *The Cambridge Handbook of Endangered Languages*. Cambridge: Cambridge University Press.

Bell, Allan, 1991c. 'The politics of English in New Zealand'. In Mark Williams and Graham McGregor (eds), *Dirty Silence: Aspects of Language and Literature in New Zealand*. Auckland, New Zealand: Oxford University Press. 65–75.

Bickerton, Derek, 1981. *Roots of Language*. Ann Arbor, MI: Karoma Publishers.

Bradley, David, 2005. 'Introduction: language policy and language endangerment in China'. *International Journal of the Sociology of Language* 173: 1–21.

Brenzinger, Matthias (ed.), 1992. *Language Death: Factual and Theoretical Explorations with Special Reference to East Africa*. Berlin and New York: Mouton de Gruyter.

Broch, Ingvild and Ernst Håkon Jahr, 1984. 'Russenorsk: a new look at the Russo-Norwegian pidgin in northern Norway'. In P. Sture Ureland and Iain Clarkson (eds), *Scandinavian Language Contacts*. Cambridge: Cambridge University Press. 21–65.

Chaudenson, Robert, 2001 (revised in collaboration with Salikoko S. Mufwene). *Creolization of Language and Culture*. London: Routledge.

Campbell, Lyle and Martha C. Muntzel, 1989. 'The structural consequences of language death'. In Nancy C. Dorian (ed.), *Investigating Obsolescence: Studies in Language Contraction and Death*. Cambridge: Cambridge University Press. 181–96.

Crystal, David, 2008. *A Dictionary of Linguistics and Phonetics* (6th edn). Malden, MA: Blackwell Publishing.

Dimmendaal, Gerrit J., 1992. 'Reduction in Kore reconsidered'. In Matthias Brenzinger (ed.), *Language Death: Factual and Theoretical Explorations with Special Reference to East Africa*. Berlin: Mouton de Gruyter. 117–35.

Dixon, R.M.W., 1972. *The Dyirbal Language of North Queensland*. London: Cambridge University Press.

Dorian, Nancy C., 1981. *Language Death: The Life Cycle of a Scottish Gaelic Dialect*. Philadelphia, PA: University of Pennsylvania Press.

Dorian, Nancy C. (ed.), 1989. *Investigating Obsolescence: Studies in Language Contraction and Death*. Cambridge: Cambridge University Press.

Dorian, Nancy, 1998. 'Western language ideologies and small-language prospects'. In Lenore A. Grenoble and Lindsay J. Whaley (eds), *Endangered Languages: Language Loss and Community Response*. Cambridge: Cambridge University Press. 3–21.

Dorian, Nancy C., 2002. 'Diglossia and the simplification of linguistic space'. *International Journal of the Sociology of Language* 157: 63–9.

Duchêne, Alexandre and Monica Heller (eds), 2007. *Discourses of Endangerment: Ideology and Interest in the Defence of Languages.* London: Continuum.

Dutton, Tom and Peter Mühlhäusler, 1984. 'Queensland Kanaka English'. *English World-Wide* 4: 231–63.

England, Nora C., 1992. 'Doing Mayan linguistics in Guatemala'. *Language* 68: 29–35.pensa

Grenoble, Lenore A. and Lindsay J. Whaley (eds), 1998. *Endangered Languages: Language Loss and Community Response.* Cambridge: Cambridge University Press.

Grimes, Barbara F. (ed.), 1988. *Ethnologue: Languages of the World* (11th edn). Dallas, TX: Summer Institute of Linguistics.

Hale, Ken, 1998. 'On endangered languages and the importance of linguistic diversity'. In Lenore A. Grenoble and Lindsay J. Whaley (eds), *Endangered Languages: Language Loss and Community Response.* Cambridge: Cambridge University Press. 192–216.

Hale, Ken, Michael Krauss, Lucille J. Watahomigie, Akira Y. Yamamoto, Colette Craig, LaVerne Masayesva Jeanne and Nora C. England, 1992. 'Endangered languages'. *Language* 68: 1–42.

Hamp, Eric P., 1989. 'On signs of health and death'. In Nancy C. Dorian (ed.), *Investigating Obsolescence: Studies in Language Contraction and Death.* Cambridge: Cambridge University Press. 197–210.

Haugen, Einar, 1972. *The Ecology of Language (Essays by Einar Haugen, Selected and Introduced by Anwar S. Dil).* Stanford, CA: Stanford University Press.

Heller, Monica and Alexandre Duchêne, 2007. 'Discourses of endangerment: sociolinguistics, globalization and social order'. In Alexandre Duchêne and Monica Heller (eds), *Discourses of Endangerment: Ideology and Interest in the Defence of Languages.* London: Continuum. 1–13.

Hill, Jane H., 2002. '"Expert rhetorics" in advocacy for endangered languages: who is listening, and what do they hear?' *Journal of Linguistic Anthropology* 12: 119–33.

Hinton, Leanne and Ken Hale, 2001. *The Green Book of Language Revitalization in Practice.* San Diego, CA: Academic Press.

Holm, John A., 1988. *Pidgins and Creoles,* vol. 1: *Theory and Structure.* Cambridge: Cambridge University Press.

Holm, John, 1989. *Pidgins and Creoles,* vol. 2: *Reference Survey.* Cambridge: Cambridge University Press.

Holm, John, 2000. *An Introduction to Pidgins and Creoles.* Cambridge: Cambridge University Press.

Holm, John and Susanne Michaelis (eds), 2009. *Contact Languages (Critical Concepts in Language Studies),* 5 vols. London: Routledge.

Hymes, Dell (ed.), 1971. *Pidginization and Creolization of Languages.* Cambridge: Cambridge University Press.

Igboanusi, Herbert and Peter Lothar, 2004. 'Oppressing the oppressed: the threats of Hausa and English to Nigeria's minority languages'. *International Journal of the Sociology of Language* 170: 131–40.

Jaffe, Alexandra, 2007a. 'Discourses of endangerment: contexts and consequences of essentializing discourses'. In Alexandre Duchêne and Monica Heller (eds), *Discourses of Endangerment: Ideology and Interest in the Defence of Languages.* London: Continuum. 57–75.

Kouwenberg, Silvia and John Victor Singler (eds), 2008. *The Handbook of Pidgin and Creole Studies.* Oxford, UK: Wiley-Blackwell.

Krauss, Michael, 1992. 'The world's languages in crisis'. *Language* 68: 4–10.

Lakoff, George, 1987. *Women, Fire and Dangerous Things: What Categories Reveal about the Mind.* Chicago, IL: University of Chicago Press.

Lefebvre, Claire, 1998. *Creole Genesis and the Acquisition of Grammar: The Case of Haitian Creole.* Cambridge: Cambridge University Press.

Lefebvre, Claire, Lydia White and Christine Jourdan (eds), 2006. *L2 Acquisition and Creole Genesis*. Amsterdam: John Benjamins.

Lewis, M. Paul (ed.), 2009. *Ethnologue: Languages of the World* (16th edn). Dallas, TX: SIL International (online version: http://www.ethnologue.com; (retrieved 6 April 2011).

Li Fengxiang, 2005. 'Contact, attrition, and structural shift: evidence from Oroqen'. *International Journal of the Sociology of Language* 173: 55–74.

Migge, Bettina and Norval Smith, 2007. 'Introduction: substrate influence in creole formation'. *Journal of Pidgin and Creole Languages* 22: 1–15.

Muehlmann, Shaylih, 2007. 'Defending diversity: staking out a common global interest?' In Alexandre Duchêne and Monica Heller (eds), *Discourses of Endangerment: Ideology and Interest in the Defence of Languages*. London: Continuum. 14–34.

Mufwene, Salikoko S., 2001. *The Ecology of Language Evolution*. Cambridge: Cambridge University Press.

Muysken, Pieter and Norval Smith, 1995. 'The study of pidgin and creole languages'. In Jacques Arends, Pieter Muysken and Norval Smith (eds), *Pidgins and Creoles: An Introduction*. Amsterdam: John Benjamins. 3–14.

Nettle, Daniel and Suzanne Romaine, 2000. *Vanishing Voices: The Extinction of the World's Languages*. Oxford: Oxford University Press.

Ostler, Nicholas, 2005. *Empires of the Word: A Language History of the World*. London: HarperCollins Publishers.

Patrick, Donna, 2007. 'Language endangerment, language rights and indigeneity'. In Monica Heller (ed.), *Bilingualism: A Social Approach*. Basingstoke, UK: Palgrave Macmillan. 111–34.

Patrick, Peter L., 2008. 'Pidgins, creoles, and variation'. In Silvia Kouwenberg and John Victor Singler (eds), *The Handbook of Pidgin and Creole Studies*. Oxford, UK: Wiley-Blackwell. 461–87.

Pensalfini, Rob, 2004. 'Eulogizing a language: the Ngarnka experience'. *International Journal of the Sociology of Language* 168: 141–56.

Sankoff, Gillian and Suzanne Laberge, 1980. 'On the acquisition of native speakers by a language'. In Gillian Sankoff (ed.), *The Social Life of Language*. Philadelphia, PA: University of Pennsylvania Press. 195–209.

Schmid, Monika S. and Kees de Bot, 2004. 'Language attrition'. In Alan Davies and Catherine Elder (eds), *The Handbook of Applied Linguistics*. Malden, MA: Blackwell Publishing. 210–34.

Schmidt, Annette, 1985. *Young People's Dyirbal: An Example of Language Death from Australia*. Cambridge: Cambridge University Press.

Siegel, Jeff, 2008. *The Emergence of Pidgin and Creole Languages*. Oxford: Oxford University Press.

Singler, John Victor, 1996. 'Theories of creole genesis, sociohistorical considerations, and the evaluation of evidence: the case of Haitian Creole and the Relexification Hypothesis'. *Journal of Pidgin and Creole Languages* 11: 185–230.

Skutnabb-Kangas, Tove and Robert Phillipson (eds), 1994. *Linguistic Human Rights: Overcoming Linguistic Discrimination*. Berlin: Mouton de Gruyter.

Te Puni Kōkiri, 2008a. *Te Oranga o te Reo Māori 2006/The Health of the Māori Language in 2006*. Wellington, New Zealand: Te Puni Kōkiri.

Thomason, Sarah G., 2001. *Language Contact: An Introduction*. Edinburgh: Edinburgh University Press.

Tryon, Darrell T. and Jean-Michel Charpentier, 2004. *Pacific Pidgins and Creoles: Origins, Growth and Development*. Berlin: Mouton de Gruyter.

Veenstra, Tonjes, 2008. 'Creole genesis: the impact of the Language Bioprogram Hypothesis'. In Siliva Kouwenberg and John Victor Singler (eds), *The Handbook of Pidgin and Creole Studies*. Oxford, UK: Wiley-Blackwell. 219–41.

Winford, Donald, 2003. *An Introduction to Contact Linguistics*. Malden, MA: Blackwell Publishing.

5

CODES AND CHOICES

Chapters 2–4 of this book have dealt mainly with the operation of languages at large in society – with scenarios of multilingualism, the nature and repercussions of language shift, the impetus for language maintenance, and the making and unmaking of languages as a result of drastic social change. In this chapter and the next we turn to a more micro level of enquiry, to look at how speakers choose different language resources in different circumstances, including not just what are regarded as separate languages but also varieties within those languages. This leads on in Chapter 6 to considering different facets of the interaction of speakers and audiences in conversation.

5.1   VARIETIES, CODES AND REPERTOIRES

The foundation of all sociolinguistics is that speakers have choices when they talk. Their choices range from the macro to the micro, from the wholesale choice between different languages to scarcely distinguishable alternative pronunciations of the same consonant. A macro choice can be between the Xhosa, Afrikaans or English languages for a South African. A micro choice can be between a glottal stop and a [t] consonant in the middle of the English word *butter* for a Cockney in London. 'Language choice' usually refers to the choice between different languages rather than micro choices within languages.

Sociolinguists use the term **variety** to cover all kinds of differences within a single language. A variety is a relatively distinguishable form of a language, often based on geographical or social differences – Chilean versus Castilian Spanish, African American versus European American English. Variety is a less loaded term than 'dialect', which lay usage tends to equate with substandard or exotic language forms. It also enables us to encompass concepts such as 'genres' or 'registers' of a language without having to commit

The Guidebook to Sociolinguistics, First Edition. Allan Bell.
© 2014 Allan Bell. Published 2014 by Blackwell Publishing Ltd.

ourselves to defining them precisely. It remains a serviceable label even though, as we shall also see later, varieties have very porous boundaries.

Both entire languages and varieties within them can be called linguistic **codes**. The term 'code' is useful in sociolinguistics because it corrals the whole range of language resources that speakers use, whether these are regarded as distinct languages or as varieties of a language. In this book I often use 'code' as a cover term when – as so often – a generalization applies equally to whole languages or to varieties within languages. The word is used particularly in the terms 'code switching' or 'code mixing', where two or more languages or varieties are intertwined (see later in this chapter). Recall also from the discussion in Chapter 1 that although distinguishing languages from varieties is useful for some purposes, there is no absoluteness in that distinction.

The suite of codes which a speaker is able to draw on makes up their linguistic **repertoire**. The term may be used to describe the linguistic range of an individual or a small group, but not of larger, more diffuse entities such as a nation or ethnic group. If the codes are varieties of the same language – such as dialects of Urdu or Japanese – the speaker's repertoire is said to be 'monolingual'. If the codes are two separate languages, as for Kazakh and Russian in Kazakhstan, the repertoire is bilingual. If three languages or more are involved, such as Mandarin, English and Hokkien in Singapore, the speaker's repertoire is multilingual. However, by focusing on the linguistic resources that a speaker draws on, the concept of repertoire tends to break down attempts to make too-ready distinctions between those codes. Contemporary sociolinguistics particularly uses the idea of repertoire to cover the fluid language mixes used by young speakers in ethnically diverse urban situations and described with terms such as 'translanguaging' and 'metrolingualism' (Busch 2012).

Exercise 5.1   Class language varieties profile

Exercise 2.2 surveyed the repertoires of class members, concentrating on the different languages that they speak. Now consider **all** the codes in their repertoires – that is including the **varieties** of languages that they speak as well as the languages. List their languages again, then ask:

1   What varieties of those languages do they speak?
2   How are these varieties distinguished from each other socially – for example, are they associated with different regions, or social groups, or ethnicities?
3   How are they distinguished from each other linguistically? Are they very different? Do the differences lie in the vocabulary, or pronunciation, or grammar?
4   What labels are used to name these varieties?
5   What are other people's attitudes towards them?
6   For some of these, can it be difficult to decide whether they should be described as a language or a variety? Why?

Log the answers in a grid (languages x varieties) to construct a variety profile of the class's languages.

In some situations the resources may configure in unusual ways, with participants happily using different languages from each other in the same interaction. In the rural situation of Misión La Paz in northern Argentina, three indigenous languages are spoken (Campbell and Grondona 2010), and marriages are typically between speakers of different languages. Each person in a household speaks in their own language, and everyone understands, but replies in their own (different) language, creating a linguistic situation that the researchers consider unique.

All languages include a range of varieties, and all normal adult speakers can control more than one variety of their language. Among the most striking types of variety are the so-called 'mother-in-law' codes which are a feature of many Australian aboriginal languages, but are also known in North American and African Bantu languages. In the Dyirbal language of northern Queensland (see Example 4.3 in previous chapter), the everyday speech style *Guwal* is replaced by an 'avoidance' style, *Jalnguy*, when certain opposite-sex relatives, especially in-laws, are present. Avoidance speech is used because the everyday language is regarded as taboo in the presence of those relatives (Dixon 1983). The avoidance code tends to maintain the phonology and syntax of the everyday language but uses alternative lexical items.

5.2 THE SPEECH COMMUNITY

You cannot go far in sociolinguistics – or even linguistics itself – without meeting the notion of 'speech community', which now becomes important to our discussion. It has been applied to all scales of human groupings, from an entity as small as a jury or a single tribal longhouse, to entire major cities and even to all women. Not surprisingly, it has also been defined by many sociolinguists and in different ways – Exercise 5.2 shows some of these. The temptation is to jettison a term which has such a broad and inconclusive range of definitions. Nevertheless, many research articles begin by laying out their authors' idea of what a speech community is for their particular study. Although nobody has been able to define it conclusively, it remains a widespread term which socio-linguistics seems to need. Alternative concepts have also been suggested, particularly social networks and community of practice, which we deal with in Chapter 8.

The notion of the speech community goes back at least as far as Leonard Bloomfield, whose 1933 book *Language* was the foundational text of American linguistics. The concept was picked up into sociolinguistics in the 1960s by three of the field's founders, Hymes, Gumperz and Labov. Each had his own inflection on the concept, reflecting his particular research interests – 'multilingualism for Gumperz, linguistic evaluation and style-shifting for Labov, ways of speaking and communicative competence for Hymes', as Peter Patrick lucidly summarizes it in an overview article (2002: 575).

Perhaps the most basic and intractable issue is whether the speech community is based on social or linguistic criteria – or both. Gumperz's was the original definition and was largely social (1962). It assumed some cohesion among members as well as a shared linguistic repertoire, although not a single language. Later he added the linguistic criterion that the speech community is differentiated from adjacent groupings by its language usage (Gumperz 1968).

Exercise 5.2   Defining 'speech community'

Here are some of the definitions that sociolinguists have given of 'speech community'. Clarify what each of them means, compare their similarities and differences, evaluate their strengths and weaknesses, and arrive at your own definition.

- Bloomfield 1933:

  A group of people who use the same system of speech-signals is a *speech-community*. Obviously the value of language depends upon people's using it in the same way ... A speech-community is a group of people who interact by means of speech. (pp. 29 and 42)

- Gumperz 1962:

  A social group which may be either monolingual or multilingual, held together by frequency of social interaction patterns and set off from the surrounding areas by weaknesses in the lines of communication. (p. 31)

- Gumperz 1968:

  Any human aggregate characterized by regular and frequent interaction by means of a shared body of verbal signs and set off from similar aggregates by significant differences in language usage. (p. 381)

- Hymes 1974:

  A social rather than a linguistic entity. One starts with a social group and considers the entire organization of linguistic means within it. (p. 47)

- Hymes 1972:

  A community sharing rules for the conduct and interpretation of speech, and rules for the interpretation of at least one linguistic variety. (p. 54)

- Labov 1972b:

  The speech community is ... defined ... by participation in a set of shared norms. (pp. 120–1)

- Labov 1966:

  New York City is a single speech community, united by a common set of evaluative norms, though divergent in the application of these norms. (p. 355)

- Kachru 2001:

  A speech community crosses political boundaries ... does not necessarily represent one religion or culture ... comprise[s] idiolects and dialects. (p. 105)

- Bolinger 1975:

  There is no limit to the number and variety of speech communities that are to be found in a society. (p. 333)

Hymes (1962) uses the term but initially does not define it, preferring 'the speech economy of a community'. He leaned explicitly towards the speech community being socially not linguistically based (1974): the researcher begins with a social grouping and then examines their linguistic repertoire. However, elsewhere Hymes implies the speech community is defined by language-related criteria (1972).

For Labov, shared linguistic norms were central (1972b), although his work was based in a geographically defined area – the Lower East Side of New York City. He found that community members all evaluate linguistic features similarly and behave accordingly in using them (see my examination of Labov's New York study in Chapter 7.1).

It seems, then, that for these three scholars, both social and linguistic criteria are needed, but that generally the social comes first. What is true is that in actual research practice, sociolinguists tend to start from a social basis, then add linguistic characteristics. They identify some grouping – a gang, profession, village, chatroom, neighbourhood, nation – and research its linguistic repertoire and behaviour. But in looser discussion about large-scale language commonalities, they will be more liable to use shared linguistic repertoire as a criterion for treating something as a speech community – the francophone community of Canada, the German-speaking community in Australia, or even 'the speech-community which consists of all English-speaking people' (Bloomfield 1933: 42). In these cases, the constituency of people involved is so scattered and diverse that most social criteria for recognizing them as a community would fail (although see the very broad definition by Kachru 2001, Exercise 5.2). But overall, Patrick's summarization seems apt, that the speech community is 'a socially-based unit of linguistic analysis' (2002: 577).

The speech community concept must allow for difference and divergence as well as for commonality or it becomes inoperable (see the rider in Labov's 1966 definition). The knotty question remains of how much difference is tolerable before the boundaries dissolve (cf. Bolinger's definition, 1975). A second and linked issue is how different speech communities relate to each other. Patrick (2002) suggests that there are at least two kinds of relationships among speech communities:

- Nesting, where one community sits inside another. A New York youth gang may be a speech community in its own right, but it also nests within a community definable as all such gangs in New York, which again is nested within the speech community of the city as a whole.
- Overlapping, where different speech communities partially cross with each other. In contemporary London, immigrant youths from 20 or more ethnic backgrounds are members both of their separate groups of origin and of wider, pan-ethnic networks, as studies of multicultural English there show (Cheshire et al. 2011).

Unlike many early sociolinguistic concepts, the idea of speech community has not progressed much since it was proposed. It has been criticized for its indefinability, deconstructed and set aside on theoretical grounds (e.g. Rampton 2009), but still often comes back into discussions as a working concept which scholars cannot do without. It has also been challenged on ideological grounds. Labov's definition of shared norms in New York City has been regarded as assuming the existence of agreement between disparately placed social groups. Milroy and Milroy (1992) argue that a model of society

Exercise 5.3   Speech communities near you

What speech community or communities do you individually belong to?

1   What are the social characteristics of your speech community/ies? What are the linguistic characteristics?
2   Do you find that the primary criteria are social or linguistic?
3   How much diversity is there within your speech community/ies?
4   If you belong to more than one speech community, what different kinds of configurations are there? – mono/multilingual, large/small, permanent or shorter-term, based on geography or age, etc.
5   How do these speech communities relate to each other? Are they, for example, overlapping or nested?
6   Pool the speech community profiles of all class members, and evaluate the conceptions and definitions they lead to.
7   Is this sociolinguistics class itself a speech community? Why/not?
8   Consider the question: What *isn't* a speech community?
9   In the light of the above discussions, revisit the definitions in Exercise 5.2 – what definition of 'speech community' emerges from your consideration?

that takes account of conflict between groups is more appropriate than a consensus model. Given this level of debate, focus has shifted to alternative concepts that have been proposed for dealing with the nature of linguistic community. These include the Milroys' Social Network model (e.g. Lesley Milroy 1987), and the Community of Practice framework associated in sociolinguistics with Penelope Eckert (e.g. 2000). We return to these approaches in Chapter 8.

5.3   DIGLOSSIA

The concept of diglossia has to do with the way in which different language codes tend to be stratified in a society. The term dates from the earliest days of sociolinguistics. It derived from the French *diglossie* (itself taken from the Greek for 'bilingualism'), was adopted into English by the American Charles Ferguson, and later extended by Joshua Fishman and Ralph Fasold.

In 1959 Ferguson published an article with the one-word title 'Diglossia'. It became the most cited and influential single paper in the history of sociolinguistics. Even older bibliographies (e.g. Fernández 1993) show literally thousands of publications that reference the concept, which has been applied to language situations all over the world. Central to diglossia is the concept of differential language functions that we first met in Chapter 3.2 in relation to multilingualism. Ferguson observed that there exist societies which have two related varieties of a language that are used in quite different sets of functions. These varieties and functions can be stratified into 'Low' and 'High' and are in complementary distribution. The Low variety is used in everyday functions such as at home, in the market and in conversation among friends. The High language is used in prestige functions such as education, media and government. The two languages are clearly related linguistically, but rather distantly.

Classic diglossia

Ferguson offered an extended definition and four defining cases of diglossia:

- Greek has Demotiki as the Low, everyday, local form, alongside Katharevousa, Classical Greek, which is the High, prestige, universal form.
- The Caribbean nation of Haiti has the local Haitian Creole that has grown up there, based partly in French and partly in African languages, alongside standard European French.
- In Switzerland there is Schwyzertütsch, Swiss German, which is a cluster of local dialects. Superposed is the pan-Germanic standard, Hochdeutsch or High German.
- Across the Arab world, varieties of colloquial Arabic are spoken alongside Classical Arabic. Colloquial Arabic is not itself a single variety but differs greatly from place to place, e.g. between Jordan and Morocco. Classical Arabic is the language of the Koran and is constant. Despite differences among varieties of Colloquial Arabic, Colloquial and Classical Arabic stand everywhere in a constant relation to each other.

Example 5.1

Defining classic diglossia

Diglossia is a relatively stable language situation in which, in addition to the primary dialects of the language (which may include a standard or regional standards), there is a very divergent, highly codified (often grammatically more complex) superposed variety, the vehicle of a large and respected body of written literature, either of an earlier period or in another speech community, which is learned largely by formal education and is used for most written and formal spoken purposes but is not used by any sector of the community for ordinary conversation.

(Ferguson 1959: 336)

Characteristics:

- the High (H) and Low (L) languages are related
- there are complementary sets of functions or domains for H and L
- H has overt prestige
- H has an admired literary heritage
- L is acquired naturally from the start
- H is book-learned later
- H is standardized in grammars/dictionaries
- H is more linguistically complex than L.

In all four of these cases, the two codes are distinct enough to jeopardize comprehension of one code for a listener who knows only the other. They tend to be labelled as the same language but are divergent enough to have characteristics of different languages.

Ferguson laid out characteristics he saw in diglossic situations (Example 5.1). The H language has overt prestige, it is openly regarded as the good language. The L language may be regarded – including by its own speakers – as a lesser language. Communities may even deny the existence of the L language. In some areas H has a more complex grammar than L. It has a literary heritage of classically established works which form a cultural deposit and serve as standard-setters for the language as a whole. Often the epitome of the literary heritage is the society's primary religious text. In Arabic, the standard is the Koran itself. In German the standard was the Lutherbibel, reformer Martin Luther's original translation of the Bible (1534).

The H language possesses codifying prescriptive texts such as dictionaries and grammars. The L language may not have these, or may acquire them much later, and its spelling may not be stable. Thus in Switzerland there may be a full slate of reference works for High German, but relatively little on Schwyzertütsch. And whereas children grow up naturally with L and learn it as their mother tongue, H is generally learned as a subject through school. It is superposed and often external. Its home base may be

Exercise 5.4   Diglossia in the twenty-first century

Towards the end of his 1959 article, Ferguson hazarded a prediction for each of the four cases in two centuries' time (to the year 2150):

Swiss German	Relative stability
Arabic	Slow development towards several standard languages based on regional L varieties
Haitian Creole	Slow development towards a unified standard based on the L language of the capital, Port-au-Prince
Greek	Unified standard based on the L language of Athens.

Half a century since Ferguson's work, how much has changed, and is the change in the direction he expected?

1 Search out more recent information on one of the four cases (e.g. Frangoudaki 2002 for Greek).
2 Compare it to Ferguson's original presentation.
3 Assuming the validity of Ferguson's original description for this case, does diglossia still operate in the same way there nowadays? What if anything has changed and how?
4 Is the situation still diglossic in Ferguson's sense?
5 Compare the outcome after some 50 years with Ferguson's long-term prognosis above. Is the case developing in the direction Ferguson envisaged or not?
6 Do any differences in the current situation challenge the basic concept of diglossia?

geographically outside the society itself (e.g. in France not Haiti) or be identified with an earlier historical period (e.g. classical Greece). Diglossia may also be stable over a very long period. In Switzerland, Hochdeutsch and Schwyzertütsch have co-existed in a diglossic relationship for centuries – although in the period since Ferguson's article, Schwyzertütsch has made inroads into prestige domains.

Fishman and Fasold extend diglossia

In the 1960s, Fishman brought together diglossia with his own sociology-of-language concepts. He noted (1967) that the stratifying of the H and L functions also occurs in societies where unrelated languages co-exist. That is, languages which are linguistically quite unrelated may still be in a socially diglossic relationship of H and L to each other. One of his examples was Spanish and Guaraní in Paraguay. These undoubtedly stratify socially in a High/Low relationship, although one is a native South American language and the other European. Fishman therefore argued for extension of the concept of diglossia to bilingual situations where any two languages are stratified.

Later still the American sociolinguist Ralph Fasold (1984) applied the term to the stratification that also occurs within single languages. Even when the linguistic codes involved are closely similar varieties of the same language, there may be a diglossic High–Low relationship between them. A typical example is that of a standard version of many of the major European languages as used in public speaking, alongside the vernacular variety used in conversation. Fasold therefore proposed extending the concept of diglossia yet again to include all situations where language codes stratify socially, regardless of the linguistic relationship between the codes. Thus repertoires which are monolingual (Fasold), bilingual (Fishman) or somewhere in between (Ferguson) could all be labelled diglossic if they fit the stratifying criteria, forming a continuum like this:

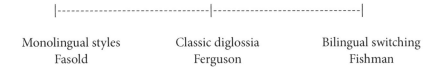

| Monolingual styles | Classic diglossia | Bilingual switching |
| Fasold | Ferguson | Fishman |

My view of these extensions is that, while I agree on the commonalities across the three cases, it makes for an unhelpful dilution of Ferguson's originally much more sharp and specific concept. I prefer to reserve the label 'diglossia' for the classic in-between language situation that Ferguson defined. Where parallel processes are evident in fully monolingual or bilingual situations, I would refer to those as 'in a diglossic relationship' rather than actual 'diglossia'.

Diglossia: caveats and critiques

Diglossia has been a very productive concept for sociolinguistics. Ferguson's original article is full of lucid and insightful generalizations and has been republished many times (e.g. in Coupland and Jaworski 2009a, volume 4). However, both the concept of diglossia, and its definition and application, raise serious issues and have been challenged:

- Scholars who are specialists in the four defining cases have questioned Ferguson's characterizations of them (e.g. Kaye 1972 asked how stable Arabic diglossia is).
- The situations in the four cases have changed over time (which Ferguson assumed). His description is now more than 50 years old and may no longer apply (see Exercise 5.4).
- Much more basically, the dichotomizing involved in diglossia is questionable (Dorian 2002). Sociolinguistic situations are scarcely ever clear-cut in this way, and the labelling involved in diglossia implies too static and monolithic a situation to suit the on-the-ground reality.
- The model presents the 'High/Low' terminology as a very uncontestable, commonsense view, but the labels are not neutral (Exercise 5.5).
- Overall the description of diglossia reflects an orientation to these sociolinguistic situations which reflects and serves the status quo (Williams 1992). The siting and valuing of the language codes is uncoupled from the social position and evaluation of their speakers, which treats a very political situation as apolitical.

These are real and principled objections mof a kind which are addressed in some of the attached exercises and which we will return to later in discussing language ideologies

---

Exercise 5.5   Apply and critique diglossia

Apply the concept of diglossia in your society:

1 Are any linguistic codes in your society in a diglossic relationship?
2 Which of Ferguson's defining characteristics do they meet?
3 Which kind of diglossia is this? Or is more than one kind involved? Or does it not really fit any of these three?
   - Ferguson's classic diglossia
   - Fishman's bilingual diglossia, or
   - Fasold's variety-based diglossia.

Now critique diglossia as a concept:

4 How much does 'diglossia' further our understanding of how languages relate in your society?
5 What is gained and what is lost through Fishman's and Fasold's extensions to Ferguson's original concept?
6 Some subsequent researchers have found Ferguson's 'High' and 'Low' labels 'unfortunate' (Williams 1992: 95) and 'invidious' (Dorian 2002: 64). Why? Can you suggest alternative labels that do not create such problems?
7 Evaluate the characteristics and definition that Ferguson offered (Example 5.1). Remembering the critiques in the text of the status-quo stance which is implied by diglossia, what alternative ways are there of thinking about the relationship between these kinds of language codes in a society?

(Chapter 10). Despite the problems, I myself find that 'diglossia' captures a basic sociolinguistic generalization about a near-universal relationship between linguistic codes in societies. However, we need to be constantly aware of and question the social and political positioning and power that underlie such a situation, and not just adopt descriptive phrasings that endorse linguistic inequities.

Diglossia continues to be frequently referenced and forms the basis of some sociolinguistic work in the twenty-first century (e.g. Snow 2010), but probably less than formerly. In origin it was a very structuralist/functionalist concept, in accordance with American social science of its time, and is less congenial to the fluidity of postmodern approaches. The issues of language choice which the concepts of repertoires, domains and diglossia seek to address underlie most of the matter in the rest of this chapter – and indeed in later chapters in the book. Understanding the social embedding and significance of language choices is arguably the key question in sociolinguistics, and we will address it in a number of ways as the book develops, including in relation to the concept of 'style' (Chapter 11) which overlaps with Fasold's monolingual diglossia.

5.4   CODE SWITCHING

Code switching is one of the choices available to bilingual and multilingual speakers. It occurs when speakers switch backwards and forwards between distinct codes in their repertoire, often within the same sentence or utterance. It is a complex and skilful type of language choice, and involves the accomplished handling of two or more languages simultaneously – structurally, psychologically and socially. Code switches often carry a lot of social meaning, and attempting to interpret and explain them can be a challenge.

Code switching is simultaneously one of sociolinguistics' most interesting and most demanding areas because of the complexity of the linguistic structures it creates. The challenges begin with radical disagreement over what counts as code switching. Definitions will often differ even between different authors in the same publication. Milroy and Muysken (1995: 12) record that a major European research collaboration and its ensuing publications had to abandon the attempt to find consensus on code switching terminology. One distinction that many researchers agree on is between inter- and intra-sentential switching – what occurs between sentences versus within the same sentence. Switching inside the one sentence is also sometimes distinguished as 'code mixing'. The quantitative sociolinguist Shana Poplack who studied Spanish–English switching in New York (1980) recognized a third category, 'tag-switching', when the switch occurs on a sentence tag, like *you know* in English. A basic issue is what stretch of language should be taken into account – the sentence, the utterance, the turn, the conversation?

Much of the research on code switching focuses on the structural linguistics of switches. One approach comes from the American contact linguist, Carol Myers-Scotton. The Matrix Language Frame model was put forward in her 1993(a) book *Duelling Languages*, and developed in later publications particularly with Janice Jake (e.g. 2009). Myers-Scotton's main contention is that in code switching, one or other language will always be dominant. This is called the 'Matrix Language', and it sets the structural frame of a code-switched sentence: the order of elements will be that of the matrix language, which also provides all the necessary structural material. The other

Example 5.2

Code switching in Kenya

This example comes from two students in Nairobi discussing their school work in Swahili and English (Myers-Scotton 1993a: 79). The hyphens identify bound morphemes, those that cannot stand alone.

Leo siku-*come* na *books* zangu

leo	si-	-ku-	-*come*	na	*books*	z-	angu
today	1 S/NEG	PAST/NEG	come	with	books	CL 10	my

'Today I didn't come with my books.'

Myers-Scotton treats Swahili here as the matrix language, and English as the embedded language. The speaker's first word is in Swahili, then there are switches back and forth on each of the remaining four words of the sentence. English provides two content words – the main verb *come* and noun *books*. The structural material comes from Swahili: the first person singular pronoun *si-*, past tense marker *-ku-*, negation marking, preposition *na*, and the prefix *z-* on the possessive *angu* (identifying the English noun *books* as belonging to class 10 out of the approximately 15 noun classes of Swahili).

language is the 'Embedded Language', which provides only content material. Although widely used, the Matrix Language Frame model has received many challenges from other scholars (e.g. Auer 2007). They point out that the matrix language can change from sentence to sentence, and it may not be easy to decide which language is in fact the matrix or how all morphemes should be classified. Example 5.2 shows a sentence with four code switches, drawn from Myers-Scotton's extensive Swahili–English research in Kenya. Extended switching among several languages simultaneously is by no means unusual, as shown for example by Migge's research (2007) on the languages of the rainforest of Suriname and Guyane in the north of South America.

5.5   THE SOCIOLINGUISTICS OF CODE SWITCHING

Code switching is often socially meaningful, and many sociolinguists have examined how this works. It also triggers strong reactions from audiences. It tends to be denigrated by popular opinion from inside as well as outside the speech communities where it occurs, and is often regarded as a corrupted semi-language. This gives rise to pejorative labels such as Spanglish (or Espanglés), Franglais or Chinglish, which represent various mixes of other languages with English. However, the research shows that code switching is a routine behaviour in all bilingual and multilingual communities. Exercise 5.6 shows an extended passage of switching whose topic, ironically, is the practice of switching itself.

Exercise 5.6 Code switching attitudes

Here is a Panjabi–English bilingual from a study by Romaine (1995: 122) discussing code switching:

I mean I'm guilty in that sense *ke ziada ʋsi* English *i bolde fer ode nal eda hʋnda ke twhadi jeri zəban ɛ̃, na? Odec hər ik sentence ic je do tin* English *de word honde* ... but I think that's wrong. I mean, *mə khəd čana mə ke, na, jədo Panjabi bolda ɛ̃, pure Panjabi bola ʋsi* mix *kərde rɛ̃ne ā.* I mean, unconsciously, sub-consciously, *kəri jane ɛ̃,* you know, *pər* I wish, you know *ke mə pure Panjabi bol səka.*

I mean I'm guilty as well in the sense <u>that we speak</u> English <u>more and more, and then what happens is that when you speak your own language, you get two or three</u> English <u>words in each sentence</u> ... but I think that's wrong. I mean, <u>I myself would like to speak pure Panjabi whenever I speak Panjabi. We keep</u> mixing. I mean unconsciously, subconsciously, <u>we keep doing it,</u> you know, <u>but</u> I wish, you know, <u>that I could speak pure Panjabi.</u>

1 In the passage identify the three kinds of code switching mentioned earlier in the text:
   • inter-sentential (at sentence or clause boundary)
   • intra-sentential (within the sentence)
   • tag switching (such as *I mean*).
2 Tease out the description that the speaker gives of code switching, and the attitudes he expresses. Evaluate them.
3 Consider the speaker's expressed attitudes to code switching in the light of the amount he uses in the excerpt itself.

Gumperz: interactional code switching

The way code switches operate in conversation was a focus of the American anthropological linguist John Gumperz, one of the founding figures of sociolinguistics. Gumperz was the originator of 'interactional sociolinguistics', which we will deal with in more detail in Chapter 6.6. He studied bilingual situations in places as diverse as India, Austria, Norway and California, summarizing much of his work in a 1982 book. His interest was in the operation of switches in the flow of conversation regardless of whether the codes involved were distinct languages or related varieties of the same language.

Gumperz noted that the conversational code switches he observed occurred in interactions that were as fluent and unitary as monolingual exchanges – except that they involved two languages not one. The switches might be salient to outsiders or to linguists, but the participants scarcely noticed them, being immersed in the meaning of the communication not its linguistic form. Seeking to identify the interactional triggers for switching. Gumperz (1982a) found that they include:

• introducing direct quotation or reported speech
• picking out a specific addressee

- interjections
- reiterations
- qualifying messages.

Take this English/Hindi switch by a bilingual university student in Delhi:

> I went to Agra,   *to maine ǝpne bhaiko bola ki,*   if you come to Delhi you must
>   (then I said to my brother that)   buy some lunch
>   (Gumperz 1982a: 76)

The switch introduces a quotation – a common use, Gumperz found. A message in one code may also be repeated or modified in the other, to clarify or amplify or emphasize what has been said. This switch involves a repetition by a Chicano professional in California who generally speaks Spanish at home and English elsewhere:

> I got to thinking   *vacilando el punto ese*   you know? I got to thinking well this and
>   (mulling over that point)   that reason.
>   (Gumperz 1982a: 78)

Gumperz suggested that in bilingual situations there tends to be a *we*-code and a *they*-code – one of the languages will generally be associated with the minority and its ingroup life, and the other with the outgroup, that is the wider society (similarly to diglossia). To investigate what code switches mean in their speech community, Gumperz played back recordings of switches and asked members to interpret them. Listeners reported that flipping the order of the languages in a code switch could make a difference because of the *they/we*-code reversal. A Puerto Rican mother was heard calling to her child in a New York street:

> *Ven acá.*   *Ven acá.*   Come here, you.
> (Come here.   Come here.)
>   (Gumperz 1982a: 92)

The listeners interpreted the switch to the *they*-code, English, as a warning to the child. But when the order was reversed and English came first followed by the *we*-code, Spanish, it sounded like an appeal:

> Come here. Come here. *Ven acá.*

One of Gumperz's most fruitful insights was the distinction between situational and metaphorical code switching, based on research in the settlement of Hemnesberget in northern Norway (Blom and Gumperz 1972). In situational switching, there is a regular association between language and social situation, and the switch lasts as long as the situation lasts. The researchers observed that the entry of outsiders to a local group in Hemnesberget triggered switches from Ranamål, the dialect, to standard speech, Bokmål. A move from business to personal subjects also caused a switch from standard to dialect. These situational switches reflect accepted norms of what is appropriate language choice for certain audiences or topics. Metaphorical switches trade on such regular associations, actively using language to inject the flavour of one setting into another, alien context. So in an otherwise standard language conversation, local forms were introduced to provide anecdotal colour. Conversely, standard forms surfaced as a claim to intellectual authority during a conversation conducted in dialect. Gumperz's situational/metaphorical distinction has been widely applied in the study of sociolinguistic style, which we look at more closely in Chapter 11.

Myers-Scotton: the Markedness Model

Myers-Scotton has developed an approach to the social operation of code switching which has parallels to Gumperz's. Her Markedness Model – detailed especially in her 1993(b) book *Social Motivations for Codeswitching* – classifies switches into either marked or unmarked choices. Unmarked choices are the default choices that tend to be expected, usual or frequent. They contrast with the 'marked' choices, which are more unexpected, unusual or rare. Markedness can be hard to tie down and assign, but the concept does capture something important about the social significance of language choices.

The Markedness Model maintains that many interactions carry the expectation of certain 'rights and obligations' which mean that one of the code choices is unmarked. Other choices in the situation are more marked because they do not meet those rights and obligations. Many of Myers-Scotton's examples (1988, 1993b) come from trilingual exchanges in Kenya, where English, the national lingua franca Swahili and various local languages interact. Swahili would normally be the unmarked choice for addressing another, apparently local African. If the person turns out to be from the same ethnic group, then the shared ethnic language is expected. But if the setting is a white-collar office in the capital, Nairobi, the unmarked choice is English. Note the similarity again to the approach through domains and diglossia.

The model stresses the proactive position of speakers, negotiating strategic choices based on their own interactional goals, the social situations they are in, and the wider sociolinguistic ecology surrounding them. Markedness works because societies have norms which – although they do not control the speaker's choices – frame the interactional and social consequences of those choices. All choices indicate a particular interpersonal balance between the participants. Marked switches usually redefine the identity of a speaker and her social distance from the addressee. They may, for example, exclude outsiders from an ingroup by switching to a language the outsiders do not understand.

As well as its similarity to Blom and Gumperz's situational/metaphorical distinction, the Markedness Model parallels other theories of sociolinguistic styling that we shall deal with in Chapter 11.3. Myers-Scotton argues that there are situations where code switching itself can operate as the unmarked choice. In these cases continuing code switching is the norm, with no specific social meaning adhering to the individual switches. It is the interplay of two languages that indicates the speakers acknowledge affiliations to, for example, both national and local identities. So young men in Harare, the capital of Zimbabwe, may keep on switching between English and Shona, the national language, because they want to affiliate with the prestige of English as well as the indigenous value of Shona (Myers-Scotton 1993b: 123).

Auer: code switching as practice

Gumperz's focus on how code switching is embedded in the flow of bilingual interaction, and what it means to community members, has been picked up by scholars such as the German conversation analyst, Peter Auer. Conversation Analysis is an approach to the study of (usually monolingual) conversation that I will not have space to discuss in its own right in this book. Suffice to say that it focuses on the orderly minutiae of everyday conversations through close analysis of, for example, how turns are taken.

Auer's original research was conducted with a group of bilingual Italian immigrant children in the German city of Konstanz on Lake Geneva. Example 5.3 comes from this study. Auer found that their language alternations were inter-sentential – between rather than within sentences – and proposed a four-part classification of how they operated (Auer 1988), which I diagram like this:

	Transfer	Code switch
Participant related	x	x
Discourse related	x	x

First, the alternations were either transfers (which were mostly lexical) or code switches. Transfers tended to be followed by a return to the previous language, while switches

Example 5.3

Wait, Pino

This example is from Auer (1988: 197). 'm' is the project fieldworker, with two of the boys taking part in the study.

((m. has taken Luziano and Pino in his car to his house. The car has stopped, the three are about to get out.))

70:	06	m:	là là si apre, là sotto
	07	Lz.:	ah là
71:	01		Pino – – willscht rau:s – wart mal
	02		wart mal Pino

Translation (Italian in lower case, German in CAPITALS)

70:	06	m:	here here you can open it, down there
	07	Lz.:	oh there
71:	01		PINO – SO YOU WANT TO GET OUT – WAIT,
	02		WAIT PINO

Auer writes that Luziano's switch in line 71:01 is part of effecting a change in the 'participant constellation'. His Italian *ah là* was addressed to the fieldworker, acknowledging his instruction about how to open the car door. Luziano then switches to German to give orders to the younger boy, Pino.

usually stayed with the new language choice. For these students, German was dominant. Almost all the code switches were from Italian to German, and the transfers inserted German words into Italian discourse. Secondly, the basis of the alternations was either participant related (e.g. due to a speaker's language preference or capability) or discourse related, that is signalling what the speaker is doing in the interaction such as changing the topic. Code switching is therefore what Gumperz called a 'contextualization cue' (1982a: 131) – one of the means by which speakers signal, and listeners interpret, their interaction and its content.

The conversational take on code switching proceeds from radically different assumptions than structural approaches such as Myers-Scotton's Matrix Language Frame model. It takes bilingualism to be not a capability but a behaviour, and being bilingual as something that speakers do rather than are (Auer 1988). The unit to be analysed is the discourse itself, and code switches can be understood only in the light of the choices that have preceded and followed. This has the advantage of emphasizing that in code switching one choice leads to another.

Auer questions whether bilingual conversation can be reduced to 'two-sided monolingual talk' (2007: 321), partly because of the difficulty of telling where one language stops and the other starts in mixed discourse. What is more, speakers can intentionally use the ambiguity of an item from related languages to trigger a switch. This example from Kathryn Woolard (1999) presents the standard opening gambit used by the Catalan comedian Eugenio in the 1980s, a period when the choice between Spanish and Catalan was particularly salient:

el	**saben**	aquel …
him	know	this-one …
'do you know this one …'		

The first word is Catalan and the third is Castilian Spanish, but *saben* 'know' is either – or both. Woolard describes *saben* as 'bivalent' – that is, belonging to both codes. Its hybridity is the source of the humour and makes it impossible to pin down precisely where the transition between the two languages occurs. Woolard's later work looks at whole texts that are bivalent: they could be read as either Spanish or Latin, intentionally composed as a strategy for enhancing the standing of Spanish from the sixteenth century (Woolard and Genovese 2007). Recall Heller's stress (in Chapter 2) on the fluidity of languages and their boundaries.

5.6   THE CASE OF OBERWART

Susan Gal's study of the bilingual community of Oberwart is one of the classics of research into individual and community code choice. The American anthropological linguist conducted her doctoral research in this town on the Austria–Hungary political border in the 1970s. It also lies on the German–Hungarian language border and has been bilingual for centuries. The name is the German translation of the Hungarian *Felsöör*, meaning 'upper sentry'. It shifted politically between Austria and Hungary as state boundaries changed but has remained part of Austria since 1921.

'Peasant men can't get wives'

Since the Second World War Oberwart has received many German-speaking immigrants and undergone expansion, urbanization and industrialization, in a pattern typical of post-war Europe. This has turned it from a rural, farming-focused community into a more city-like environment. Gal's study (published 1979) offers a rich and winsome characterization of the social traits of the town and its peoples, telling a story of social division that is manifested in history, architecture, urban planning, lifestyles – and language. Although the bilinguals of Oberwart control a range of styles in both their languages, and use this range for various social functions, their main linguistic choice is between their two languages: 'The choice *between* languages is more salient linguistically and more important socially than style differences within each language' (Gal 1979: 97).

In 1970s Oberwart, Hungarian symbolizes peasant status and is deprecated because peasant status itself is no longer respected. Gal characterizes the label 'peasant' as a 'native cultural category' – it is a label that the people use to describe themselves or others, *Bauer* in German. Young people want the newly available status of being employed workers, not peasants, and the world of work speaks German. For this reason, German carries more prestige than Hungarian – 'you can't go far without German' is a frequent local saying that applies geographically and socioeconomically. In diglossic terms, German is the H language and Hungarian the L. One consequence of the growing social and linguistic divide is, in the lucid title of a 1978 article by Gal, 'Peasant men can't get wives.' The young women of Oberwart do not want to 'shovel cow manure', and this affects their marriage decisions. Another consequence is that children of a marriage between a monolingual German and a bilingual learn only German, not Hungarian.

Language choice in Oberwart–Felsöör

In this context the choice between the two languages is socially meaningful. Table 5.1 shows the choices that Gal observed for 14 individual bilingual women (in the rows) in their interactions with 11 classes of interlocutors (columns) – in her 1978 article, Gal concentrated particularly on women and their role in the language shift. The table is an implicational scale, a technique not much used nowadays but which in skilled hands such as Gal's offers an enlightening way of displaying individual sociolinguistic behaviour on a continuum (1979: 19). Each cell represents one set of speaker × interlocutor relationships and the language choice favoured for them. For example, the cell where row 12 intersects with column 9 represents the language choice of a 64-year-old woman when talking to her children – in Hungarian. 'Implicational' means that the occurrence of the languages in the cells is expected to pattern so that if H (Hungarian), for example, occurs in a particular cell, all cells below and to the left of that will also have H (as happens for the cell at row 12 × column 9). And if G (German) occurs in a cell, all the cells above and to the right should also show G (as for row 2 × column 5). As a result, one corner of the table will have only Hungarian (here, the bottom left) and the opposite corner only German (top right). If the scale were perfect, the Gs and the Hs would meet in between. Both might occur in the same cells where they meet, but in a perfect scale

Table 5.1 Women's choice of German or Hungarian when speaking to different interlocutors, according to researcher's observation

Speaker		*Interlocutors*										
No.	*Age*	*1*	*2*	*3*	*4*	*5*	*6*	*7*	*8*	*9*	*10*	*11*
1	25	H	HG	HG	G	G	G	G	G	G	–	
2	15	H	HG		HG	G	G	G			–	
3	23	–	H	HG	HG	–	HG	G		HG	–	
4	27	–	H		HG	G	G	–			–	
5	39		H		HG	–	HG	G	G	G	–	
6	52	H	H	–	HG	HG	–	–	HG	G	–	G
7	17	H	H		HG	–	HG	–			–	
8	59	H		H	H	H	H	H	H	HG	–	HG
9	43	H			H	–	–	–	HG	HG	–	
10	54	H		H	H	H	H	–	H	HG	–	–
11	63	H				H	H	H	H	H	–	HG
12	64	H				H	–	–	H	H	–	HG
13	66	H				H	H	–		H	–	HG
14	71	H				H		H		H	–	H

Interlocutors
1 God
2 grandparents and their generation
3 black market clients
4 parents and their generation
5 peers
6 siblings
7 salespeople
8 spouse
9 children and their generation
10 government officials
11 grandchildren and their generation

Notes:
Empty cells = no data, not applicable
Dash – = not enough data
Source: Adapted from Gal (1979), table 4.1

they would never cross over. The scale is ordered to produce the best fit, that is with the least number of crossover cells showing an H in G 'territory' (as in row 3 × column 9) or vice versa. The number of cells that are out of order tells how good the fit is. In Table 5.1, the fit is good, with only three deviant cells (empty cells do not count).

Looking at the ages shown in the table, notice that the scaling has produced an approximate ordering from younger to older speakers from top to bottom. And the order across the page for interlocutors who are relatives is cleanly from the oldest interlocutors on the left (column 2) to youngest on the right (11). The speakers are arranged this way to produce the most consistent pattern of Gs and Hs, not directly because of their age. This means that the age ordering displayed in the table is actually a finding from the data not a prior decision. That is, the table gives the evidence that the younger you are, the more German you are likely to use. And the younger your addressee is, the more German is likely to be used to them – and vice versa for Hungarian.

As well as the age pattern, there is also a gradient from left to right across the table from more intimate contexts to more public ones. This horizontal ordering can be reduced, Gal writes (1979: 126), to a single association – that of 'urban' or 'Austrian', as opposed to peasant/Hungarian – although this correlates closely with age. Gal's conclusion – and one that we will have reason to return to when we deal with language style in Chapter 11 – is that 'only the identity of the participants determines language choice' (1979: 120). In many sociolinguistic situations, such as this, who is the speaker and who the addressee is the overwhelmingly important factor in code choice.

It is also an issue whether Oberwart represents a case of diglossia (see Exercise 5.7). In terms of its social standing, Hungarian has many of the characteristics of a High language – dictionaries, grammars, literature, etc. (Gal addresses the sociopolitics of Hungarian in later work, Gal and Woolard 2001). Within Hungary, it operates as an H language to minority languages which are Ls. Can it simultaneously be an L language to German as H in Oberwart? The situation reminds us that the social positioning of languages is not immutable across space or time. The same language may be regarded as prestigious in one place and denigrated in another. In Mexico, Spanish is the H language to Mayan languages as L; while next door in the United States, Spanish becomes the L language to English as H.

The social valuing of languages can differ over time as well as between places. The use of Hungarian in church (interlocutor 1) remains as a reminder of the former sociolinguistic norms of this society. Until after the First World War, Oberwart was part of Hungary, and Hungarian rather than German was the national language.

Exercise 5.7   Interpreting language choice in Oberwart

Identify and explain the language choice patterns in Table 5.1, for example:

1 'God' as an addressee refers to language use in a public church service (Gal 1979: 125). Everyone says they use Hungarian in church. Why do you think this is?
2 Explain the language used to black market clients (3). These are people, Gal writes (1979: 126), who come to the speaker's home to provide a service, such as repairs or renovation, which they are not licensed to perform.
3 Look across the age/generation columns for relatives, from grandparents to grandchildren (2, 4, 6, 8, 9, 11). Examine the patterns of choice, and suggest reasons for what you find. For example, explain why language usage to grand-children (11) is the most bilingual of all the columns.
4 The table shows that language choice is strongly age graded according to both speakers and interlocutors. What do you think these gradients mean for the futures of the two languages?
5 Do you assess that Oberwart is a case of diglossia (in Fishman's definition)? Evaluate the relationship of Hungarian and German against the criteria in 5.3. Is it possible for Hungarian to be a 'Low' language in Austria and a 'High' language in Hungary?
6 What other patterns do you observe in the table, and what are the reasons for them?

It operated as the superposed language in education, bureaucracy, media and church until 1921 (Gal 1979: 161), when the area was transferred to Austria, and German became the national language. The religious standing of Hungarian is the residue of the language's former prestige. Chapter 10 will focus on such language ideologies, including Gal's later work.

Finally, Gal notes that in this speech community, code switching is rare (1979: 118), in contrast to the extreme level of switching shown in Exercise 5.6, for instance. Code switching is not rife in all bilingual situations.

5.7   RESEARCH ACTIVITY
OBSERVATION VERSUS SELF-REPORT

The standard method of gathering language choice information in the sociological and social psychological traditions is, as we saw in Chapter 2, the survey questionnaire. The data in Table 5.1 however, are the result of Gal's **observation** of people's language choice in Oberwart. This involved a year spent living in the community, for example sitting in farm kitchens noting the language behaviours that were going on. Her long-term involvement with the community enabled this and is typical of an anthropological research approach, as we shall see in the next chapter. However, in the middle of that year of participant observation, Gal also conducted a survey with these same people, using a questionnaire to have them report on their own usage (1979: 98). These findings are shown in Table 5.2.

Table 5.2   Women's choice of German or Hungarian when speaking to different interlocutors, according to self-reported questionnaire

| Speaker | | Interlocutors | | | | | | | | | | |
No.	Age	1	2	3	4	5	6	7	8	9	10	11
1	25	H	HG	HG	HG	G	G	G	G	G	G	
2	15	H	HG		G	G	G	G			G	
3	23	H	H		H	HG	H	G		HG	G	
4	27	H	H		HG	G	G	G			G	
5	39	H	H		H	HG	HG	G	G	G	G	
6	52	H	H	H	HG	H		H	HG	G	G	G
7	17	H	H		H	HG	G	G			G	
8	59	H	H	H	H	H	H	H	H	H	H	
9	43	H	H		HG	HG		G	HG	HG	G	
10	54	H	H	H	H	H	H	H	H	H	H	
11	63	H	H		H	H	H	H	H	H	H	HG
12	64	H	H		H	H	H	H	H	H	H	H
13	66	H	H		H	H	H	H	H	H	H	HG
14	71	H	H		H	H	H	H	H	H	H	H

Source: Adapted from Gal (1979), table 4.3

Gal's use of both these methods offers the opportunity for a rare research activity. We can 'triangulate' the two approaches, that is, compare findings about the same issue gathered by different means. We focus here on identifying and understanding any differences between the results of direct observation and of self-report. Gal does not make this comparison herself, but I have extracted from her tables those 14 speakers who could be clearly identified in both (by means of their unique age). Although self-report is the main source of language choice information, researchers know that as a method it must be handled with care and reservation. Recall Figure 3.1: this showed a steep rise in Māori fluency in a short time, which I interpreted as representing increased motivation to report fluency more than an increase in fluency itself. The comparison in Oberwart enables us to calibrate self-report against what the researcher has actually observed.

The most obvious difference between the two tables shows up at a glance: the self-report table has many more filled cells than the observation table. You can count them and calculate the number of cells that are filled in each table out of the maximum possible total of 154 cells (14 speakers × 11 interlocutors). The reason for the difference is also obvious but worth making explicit: whereas you can ask informants about what they do in any situation, you are unlikely to be able to observe everyone in all situations. Thus, Gal did not observe all 14 speakers in church, but all of them reported on their church usage. There are also some kinds of situations (e.g. with government officials or black market clients) which will routinely occur behind closed doors. Other situations may no longer be observable – a researcher can ask someone how they used to talk to their grandparents when they were alive, but cannot observe that for herself. The coverage of the questionnaire was therefore much more complete than was observation.

The key question to ask about the two sets of findings now is this:

- Are there differences between the information Gal obtained about language choice through direct observation (Table 5.1) compared to the choices speakers reported for themselves when interviewed (Table 5.2)? If so, what do they mean, and how can they be explained?

Exercise 5.8 addresses this overall issue through a number of specific sub-questions, after working through a method for comparing the two tables.

Once the comparison exercise has been completed and your conclusions drawn, we can close by comparing the pros and cons of observation and self-report. The central issue between them is a trade-off between time and reliability. It is much quicker to administer a questionnaire than it is to sit and observe. We also presume that observation is more reliable than self-report in the sense that people may offer inaccurate reports, either because they are unaware of their behaviour or are misleading the researcher. But remember that observation is itself partial, in both senses of the word – it is incomplete and represents one observer's viewpoint.

The comparison we have run here shows differences between the two methods – but more striking is their close fit. About 85 per cent of the cells that are filled in both tables are the same through both methods. When you factor in the amount of time the two methods take – a year devoted to the community versus the much shorter and easier time for doing a survey – it is understandable that researchers tend towards using

Exercise 5.8 Comparing observation and self-report

To make a detailed comparison of the two tables, use Table 5.2 (self-report) as the basis. Ignore cells that are empty in one or other table, mark only cells that are filled in both tables. Go carefully along each row in Table 5.2, marking any cell that is different from Table 5.1. For example, speaker 1 × interlocutor 4 drops H to go from HG in Table 5.2 to G only in 5.1, and speaker 10 × interlocutor 9 adds G to the existing H to create an HG cell. Although this exercise looks complicated, it is in practice quite straightforward if not rushed, and can readily be done in class by individuals or groups.

This comparison should identify just 12 cells that are different between the two tables. Look at these differences, and address the following questions:

1 Which language was observed more than it was self-reported? That is, how many Gs does your comparison between Table 5.2 and 5.1 add, and how many Hs? Is there a pattern? If so, what do you think is the explanation?
2 Conversely, which language was observed less than it was self-reported? That is, how many Gs were lost in your comparison, and how many Hs? Is there a pattern? Explain.
3 Was more or less mixed-language use observed than self-reported? That is, does your comparison find more HG cells in Table 5.1 than in 5.2, or fewer? You can work this out by calculating the number of HG cells out of all filled cells. Does this mean people's reports are more variable or their actual behaviour? Why do you think this is?
4 Taking these comparisons, relate them to the interlocutors. Are there any interlocutors for whom there are a lot of differences between observation and self-report? Explain.
5 Overall, what is the key generalization that can be made on language choice in Oberwart from the above comparisons between observation and self-report? And what do you take to be the reasons behind the difference?
6 What can this comparison tell us about observation and self-report as research methods, and the relationship between the findings that result from them?

self-report. It is rapid and, at least in Gal's study, apparently quite accurate. It offers a ready means of first approach to language choice in a speech community. What it does miss out on – and many researchers would argue this is central to understanding, not peripheral – is the texture of ethnographic context and detail that participant observation garners, and that Gal presents so richly in her book.

5.8   SUMMARY

- Linguistic choice is foundational to all sociolinguistics. 'Language choice' usually refers to the option between different languages rather than between varieties – a term sociolinguists use rather than 'dialect' to cover all kinds of differences within a single language. Both varieties and whole languages can be covered by the term 'code'. The range of codes which speakers are able to draw on makes up their linguistic repertoire.

- The speech community is a contested notion, with three founding sociolinguists proposing different definitions. At one end the term has encompassed small, specific groups; at the other, enormously broad categories like 'English speakers'. It remains a widespread concept which sociolinguistics seems to need, and has been best defined by Peter Patrick as a socially based unit of linguistic analysis.
- Ferguson's concept of diglossia describes situations where two linguistically related codes are used in different sets of social functions, stratified between 'Low' and 'High'. In classic diglossia, the two codes are related linguistically, as for Arabic, Greek, Swiss German and Haitian Creole. Fishman extended the notion of stratification to clearly different languages, and Fasold extended it further to varieties in monolingual situations. Diglossia has been a very productive notion, although it can be criticized for its status-quo implications.
- Code switching occurs when speakers switch back and forth between distinct codes in their repertoire, often within the same sentence or utterance, and often carrying social meaning. Myers-Scotton originated the Markedness Model to describe the sociolinguistics of code switching, and argues that in some situations code switching itself is the socially unmarked choice. Gumperz proposed an interactional approach, distinguishing a *we*-code from a *they*-code, and situational from metaphorical switching. Auer sees code switching as organized conversational practice, which is either participant-related or discourse-related.
- Gal's study of the Austrian town of Oberwart shows how the choice between German and Hungarian there patterns according to the age and urbanness of speakers, and the effect of different interlocutors. Her use of both observation and a self-report questionnaire enables us to calibrate these two methods, showing that self-report gives broadly similar findings to observation.

5.9   FURTHER READING

Early work by Gumperz (1962), Hymes (1962) and especially Labov (1972b) dealt with the notion of the speech community – Labov's view is critiqued in Milroy and Milroy (1992). Peter Patrick's overview article (2002) offers the best available coverage; see also Rampton (2009), which deconstructs the concept.

Ferguson's original article on diglossia (1959) has been republished often, including in Li Wei's reader (2000) alongside Fishman's 1967 paper that extends the concept. Ferguson became founding Director of the Center for Applied Linguistics (CAL) in Washington, DC, under whose umbrella some of the most influential early sociolinguistic research was conducted or published (e.g. Labov 1966; Shuy, Wolfram and Riley 1968). CAL remains an important focus for socio- and applied linguistic research in the twenty-first century, with a useful website. Hudson (1992) is an accessible bibliography with 1,000 references to diglossia-based work up till that time. Issue 157 of the *International Journal of the Sociology of Language* (2002) is devoted to diglossia, with a long introductory overview by Hudson (2002). Glyn Williams's detailed evaluation of diglossia comes as part of his more general sociological critique of sociolinguistics (1992). The book is a useful exposé of the ideological underpinnings of concepts and approaches that many sociolinguists have taken for granted.

In code switching, the most accessible presentation of Myers-Scotton's approach is in her two 1993 books, one dealing with structural and the other sociolinguistic aspects. Later developments are found in e.g. Myers-Scotton and Jake (2009). Gumperz (1982a) is the main text on interactional work, plus his 1982b edited collection. Peter Auer's deconstruction of code switching and multilingualism is encapsulated in his 2007 article, and Auer (1988) summarizes his research on Italian/German alternation in Konstanz. Gafaranga (2007) offers a considered overview of the three approaches to code switching distinguished earlier, building mainly on Auer to stress code switching as orderly alternation. Gardner-Chloros's 2009 text is a useful introduction. Collections include Auer (1998), Milroy and Muysken (1995), Bullock and Toribio (2009), and two edited by Monica Heller (1988, 2007a). Volume 3 of Li Wei (2010) republishes leading papers on the sociolinguistics of code switching, with the linguistics covered in volume 1. The collections on overall bilingualism referenced in earlier chapters, such as Li Wei (2000) and Bhatia and Ritchie (2004), carry chapters on code switching. Many papers on the topic appear in the main journals of sociolinguistics and bilingualism (e.g. De Fina 2007).

Gal's Oberwart research is detailed in her 1979 book, with a distillation in the 1978 *Language in Society* article. As we shall see in Chapter 10, her subsequent work has been foundational in the investigation of language ideologies (e.g. Gal and Irvine 1995, Gal and Woolard 2001).

REFERENCES

Auer, Peter, 1988. 'A conversation analytic approach to code-switching and transfer'. In Monica Heller (ed.), *Codeswitching: Anthropological and Sociological Perspectives*. Berlin: Mouton de Gruyter. 187–213.

Auer, Peter (ed.), 1998. *Code-switching in Conversation: Language, Interaction and Identity*. London: Routledge.

Auer, Peter, 2007. 'The monolingual bias in bilingualism research, or: why bilingual talk is (still) a challenge for linguistics'. In Monica Heller (ed.), *Bilingualism: A Social Approach*. Basingstoke, UK: Palgrave Macmillan. 319–39.

Bhatia, Tej K. and William C. Ritchie (eds), 2004. *The Handbook of Bilingualism*. Malden, MA: Blackwell Publishing.

Blom, Jan-Petter and John J. Gumperz, 1972. 'Social meaning in linguistic structure: code-switching in Norway'. In John J. Gumperz and Dell Hymes (eds), *Directions in Sociolinguistics*. New York: Holt, Rinehart & Winston. 407–34.

Bloomfield, Leonard, 1933. *Language*. New York: Henry Holt & Co.

Bolinger, Dwight, 1975. *Aspects of Language* (2nd edn). New York: Harcourt Brace Jovanovich.

Bullock, Barbara E. and Almeida Jacqueline Toribio (eds), 2009. *The Cambridge Handbook of Linguistic Code-switching*. Cambridge: Cambridge University Press.

Busch, Brigitta, 2012. 'The linguistic repertoire revisited'. *Applied Linguistics* 33: 503–23.

Campbell, Lyle and Verónica Grondona, 2010. 'Who speaks what to whom? Multilingualism and language choice in Misión La Paz'. *Language in Society* 39: 617–46.

Cheshire, Jenny, Paul Kerswill, Sue Fox and Eivind Torgersen, 2011. 'Contact, the feature pool and the speech community: the emergence of Multicultural London English'. *Journal of Sociolinguistics* 15: 151–96.

Coupland, Nikolas and Adam Jaworski (eds), 2009a. *Sociolinguistics (Critical Concepts in Linguistics)*, 6 vols. London: Routledge.

De Fina, Anna, 2007. 'Code-switching and the construction of ethnic identity in a community of practice'. *Language in Society* 36: 371–92.

Dixon, R.M.W., 1983. *Searching for Aboriginal Languages: Memoirs of a Field Worker*. St Lucia, Queensland: University of Queensland Press.

Dorian, Nancy C., 2002. 'Diglossia and the simplification of linguistic space'. *International Journal of the Sociology of Language* 157: 63–9.

Eckert, Penelope, 2000. *Linguistic Variation as Social Practice: The Linguistic Construction of Identity in Belten High*. Malden, MA: Blackwell Publishers.

Fasold, Ralph, 1984. *The Sociolinguistics of Society*. Oxford, UK: Basil Blackwell.

Ferguson, Charles A., 1959. 'Diglossia'. *Word* 15: 325–40.

Fernández, Mauro, 1993. *Diglossia: A Comprehensive Bibliography, 1960–1990*. Amsterdam: John Benjamins.

Fishman, Joshua A., 1967. 'Bilingualism with and without diglossia; diglossia with and without bilingualism'. *Journal of Social Issues* 23: 29–38.

Frangoudaki, Anna, 2002. 'Greek societal bilingualism of more than a century'. *International Journal of the Sociology of Language* 157: 101–7.

Gafaranga, Joseph, 2007. *Talk in Two Languages*. Basingstoke, UK: Palgrave Macmillan.

Gal, Susan, 1978. 'Peasant men can't get wives: language change and sex roles in a bilingual community'. *Language in Society* 7: 1–16.

Gal, Susan, 1979. *Language Shift: Social Determinants of Linguistic Change in Bilingual Austria*. New York: Academic Press.

Gal, Susan and Judith T. Irvine, 1995. 'The boundaries of languages and disciplines: how ideologies construct difference'. *Social Research* 62: 967–1001.

Gal, Susan and Kathryn A. Woolard (eds), 2001. *Languages and Publics: The Making of Authority*. Manchester, UK: St Jerome Publishing.

Gardner-Chloros, Penelope, 2009. *Code-switching*. Cambridge: Cambridge University Press.

Gumperz, John J., 1962. 'Types of linguistic communities'. *Anthropological Linguistics* 4: 28–40.

Gumperz, John J., 1968. 'The speech community'. In David L. Sills (ed.), *International Encyclopedia of the Social Sciences*. New York: Macmillan and Free Press. 381–6.

Gumperz, John J., 1982a. *Discourse Strategies*. Cambridge: Cambridge University Press.

Gumperz, John J. (ed.), 1982b. *Language and Social Identity*. Cambridge: Cambridge University Press.

Heller, Monica (ed.), 1988. *Codeswitching: Anthropological and Sociological Perspectives*. Berlin: Mouton de Gruyter.

Heller, Monica (ed.), 2007a. *Bilingualism: A Social Approach*. Basingstoke, UK: Palgrave Macmillan.

Hudson, Alan, 1992. 'Diglossia: a bibliographic review'. *Language in Society* 21: 611–74.

Hudson, Alan, 2002. 'Outline of a theory of diglossia'. *International Journal of the Sociology of Language* 157: 1–48.

Hymes, Dell H., 1962. 'The ethnography of speaking'. In Thomas Gladwin and William C. Sturtevant (eds), *Anthropology and Human Behavior*. Washington, DC: Anthropological Society of Washington. 13–53.

Hymes, Dell, 1972. 'Models of the interaction of language and social life'. In John J. Gumperz and Dell Hymes (eds), *Directions in Sociolinguistics*. New York: Holt, Rinehart & Winston. 35–71.

Hymes, Dell, 1974. *Foundations in Sociolinguistics: An Ethnographic Approach*. Philadelphia, PA: University of Pennsylvania Press.

Kachru, Braj B., 2001. 'Speech community'. In Rajend Mesthrie (ed.), *Concise Encyclopedia of Sociolinguistics*. Oxford, UK: Elsevier. 105–7.

Kaye, Alan S., 1972. 'Remarks on diglossia in Arabic: well-defined vs. ill-defined'. *Linguistics* 81: 32–48.

Labov, William, 1966. *The Social Stratification of English in New York City*. Washington, DC: Center for Applied Linguistics.

Labov, William, 1972b. *Sociolinguistic Patterns*. Philadelphia, PA: University of Pennsylvania Press.

Li Wei (ed.), 2000. *The Bilingualism Reader*. London: Routledge.

Li Wei (ed.), 2010. *Bilingualism and Multilingualism: Critical Concepts in Linguistics* (4 vols). London: Routledge.

Milroy, Lesley, 1987. *Language and Social Networks* (2nd edn). Oxford, UK: Basil Blackwell.

Milroy, Lesley and James Milroy, 1992. 'Social network and social class: toward an integrated sociolinguistic model'. *Language in Society* 21: 1–26.

Milroy, Lesley and Pieter Muysken (eds), 1995. *One Speaker, Two Languages: Cross-disciplinary Perspectives on Code-switching*. Cambridge: Cambridge University Press.

Migge, Bettina, 2007. 'Code-switching and social identities in the Eastern Maroon community of Suriname and French Guiana'. *Journal of Sociolinguistics* 11: 53–73.

Myers Scotton, Carol, 1988. 'Code-switching as indexical of social negotiations'. In Monica Heller (ed.), *Codeswitching: Anthropological and Sociological Perspectives*. Berlin: Mouton de Gruyter. 151–86.

Myers-Scotton, Carol, 1993a. *Duelling Languages: Grammatical Structure in Codeswitching*. Oxford: Oxford University Press.

Myers-Scotton, Carol, 1993b. *Social Motivations for Codeswitching: Evidence from Africa*. Oxford: Oxford University Press.

Myers-Scotton, Carol and Janice Jake, 2009. 'A universal model of code-switching and bilingual language processing and production'. In Barbara E. Bullock and Almeida Jacqueline Toribio (eds), *The Cambridge Handbook of Linguistic Code-switching*. Cambridge: Cambridge University Press. 336–57.

Patrick, Peter L., 2002. 'The speech community'. In J.K. Chambers, Peter Trudgill and Natalie Schilling-Estes (eds), *The Handbook of Language Variation and Change*. Malden, MA: Blackwell Publishing. 573–97.

Poplack, Shana, 1980. 'Sometimes I'll start a sentence in Spanish Y TERMINO EN ESPAÑOL: toward a typology of code-switching'. *Linguistics* 18: 581–618.

Rampton, Ben, 2009. 'Speech community and beyond'. In Nikolas Coupland and Adam Jaworski (eds), *The New Sociolinguistics Reader*. Basingstoke, UK: Palgrave Macmillan. 694–713.

Romaine, Suzanne, 1995. *Bilingualism* (2nd edn). Oxford: Blackwell Publishers.

Shuy, Roger W., Walt Wolfram and William K. Riley, 1968. *A Study of Social Dialects in Detroit*. Washington, DC: Educational Resources Information Center.

Snow, Don, 2010. 'Hong Kong and modern diglossia'. *International Journal of the Sociology of Language* 206: 155–79.

Williams, Glyn, 1992. *Sociolinguistics: A Sociological Critique*. London: Routledge.

Woolard, Kathryn A., 1999. 'Simultaneity and bivalency as strategies in bilingualism'. *Journal of Linguistic Anthropology* 8: 3–29.

Woolard, Kathryn A., and E. Nicholas Genovese, 2007. 'Strategic bivalency in Latin and Spanish in early modern Spain'. *Language in Society* 36: 487–509.

6

SITUATED LANGUAGE

Language does not occur in a vacuum. It is situated, contextualized. There are speakers and hearers, a time and a place, a topic and a purpose. This chapter introduces the main ways in which sociolinguists have tried to describe and make sense of how everyday language is moulded by – and moulds – the situation of its usage.

We then go on to examine several approaches to how language operates as part of interaction. The chapter deals with the use of language to do things through speech acts, and the ways in which politeness (or impoliteness) affects how we address another person. It looks in detail at the sociolinguistics of interaction, how that can lead to miscommunication between people, and the ways in which gender dynamics affect conversational patterns such as turn taking. Underlying this is a concern for the micro detail of everyday conversation that is informed by the methods and theories of anthropology, in particular by ethnographic approaches.

6.1   SITUATIONS, CONTEXTS AND DOMAINS

A situation is the extended social occasion within which speech occurs (Hymes 1972). Situations are as variegated as human encounters – 'card games, ball-room couplings, surgical teams in operation, and fist fights', as Erving Goffman put it in a brief early paper on 'the neglected situation' (1964: 135). Language is one player in situation, although most situations are not primarily defined by language but by the shared activity. They may, however, contain conventional language elements, and speech may even be the main activity or prerequisite of what occurs. A committee meeting, a trial in court, a school class are all speech situations – they cannot in fact take place without speaking, and speaking that is appropriate to the specific situation.

The Guidebook to Sociolinguistics, First Edition. Allan Bell.
© 2014 Allan Bell. Published 2014 by Blackwell Publishing Ltd.

Exercise 6.1   Evaluating context

'Context' is a term that is widely used in sociolinguistics even when scholars question its appropriateness.

- How justifiable is it to treat language and context as separate entities?
- How practical is it *not* to treat them as separable?

See for example the essays in Duranti and Goodwin (1992).

Closely related to situation is the notion of context. This assumes that a situation consists of two elements: a core event or activity, and the field of action in which it is embedded – the context. Traditionally, these have been treated as two relatively separable components (Goodwin and Duranti 1992), and interaction between them has been regarded as essentially one-way, from the context to the language. But sociolinguists became increasingly aware that language itself shapes and re-shapes the context, and therefore the overall situation of its own use. Even at the most basic level of who counts as a participant in a situation, language choice can define people as in or out of the frame. In an early phrasing that could represent much of the sociolinguistic work of the early twenty-first century, John Gumperz wrote: 'Sociolinguistic variables are themselves constitutive of social reality' (1982a: vii).

Fishman (e.g. 1965) offers a series of questions about language use in society which have been widely used as a shorthand way of characterizing sociolinguistic situations:

- who uses
- what variety
- of what language
- to whom
- when
- where
- about what
- and to what end.

A good deal of sociolinguistic enquiry can be pursued through these questions, and throughout this book we address the issues they raise in different guises (see Gal's study in Chapter 5.6, for example). Such a series of questions seeks to investigate 'the norms of language usage – that is to say, the generally accepted social patterns of language use and of behavior and attitude toward language' (Fishman 1971: 219). These questions can be used, for example, to examine the choice between polite and familiar second person pronouns, a common feature of many languages. The so called 'T/V' pronouns in European languages (e.g. French *tu* versus *vous*) were the focus of a pioneering study by Brown and Gilman (1960) which characterized them as encoding solidarity versus power.

Exercise 6.2   Address systems

In a classic article, Susan Ervin-Tripp (1972), one of the founding sociolinguistic scholars, proposed a framework of 'alternation and co-occurrence'. She built on the work of Brown and Ford (1964) on address terms in American English. These terms involve choices between addressing your interlocutor by their first name, or by title plus last name, and so on – 'Julia' versus 'Mrs Child'. Ervin-Tripp diagrams a flow chart which offers a series of binary alternatives according to the addressee's gender, relative age, etc.

Address systems differ across languages and in different dialects of English. Read the relevant section at the beginning of Ervin-Tripp's article, then interview each other about address terms in your respective languages and dialects:

1 What terms are available in the address system of your informant's language or dialect (e.g. first name, titles, etc.)?
2 Give examples of how these terms combine to make different forms of address.
3 What are the factors that influence choice of address terms in your informant's language or dialect?
4 List these factors and diagram them in a flow chart similar to Ervin-Tripp's. If there are too many factors or outcomes, just diagram the main parts of the system.
5 Report back and draw generalizations and conclusions on the basis of the class's findings.

Domains of use

Fishman also approached context through his concept of **domains** (1972). The choice of which code to use in habitual situations in a bilingual or multilingual society is not random. Fishman writes about a Belgian official who tends to use one code (standard French) at the office, another (standard Dutch) at his club, and a third (a local variety of Flemish) at home. The domain proposal aims to capture the regularity of these uses without losing the possibility of individual choice and fluctuation. The description here may represent the official's typical code choices, but he will occasionally use Flemish at the office, French at the club, and standard Dutch at home.

Note the links between domain and 'language function', which I introduced in Chapter 3. Function is a macro-level concept which focuses on how languages operate across a whole nation or society. Domain is a parallel micro-level notion, which is concerned with the code choices that individuals or small groups make in particular interactions. Typical combinations of three main elements feed in to make up a domain – the topic of talk, the locale or physical setting and the expected role relations between participants (Table 6.1). The different factors buttress each other, and the likelihood of a particular language code occurring becomes stronger. In the Education domain, for example, there is typically a clustering of participants in defined role relationships (teacher and students), meeting in an educational institution and discussing the content of a course of study. In a bilingual

Table 6.1   Characterizing domains

Domain	Participants	Setting	Topic
Education	teacher	school	coursework
Religion	priest	church, temple	religious practice
Employment	employer	workplace	tasks at hand
Family	parent	home	domestic matters
Friendship	friend	café	common interests

Source: Adapted from Fishman (1972), 445

Exercise 6.3   Applying and evaluating domain

Apply the concept of sociolinguistic domains in your setting:

1 How well do the five domains in Table 6.1 apply to interactions in your society? Do they involve the listed participants, settings and topics, or different ones?
2 What further domains can you identify? How are they defined in terms of participants, settings and topics?
3 Do a domain analysis of one event in your culture such as a workplace interaction or a religious service.

Evaluate domain as a concept:

4 Does 'domain' further your understanding of how languages are used by people and groups in your own society? How?
5 Are there any ways in which it limits or skews our understanding? For example, is it too static to capture some – or many – situations? Does it close off alternative ways of looking at individuals' language choices and behaviours?

---

society, this educational domain will characteristically favour one language rather than another – for example, English in Malawi (Chapter 3), or Spanish in Mexico.

Research has tended to emphasize those domains associated with institutional public areas such as religion, education or media. However the more private situations with family and friends are also included, as Table 6.1 shows. Domains continue to be used as an organizing principle, for example in Kelly-Holmes's study (2010) of marketing language.

6.2   ETHNOGRAPHIES OF COMMUNICATION

Situated language has long been the interest of broadly anthropological approaches to sociolinguistics which provide much of the substance of this chapter. The most comprehensive early proposals came from Dell Hymes. Starting with a pioneering article in 1962, he developed a framework which he first called the 'ethnography of speaking'. Ethnography is the core method of social anthropology. It involves a close description of a community's way of life – what they do together, how they interact with each other, how they see themselves and the world. It is mainly the fruit of participant observation: the researcher observes the everyday life of the group through long-term involvement and experience, whether a plateau village in Madagascar (Keenan 1989) or a gang of teenage Latina girls in northern California (Mendoza-Denton 2008). The ethnographer learns the group's language and practices, often over the course of a year or more and with subsequent return visits. She keeps detailed fieldnotes of what she sees and hears, makes audio or video recordings, asks questions, probably conducts interviews. She aims to set aside her own preconceptions and to understand the group in its own terms, but also to maintain an independent view on what she finds. The result is a 'thick' description which leads to an understanding of the group and its practices – including clarifying in what sense it is a 'group' at all.

Blending ethnography into the study of language, Hymes's formulation of the ethnography of communication was typical for the early stages of an academic discipline. He advocated the value of developing a **taxonomy** – a structured and stratified list of the elements of a communication situation, like that used to classify plants into families, species and so on. This taxonomy aimed to help the ethnographer of communication observe, specify and interpret the patterns of a group's communicative behaviour.

In a series of publications Hymes offered related – although not identical – listings of the 'components' of the speech situation. The best-known and most complete list contains 16 terms (Hymes 1972), which he groups under eight headings whose initials form a mnemonic spelling out the word SPEAKING (Table 6.2). Many of these components have been mentioned in earlier chapters, and others will come up later. This is no surprise since they include most of the basic parameters surrounding the use of language. The research activity at the end of this chapter applies the SPEAKING taxonomy to analysing the classroom situation.

Situation consists of the circumstances in which a particular communication occurs. **Setting** (1 in Table 6.2) means the physical parameters of time and location – for example, 6.00 pm on a commuter train in New York City. **Scene** (2) is the culturally defined occasion that is involved – language happens very differently at a rock concert compared to a cocktail party.

Participants are the people who are taking part in a situation where language is being used. Classifying and illustrating participant roles and the part they play in language situations has attracted attention from successive sociolinguists because participants are arguably the key component of any interaction. I deal with Hymes's version of these roles only briefly, and return later in the chapter to look at more detailed formulations. Two of Hymes's four categories identify the people producing the language. The **Speaker/ sender** (3) is the authority behind something that is being communicated, the person responsible for the message. The **Addressor** (4) is the physical producer of the speech, the voicebox. Two categories distinguish types of receivers – **Hearers/audience** (5) who are not being directly targeted, and the **Addressees** (6) who are.

Ends are the purposes of a particular communication. Hymes divides this into two: **Outcomes** (7) are the general goals of an activity within a culture. For example, a university graduation ceremony involves staff and students acting out a rite of passage in front of a supporting audience. **Goals** (8) on the other hand are individual participants'

Table 6.2 The SPEAKING taxonomy

1	**Setting**	SITUATION
	time, place, circumstances	
2	**Scene**	
	'psychological setting' – the cultural definition of an occasion	
3	**Speaker/sender**	PARTICIPANTS
	person/authority behind the message	
4	**Addressor**	
	person who voices the message, spokesperson	
5	**Hearer/audience**	
	person/s who hear the message	
6	**Addressee**	
	person directly addressed	
7	**Purposes – outcomes**	ENDS
	general purposes within the culture	
8	**Purposes – goals**	
	individual participants' goals	
9	**Message form**	ACT SEQUENCE
	how things are said	
10	**Message content**	
	topic, theme	
11	**Key**	KEY
	tone or manner in which something is said	
12	**Channels**	INSTRUMENTALITIES
	spoken, written, etc.	
13	**Forms of speech**	
	language codes – varieties, languages, etc.	
14	**Norms of interaction**	NORMS
	cultural 'rules' for conducting conversations	
15	**Norms of interpretation**	
	listeners' or observers' interpretations of the rules	
16	**Genres**	GENRES
	language associated with particular speech events	

Source: Drawn from Hymes (1972)

intentions in relation to the overall event, for example family members who come to support a graduand. The difference between outcomes and goals is most obvious when there is a clash between the general and the individual purposes. Say a political dispute is underway between students and university management, and some students at the graduation ceremony voice their protest – then their goals differ from the outcome and from the goals of most other participants. The importance of participants' goals in communication has been a particular interest of social psychologists of language.

   Act sequence involves two components. The **Message form** (9) covers the way things are said – in fact, the stuff of most language analysis. The **Message content** (10) is what is said – the topic or theme. Different topics will often trigger different ways of speaking – we discuss road deaths differently from local gossip.

> ### Exercise 6.4 Topic and language choice
>
> Topic is an important category in sociolinguistic enquiry – note for example its role in Fishman's domain construct. In many workplaces around the world, technology may be discussed in English because technological advancement is associated with English. And surprisingly, in a traditional society an external language such as English may be used for intimate topics because traditional norms simply do not allow them to be discussed in the indigenous language. Rickford and McNair-Knox (1994) detail how one speaker, Foxy, shifted her linguistic style depending on what she was talking about – from teen pregnancies to career issues to drugs to race relations.
>
> * Do you believe the topic you are discussing affects the way you and other people in your speech community talk? How? For example, are some topics discussed in one language but not another? Why?

Key (11) is the manner or tone in which something is presented. What is superficially the same thing may be said in different ways. Conversationalists, like actors, can impart to a line widely different 'readings' through different keyings. The most obvious manifestation of key is when the way something is said subverts the meaning so that it becomes the opposite of what the surface of the words appears to intend – that is, irony. A change of key is often marked in the intonation. In English 'That's brilliant!' with a falling intonation is a criticism, the opposite of the same exclamation with a neutral rise-fall intonation.

Instrumentalities include the **Channels** (12) by which the language is carried, such as writing versus speech, or sung versus spoken. This has become an increasingly important dimension as technological change has created new communication media, especially through the many affordances of the internet. **Forms of speech** (13) covers the repertoire of codes that are available to speakers in a community (see Chapter 5).

Norms are the rules governing the production and interpretation of language in a situation. **Norms of interaction** (14) are the community's rules for communication, and are most easily visible when someone breaks them, for example in an encounter between two contrasting cultures. They include such things as when it is appropriate to take a turn at speech and when to keep silent. For example, Athabaskans leave more silence between speaking turns than do mainstream North Americans (Scollon and Scollon 1981). Such rules for turn taking in conversations are studied in particular detail by Conversation Analysts. The **Norms of interpretation** (15) show how interactants interpret each other's practices. When Athabaskans and mainstream North Americans interact, both follow their own norms for silence after each turn. The Athabaskans find the others rude or dominating because they themselves can never get a word in edgeways. The others think the Athabaskans are sullen or superior because they will not talk. Both groups end up confused and frustrated by each other.

Genres involve the language associated with a particular kind of speech event: a story, a job application, a blog, and so on. Different **Genres** (16) have different rules

Exercise 6.5   New genres on the internet

The internet has opened up new channels of communication that did not exist until the late twentieth century. It has also created new genres, and changed existing genres (see for example Rowe and Wyss 2009, Thurlow and Mroczek 2011). Many people believe it is having a major impact on our language (see e.g. Crystal 2006).
   Consider these questions:

1   What new genres have been developed on the internet? List as many as you can, and describe their similarities and differences, using appropriate terms from the SPEAKING framework. Have they introduced linguistic changes?
2   Also consider how new these genres in fact are – did they originate in pre-internet channels and genres? (see for example McNeill 2009 on the origins of the blog in hard-copy personal diaries).
3   How have traditional mass media (such as press, radio, television) colonized the internet? How has this changed them and their language? (Use the SPEAKING framework to compare for example a hard-copy edition of a newspaper and its internet site on the same day – see Bell and Smith 2012.)

for language choice and use. New technologies create new genres, most obviously in the burgeoning of internet forms. Genre is a slippery concept which eludes easy definition but which many analysts have found indispensable to understanding language use.

   The research activity later in the chapter offers the chance to apply and evaluate Hymes's taxonomy. In the process, it will become clear that some of the terms are overlapping, obscure, counter-intuitive, or simply selected to fit the mnemonic. Despite this, Hymes's listing serves as a wide range where sociolinguists may browse and find something appropriate and usable for their analysis. Later sociolinguists have adapted this kind of taxonomy for their own purposes, for example Scollon and Scollon's 'grammar of context' in intercultural communication (2001). Applied judiciously and perceptively, the analysis of such components makes a good starting point for understanding how language works in specific situations.

6.3   SPEAKERS IN SITU

Earlier we saw briefly how Hymes, as part of his SPEAKING taxonomy, distinguished just two speaker and two hearer roles. A more detailed approach comes from Erving Goffman, the sociologist of everyday life. Goffman's construct of the 'interaction order' was an important influence on sociolinguistic approaches to speaking situations, and in his later work he himself engaged extensively with sociolinguistic issues. In an essay on 'footing', Goffman (1981) laid out what he called the 'production format' in which speakers operate, recognizing three speaker roles: the Animator is the voice box, the Author is the strategist who formulates the message and the Principal is the authority

Table 6.3 Roles in language production

Hymes 1972	Goffman 1981	Bell 1991b
Sender	⎧Principal ⎨ ⎩Author	Principal ⎧Author ⎨ ⎩Editor/s
Addressor	Animator	Animator

Source: Bell (1991b), table 3.1

behind the words. Goffman thus splits Hymes's role of 'sender' into two (see Table 6.3). In the default case of ordinary face-to-face conversation, the speaker is the sole 'first person', playing all three of Goffman's roles simultaneously.

But even these prove to be not fine enough for the complexities of many institutional production formats, especially in mediated communication, where a fourth role is required. In my own research on the generation of news language (Bell 1991b), I subdivided the 'author' role again to allow for the fact that there can be numerous 'authors' but not all of them play the same function towards the text (Table 6.3).

The **principal** is the institutional authority behind a speech or text, whose position or stance is being expressed. There is an initial **author** who originates the first draft of a news story. But that story then passes through the hands of a number of **editors** who process and modify the text until it is presented or published in its final form by the **animator**. These roles can be applied to the analysis of language events of all kinds, including internet texts.

The straight listing of roles implies a linear chain, which in Table 6.3 looks like a production line from Principal →Author → Editors → Animator. But what is going on can better be regarded as an embedding or layering or nesting of one role within the next rather than as a line, as Goffman noted (1981: 147ff.). To illustrate again through the news process: each separate role in fact represents its own distinguishable speech event which could be characterized using the full apparatus of Hymes's SPEAKING taxonomy. Journalists work in a particular setting, with particular purposes and norms of interaction. They pass a text to copy editors, who are working in their own, different situation, then on to newsreaders in theirs, and so on. And each of these situations and their resultant texts is embedded within the next (Bell 1991a). Clearly such a detailed description would be large and cumbersome, but traces of the many layers sometimes show through in the finished product, the published text. When a story published in New Zealand describes a location as '129 kilometres west of London', we can safely deduce that the original said '80 miles', but the copy editors have neglected to round up the conversion to '130 kilometres'.

The concept of embedding is extraordinarily important for understanding how a lot of both everyday conversation and mediated language production work. Goffman describes the layerings or 'laminations' which speakers routinely introduce into their talk as they recount stories or incidents about themselves or others. The production format of the story scenario is embedded into that of the story's telling. Each such embedding changes the speaker's footing – their 'alignment, or set, or stance, or posture, or projected self' (Goffman 1981: 128). Contemporary sociolinguistic work also focuses

---

Exercise 6.6   Applying and critiquing production roles

1   Review the three approaches to speaker roles (Hymes, Goffman, Bell) outlined in Table 6.3.
2   Choose one situation of institutional face-to-face communication – e.g. a service encounter in a government office, or a trial in court – and apply each of the three frameworks to it in turn, especially with reference to any instances of 'embedding'.
3   Or: choose one genre of traditional media communication, such as production of a newspaper advertisement or television commercial, and apply each of the three frameworks to it.
4   Or: choose one internet genre such as production of a blog or social network site wall, and apply each of the frameworks to it.
5   Use your analysis to compare and assess the usefulness of each framework. Are the greater complexities in the Goffman and Bell frameworks justified by the increases they bring in insight? How appropriate and helpful is the concept of 'embedding/layering'.
6   How would you modify the frameworks in the light of the analyses you have done?

---

on how speakers take up different footings, for example in the course of a US presidential campaign where inconsistency or 'flip-flopping' of candidates' stances may itself become an issue (Lempert 2009).

Bakhtin (1981) has maintained that much of our spontaneous speech consists of words that come from the mouths of others, and this is nowhere more evident than in news discourse. Most news is based on talk. The information that journalists write up is gleaned mainly from interviews and documents. Fragments from these texts are embedded into the story, most obviously as written quotations or audio and video clips. As a result, the news story you read or watch consists of a set of textual laminations which would be almost impossible to unravel to its origins.

6.4   AUDIENCES FOR LANGUAGE

Speakers require listeners. The audience makes up the complementary dimension of language interaction, the second and third persons of the pronoun paradigm. We saw in Table 6.2 how Hymes distinguished between addressees and a wider set of hearers who are not being addressed. Goffman, however, points out that 'an utterance does not carve up the world beyond the speaker into precisely two parts, recipients and non-recipients' (1981: 137). He makes finer distinctions between ratified and unratified participants (Table 6.4).

Building on Goffman's proposals, I developed a set of roles as part of the 'Audience Design' framework, systematizing and labelling them as in Table 6.4. Audience Design (Bell 1984) treats the speaker, the first person, as the primary participant at the moment

Table 6.4 Audience roles

Hymes 1972	Goffman 1981	Bell 1984	Participant status
Addressee	Addressed recipient	Addressee	Addressed
	Unaddressed recipient	Auditor	Not addressed
Hearer/audience	Bystander: Overhearer	Overhearer	Not ratified
	Bystander: Eavesdropper	Eavesdropper	Not known

of speech, qualitatively apart from other interlocutors. It then ranks the audience roles according to whether or not the persons are addressed, ratified or known by the speaker. The main audience role is the second person, the **addressee**, who meets all three criteria – known, ratified and addressed. Other, present third persons may be licensed to participate, but they are not directly addressed – I term these **auditors**. Beyond them, talk often has a wider audience of unratified third parties. Those whom the speaker knows to be present, but who are not ratified participants in the conversation, are **overhearers** – parties within innocent earshot of the conversation. Other parties whose presence is unknown to the speaker are **eavesdroppers**, whether they are intentionally and maliciously hiding 'behind the arras', or whether they hear by chance because they just happen to be within earshot but out of sight. The specific configuration of all these roles and relations during any given utterance is, to use Goffman's term, the 'participation framework' of that moment of talk.

These four audience roles are implicationally ordered according to their status as addressed, ratified and known. Often in an interaction, the physical distance of audience members from the speaker coincides with their role distance, with the addressee physically closest and eavesdropper farthest away. Audience roles are assigned by the speaker, and visual criteria such as physical placement, body orientation or direction of gaze are often crucial to identifying who is who.

The differences between these audience roles have significant sociolinguistic repercussions. We have seen in preceding chapters how speakers choose their language code depending on who their specific addressee is. This is most obvious when the repertoire is multilingual rather than monolingual. In a bilingual group, the language you choose to use may in fact be enough to nominate who it is that you are addressing. Gal (1979: 121) reports an instance from her Oberwart study where two younger people in a farm kitchen were joking together in German. The young man switched out to Hungarian when he wanted to ask his mother something. The change in language choice briefly and directly re-classified the mother as his addressee, whereas she had been just auditor to the German conversation of the younger ones.

One case where production and audience roles quickly become very complex occurs with translation or interpretation from one language to another. Vigouroux (2010) describes the role and footing complexities involved in a Pentecostal church service for Congolese migrants in South Africa, where the pastor's French-language sermon must be simultaneously translated into English. Within a monolingual code, speakers can adjust their pronunciations very finely to cater for changes in audiences (Bell 1984: 172ff.) – we return to these kinds of styling abilities in Chapter 11.

Exercise 6.7 Applying and critiquing audience roles

Use the questions from Exercise 6.6 but apply them to audience instead of producer roles.

- Specify audience roles in terms of the addressed-ratified-known criteria (Table 6.4), which are especially relevant to distinguishing different internet genres or sites such as blogs or chatrooms.
- What light do these roles throw on the issue of what is public and what is private on the internet, e.g. on a social media site?

Language choice can be influenced not just by the addressee but by the outer audience roles, the auditor and the overhearer. It is common practice in many bilingual communities for even a single monolingual speaker joining a group (thus becoming an auditor) to trigger a switch by the whole group to the monolingual's language so as to include the person as a participant. Continuing use of a language that one participant does not understand would define the uncomprehending hearer as unratified, outside the group. Even overhearers can have this kind of effect on speakers' language choice. Gumperz found an absolute overhearer-determined rule operating in a bilingual Slovenian/German community in southwestern Austria: 'So strong is the injunction against speaking Slovenian in mixed company, that tourists can live in the village for weeks without noticing that any language except German is spoken' (Gumperz 1982a: 47). But overhearer-oriented choices are generally less determined. Gal and Dorian record identical incidents from their two communities, but with opposite results. In Oberwart, a group of bilinguals at an inn switched from Hungarian to German when overhearers at a nearby table requested it. But in East Sutherland, a group of bilinguals in a bar refused a similar request to switch from Gaelic to English.

Just as the media situation complicates the roles we need to describe the language producers, so it complicates the audience roles through the kind of embedding discussed earlier. Since each interaction situation becomes embedded inside the next, audience roles as well as speaker roles are laminated. A concert performance in front of a live audience can be broadcast (in real time or recorded). The live performance is a situation with its own full set of audience roles. When that performance is then broadcast, embedding it in the mediated situation, the wider audience generates its own, further set of roles. This can lead to trouble: the concert becomes technologically available to an audience which includes groups who were not targeted in the live event. Through mass media, everyone may become overhearers. And through the internet, everyone is potentially an eavesdropper – unaddressed, unratified, unknown but there – as many have discovered to their cost.

6.5 SPEECH ACTS AND POLITENESS

Speaker and audience roles are central to the study of speech acts – the abiding interest of the field of pragmatics, which is one of sociolinguistics' nearest disciplinary neighbours. Pragmatics focuses on language use and users. In its narrowest definition, it is concerned with those aspects of the context of communication that get encoded in the language itself – most obviously deictics such as pronouns (who 'she' means in a discourse can only be specified by reference to the context). More broadly, pragmatics deals with the many ways in which discourses are internally organized and related to their context. Its interests therefore overlap with much sociolinguistic work on syntax and discourse.

The study of speech acts is founded on the work of the British philosopher, J. L. Austin. In 1955 he presented his central ideas as the William James Lectures at Harvard University, although he died before these were published in 1962. His *How to Do Things with Words* is a book written with that shining clarity of style which some philosophers have achieved on difficult linguistic subjects.

Speech acts are **performatives**, Austin argued – utterances that actually perform the action they express. If I say, 'I promise to pick you up at midday', just by saying the verb 'promise', I perform the act of promising. Austin suggested that while statements can be true or false ('I picked you up at midday' – 'No you didn't' – 'Yes I did'), performatives can be either 'happy' or 'unhappy'. That is, they have to meet certain 'felicity' conditions, such as the right configuration of participants. Consider the words, 'I pronounce you husband and wife.' In most countries, the conditions for 'happy' performance of this kind of utterance are severely restricted. The law prescribes who is allowed to say it (a limited set of qualified celebrants), who it can be said to, where it can be said, and even the attitude of the couple.

Austin (1962) distinguished three aspects of the speech act:

- The locutionary act is the activity of uttering the appropriate wording.
- The illocutionary force denotes what act is performed through the utterance, such as complimenting or requesting.
- The perlocutionary effect indicates what the act actually achieves with its hearer – an apology accepted, an offer taken up.

The difference between the locutionary and illocutionary act is important. Many different forms of wording can be used to express the same illocution. 'I ask you to do *x*' may be the most overt form of requesting in English, but phrases such as 'would you please' are the more common locutions.

Austin found that his initial distinction between 'constatives' (statements) and performatives could not be easily sustained. This opened the way for John Searle, a student of his, to develop a general theory of speech acts (1969), including dividing them into five classes:

- assertives (or representatives), such as to state or describe
- directives: order, permit, request
- commissives: promise, pledge
- expressives: thank, apologize
- declarations: appoint, declare.

(Searle 1976)

Sociolinguists and speech acts

Pragmatics scholars and philosophers approach speech acts quite abstractly, using invented examples to illustrate points, but sociolinguists engage with them as they occur in natural language data. Apologies, compliments and complaints offer a very obvious zone for investigating the social workings of language. The earliest research counted and compared the numbers of particular speech acts used by different groups, along with their topics and functions. Much of that work focused on gender language differences in English (see Exercise 6.11).

In many speech acts, the exact configuration of participants is crucial to the success or interpretation of the discourse and interaction, bringing us back to the detail of speaker and audience roles laid out earlier. Some speech acts may be incomplete unless the addressee responds appropriately. 'I bet you –' is successful only if the addressee accepts the bet. When a complaint is produced before an auditor, that person functions as witness to the complaint, and their response helps determine what the outcome will be. Researching interactions within a Montreal family, Laforest (2009) found that the auditor/witness usually affiliates with the complaint and so collectivizes it, but also works to ensure the situation does not deteriorate too far (Exercise 6.8). Even an unratified over-hearer lurking unintentionally on the edge of interaction may play a role, for example inducing a speaker to mitigate an uttered threat.

But researching speech acts does raise issues for sociolinguists. Real recorded data is much less tidy than constructed examples, and it can be difficult to decide which speech act is being performed. Very many locutionary acts seem to perform more than one illocution at the same time, and often apparently deliberately so. Is 'How do you feel about coming with me?' a question, request or offer? Or is the speaker relying on just that ambiguity to hedge her positioning between imposing on the hearer or exposing herself to a face-threatening refusal? Researchers are now very conscious that speech acts are multi-functional, that they need to take thorough account of the wider discourse and context in which they occur in order to interpret their meaning, and that the same speech acts may operate differently in different languages and societies.

Politeness

A major strand of the pragmatic approach to language in use, and especially speech acts, is the politeness model proposed by Brown and Levinson (1987). The term unfortunately conjures up everyday perceptions of 'polite society', etiquette and manners, but here it receives a broader definition. The central construct is 'face', a person's public self-esteem, which Brown and Levinson take over from Goffman's analysis of relations in everyday life. Building on common notions like 'losing face' and 'saving face', they distinguish two dimensions: positive face is a person's desire to be actively appreciated, negative face is the desire not to be imposed on. Behaviour that caters to the first desire is **positive politeness**, and to the second, **negative politeness**.

Central to the approach is the notion of the **face threatening act** (FTA), and the many ways in which interactants handle these. Obvious FTAs include warnings and commands,

Exercise 6.8   Complaints and witnesses

From Laforest's study in a Montreal family (2009), consider the course of this complaint sequence and especially the mother's role:

23 *	Père	Je te trouve bien des affaires à la dernière minute.
24	Fille	Ben non.
25 →	Mère	Tu te laisses pas le temps de réfléchir [entre tes:entre tes
26	Père	[Bien oui.
		Ça c'est: faut que ça retombe la poussière à un moment donné.

23 *	Father	I think you do a lot of things at the last minute.
24	Daughter	Not really.
25 →	Mother	You don't give yourself the time to think [between your: between your
26	Father	[Yeah.
		Well that's: the dust has to settle sometime.

*	complaint
→	witness's reaction
[	overlapping speech

- What is the nature of the daughter's response to her father's complaint?
- Who does the mother align with?
- What stance does she take towards the complaint itself?
- What effect does that have on the force of the complaint?
- What function does the father's closing remark have?

but gentler speech acts such as requests and advice also embed latent threats (to the hearer's negative face). FTAs can be classified on whether they threaten speaker or hearer, and their positive or negative face. An apology constitutes a threat to the speaker's own positive face, since it implies a past shortcoming of theirs. An FTA is said to be **on record** when a clear single intention is obvious behind it, while for **off record** the intention remains ambiguous. The most direct, bluntly expressed FTA is **bald** – 'Sit down' – compared with the many **redressive actions** by which speakers mitigate the face threat: 'Please pull up a chair', 'Won't you take a seat.'

The politeness model has triggered a great deal of sociolinguistic research over more than 30 years in many cultures, languages and genres, often focusing on gender differences. It has also faced many refinements and challenges (e.g. Watts 2003). Probably the main issue has been Brown and Levinson's original claim to universality – their subtitle was 'Some Universals in Language Usage' (1987). In particular, face wants are not necessarily the drivers of politeness in all cultures. An ongoing site for research on the nuances and relationship of politeness and face is the use of honorific forms in

Exercise 6.9 Face attack in a Kenyan hospital

Politeness interacts with power, as Watts's text argues (2003). Despite a charter which entitles patients in Kenyan hospitals to respect, Ojwang, Matu and Ogutu (2010) found patients are subjected to frequent face-attacks by nurses. This reflects the power which nurses as professionals hold over patients, overriding usual considerations of politeness. Ojwang et al. give examples of eight types of speech acts from their data (2010: 505):

Why do you keep disturbing us?
Don't you know that you must pay for drugs?
I don't want to see that woman here.
The problem with you is that you don't understand.
Why follow me in hospital as if I were your debtor?
Take that woman out of here now.
You are adults but you behave like children.
If you try to be clever here, you will regret.

- What are the speech acts involved here? In Brown and Levinson's terms, which are on- or off-record – with a clear single intention versus ambiguous? Which are baldly put, and which have some mitigating redressive wording? In what cases is it hard to say?

While some patients tried to repair the damage to their dignity or launched a counter-attack on the nurse's face, most responded with a silence that reflected the power the nurse held over them. A teenage girl in labour was reprimanded and humiliated when she appealed for assistance (2010: 506):

a. Patient: Sister *nisaidie nakufa na maumivu.*
'Sister, help me I am dying of pain.'
b. Nurse: *Si ungemaliza shule kwanza ndiyo ushike mimba wewe msichana?*
'Why didn't you complete school before conceiving you girl?'
(Silence)
c. Nurse: *Sasa ndio utashika adabu*
'It is now that you will learn manners.'
(Silence)

- Interpret how the Nurse's words in this extract threaten the patient's positive and negative face.

Japanese, by which levels of respect are encoded in grammatical forms such as prefixes (see for example a *Journal of Pragmatics* theme issue, 43/15, 2011).

6.6 THE SOCIOLINGUISTICS OF INTERACTION

Sociolinguistic research into speech acts involves attention to the fine detail of how participants interact in everyday situations. It forms part of a wider interest in how we make ourselves and our communicative intentions understood in daily interaction. This was the pioneering work of John Gumperz, whose name is inextricably linked with Dell Hymes because of their co-editorship of the foundational *Directions in Sociolinguistics* collection (1972). But their work, approaches and contributions were very different. Hymes saw the big picture of the emerging field, taxonomizing and theorizing, and presenting little empirical language analysis of his own. Gumperz's focus was micro, as my Chapter 5 discussion of his research on code switching showed. He examined the minutiae of everyday conversations, and how these functioned to enable individuals to communicate and understand one another. His 'Interactional Sociolinguistics' was hands-on rather than programmatic.

Gumperz's work relates, often quite explicitly, to several of the approaches presented in this chapter. Goffman's 'interaction order' (section 6.3) offered a framework for studying everyday social dealings for which Gumperz looked to work out principles specific to language use. Gumperz (1982a: 156) also built on the thinking of speech act philosophers such as Austin and Searle (section 6.5), and particularly the approach of H.P. Grice. Grice had developed the 'Cooperative Principle' (1975), which spelt out four maxims for the conduct of conversations: that contributions need to be informative, true, relevant and clear. Gumperz's consideration of what was below the surface of conversations drew on Grice's other main construct – 'conversational implicature'. He took the proposals of the philosophers and sociologists and operationalized them for actual everyday conversation.

Gumperz's leading concept was the **contextualization cue**, presented in his foundational book *Discourse Strategies* (1982a). Contextualization cues are 'constellations of surface features of message form ... by which speakers signal and listeners interpret what the activity is, how semantic content is to be understood, and *how* each sentence relates to what precedes or follows' (Gumperz 1982a: 131). They offer overt clues to what is otherwise only presupposed or implied below the surface of a conversation. The cues can be of almost any linguistic (and non-linguistic) kind – vocabulary, phonology, syntax, code switching, use of formulae, and (particularly) intonation patterns or 'prosody'. They function to 'key' (as in Hymes's SPEAKING framework, Table 6.2) the interpretation which the speaker expects the hearer to reach. At the start of an interaction, a speaker and a listener will spend some time negotiating the basis of continuing conversation. In this process, the interpretive weight placed on contextualization cues is much greater than their surface linguistic importance. If the interactants coordinate successfully, they have achieved 'conversational synchrony' and move forward in tune with each other.

But if interactants do not share a common set of contextualization cues, trouble follows. Miscommunication brings to the surface presumptions that are usually hidden. Gumperz focused on such misfires, investigating communication problems and seeking to interpret where, how and why such breakdowns had occurred. Much of his early empirical work looked at interactants who share the same language but come from very different background cultural situations, such as Indian speakers of English in conversation with British or American speakers. He analyses in depth (1982a: 174) one employment counselling interview between a (white) British counsellor and an Indian teacher which lasts over an hour in a state of continual misunderstanding and increasing conflict. Their purposes for the conversation clash in the manner of Hymes's Goals/Outcomes distinction (Table 6.2).

Exercise 6.10 Question or request?

Here are two examples from Gumperz's early research on contextualization cues (1982a: 135):

A   A husband sitting in his living room is addressing his wife ...

     Husband   Do you know where today's paper is?
     Wife   *I'll* get it for you.
     Husband   That's O.K. Just tell me where it is.
                      I'll get it.
     Wife   No, I'LL get it.

B   A mother is talking to her eleven year old son who is about to go out in the rain:

     Mother   Where are your boots?
     Son   In the closet.
     Mother   I want you to put them on *right* now.

1   What sort of speech acts do you think these are? – questions seeking information, or indirect requests for action?
2   Notice the occurrence of strong word stresses in the last utterance of each example. What do these express?
3   When Gumperz played the two interactions to sets of listeners, those who heard the opening line of each example as a request also felt the tone adopted in the closing lines was justified. Why?
4   The husband in A is American, while the wife in A and mother in B are both British. Listeners who were British tended to give different interpretations from Americans. Which variety do you think would favour the question reading, and which the request? (See Gumperz's finding at 1982a: 139.) What could this mean for cross-varietal/cultural communication?

The difficulties that questions 1–3 pose for non-native English speakers, and 4 for non-Americans/British, illustrate how subtly and culturally determined is the knowledge required to interpret such everyday interactions.

Contextualization cues are central to the communicative competence of speakers – recall Dorian's characterization of the interpretive skills of semi-speakers in her Gaelic community (Exercise 4.7). Many of these cues are subtle, specific to sub-groups, and learned through long-term, face-to-face interaction with ingroup members. But the very absence of these skills contributes to limiting the amount and kind of contact that would produce their acquisition by the outsider.

Gumperz's wider research interest was in the sociopolitical repercussions of these kinds of cross-cultural misunderstandings, though his legacy is in many ways the least sharply defined of the sociolinguistic founders. **Interactional Sociolinguistics** is the name given to the body of work that has built on Gumperz's methods (2001). It shares not so much a cohesive theory as a methodological conviction that the detailed workings of everyday conversations are interactionally important. This it has in common with the fine-grained methods of Conversation Analysis. It has fed into the approaches of socio-linguists whose work we have discussed earlier, such as Gal, Levinson, Heller and Auer (some of whom were Gumperz's students). Best known is Deborah Tannen, collaborator with Gumperz on the development of contextualization cues, whose study of 'conversa-tional style' (1984) is a comprehensive application of the interactional approach. It analyses talk over a dinner (for American Thanksgiving) among six friends in California. Three came from New York, two from California, and one from England. The New Yorkers had what Tannen called a 'high-involvement style': fast and simultaneous speech, rapid questions, quick turn taking. This left the other three participants – who had a 'high-considerateness style' – feeling dominated and sidelined. In Hymes's terms (Table 6.2), there was a clash of norms.

6.7   GENDER AND CONVERSATION

Such research on communicative cross-purposes led Tannen to publish books like *You Just Don't Understand* (1990), which popularized the role of gender difference in con-versation to the broader American and international public, particularly with her con-trast between men's 'report-talk' and women's 'rapport-talk'. This was part of an upsurge in sociolinguistic work on gender and language, one strand of which treated gendered distinctions in language as a form of cross-cultural **difference**. Extending Gumperz's approach into cross-gender communication, Maltz and Borker (1982: 212) treated American boys and girls as being socialized in different worlds:

> What we are suggesting is that women and men have different cultural rules for friendly conversation and that these rules come into conflict when women and men attempt to talk to each other as friends and equals in casual conversation.

Early research examined differences, for example in speech acts such as compliments in English (e.g. Holmes 1988, in New Zealand). The general findings were that women give and receive more compliments than men. Rees-Miller (2011) replicated such studies in the United States decades later. In 'unstructured' settings, compliments by women to women were largely (74%) about appearance, while male-to-male compliments on appearance were very rare. Most compliments between men were about performance (64%), particularly in sport (see Exercise 6.11).

A second approach takes a **deficit** line. The earliest gender language research implied that women's language is in some ways deficient rather than just different. Robin Lakoff's short book *Language and Woman's Place* (1975) focused on language forms which indicated subservience and, she believed, were typical of women's English rather than men's, for example:

> ## Exercise 6.11   Compliments and gender
>
> Consider these three compliments and their reception (Rees-Miller 2011):
>
> 1 M: Hey bro, good game tonight; you played really well.
>   M: Hey thanks, man; it was a tough one.
>
> 2 F: That color goes great with your eyes.
>   F: Thank you for noticing.
>
> 3 M: I like that shirt on you.
>   M: Thanks, I like your face.
>
> - Describe and interpret the gender mix of participants, the topics and the reception of these compliments. Note the linguistic details such as the use of solidary address terms in 1 (see Kiesling's study on 'dude', 2004).
> - Exactly how and why is the response to 3 odd? What do you think it means socially? – for speaker, for hearer, and for the relationship between them? (see Rees-Miller 2011: 2685 for the researcher's interpretation).
> - Why were compliments 1 and 2 accepted and 3 not?

Pragmatic markers	*you know, sort of*
Tag questions	*isn't it? can't we?*
Intensifiers	*so much, just great*
'Empty' adjectives	*sweet, adorable*
Precise colour terms	*beige, lavender*

While her book was the foundation of gender language studies, Lakoff was soon criticized on at least three grounds: aspects of her approach implied women's deficiency, the linguistic forms were not at all neatly distributed according to gender, and their functions were much more variegated than just indicating lack of confidence. Many of these are typical Gumperz-type contextualization cues, the pragmatic lubricant which eases the course of conversation, while others are politeness moves which attend to an interlocutor's face needs. And it was not long before feminist sociolinguists questioned why women's language should be regarded as the deviation from men's language rather than vice versa.

The third approach views gender language as involving **dominance**. Lakoff's explicit statements on the matter make it quite clear that she believed the root cause of the 'deficiencies' was in fact dominance:

> The ultimate effect of these discrepancies is that women are systematically denied access to power, on the grounds that they are not capable of holding it as demonstrated by their linguistic behavior along with other aspects of their behavior. (Lakoff 1973: 48)

Gender differences – both in language and generally in society – are not random or neutral alternatives. Gender is itself a significant form of social stratification: there is no known society where women have more power than men (Giddens 2009). That power relation often surfaces in the patterns of conversation. In an article on 'the work women do' in interaction, Pamela Fishman (1978) found that women provided most of the support in conversations with their partners – for example, they asked three quarters of the questions. On the other hand, men did three-quarters of the interrupting in West and Zimmerman's research (1983) on the 'small insults' embodied in conversational interruptions. It was not long before O'Barr and Atkins (1980) concluded, on the basis of comparing male and female witnesses in court, that it was not a matter of women's language but of 'powerless language'.

Gender language research is now a large and varied field, and we return to different facets of it in the following chapters, including nuancing the definition of gender and how it is enacted. We will also see that the deficit–difference–dominance paradigms apply as well – not surprisingly – to other dimensions of social differentiation, particularly ethnicity (Chapter 7).

6.8 THE CASE OF SLANG IN RIO

The South Zone is the wealthiest area of the Brazilian mega-city of Rio de Janiero. It has spectacular hills and beaches and the most expensive real estate in South America. It is also the location of a number of *favelas* – shanty towns. These side-by-side contrasts of rich and poor have, as so often, an ethnic and gender reflex. Poor black young men in the area are some of Brazil's 'most disenfranchised citizens', according to an ethnographic study by the American sociolinguist Jennifer Roth-Gordon (2007: 323).

Research into the language of disadvantaged black male urban youth has a long tradition in sociolinguistics, stretching back to pioneer studies in the 1960s of New York City teenage gangs (Labov 1972a – see Chapter 7, this volume). The methods needed to research language in such situations are necessarily ethnographic. Researchers have to win access to and earn the trust of the people they wish to work with. Roth-Gordon's approach was typical of a linguistic-ethnographic study in its use of multiple data sources, long-term involvement, and collaboration with the participants. She interacted with her informants over a period of 18 months. Data collection began with written surveys and interviews at a high school. This led on to recording casual conversations with a peer group, the central data pool of the project. One group member acted as the researcher's mentor, guide and interpreter to the group and its language. He reviewed the recordings, identifying and translating target expressions from the Portuguese, which made participants' intuitions and judgements central to defining the data of the study. Finally, the researcher took selected excerpts from the recordings and played them back to different groups – the participants themselves, their parents, other adults, and middle-class youth.

Pragmatic markers

The Rio de Janiero study focused on the role of *gíria* or 'slang' in the marginalization of these young men of the *favelas*, and specifically on the role of four 'pragmatic markers' in *gíria*. Sometimes also called discourse markers or pragmatic particles, these are the small bits of language which provide much of the discoursal and interactional glue that hold our conversations together (Schiffrin 1987). In English, expressions like 'all right', 'actually', 'I mean', 'and so on' pepper our conversation, constantly signposting the structure and significance of what we say and the way in which we want to relate to our interlocutors. They are, in Gumperz's terms, some of the leading contextualization cues. Ethnographic, qualitative methods are suited to researching these kinds of linguistic forms, which require a situation where speakers are at ease and analysts can retrieve enough context to interpret the usages.

But there is a sociolinguistic issue here as well as a pragmatic one: the markers are often denigrated, especially in the speech of non-mainstream groups. They change frequently and spread quickly – and are commonly despised by, *you know*, older people as *sort of* indicative of the inadequate language skills of, *like*, younger people? There can be little doubt, however, that these critics will themselves be using pragmatic markers in their own conversation. Everyone does.

The pragmatics of *gíria*

The outsider groups routinely described the *gíria* users' speech as incomprehensible, and pointed especially to their high use of several pragmatic markers that are both textual and interactional. Roth-Gordon studied four expressions: sound words, obscenities, address terms and addressee-oriented tags. Example 6.2 shows multiple occurrences of the first three of these. We will look at just two of them.

Sound words are in fact non-words, phonologically graphic expressions that have also been studied in other languages such as Greek, where they are frequent in narratives (Tannen 1986). Most sound words imitate noises of contact or conflict like *bam!* or *pá!* Often preceded or followed by a pause in *gíria*, they behave almost like spoken commas, punctuating narratives and foregrounding new and important information (see Example 6.2) – classic contextualization cues. These loud, fast-spoken items are widely used in the male peer group, although speakers of standard Portuguese would not even regard them as words. The parents and middle-class Brazilians, whom Roth-Gordon surveyed for comment, know that these are part of stigmatized *gíria* speech and say that they hamper the coherence of the discourse. Since the function of pragmatic markers is to do just the opposite – to organize and structure discourse – the perception of incoherence appears to be a reaction to the speakers rather than to their speech.

Addressee-oriented tags are among the most common interactional devices in language – classically in English *y' know* (Example 6.1). The most distinctive addressee-oriented tag in *gíria* is *tá ligado* 'are you connected/paying attention?', which has been popularized by Brazilian rappers to reference black unity and political consciousness. It therefore functions both linguistically and sociopolitically in the same way as two pragmatic markers in African American Vernacular English – *aite* 'all right' and *na mean* 'you know what I mean' (Reyes 2005).

Pragmatic markers in English

Example 6.1

Pragmatic markers have been heavily researched in sociolinguistics for decades, in English and other languages – in women's and men's speech (Holmes 1995), academic lectures (Chia-Yen Lin 2010), workplace discourse (Holmes 2006), and (Spanish) classroom interaction (De Fina 1997).

One study of my own looked at markers in the peer conversations of young New Zealanders (Bell and Johnson 1997), especially addressee-oriented markers which serve to check the listener's comprehension of and empathy with what the speaker is saying. *Y'know* turned out to be especially common, occurring up to 200 times in a single interview. (Discourse markers often have reduced phonetic realizations, so linguists write them accordingly – *y'know* 'you know', *aite* 'all right'.) One speaker produces frequent clusterings of *y'know* as he talks, sometimes up to 10 tokens in a run, and even the occasional pair of two *y'know*s directly after each other. By contrast, tag questions such as *aren't they?* are very rare in real talk despite their being taught to learners as essential colloquial expressions.

Hustling in Brazilian *gíria*

Example 6.2

The *gíria* speaker 'Karate' describes watching street vendors hustle bystanders into playing a gambling game. He uses three of the four pragmatic markers studied – sound words (three times), obscenities (three times) and address forms (twice). Their frequency 'dramatically alters the rhythm of his speech' (Roth-Gordon 2007: 327) and constitutes a distinctive *gíria* style.

Karate: **Caralho**, *tirou dez mingau do bolso.* **Pum**! *Botou na parada.* **Bum**! **Caraca**, *ganhou os dez mingau.* **Caralho**, *ganhou quarenta merréis. Ih,* **mané**, *é mole!* [....] *Os outros cara tão apostando também junto com ela.* **Bá**! *Ganhando, perdendo, mas o mesmo,* **cara**.

Caralho ('shit'), he took ten bucks out of his pocket. **Pum**! Put it in the game. **Bum**! **Caraca** ('gosh'), he won the ten bucks. **Caralho** ('shit'), he won forty big ones. Oh, **mané** ('man'), it's easy! [....] The other guys are also betting along with her. **Bá**! Winning, losing, but it's all his money, **cara** ('man').

'One normal word in ten'

However, the salient thing for listeners is not so much that *gíria* speakers use their own distinctive addressee-oriented tags as the frequency with which they use the standard tags, particularly *sabe* '(you) know'. Some of the outsiders that Roth-Gordon surveyed describe slang speakers as 'speaking one normal word for every ten words' (2007: 332). The markers are indeed frequent in Example 6.2, but in fact they constitute there only one word in five rather than nine words out of ten.

Exaggerating the prevalence of a handful of features is a common stereotype of youth speech in different languages and locations, from Brazilian *gíria* to Californian female youth language to British 'chavspeak' (Mendoza-Denton 2008) – see Exercise 6.12. Yet study after study has found that discourse markers are widespread in everyday speech from all kinds of speakers. As Roth-Gordon concludes, these *gíria* speakers 'present a coherent linguistic style that makes extensive use of pragmatic expressions to organize textual information, manage interpersonal relationships between speaker and listeners, and convey speaker stance towards content and audience' (2007: 339). Standard Portuguese speakers make their judgement of *gíria* on social not linguistic grounds – on the marginalized position of its speakers, and on the way in which *gíria* challenges convention.

Exercise 6.12   The image of pragmatic markers

'Discourse markers in general suffer from an image problem,' observes Norma Mendoza-Denton (2008: 285), whose study investigated Latina gang use of various markers.

1 Are there any such frequent but stigmatized markers in your language and dialect? If so, what are your impressions of how they are used and by whom, what are their discourse and social meanings, and what are general attitudes to them? How did you form your impressions?
2 Use internet and library resources to research these questions further – see for example articles and books by Janet Holmes, and many papers in the *Journal of Pragmatics*.
3 Locate YouTube clips of media representations of this kind of language – such as *Little Britain* and *The Catherine Tate Show* for British chavspeak (see also Bennett 2012), and *Saturday Night Live* performances of young California female talk. Assess the accuracy of these performances, and their part in the social evaluation of the varieties.
4 Consider the role that these pragmatic markers play in stereotyping and marginalizing their users. Why do they attract such negative evaluations? What are the means by which these evaluations get circulated in a society? Should anything be done about them?

See Chapter 10 for further discussion of language ideologies and standards and their repercussions.

6.9   RESEARCH ACTIVITY
ETHNOGRAPHING THE CLASS

Apply Hymes's framework as displayed in Table 6.2 to the class you are in. I have expanded Hymes's terms for participants by introducing the finer distinctions shown in Tables 6.3 and 6.4.

Then use the activity to assess the framework. How much does it further your understanding of language use in the classroom? What are its limitations? Can you suggest improvements?

Setting
Time and place where the class is held.
Physical setup, e.g. of seating. Does 'place' signify more than just location?

Scene
What is the cultural definition of this occasion?
Is it a formal lecture? Or some other format – seminar, tutorial? What are the rules?

Animator, Editor, Author, Principal
Who does the talking? Who voices the messages?
Who is the author? Are there any 'editors'?
To what extent is the lecturer conveying content generated by others? Is there a 'tradition' being handed on? Is there much quotation, direct or paraphrased?
Who is the authority standing behind the messages? Who is responsible for the content of the class? Do class members generate content?
Does the institution (department, university management) have a role? How and when might that become an issue?

Addressee, Auditor, Overhearer, Eavesdropper
Who hears the message? The whole class? And only the class?
Are all class members being addressed, or are some of them auditors (ratified but not addressed)?
Are any unratified hearers present – overhearers?
Are all the hearers being addressed all of the time?
Are there any eavesdroppers?!
How do both producer and audience roles change when lecturer or student asks a question? Or when the class breaks out into small groups?

Outcomes
What is the overall purpose of the class?

Goals
Do all class members share this purpose? Does the lecturer?
How can differences between outcomes and goals show up?

Message form
How are things said – by lecturer, by class members? What is the mix of formal and
   informal?

Message content
What is the overt theme, topic? How is this approached and presented? Is it adhered to?

Key
What is the manner or tone of what is said? Is it always straight and serious, or are there
   other keyings such as humour, irony?
Are there non-verbal aspects?

Channels
What are the channels of communication – spoken, written, audio, visual?
Are there handouts, graphs, powerpoint, video playback, internet materials, etc.?

Forms of speech
What languages are used, and what varieties? Who by? What codes from participants'
   repertoires are *not* used?

Norms of interaction
What are the rules for turn taking in the class? Who is licensed to speak? When and how?
Do all interactions take place across the whole class, or are there 'breakouts' such as
   pair work?

Norms of interpretation
Does everyone interpret the norms in the same way? Are there any clashes between lecturer and students, or between different class members? Why?

Genre
Should this really be classified as a lecture? Or is it some other related genre? What are
   the criteria?

6.10   SUMMARY

This chapter has interwoven several broadly anthropological approaches to language use
and users, introducing a large battery of concepts and terms.

- 'Situation' is the social occasion where language occurs. It involves interplay
  between language and its context, with language in part shaping the situation of its
  own use.
- Fishman's concept of domains reflects that there are typical combinations of participants, topics and settings in, for example, educational or religious contexts, and these
  tend to trigger particular code choices.

- The founding approach to situated language was Dell Hymes's 'ethnography of communication', focused in the SPEAKING taxonomy which identifies the components of speech situations.
- While Hymes recognized only two speaker and two hearer roles, Goffman then Bell advocated for finer divisions. Within the construct of 'speaker', roles from the Principal (authority behind a text) through Author and Editors to Animator (the voicebox) need to be differentiated.
- Audience roles are also ranked in centrality from the targeted Addressees outwards through the unaddressed Auditors and unratified Overhearers to any unknown Eavesdroppers. These finer roles can be seen at work in media and internet production and reception, and are best conceived as embedded within or layered upon each other.
- Participant roles have major implications for language choices, and also for the operation of speech acts, a focus in the neighbouring field of pragmatics. Austin identified performative expressions like 'I promise' which do the action they name. Speech acts have different 'illocutionary forces' such as asking or threatening.
- Early sociolinguistic research in speech acts focused on counting and comparing gender differences in acts such as apologies. Later research attends to the multiple functions and nuances that such speech acts may carry in the context of discourse.
- In the 'politeness' framework of Brown and Levinson, speech acts relate to participants' 'face' needs, especially when confronted with face-threatening acts.
- Gumperz's work in Interactional Sociolinguistics focuses on how we make our communicative intentions understood through the minutiae of everyday interaction. His concept of the contextualization cue identifies surface features by which speakers signal to listeners what is otherwise only implied in a conversation. If interactants do not share a common set of contextualization cues, trouble follows. Gumperz focused on such communication breakdowns especially in cross-cultural encounters.
- Gendered language differences show in conversation. The 'difference' approach regards men and women as coming from communicatively distinct subcultures, shown for example in their complimenting behaviours. The deficit perspective evaluates women as conversationally unconfident and subservient, while the dominance approach sees the differences as the result of men's power in society, exemplified in more frequent interrupting behaviour.
- The chapter's case study is Roth-Gordon's ethnography (2007) of disadvantaged black youth in Rio de Janiero, involving long-term close observation of their way of life, recording their interactions, and eliciting their interpretations. *Gíria* or 'slang' is a key part of their identity and marginalization, and is especially expressed in the high use of pragmatic markers, which is denigrated by standard Portuguese speakers.

6.11   FURTHER READING

For overviews of ethnographic/anthropological approaches, see the complementarily titled texts by Duranti (*Linguistic Anthropology*, 1997) and Foley (*Anthropological*

Linguistics, 1997). Duranti has also edited two readers (2004, 2009). The five-volume Schieffelin and Garrett compendium (2011) assembles an invaluable set of classic and recent articles. For considerations of situation and context, see Duranti and Goodwin's collection (1992) and van Dijk's recent monograph from a text discourse perspective (2009). Saville-Troike's *The Ethnography of Communication* (2003) gives an extensive exposition of Hymes's SPEAKING framework plus several worked examples. The book-length studies by Eckert (2000) and her one-time student Mendoza-Denton (2008) offer insightful expositions and reflections on the doing of ethnography. The *Journal of Linguistic Anthropology* gives the flavour of current research, as do articles in *Language in Society* and *Journal of Sociolinguistics*.

Like his contemporary, Fishman, Hymes was central in shaping the field through his work as an essayist (e.g. 1972), journal and collection editor. In 1972 he founded the original sociolinguistic journal, *Language in Society*, and edited it for over 20 years. He also (co-)edited still-relevant early collections (Hymes 1964; Gumperz and Hymes 1972). Hymes's work is most accessible through his 1974 collected works *Foundations in Sociolinguistics*. He is not a tidy thinker or writer, but his thought is stimulating and foundational. See biographical essay in Wodak, Johnstone and Kerswill (2011).

Studies of participation and audience frameworks trace their roots back to Hymes (1972) and Goffman (1981). My own take is in Bell (1984, 1991a), and sociolinguists continue to revisit and refine these basic constructs (see articles in the *Journal of Pragmatics*).

On speech acts, Austin's founding book *How to do Things with Words* (1962) is an essential and elegant read. Collected readers at the more abstract/philosophical end of pragmatics include Kasher (1998) and Allan and Jaszczolt (2012). For empirical sociolinguistic studies, the *Journal of Pragmatics* – at nearly 4,000 pages per year in 15 issues – is a compendium of up-to-date research, especially on speech acts, politeness and discourse markers. The International Pragmatics Association runs conferences and publishes (see website).

Brown and Levinson (1987 – first published in 1978 as the major part of a collected volume) is the foundation document of the politeness framework. There is a *Journal of Politeness Research* devoted to the topic. Watts's reframing text (2003) challenges many of its assumptions and presents politeness as involving a discursive struggle for power. Janet Holmes's research, especially on workplace interaction, forms a major body of work on speech acts, discourse markers and politeness (e.g. 1995, 2006; Holmes and Stubbe 2003; Holmes, Marra and Vine 2011).

Gumperz's 1982(a) monograph is the basic text of Interactional Sociolinguistics, twinned with his edited collection (1982b) of chapters by students and colleagues. The biographical and contextual essay by Gordon in Wodak, Johnstone and Kerswill (2011) provides a good overview of Gumperz's work. Eerdmans, Prevignano and Thibault's *Discussions with John J. Gumperz* (2002) offers a fascinating roundup of his own approach and its successors. Volume 3 of Coupland and Jaworski's collection (2009a) covers *Interactional Sociolinguistics* (although oddly Gumperz's own work appears in other volumes). Tannen's books, both academic and popular (1984, 1990, 1994) probably constitute the most sizeable corpus of overtly interactional sociolinguistic work. Gender/language reading will be summarized in Chapter 7, except to note Pavlidou's very useful overview of 'gender and interaction' (2011).

References

Allan, Keith and Kasia M. Jaszczolt (eds), 2012. *The Cambridge Handbook of Pragmatics*. Cambridge: Cambridge University Press.

Austin, J.L., 1962. *How to Do Things with Words*. Cambridge, MA: Harvard University Press.

Bakhtin, M.M., 1981 [1935]. 'Discourse in the novel'. In M.M. Bakhtin, *The Dialogic Imagination*. Austin, TX: University of Texas Press. 259–422.

Bell, Allan, 1984. 'Language style as audience design'. *Language in Society* 13: 145–204.

Bell, Allan, 1991a. 'Audience accommodation in the mass media'. In Howard Giles, Nikolas Coupland and Justine Coupland (eds), *Contexts of Accommodation: Developments in Applied Sociolinguistics*. Cambridge: Cambridge University Press. 69–102.

Bell, Allan, 1991b. *The Language of News Media*. Oxford, UK: Basil Blackwell.

Bell, Allan and Gary Johnson, 1997. 'Towards a sociolinguistics of style'. *University of Pennsylvania Working Papers in Linguistics* 4: 1–21.

Bell, Allan and Philippa Smith, 2012. 'News discourse'. In Carol A. Chapelle (ed.), *The Encyclopedia of Applied Linguistics* (1st edn). Oxford and Malden, MA: Wiley-Blackwell (online at http://onlinelibrary.wiley.com/book/10.1002/9781405198431; retrieved 1 February 2013).

Bennett, Joe, 2012. '"And what comes out may be a kind of screeching": the stylisation of *chavspeak* in contemporary Britain'. *Journal of Sociolinguistics* 16: 5–27.

Brown, Penelope and Stephen C. Levinson, 1987. *Politeness: Some Universals in Language Usage*. Cambridge: Cambridge University Press.

Brown, Roger and Marguerite Ford, 1964. 'Address in American English'. In Dell Hymes (ed.), *Language in Culture and Society*. New York: Harper & Row. 234–44.

Brown, Roger and Albert Gilman, 1960. 'The pronouns of power and solidarity'. In Thomas A. Sebeok (ed.), *Style in Language*. Cambridge, MA: MIT Press. 253–76.

Coupland, Nikolas and Adam Jaworski (eds), 2009a. *Sociolinguistics (Critical Concepts in Linguistics)*, 6 vols. London: Routledge.

Crystal, David 2006. *Language and the Internet* (2nd edn). Cambridge: Cambridge University Press.

De Fina, Anna, 1997. 'An analysis of Spanish *bien* as a marker of classroom management in teacher–student interactions'. *Journal of Pragmatics* 28: 337–54.

Duranti, Alessandro, 1997. *Linguistic Anthropology*. Cambridge: Cambridge University Press.

Duranti, Alessandro (ed.), 2004. *A Companion to Linguistic Anthropology*. Malden, MA: Blackwell.

Duranti, Alessandro (ed.), 2009. *Linguistic Anthropology: A Reader* (2nd edn). Malden, MA: Wiley-Blackwell.

Duranti, Alessandro Duranti and Charles Goodwin (eds), 1992. *Rethinking Context: Language as an Interactive Phenomenon*. Cambridge: Cambridge University Press.

Eckert, Penelope, 2008. 'Variation and the indexical field'. *Journal of Sociolinguistics* 12: 453–76.

Eerdmans, Susan L., Carlo L. Prevignano and Paul J. Thibault (eds), 2002. *Language and Interaction: Discussions with John J. Gumperz*. Amsterdam: John Benjamins.

Ervin-Tripp, Susan M., 1972. 'On sociolinguistic rules: alternation and co-occurrence'. In John J. Gumperz and Dell Hymes (eds), *Directions in Sociolinguistics*. New York: Holt, Rinehart & Winston. 213–50.

Fishman, Joshua A., 1965. 'Who speaks what language to whom and when'. *La Linguistique* 2: 67–88.

Fishman, Joshua A. (ed.), 1971. *Advances in the Sociology of Language*, vol. 1: *Basic Concepts, Theorys and Problems – Alternative Approaches*. The Hague: Mouton.

Fishman, Joshua A. (ed.), 1972. *Advances in the Sociology of Language*, vol. 2: *Selected Studies and Applications*. The Hague: Mouton.

Fishman, Pamela M., 1978. 'Interaction: the work women do'. *Social Problems* 25: 397–406.

Foley, William, 1997. *Anthropological Linguistics: An Introduction*. Malden, MA: Blackwell.

Gal, Susan, 1979. *Language Shift: Social Determinants of Linguistic Change in Bilingual Austria*. New York: Academic Press.

Giddens, Anthony, 2009. *Sociology* (6th edn). Cambridge, UK: Polity Press.

Goffman, Erving, 1964. 'The neglected situation'. *American Anthropologist* 66/6, part 2: 133–6.

Goffman, Erving, 1981. *Forms of Talk*. Philadelphia, PA: University of Pennsylvania Press.

Goodwin, Charles and Alessandro Duranti, 1992. 'Rethinking context: an introduction'. In Alessandro Duranti and Charles Goodwin (eds), *Rethinking Context: Language as an Interactive Phenomenon*. Cambridge: Cambridge University Press. 1–42.

Grice, H.P., 1975. 'Logic and conversation'. In Peter Cole and Jerry L. Morgan (eds), *Speech Acts*. New York: Academic Press. 41–58.

Gumperz, John J., 1982a. *Discourse Strategies*. Cambridge: Cambridge University Press.

Gumperz, John J. (ed.), 1982b. *Language and Social Identity*. Cambridge: Cambridge University Press.

Gumperz, John J., 2001. 'Interactional sociolinguistics: a personal perspective'. In Deborah Schiffrin, Deborah Tannen and Heidi E. Hamilton (eds), *The Handbook of Discourse Analysis*. Malden, MA: Blackwell. 215–28.

Gumperz, John J. and Dell Hymes (eds), 1972. *Directions in Sociolinguistics*. New York: Holt, Rinehart & Winston.

Holmes, Janet, 1988. 'Paying compliments: a sex-preferential politeness strategy'. *Journal of Pragmatics* 12: 445–65.

Holmes, Janet, 1995. *Women, Men and Politeness*. London: Longman.

Holmes, Janet, 2006. *Gendered Talk at Work: Constructing Gender Identity through Workplace Discourse*. Malden, MA: Blackwell Publishing.

Holmes, Janet, Meredith Marra and Bernadette Vine, 2011. *Leadership, Discourse and Ethnicity*. New York: Oxford University Press.

Holmes, Janet and Maria Stubbe, 2003. *Power and Politeness in the Workplace: A Sociolinguistic Analysis of Talk at Work*. London: Longman.

Hymes, Dell H., 1962. 'The ethnography of speaking'. In Thomas Gladwin and William C. Sturtevant (eds), *Anthropology and Human Behavior*. Washington, DC: Anthropological Society of Washington. 13–53.

Hymes, Dell (ed.), 1964. *Language in Culture and Society: A Reader in Linguistics and Anthropology*. New York: Harper & Row.

Hymes, Dell, 1972. 'Models of the interaction of language and social life'. In John J. Gumperz and Dell Hymes (eds), *Directions in Sociolinguistics*. New York: Holt, Rinehart & Winston. 35–71.

Hymes, Dell, 1974. *Foundations in Sociolinguistics: An Ethnographic Approach*. Philadelphia, PA: University of Pennsylvania Press.

Kasher, Asa (ed.), 1998. *Pragmatics: Critical Concepts* (6 vols). London: Routledge.

Keenan, Elinor, 1989. 'Norm-makers, norm-breakers: uses of speech by men and women in a Malagasy community'. In Richard Bauman and Joel Sherzer (eds), *Explorations in the Ethnography of Speaking* (2nd edn). London: Cambridge University Press. 125–43.

Kelly-Holmes, Helen, 2010. 'Rethinking the macro–micro relationship: some insights from the marketing domain'. *International Journal of the Sociology of Language* 202: 25–39.

Kiesling, Scott F., 2004. 'Dude'. *American Speech* 79: 281–305.

Labov, William, 1972. *Language in the Inner City: Studies in the Black English Vernacular*. Philadelphia, PA: University of Pennsylvania Press.

Laforest, Marty, 2009. 'Complaining in front of a witness: aspects of blaming others for their behaviour in multi-party family interactions'. *Journal of Pragmatics* 41: 2452–64.

Lakoff, Robin, 1973. 'Language and woman's place'. *Language in Society* 2: 45–80.

Lakoff, Robin, 1975. *Language and Woman's Place*. New York: Harper & Row.

Lempert, Michael, 2009. 'On "flip-flopping": branded stance-taking in U.S. electoral politics'. *Journal of Sociolinguistics* 13: 223–48.

Lin, Chia-Yen 2010. '. . . that's *actually sort of you know* trying to get consultants in . . .': functions and multifunctionality of modifiers in academic lectures'. *Journal of Pragmatics* 42: 1173–83.

Maltz, Daniel N. and Ruth A. Borker, 1982. 'A cultural approach to male–female miscommunication'. In John J. Gumperz (ed.), *Language and Social Identity*. Cambridge: Cambridge University Press. 196–216.

McNeill, Laurie, 2009. 'Diary 2.0? A genre moves from page to screen'. In Charley Rowe and Eva L. Wyss (eds), *Language and New Media: Linguistic, Cultural and Technological Evolutions*. Cresskill, NJ: Hampton Press. 313–25.

Mendoza-Denton, Norma, 2008. *Homegirls: Language and Cultural Practice among Latina Youth Gangs*. Malden, MA: Blackwell.

O'Barr, William M. and Bowman K. Atkins, 1980. '"Women's language" or "powerless language"?' In Sally McConnell-Ginet, Ruth Borker and Nelly Furman (eds), *Women and Language in Literature and Society*. New York: Praeger. 93–110.

Ojwang, Benson Oduor, Peter Maina Matu and Emily Atieno Ogutu, 2010. 'Face attack and patients' response strategies in a Kenyan hospital'. *Journal of Sociolinguistics* 14: 501–23.

Pavlidou, Theodossia-Soula, 2011. 'Gender and interaction'. In Ruth Wodak, Barbara Johnstone and Paul Kerswill (eds), *The Sage Handbook of Sociolinguistics*. London: Sage. 412–27.

Rees-Miller, Janie, 2011. 'Compliments revisited: contemporary compliments and gender'. *Journal of Pragmatics* 43: 2673–88.

Reyes, Angela, 2005. 'Appropriation of African American slang by Asian American youth'. *Journal of Sociolinguistics* 9: 509–32.

Rickford, John R. and Faye McNair-Knox, 1994. 'Addressee- and topic-influenced style shift: a quantitative sociolinguistic study'. In Douglas Biber and Edward Finegan (eds), *Sociolinguistic Perspectives on Register*. New York: Oxford University Press. 235–76.

Roth-Gordon, Jennifer, 2007. 'Youth, slang, and pragmatic expressions: examples from Brazilian Portuguese'. *Journal of Sociolinguistics* 11: 322–45.

Rowe, Charley and Eva L. Wyss (eds), 2009. *Language and New Media: Linguistic, Cultural and Technological Evolutions*. Cresskill, NJ: Hampton Press.

Saville-Troike, Muriel, 2003. *The Ethnography of Communication: An Introduction* (3rd edn). Malden, MA: Blackwell.

Schieffelin, Bambi B. and Paul B. Garrett (eds), 2011. *Anthropological Linguistics (Critical Concepts in Language Studies)*, 5 vols. London: Routledge.

Schiffrin, Deborah, 1987. *Discourse Markers*. Cambridge: Cambridge University Press.

Scollon, Ron and Suzanne Scollon, 1981. *Narrative, Literacy and Face in Interethnic Communication*. Norwood, NJ: Ablex.

Scollon, Ron and Suzanne Wong Scollon, 2001. *Intercultural Communication: A Discourse Approach* (2nd edn). Malden, MA: Blackwell Publishers.

Searle, John R., 1969. *Speech Acts: An Essay in the Philosophy of Language*. Cambridge: Cambridge University Press.

Searle, John R., 1976. 'A classification of illocutionary acts'. *Language in Society* 5: 1–23.

Tannen, Deborah, 1984. *Conversational Style: Analyzing Talk among Friends*. Norwood, NJ: Ablex.

Tannen, Deborah, 1986. 'Introducing constructed dialogue in Greek and American conversational and literary narrative'. In Florian Coulmas (ed.), *Direct and Indirect Speech*. Berlin: Mouton de Gruyter. 311–32.

Tannen, Deborah, 1990. *You Just Don't Understand: Women and Men in Conversation*. New York: William Morrow.

Tannen, Deborah, 1994. *Talking from 9 to 5: Women and Men at Work – Language, Sex and Power.* New York: William Morrow.

Thurlow, Crispin and Kristine Mroczek (eds), 2011. *Digital Discourse: Language in the New Media.* New York: Oxford University Press.

van Dijk, Teun A., 2009. *Society and Discourse: How Social Contexts Influence Text and Talk.* Cambridge: Cambridge University Press.

Vigouroux, Cécile B., 2010. 'Double-mouthed discourse: interpreting, framing and participant roles'. *Journal of Sociolinguistics* 14: 341–69.

Watts, Richard J., 2003. *Politeness.* Cambridge: Cambridge University Press.

West, Candace, and Don H. Zimmerman, 1983. 'Small insults: a study of interruptions in cross-sex conversations between unacquainted persons'. In Barrie Thorne, Cheris Kramarae and Nancy Henley (eds), *Language, Gender and Society.* Rowley, MA: Newbury House. 102–17.

Wodak, Ruth, Barbara Johnstone and Paul Kerswill (eds), 2011. *The Sage Handbook of Sociolinguistics.* London: Sage.

7

VARIATION IN LANGUAGE

This chapter introduces the field of variation research that has grown from the pioneering work of William Labov in the 1960s to become the most cohesive and dominant strand of sociolinguistics. The study of sociolinguistic variation had its roots in the tradition of dialectology practised in Europe and North America. This involved surveys of rural communities, concentrating on disappearing dialectal words and pronunciations, and mapping their distribution. Until the mid twentieth century, there had been no such work in urban areas but that changed with Labov's innovative research in New York City.

The 'variationist' strand of sociolinguistics studies the nexus of both variation and change. This chapter concentrates on sociolinguistic variation, as far as possible reserving discussion of linguistic change for the next chapter. Variation is wider than change: a feature may vary without changing, but it does not change without varying. Here we focus on three of the five main social dimensions on which language varies between speakers: class, ethnicity and gender. Chapter 8 will cover another, age, together with change, and Chapter 9 deals with region, including geographical variation. Many of the examples here are from English, reflecting the preponderance of the research. Variation analysis deals in linguistic detail, and so technical terminology will be required in this and subsequent chapters to specify the phonetics of variation with the necessary precision.

7.1   FOUNDATIONS: NEW YORK CITY

Doing sociolinguistic interviews

Labov began his doctoral research in the Lower East Side of Manhattan in 1962, aiming to investigate the English of New York City, map its social distribution and identify how it was changing. The Lower East Side was an economically and ethnically mixed area that

The Guidebook to Sociolinguistics, First Edition. Allan Bell.
© 2014 Allan Bell. Published 2014 by Blackwell Publishing Ltd.

was broadly typical of the city as a whole (Labov 1966, 2006). It had a cross-section of socioeconomic levels, ranging from lower working class (LWC) through to upper middle class (UMC). Labov struck an early windfall: there had been a large and detailed random social survey of the area the previous year. He was able to coat-tail on this information and target a sub-sample who were native speakers of English and had lived in the area for at least two years. Persuading people to be interviewed, however, often involved allaying the 'suspicion of strangers [that] is an important element in the psychology of the residents of the Lower East Side' (Labov 2006: 89). The ingenious pilot study that preceded his main interviews, however, had no difficulty getting people to talk (Example 7.1).

The Lower East Side interviews included questions on language background, word and concept definitions, childhood games, pronunciation tasks, and language perceptions and attitudes. In particular, Labov concentrated on eliciting five different 'styles' of speech, with speakers paying increasing amounts of attention as they move from style A to D1:

A   Casual conversation
B   Careful conversation, which he describes as the default style of the interview – quite formal, as befits a question-and-answer exchange between strangers
C   Reading passage with target words and sounds embedded
D   Word lists of the target words/sounds
D1 Minimal pairs of words whose pronunciations differ by only one sound, like *pin* and *pen*, or *dock* and *dark* (testing for (r) pronunciation).

We will examine more closely and critique the nature of these styles in Chapter 11.1.

Example 7.1

Looking for the fourth floor

As a pilot study for the Lower East Side survey, Labov (1966, 1972b) devised a creative technique of rapid and anonymous interviews to test for New York City stratification of the postvocalic (r) variable as in *fourth floor*. Hypothesizing that the social rankings of department stores would be reflected in their workers' pronunciations, he chose three large stores that catered for very different social levels of customers: Saks Fifth Avenue with a very upper-class clientele, Macy's with mid-level customers, and S. Klein with the lowest ranking.

Labov went around each of these stores asking different salespeople about the location of goods which he knew to be on the 'fourth floor'. He would pretend not to hear the answer, and get them to repeat it again emphatically. He then slipped out of sight, noted down their four pronunciations (with or without an 'r') and characteristics like gender and race, and moved on to the next person. Labov reports that for 274 brief encounters this took 6½ hours (about 1½ minutes per speaker).

The study produced findings stratified similarly to the Lower East Side survey which followed. With 62% pronouncing at least one /r/, workers in Saks used more /r/ than Macy's (51%), who in turn used more than Klein's (21%). You can read the detail in chapter 2 of Labov (1972b).

The sociolinguistic variable

A total of 122 speakers – nearly two-thirds of the target sample – were eventually interviewed, mostly by Labov himself, resulting in 150 hours of recordings. Analysing these speakers' language involved an innovative construct that remains still at the heart of the variationist enterprise – the sociolinguistic variable. A variable offers speakers the choice between two or more alternative linguistic forms which have the same meaning (but usually different social significances). Labov examined five main sociolinguistic variables, three consonants and two vowels, plus a sixth which proved very productive: the alternation between velar [ŋ] and alveolar [n] in the suffix -*ing* in words like 'walking' (see Example 7.2). In the notation, parentheses (r) denote a variable, slashes /r/ the phoneme, and square brackets [r] the phonetic pronunciation.

Example 7.2

Counting sociolinguistic variation

With binary variables, usually one variant is regarded as a standard pronunciation and may be reflected in the spelling, e.g. [ŋ] in *driving*, and another as non-standard, [n] – *drivin'*. The researcher codes all pronunciations of ING, distinguishing the velar [ŋ] variant over against the alveolar [n]. The number of occurrences of each variant can be counted, and then the ratio is calculated as the number of times each variant actually occurred out of the times it could have potentially occurred but did not (because the alternative form was used).

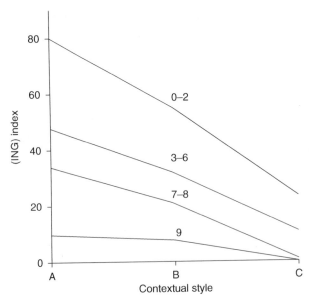

Figure 7.1   Class × style stratification of ING in New York City (white adults only), percentage of non-standard *in* variants

Classes: lower working class (LWC) 0–2, upper working class (UWC) 3–6, lower middle class (LMC) 7–8, upper middle class (UMC) 9

Styles: A = Casual, B = Careful, C = Reading

Source: Labov (2006), figure 10.7

Figure 7.1 shows what Labov found in New York City for the variable ING, which will be the subject of the case study later in this chapter. The graph has three elements which need to be understood:

- The vertical (*y*) axis shows the percentage of pronunciations that were non-standard *in*. If all were *in*, the index would be 100%, completely non-standard. If all were *ing*, it would be 0%, fully standard.
- The horizontal (*x*) axis has three points on it representing styles from A (casual), through B (careful), to C (reading passage), as defined earlier.
- Each of the four lines represents the pronunciations of all the speakers in one socio-economic class. The demographic survey constructed a single socioeconomic index by combining speakers' data on scales for occupation, education and income. This resulted in 10 socioeconomic strata (0–9), which Labov has here lumped into four classes.

Style × social stratification

The graph therefore shows the social × style pattern of the ING variable. Looking only at Style A, casual speech, which is displayed on the far left of the graph, see that the index ranges from 10% *in* for the upper middle class, increasing through the two central groups, and up to the lower working class at 80%. This means that the UMC are almost always using *ing*, and the LWC almost always *in*. Note also that the stratification between the four classes, shown by the vertical distance between the lines on the graph, is clear and consistent in each of the styles. No line crosses any other line, all four classes are perfectly stratified in the three styles. That is, LWC speakers always use the most of the non-standard *in* variants regardless of style, the UMC always use the most standard variants, and the other two classes position cleanly in between.

The slope of the lines shows the degree of style shift that each group makes from casual conversation (A) through to reading style (C). The UMC does not shift much, but then it does not have far to go from a starting point of 10% to zero. In reading style, all UMC speakers always produced fully standard *ing* pronunciations. The LMC (lower middle class) and UWC (upper working class) groups shift more, and the LWC shift steeply. Starting at 80% in casual speech, they end up at only 24% in reading style pairs. This represents a shift of 56%, from mostly using *in* in casual speech to mostly using *ing* in reading style. Interpreting displays such as Figure 7.1 is an essential skill in understanding variationist research, so it is worth ensuring you have followed all of the exposition. Nevertheless, there are issues over the social meaning of such styles and their stratification, which we return to in Chapter 11.

Labov concluded that this kind of clean stratification is typical of variables that are stable in the community's speech. The other variables were less tidy, indicating that change was in progress. Labov cross-analysed his data by gender and ethnicity, not just class, indicating how women and men and different ethnic groups tended to differ in their pronunciations. The study was pioneering on all fronts:

- the conception and design of the project and sample – urban, random, comprehensive
- the methodology of the sociolinguistic interview for eliciting different styles, especially casual speech
- the analytical method for quantifying linguistic variation and correlating it with social difference, especially the construct of the (socio)linguistic variable, and the discovery of systematic social and stylistic structure in language
- establishing that the same linguistic variable serves to signal both social and style stratification. In Labov's lucid phrase, 'it may therefore be difficult to interpret any signal by itself – to distinguish, for example a casual salesman from a careful pipefitter' (1972b: 240).

Since then, there has been variationist research on a wide variety of languages – English predominates, but there is a substantial body of work on (in descending order) French (especially Québec), Spanish and Portuguese (especially in the Americas). From the 1970s the variationist approach quickly became dominant in North America, where there is some tendency to equate it with the whole of sociolinguistics. Variationism has its own annual conference, NWAV (New Ways of Analyzing Variation) and journal, *Language Variation and Change*. A scan of recent journal issues shows articles on the four languages already mentioned plus Arabic, Dutch, Russian, Greek, Italian, Guaraní, Hebrew, Māori and Australian Sign Language. We now turn in the remainder of this chapter to dealing with variation according to class, ethnicity and gender.

7.2   CLASS IN LANGUAGE

Figure 7.1 is the iconic class stratification graph of sociolinguistics, a format on which hundreds of displays in dozens of studies have been patterned. It shows clean stratification of sociolinguistic variation by class in New York City, and the classes' shared pursuit of the standard variant across the style spectrum. The figure presents the measurement of language variability in a luminously unmissable way. Here the vision of class stratification is self-evident: this graph talks. Although Labov's prime interest after the 1960s was linguistic change, it is arguably such displays of sociolinguistic variation that constituted his founding breakthrough.

A second pattern of stratification that emerged in New York is shown in Figure 7.2, the graph for the variable (r), pronunciation or omission of postvocalic /r/ in words like *card*. This graph combines the 10 social levels of the survey into 6 classes, and displays all 5 styles. Mostly it shows the same kind of clear, fine stratification as for ING, but there is also a difference. In the two most formal styles, the LMC considerably outdo their betters, the UMC, in the pronunciation of prestige /r/. Why?

Labov describes it as hypercorrection: in their pursuit of prestige, the class that is just below the most prestigious actually overshoots their model. This became known as the lower-middle-class crossover effect. The pattern, which also showed out for both the New York vowel variables, is parallelled and illuminated by interviewees' language perceptions – how they evaluated the specific sociolinguistic variables when they heard them. The lower middle class reacted more than any other group to whether /r/ was pronounced or not by other people. Their hypersensitivity reflects

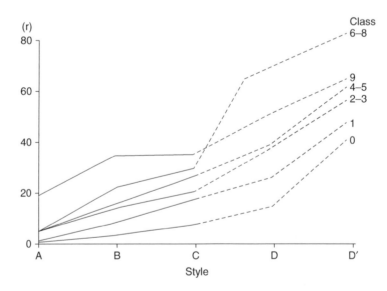

Figure 7.2   Lower-middle-class crossover: class × style stratification of (r) in New York City per-centage of prestige r-ful variants

Classes: lower class 0–1, working class 2–5, lower middle class 6–8, upper middle class 9
Styles: A = Casual, B = Careful, C = Reading, D = word lists, D′ = minimal pairs
Source: Labov (2006), figure 7.11

Exercise 7.2 Sharp and gradient stratification

What we have seen of New York pronunciations in Figures 7.1 and 7.2 is **gradient stratification**, that is relatively gradual differences between classes. This turns out to be typical of phonological variables, but grammatical variables may show **sharp stratification**. Below are data from African American speakers in Detroit (taken from Wolfram and Schilling-Estes 2006: figures 6.1 and 6.2). The phonological variable is (r) again, only here it is quantified in the opposite direction from Figure 7.2: the percentage is for /r/ absence rather than presence. The morphological variable is the absence of inflection to mark the third person present tense of verbs – *she go to the store* not *goes*.

	Absence of postvocalic /r/	Absence of third person -s
Upper middle class	21%	1%
Lower middle class	39%	10%
Upper working class	61%	57%
Lower working class	72%	71%

- Identify the gradient stratification for (r) and sharp stratification for -s. Is all the -s stratification sharp? Explain why/not.
- Why do you think grammatical variables show sharper stratification than phonological ones?

linguistic insecurity and matches their extreme style shift, indicating that they are taking the lead in change for variables like (r). We return to such sociolinguistic perceptions in Chapter 10.3.

What is class?

So far we have begged a crucial sociological question: what is class and how do we measure it? Class can be defined as structured inequality between groups. In modern western societies, it tends to have several characteristics (Giddens 2009). It is:

- fluid rather than clear cut (as 'caste' is)
- at least partly achieved rather than just ascribed by birthright
- economically based in material possessions not, for example, racially based
- large-scale and impersonal, for example not located in individual master–slave relationships.

Typically there is a small upper class, and perhaps sizeable underclass. In between are the working class, a shrinking group in western societies, and an expanding and highly diverse middle class. The two main sociological theories of class have been Marxist and structural-functionalist, which was accepted in American social sciences in the mid twentieth century. Labov uses this model and deals with its operationalization in some detail in his thesis (1966/2006). Stratification was seen as measurable through scales based on informants' answers to questions about things like occupation, education and income, in the manner described earlier for the New York survey. This still seems a very commonsense way to measure class: we are used to being asked these things in marketing surveys or seeing them reported in opinion polls. Most subsequent major sociolinguistic projects applied similar indexes not just in the United States, but also in countries like the UK, Canada, Brazil, Egypt, Argentina and Japan.

There are, however, issues around the detailed workings of these scales. Even in some western societies, they may not apply easily – in New Zealand we have found it very difficult to sort middle class from working class, let alone distinguish lower from middle from upper sub-classes. Nor should we expect to transplant these measures to non-western nations. However, the results demonstrate that such scales do locate social stratification, if only because the social divisions they identify are gross enough to make them impervious to upset by marginal, outlier and contrary cases, or by more subtle sociocultural factors.

Prestige and counter-prestige

Why, then, do class differences manifest themselves in language? Look at the style dimension in Figures 7.1 and 7.2. As well as the differentiation between classes, we see the shared pattern of style shifting. The style slope represents the common norm across New York City, which is for Labov the defining characteristic that makes it a speech community (recall his definition back in Exercise 5.2). All groups, highest and lowest, share similar responses. All acknowledge the one standard for both ING and (r).

In a sense then there is agreement on standardized norms, reflected in attitudes and behaviours. But there is also rejection of those standards. The standard pattern raises a question of its own: if all groups have the same evaluations and the same target – in Figure 7.1 zero ING, in Figure 7.2 100 per cent (r) – why do they not always speak how they want to, or at least how they think they ought to? In their most formal styles the lower classes approach the highest class's casual style. Why do they not do that all the time so that they can sound like the upper middle class in ordinary speech? The reason is that the overt prestige of standard forms like *ing* is not the whole story. There exists a countervailing set of attitudes which reject the standard and align instead with an oppositional vernacular norm, in this case *in* for ING. We explore this further in the case study of ING (section 7.6), and examine prestige, covert prestige and related concepts in Chapter 10.

Conflict or consensus?

One of the main sociological critiques of the structural-functionalist approach is that it treats stratification as if it were neutral, value-free. That results in endorsement of the status quo, an inherent conservatism. It assumes consensus within society. But the

Exercise 7.3   Class as consensus or conflict

Labov describes the structural-functionalist approach he adopted for measuring social stratification in New York as:

> ... simply that the normal workings of society have produced systematic differences between certain institutions or people, and that these differentiated forms have been ranked in status or prestige by general agreement. (1972b: 44)

Compare this with Rickford's view (1986: 218), based in the very different positioning of the Estate Class speakers of 'Cane Walk', Guyana:

> These fieldworkers essentially share a Marxist view of society – some of them explicitly identify it as such – seeing the assigned value of English as just another aspect of ruling class ideology, and aspiring to socioeconomic improvement through class struggle and change in the social order itself ... Many EC speakers use creole rather than standard English as a matter of choice, as a revolutionary act, as a means of emphasizing social solidarity over individual self-advancement and communicating political militancy rather than accommodation.

- Consider these two statements and their wordings very carefully (their 'discourses'). Identify, contrast and critique the views of society stated or implied in them.
- Could Labov's premise be transplanted to Guyana? Would Rickford's premise work in New York? Which best fits the social structures in your nation?
- What different kinds of sociolinguistic behaviours, policies and research would these different views result in?

Rickford ends his article with a plea for sociolinguists to benefit from the theories developed in the social sciences rather than trying to create their own as they go along. See Chapter 12 for discussion of sociolinguistics and social theory.

- From your knowledge of sociology, psychology or other social sciences, what theories from those fields might be particularly applicable in sociolinguistics?

alternative to consensus is conflict, in line with the social theories of Marx and Weber. This contrasting view comes in the work of John Rickford, a leading scholar of African American English and the creoles of the Caribbean. In a reflective 1986 publication, Rickford argues that structural-functionalist scales risk minimizing or overlooking the operation of power, the distribution of wealth and resources, and the role these play in creating and sustaining social disadvantage.

Rickford's doctoral work in his native Guyana (supervised by Labov) studied the creole–standard continuum of the village of 'Cane Walk' near the capital Georgetown. He saw that an American-style functional scale would not work in this East Indian, sugar-cane community. Local discourses revealed just two, clear-cut classes – manual labourers on the sugar estates, called the Estate Class (EC), and the others, Non-Estate (NEC). The social and economic differences between the two groups were clear cut, and were reflected in a dramatic difference between their Englishes. One was overwhelmingly creole, the other much closer to standard English. For a set of pronoun alternates, such as basilectal *mi* versus meso/acrolectal *ai* for the first person, their usages were poles apart – 18 per cent standard forms for the EC, 83 per cent for the NEC. This was despite the EC class agreeing with the NEC in associating the standard language with the highest jobs and creole with the lowest. The NEC members evaluate standard variants as part of getting ahead socially – like the lower-middle-class New Yorkers for (r). But the EC labourers see attempts to better themselves through standard English as making little difference.

Linguistic stratification is not a neutral social fact any more than social stratification itself is. Rather, it is a reflex always of inequality, usually of disadvantage, and often of exploitation. In earlier chapters we noted the existence of inequality between majority and minority languages, between established and immigrant languages, between 'low' and 'high' languages in diglossia, between pidgins/creoles and standard languages. The same stratification operates in monolingual configurations, and its basis – as Guy notes in his overview of class in sociolinguistics (2011) – is power: social, economic and political power.

Structural functionalism minimizes intergroup conflict but stresses the opportunity for individuals to compete and rise through the class layers. What it ignores is that a person's life chances are circumscribed (although not dictated) by their origins, by the place they inherit in the structure. As Labov's dedication of his book on African American youth vernacular puts it: 'To the Jets, the Cobras, and the Thunderbirds who took on all odds and were dealt all low cards' (1972a: v). Labov's very evident decades-long commitment to sociolinguistic equity comes in spite of rather than because of the social theory he adopted. Alternative views of class in sociolinguistics regard stratification as a process rather than a structure, not something given but the fruit of ongoing socioeconomic and political forces (Lesley Milroy and James Milroy 1992). They have proposed alternative or complementary models for understanding social patterns, three in particular – social networks, communities of practice and the linguistic marketplace. Because of their close association with the mechanisms of language change, we will deal with these in Chapter 8. They all represent attempts to access more of the cultural life-blood of 'class' differences in lived-out experience, particularly of those on the social margins.

7.3   ETHNICITY IN LANGUAGE

The sociolinguistic significance of ethnicity is reflected in the many ways it has already surfaced earlier in this book:

- in Chapter 2, Fishman's focus on ethnicities and their languages and Giles's ethnolinguistic vitality paradigm
- the place of ethnic identity in language maintenance and shift (Chapter 3)
- the racial dimension of pidgin and creole origins (Chapter 4)
- the role of shared ethnicity in language choice (Chapter 5)
- Gumperz's research on cross-ethnic misunderstandings (Chapter 6).

Example 7.3

A new pronoun in Portuguese

Portuguese is one of the most researched languages using variationist methods. The phrase *a gente* means, literally and historically, 'the people', but a study by Ana Zilles (2005) shows that in Brazilian Portuguese over the past hundred years, *a gente* has increasingly replaced the traditional first person plural pronoun *nós* for 'we'. The same kind of change has gone on in French, where the indefinite pronoun *on* has now nearly replaced the traditional first person plural *nous* in everyday speech. These changes affect both the language's pronoun system and its pattern of inflections on verbs.

One of the speakers in Zilles's recordings used both *nós* and *a gente* in this utterance (2005: 25):

Condução, bom, *nós não temos* condução própria.
Então *a gente depende* do ônibus.

Transportation, well, we don't have our own [car].
So we depend on the bus.

A gente seems to have arisen first from speakers of lower social status and then spread to higher classes, and remains less used in formal than informal speech. Zilles found that speakers in the large southern Brazilian city of Porto Alegre chose *a gente* 69% of the time. Using education as a measure of social stratification, the main difference was between those who had only elementary education (54% *a gente*) and all those with higher levels of education (67–74%). But as often, stratification interacted with gender: the elementary-educated women used about the same level as others (72%), but the men with elementary education used only half as much (37%). Zilles explained this as lower-educated men not wanting to use a form associated with women. See the case study of ING in 7.6 for a similar pattern.

And in Chapters 10 and 11 we will see how language ideologies tie in with ethnicity and how language can be used to claim an ethnicity. In this chapter we concentrate on the study of ethnically related variation within languages – primarily English, where most of the research has been done.

What is ethnicity?

Ethnicity is one of the most slippery social dimensions. It has to do with a group sharing sociocultural characteristics – a sense of place, an ancestry, a common history, religion, cultural practices, ways of communicating, and often a language. When sociolinguists question their informants about ethnicity, they are nowadays most likely to ask what ethnic group a person identifies with, indicating the socially constructed

Exercise 7.4   Defining ethnicity

1   Do you see a difference between 'race' and 'ethnicity'? What does your answer mean for language in society, and for research on language and ethnicity?
2   In his essay 'Language, ethnicity and racism', Fishman (1985: 4) characterizes ethnicity as 'collective intergenerational cultural continuity', and suggests these as central questions:

> Who are we?
> From where do we come?
> What is special about us?

Answer these questions in relation to your own ethnic affiliation/s. Then consider the questions themselves: what definition of ethnicity do they imply?
3   Consider the sociolinguistic implications of the four stances towards ethnic relations listed in the text – deficit, difference, dominance and discourse. What different kinds of language behaviours, policies and research would these different views result in? See the useful table in Harris and Rampton (2003: 9).
4   Think of ethnic minority groups in your own country. Which of the four approaches in question 3 characterizes the way they are actually treated by other minorities, by the majority and by the state? What role does their language or variety play in those attitudes and behaviours?
5   Majority groups often do not perceive themselves as ethnicities: they are just the default against which others' differences are defined. The home page of the New Zealand Government's Office of Ethnic Affairs states:

> The Office of Ethnic Affairs is focused on people whose culture and traditions distinguish them from the majority in New Zealand. This website celebrates New Zealand and its ethnic communities. Ethnic people and their families are part of New Zealand's national identity and support our nation's economic transformation.

Analyse how these statements construct ethnicities in New Zealand, including the majority.

nature of ethnicity. 'Race' involves treating a biological characteristic, such as skin colour, as socially significant. But recent history is littered with conflicts in which race determined which side you were on and whether you lived or died, and this heritage still remains with us. The legacy of enslavement of Africans by Europeans underlies the deep racialization of American society which is one reason for the enormous amount of research undertaken on African American English by both white and black researchers.

Harris and Rampton (2003) distinguish four positions on ethnicity, which parallel those identified in the previous chapter for gender:

- Deficit: other races are inferior to us.
- Difference: you are not inferior to us, but you are different.

- Dominance: acknowledging that ethnic relations have routinely meant the domination of one group by another, often through imperial power.
- Discourse (diversity): the previous three categories, ethnic groups, and 'ethnicity' itself are socially constructed and reproduced.

Often a theory of difference has involved a de facto stance of deficit, leading in practice to dominance – as, for example, under apartheid in South Africa. Much sociolinguistic work has concentrated on challenging the deficit approach and advocating the acknowledgement of difference and even dominance. It has often been concerned to address the difficult questions of ethnic disadvantage, although sometimes working with quite simplistic definitions of ethnicity. More recent research has tended to problematize this, stressing that ethnicities are fluid, and language is not just a correlate or product of ethnicity but also a component of it. This same deconstructive trend in the social sciences applies also to gender and other 'categories'. See Exercise 7.4 to take your consideration of the nature of ethnicity further.

The ethnicity–language interface

As we found in Chapter 3 on language maintenance, many minority ethnicities see language as a core part of their identity. Some theorists – most obviously Fishman – agree. In this chapter we are concerned not with the heritage languages of minorities but rather with the effect those languages have had on the minority's variety of the dominant language. We find two main kinds of sociolinguistic situations behind ethnic variation, both resulting from migrations and usually the fruit of colonization or globalization:

- When an indigenous group is outnumbered (or at least outgunned) by a colonizing majority, they will in due course usually start to adopt the majority's language. Their variety of that language will bear traces of the differences between it and their own language. Here the indigenous language is called the 'substrate' (as in pidgin/creole studies, see Chapter 4). This is the situation for the First Nations of Canada and Māori of New Zealand.
- When immigrants arrive in a new nation with a different language, their descendants will quickly shift to adopt the majority language. Their own language is termed the 'adstrate' which affects the way they speak the majority language. This is the situation of Korean immigrants living in Australia or Moroccans in the Netherlands.

In both these situations, the ad/substrate may produce a variety of the majority language that is hearably different from the mainstream version. A few of the differentiating features may be unique to the minority's variety, but most differ in frequency only. Researchers may call such a variety an 'ethnolect' (see Exercise 7.5) and give it a name such as 'African American Vernacular English'. A third situation involves a variety that is so radically different from the standard, and has such a distinctive history, that it is different in kind: a creole language and its former colonizing lexifier language may blend in a 'post-creole continuum' (Chapter 4.3), as with Caribbean Englishes.

Exercise 7.5   Ethnolect or repertoire?

Sarah Bunin Benor (2010) questions the label 'ethnolect' because it does not take account of five kinds of fluidity found in ethnic variation:

1 Intragroup variation – between different speakers in an ethnic group.
2 Intraspeaker variation – individual speakers shift between the ethnic variety and the majority standard depending on the situation.
3 Outgroup use: non-members who associate closely with the group may use the variety.
4 Ethnic groups do not have sharp boundaries that define clearly who is in and who is out.
5 Ethnolects similarly have fuzzy linguistic boundaries, most differences are by degree not absolute.

• Benor proposes the term 'ethnolinguistic repertoire' as more fluid and appropriate than ethnolect. Do you agree? Why?

She also questions the way we identify what is distinctive about an ethnic group's language. Distinctive from what? From 'the standard' – 'mainstream' – 'white' (in the US)? She suggests the term 'unmarked variety', while questioning the implication that minority groups and their varieties are 'marked'.

• List the ethnic varieties or repertoires that people tend to recognize in your own society. Do these get named? What groups are they associated with? What are their histories? What are people's attitudes towards the groups and their varieties? – deficit? difference? dominance? discourse?
• Answer the same questions for the majority variety/ies.
• What measure would you use of the distinctiveness of ethnic varieties or repertoires in your society? What term would you give to that measure? – standard, mainstream, marked, or something else? Why?
• What do your answers to the above questions indicate about relations between language and ethnicity in your society? And in sociolinguistic theory?

7.4 ETHNIC VARIETIES OF ENGLISH

African American Vernacular English

It was the background of problematic race relations and disadvantage among urban African Americans that triggered the first sociolinguistic projects after Labov's New York City study. Labov himself led a project from the mid 1960s which researched three New York adolescent gangs. This was an innovative ethnographic study, where two white linguists collaborated with two local black field workers (recall Roth-Gordon's research practice in Rio de Janiero in Chapter 6). The outcomes were significant, published in Labov (1972a):

Example 7.4

The grammar of AAVE

African American Vernacular English shares by far the majority of its grammar with standard English, but the non-standard forms are salient to outsiders even though most are easily enough understood. While a few of these forms are specific only to AAVE, most (like *ain't*) are shared with other vernacular Englishes:

it's a lot of girls	Existential *it is* (instead of *there is*)
the dog live in the swamp	Absence of verbal *-s* marking
people ∅ crazy, people are stone crazy	Zero copula (absence of verb *to be*)
it mostly be in the evening	Invariant habitual *be* (for repeated actions)
they done tore the school up	Perfective *done*
she might could do the work	Multiple modals
they didn't never do nothing to nobody	Negative concord/multiple negation
he came over to that girl house	Absence of possessive *-s* marking
he the man [who] got all the old records	Absence of subject relative pronoun

- description of black youth rhetorical styles, especially in the use of ritual insults – 'your mother so old she got spider webs under her arms'
- study of the structure of conversational stories, seeding what became the foundational framework for narrative analysis in sociolinguistics
- and most sociopolitically significant, the conclusion that inner-city ethnic vernaculars were not illogical, substandard linguistic codes, but had their own systematicity – 'the logic of non-standard English', as Labov's title went in a seminal paper (in 1972a).

Hundreds of studies and thousands of publications later, we now know more about African American Vernacular English (AAVE) than any other variety on the planet – an irony considering its continuing stigmatized status. Its features have been comprehensively analysed and quantified, including on a wide range of sociodemographic dimensions – regional differences throughout the US, isolated relict communities, individual case studies of young and old, contrasts between women and men, between middle and working class, and the developmental paths of African American children. Since the 1970s successive generations of African American sociolinguists have taken the lead in much of this research, and the labelling has shifted with the times from NNE 'Non-standard Negro English', through BEV 'Black English Vernacular', to AAVE since circa 1990.

In the 1980s and 90s the repercussions of sociolinguistic findings on AAVE came into the public arena through three major controversies:

- Sociolinguists testified as expert witnesses in the 1979 'Ann Arbor case' in Michigan, supporting the right of African American students to be taught language through their own vernacular. The case was won (Labov 1982).

- The black/white English divergence hypothesis: in 1986 Labov published a study with Wendell Harris which claimed inner-city Black and White vernaculars were diverging, and that this reflected and strengthened social division. Their interpretation was widely publicized and debated, supported by some researchers and challenged by others (Fasold et al. 1987).
- In 1996, the Oakland School Board (California) authorized AAVE as a language-teaching medium in their schools, sparking a controversy about 'Ebonics' (AAVE). Many sociolinguists were called on to take public positions and explain the character and structure of AAVE, and the Linguistic Society of America immediately passed a resolution in support (Rickford 1999; Lippi-Green 2012).

The question of the origins of AAVE has triggered a vast amount of research in its own right, with positions often polarized – linguistically and politically – between a creole-origins hypothesis (see Chapter 4) and an 'anglicist' theory that AAVE developed from the input British dialects and parallel to white varieties (see e.g. Rickford 1998; Poplack 2000).

Ethnic variation in Englishes worldwide

The quantitative variationist techniques pioneered by Labov, especially the sociolinguistic variable, are ideal for identifying the relative differences which are the main markers of ethnic varieties of languages. Such research has spread around the world over the past 40 years, most of it on English and much of that on ethnic variation. Some examples:

Lumbee Indian English, North Carolina: The Lumbee are an unusual group of Native Americans. They have spoken English for well over 200 years but no one knows why they acquired the language so early and from whom. Nor does their current variety retain any hints of what the group's ancestral language/s may have been. Because of this unclear ethnolinguistic history, they have in fact had some trouble convincing authorities that they are an ethnic group at all. Walt Wolfram and colleagues' studies of Lumbee English (e.g. Dannenberg and Wolfram 1998) show that the group have forms and functions of the verb *to be* that are relics of earlier British-dialect forms. These have receded in other local varieties but been retained by the Lumbee, with the result that they serve as ethnolinguistic markers in their speech.

Māori English, New Zealand: Until circa 1990, New Zealand linguists had not managed to establish that a Māori English existed let alone described its features, despite most New Zealanders believing they could hear it. This was probably because we were looking for absolute differences from general NZ English. But when we started to search for relative differences, we found that Māori and Pakeha used the same features but at different frequencies. Taken together, a cluster of intonations, morphological and syntactic forms, and especially phonological differences, made for a hearably different variety of English (e.g. Bell 2000; Holmes 2005). For example: general NZ English has a very centralized, schwa pronunciation for the short /ɪ/ vowel, known as the KIT vowel. (Sociolinguists tend to refer to vowels using a set of key words invented by Wells 1982, in which the word represents the vowel – this helps avoid confusion in identifying vowels across different dialects.) But some Māori use a close front [ɪ ~ i] variant of KIT that sounds more like British Received Pronunciation or Australian than mainstream NZ English. In our study in Porirua near Wellington, there were five Māori people who used this pronunciation (Bell 1997b). These were also the sample's only fluent speakers of Māori, which has a close, front pronunciation of short /ɪ/. The five speakers' Māori language influenced their English pronunciation, a substrate effect that created a distinctive ethnic feature.

Italian Australian English: Not all heritage languages produce persistent traces in an immigrant group's dialect. In Barbara Horvath's research on the vowels of English in Sydney, Australia (1985), she found that most of the Greek and Italian adults – the first-generation immigrants – had a 'broad ethnic' accent influenced by their first language, with quite different vowels from the core of the Sydney community. But the next generation, the teenagers, used even more native vowels than the natives. Why? They appear to have been distancing themselves from their parents' ethnically marked L2 English: they did not want a stigmatized accent like their parents. Labov had found the same thing for Jewish and Italian descendants in New York. Psychologically this 'anti-adstrate' shift fits with the tendency we noted in Chapter 3 for second-generation immigrant children to reject their heritage first language.

7.5   GENDER IN LANGUAGE

Gender is a major influence on language choice. In the languages of western societies, differences between women's and men's speech are mostly matters of degree, but there are communities where wives and husbands do not even speak the same language to each other (see example in Chapter 5.1 from Misión La Paz, Argentina). This is an extreme case, but many languages have alternative forms or features used only by women or by men. The lexicon holds the most obvious differences, with taboo words forbidden or at least disfavoured for women. In some societies, the names of male in-laws are taboo to women – and so are any words that sound like those names. But there do not appear to be any societies with parallel restrictions on men. The grammar of some languages may encode male/female speaker differences. In Yanyuwa, from the Northern Territory of Australia, women and men speak different dialects: they use the same vocabulary but apply different sets of grammatical affixes to the base words. Yanyuwa boys face a challenge growing up: they are raised by the women so they learn the female dialect, and therefore have to shift to the men's dialect at puberty. One man narrated (John Bradley 2011: 15):

> When I spoke like a woman my father said to me, 'Where are your breasts and woman's parts?' I was really shamed. I was very careful for a while after that to speak the men's words.

Gender often forms the most salient dimension of sociolinguistic variation in a community. On the basis of research findings from the New York City study onwards, Labov

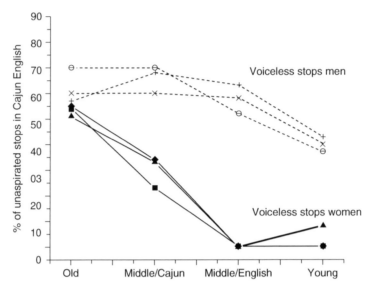

Figure 7.3   Unaspirated stops (p, t, k) in Cajun English, by age and gender
'Middle/Cajun' = middle-aged, brought up speaking French, versus 'Middle/English'
Source: Dubois and Horvath (1999), figure 2

has proposed the 'general linguistic conformity of women' as one of several principles of sociolinguistic structure (2001a: 266):

> For stable sociolinguistic variables, women show a lower rate of stigmatized variants and a higher rate of prestige variants than men.

He surveys studies not only from many varieties of English, but from Canadian French and Spanish in Latin America and Europe. For example, nine out of ten variables researched in Detroit English show that women used more standard forms than men (Wolfram 1969). This pattern holds for the most stable English variable of all, ING – see the case study in the next section.

Gender is usually a major factor in the usage of sociolinguistic variables that are unstable – that is, changing. Cajun English is the ethnic variety used by originally French-speaking communities in rural Louisiana (Dubois and Horvath 1999). Its pronunciation is influenced by the French-language lack of aspiration on the stops /p, t, k/. Cajun English tends not to aspirate these stops, pronouncing them [p t k] rather than the standard English [pʰ tʰ kʰ]. Figure 7.3 shows three age groups of Cajun English speakers, and in every case men use more Cajun-style unaspirated stops than women. The gender difference is quite small for the older generation, about 15 per cent, but widens markedly for the middle-aged and young.

The researchers explain the shift for the middle-aged women as a reflection of girls spending longer at English-language school than boys. The maintenance of non-aspiration by the youngest men comes from their greater involvement in the late-twentieth-century renaissance of Cajun culture. Note how the social dimensions intertwine here: region with ethnicity, ethnicity with gender, and gender with age. The age differences reflect change in progress, the subject of the next chapter. And there is also a class reflex, since Cajuns and their language have been marginalized. Many studies show women and men from the same class differing radically in their use of the same sociolinguistic variable.

In early research the most common explanation for women's use of more standard forms was that they are more inclined than men to seek prestige through language: women are more status-conscious and therefore use more standard forms. This was a difference or even deficit interpretation, in the terms introduced in Chapter 6.7. Eckert reviews the evidence on this and agrees that women are using language as a symbolic means to assert themselves, but she suggests a dominance interpretation: women are more status-*bound* than men – 'deprived of power, women must satisfy themselves with status' (1989: 256). Cheshire (2002) challenges the principle of women's conformity itself, on two main grounds:

- The findings are a reflection of the methods used to reach them, especially in the construction of social class – most obviously, in the assignment of women to a class on the basis of their husband's positioning.
- The definition of what is 'standard' is notoriously slippery and variable (see Chapter 10.5).

The gender patterning of language has repercussions for men as well as women, for masculinity as well as femininity, as the case study of ING to which we now turn will show. Chapter 11.4 returns to the issue of gender and how it can be performed linguistically.

7.6   THE CASE OF ING

The alternation between *ing* and *in* in the suffix of 'walking', which we touched on in the New York City study (Figure 7.1), is one of the most widely salient sociolinguistic variables of English. 'Dropping the g' marks social or formality levels in all Englishes – although there is no phonetic 'g' involved. It is a choice between a (standard) velar pronunciation [ŋ] for the nasal versus a (non-standard) alveolar/apical [n]. As a variable ING is also very stable – there is no evidence anywhere of significant change in its frequency or usage (Labov 2001a: 86). For these reasons, it is also the most researched variable in English. Here I bring together several different approaches to ING from research around the world in the past 60 years (the dates used are for publication of studies which were often conducted several years earlier).

New England, USA, 1958

The first quantitative research on ING was undertaken in 1954. While making recordings for an educational research project in a New England village, Fischer (1958) noticed and calculated variation in children's *in ~ ing* usage. His conclusion was that their alternations correlated with sex, class, personality, mood, formality, and the specific verb used. Fischer also quantified the individual behaviour of one pair of students, a well-behaved 'model' boy and a mischievous 'typical' boy:

	ing	in	Total	Per cent use of in
'Model' boy	38	1	39	3
'Typical' boy	10	12	22	55

Despite the slightly bizarre labellings, to whose social meanings we return later, there is a clear difference between one boy's near-total *ing* pronunciations and the other's mix of both forms. Fischer also found that the 'model' boy showed clear ability to shift his style to suit different situations:

	ing	in	Total	Per cent use of in
Story-telling test	38	1	39	3
Formal interview	33	35	68	51
Informal interview	24	41	65	63

The study thus touched on both the dimensions that Labov would soon research in New York – differences between socially different speakers, and stylistic differences within the speech of the same speaker. Fischer's study is cited frequently for its pioneering status, particularly by Labov, despite being very slight, but he did also outline a prophetic wider programme for researching variation and change.

New York City, USA, 1966

Labov's New York City study (1966, 1972b) outlined earlier in 7.1 was the major founding analysis of ING. Look back at Figure 7.1 which displays his findings for class by style stratification, interpreted there in the adjacent text. In the following two decades, ING was researched in small and large studies of English varieties all round the world including Los Angeles (Wald and Shopen 1981), Yorkshire (Petyt 1985) and Australia (e.g. Horvath 1985).

Norwich, UK, 1974

A few years after the New York study, the British sociolinguist Peter Trudgill surveyed the English of Norwich (1974), deriving his methodology from Labov, with a division into five social classes and four styles. His results showed that ING was also socially stratified in this British dialect, and that *in* was typical of males as well as working-class speakers. Men tended to use more *in* and women more *ing* (Table 7.1) and this pattern held for most of the 20 linguistic variables he examined. This was also the finding of many other early quantitative studies of stable linguistic variables, leading to Labov's principle of 'the linguistic conformity of women' mentioned earlier.

Trudgill (1972) explains the association of working-class speech with toughness and masculinity as 'covert prestige' – a positive but hidden evaluation of non-standard pronunciation. This is concealed from general social display but surfaces in the claim by most Norwich men to be using more non-standard forms than they actually do, while women profess the opposite. Trudgill's explanation for women's behaviour on ING was one that has in part been overtaken by social change, and was critiqued by some feminist sociolinguists (see Exercise 7.6).

Table 7.1   Class × gender × style stratification of ING in Norwich, UK, percentage of non-standard *in* variants

Class	Gender	Casual speech	Formal speech	Reading passage	Word list
LWC	M	100	100	100	66
	F	100	97	54	17
MWC	M	97	91	43	24
	F	88	81	46	20
UWC	M	95	81	18	0
	F	77	68	13	11
LMC	M	17	27	20	0
	F	67	3	0	0
MMC	M	31	4	0	0
	F	0	0	0	0

Classes: LWC – lower working class, MWC – middle working class, UWC – upper working class, LMC – lower middle class, MMC – middle middle class
Source: Adapted from Trudgill (1974), table 7.2

The table offers an exercise in interpreting quantitative data. What are the relationships between gender, classes and styles in the table? Graphing selections from the table (on a grid like Figure 7.1) will help show the relationships – e.g. graph men or women only, or each class separately.

1   Look at the gender stratification: in how many class × style pairs do men use more *in* than women? And vice versa? How many are the same? What generalization can you make?
2   Look at the class stratification: compare the men within each style column (vertically), and then the women. Are there any deviations from clean stratification? What conclusion can you draw?
3   Do the same with the style structure by comparing horizontally along each class × gender row. Are there any deviations from clean style shift?
4   What do you conclude about the stratification of ING in Norwich? How does it compare to New York (Figure 7.1)?

Exercise 7.6 Interpreting gender variation in ING

Trudgill (1972: 182) speculated on the reasons that women in his study used more standard variants of ING and other linguistic variables than men did:

- Women in British society are generally more status-conscious than men, because:
- their social position is less secure than and usually subordinate to men's, so they use language to signal their status, and:
- men can be rated by what they do, such as their occupation, whereas women tend to be rated on how they appear, including linguistically.

Some feminist sociolinguists partly endorsed Trudgill's interpretation (e.g. Eckert 1989, quoted in the last section), but others challenged it. Deborah Cameron (1992: 63) wrote:

> Trudgill took it that women wished to identify themselves with a higher social class, and thus that their status aspirations were higher than men's... But surely it is possible that the women's assessments might just as well have reflected their awareness of sex stereotypes and their consequent desire to fulfil 'normal' expectations that women talk 'better' ... Furthermore the finding itself – that women in each class use more standard forms than men – ... may be at least partly an artefact of the methodology used to assign speakers to social classes ... the husband's occupation defined the class of the wife.

- Read Trudgill's article, Eckert's article, and the section in Cameron's book (pp. 61ff.).
- Consider Trudgill's findings, the methods behind them, and the different premises that he, Eckert and Cameron have brought to interpreting them. Make your own interpretation and present the arguments for it. The class could divide into groups adopting the three positions and debate them.

Wellington, New Zealand, 1992

In 1989, Janet Holmes, Mary Boyce and I conducted the first full-scale sociolinguistic survey of New Zealand English. We found that New Zealanders use the *in* variant less than American and British speakers, and the variation is less stratified, but its structure is similar. Men use much more *in* than women, and the working class more than middle class (Bell and Holmes 1992).

Sociolinguistic variables are influenced by linguistic as well as social factors. All variationist research now allows for this – although in this book, I will concentrate on *socio*-linguistic variation, and largely set aside the intra-linguistic dimension. ING is affected by two main linguistic factors: the phonetics of the sound that follows it, and the grammatical category of the word where ING occurs. As well as showing percentages, Table 7.2 lays out the 'Varbrul' weights associated with the different linguistic factors. Varbrul (and its derivatives, Goldvarb and Rbrul) is a statistical program standardly used by variationists. Its output indicates how much – with what 'weight' – a particular factor or category affects the probability of a linguistic variable. The neutral point is .5. Numbers above .5 favour the use of *in*, and numbers below that disfavour *in* (and

Table 7.2 Effect of linguistic factors on proportion of *in* for ING in Wellington, New Zealand

Linguistic factor	Percentage	Varbrul weight	N
Following phonetic segment:			
Velar	21	.381	159
Alveolar	40	.600	668
Word category:			
noun/gerund	13	.253	217
adjective/modifier	29	.480	245
verb/participle	40	.576	1525
gonna	85	.932	138

therefore favour *ing*). Broadly speaking, the weights and the percentages tend to tell a similar story, especially when only two factors are involved.

The most common kind of linguistic conditioning is for a phonological variable to be affected by the sounds before and after it, for example whether the place of articulation is shared or not. This holds for ING. Table 7.2 shows that when there is a following alveolar consonant, the alveolar variant of ING [n] – as in *walkin' down* – is more frequent (40%). When there is a following velar as in *walking girl*, *in* is less frequent (21%). In probability terms, following alveolar favours the 'homorganic' alveolar [n] pronunciation (.600, that is, above the .5 neutral point). By contrast, a following velar disfavours [n] at .381 – and therefore favours the alternative velar pronunciation [ŋ] which shares the same place of articulation with the following sound.

More intriguing is the grammatical conditioning shown in Table 7.2. Verbs and participles such as *crossing roads* favour *in* (.576), while nouns and gerunds – *pedestrian crossing* – disfavour it (.253). In between are the adjectives and modifiers – *the crossing place* – at .480. It turns out that the only explanation for these preferences is an historical one (Labov 2001a: 88). In Old English, the verbal noun ending was *-inge*, and the participle ending *-inde*. Although the two have long since merged into the modern 'ing' spelling, a residue of the grammatical difference remains and still influences contemporary speakers' choice of *in/ing* pronunciations. Finally in Table 7.2, we see *gonna*, the 'periphrastic future' *going to*, treated as a separate factor. Sociolinguists spell it this way to recognize that it behaves as a unit, differently from the lexical 'I am *going to* (the city). *Gonna* has an overwhelming frequency of the [n] variant in its pronunciation (here 85%, .932). Frequently occurring function words such as *gonna* and *just* are treated separately in variable analysis because they tend to behave differently.

Masculinity and ING in America, 1998

Most of the studies of ING through to circa 1990 were community-wide projects modelled on New York City and its methods. And most of those – except in fact in New York – have shown that men use the alveolar variant *in* more than do women. As variation work has matured, researchers have begun to go deeper into the operation and social significances of variables such as ING in particular groups. One such study is Scott Kiesling's research (1998) on the role of *in* in marking masculinity in a US college fraternity group. Kiesling's study is typical of more recent variationist work in targeting a specific cohesive social group rather than a whole community, in recording natural discourse as it occurs within the group, and in complementing quantification with qualitative analysis of how a variable functions online in stretches of talk.

The apparently simple demographic category of biological **sex** has also shifted to **gender** as a social construct that speakers 'do' rather than 'are' (see Chapter 11.4). And where social prestige was a key concept in Labov and Trudgill, in Kiesling's study, 'power' is central: in fraternity meetings, ING use related to power. Three fraternity members almost always used *in* during meetings, while the rest shifted to a much lower level of *in* than when they were just socializing casually. Kiesling concludes that these three are indexing an image of hard work, physicality and working-class 'vernacular' power – working-class men need to demonstrate physical power because of their lack of economic power. This focuses particularly in the expletive *fuckin'*, rhetorically powerful because of its taboo value, and almost always pronounced with *in* not *ing*. In this excerpt *fuckin'* and other *in* pronunciations cluster in a meeting speech from 'Mick' (Kiesling 1998: 90):

> I swear to God **fuckin**' every semester all we have do is sit around and argue about money money money money.
> And I'm not **gonna** pay this **fuckin**' money. All right?
> Yeah: you guys **sittin**' back
> I know you guys are **thinkin**' I'm **gonna** pay this **fuckin**' money just 'cause I *have* money.
> I'll tell you what, I ain't **gonna** pay a **fuckin**' thing. All right?

Note that as well as the tokens Kiesling marks (bolded), there are several occurrences of *gonna*. In a style contrasting to Mick's, 'Mack', a very senior fraternity member, speaks from a position of recognized structural authority within the group, lays down the law about how things shall be done – and uses very little *in*. Linguistic variables such as ING, then, are not simple reflections of social categories but are resources that speakers can use strategically to their own ends in particular interactions. In Chapter 10.3, we will touch on ING again as an example not of production but of listener perceptions and attitudes towards a variable.

7.7   RESEARCH ACTIVITY
DOING A PROJECT (2) – DATA COLLECTION

In Chapter 3.6, I outlined the first phase of undertaking a research project, in three steps. We now move on to the second phase, actually collecting the data, in two related steps (4–5 below):

1   Aims, rationale
2   Literature review
3   Design and method

4   Getting the data: how to interview
5   Processing the data

If you are working on stretches of language that are already recorded in some way (e.g. written down, extracted from a blog, recorded in a sound file), data collection may be relatively straightforward. But it is more demanding if you are recording language yourself with a microphone, or using a questionnaire or interview. Even if an interview does not use a full-scale formal questionnaire, an 'interview schedule' will be necessary to guide you through what you need to cover with your informant. Focus groups require most of the same skills as interviews. And regardless of whether you record yourself or use existing recordings, your data will need ordering (cataloguing, timing, logging, etc.).

Any research with 'human subjects' will normally need to be conducted under an approval from the university's ethics board. For coursework, this may be a generalized approval for members of a class to conduct small projects under a teacher's supervision. For a more major, stand-alone project such as a thesis, specific ethical approval will be needed. The application form is likely to be a major document and require detailed individual guidance from a supervisor. The Ethics Statement of the Linguistics Society of America at http://www.linguisticsociety.org/ethics is a good place to start for further information. See also Exercise 3.11 earlier.

Step 4: getting the data: how to interview

Questionnaire
For questionnaire design, see for example Wray and Bloomer 2012, chapter 14. Lay the questionnaire out as clearly as you can, giving yourself plenty of space to write on hard copy or annotate the file, both during interview and afterwards while coding and analysing. Make more hard copies than you need.

Who to interview
Unless you are aiming for a random sample (which most student projects would not do), it is usually best to contact potential informants through people you know.

Piloting
Any questionnaire or interview schedule should be pilot-tested. This means you do at least two trial interviews if possible before using a questionnaire in earnest, perhaps with appropriate friends or family. Piloting serves two purposes – it shows you what questions you need to revise, and it gets you accustomed to doing interviews. It can take only a few minutes of pilot interviewing to make it clear some questions are unclear or mis-ordered.

Where to interview
In a quiet room, with only the interviewee. Noise from traffic or television or children can be loud enough to make recorded answers inaudible. This matters particularly if you are studying the features of people's speech not just asking them for information.

Unless you are actually researching group interaction or opinions as such, having other people around can be distracting, and may affect the answers your informant gives. Note Goodwin's advice (1993: 188): 'Many people seem to think that somewhere a set of magic filters exist that will turn bad field sound into crystal clear audio. Some people also believe in Santa Claus.' Goodwin's is a wonderful article on the practicalities of recording: although its equipment specifics have been entirely superseded by digital technology, the advice on how to do it is timeless.

How to interview
Even if you are using a formal questionnaire, administer it during an interview with an informant rather than just giving them the questionnaire to fill in. And record the interview. Write down the answers yourself rather than giving the informants the questionnaire. Note down anything you observe that seems important.

Before interviewing
Check you have everything you need – recorder, microphone, connections, laptop, questionnaires, information sheets, consent forms, pens, paper.

Ready to record
If you are recording interviews, know your equipment well before going out. Practise setting it up, how to use it, and getting good recording levels. Accustom yourself to it through the pilot interviews.

Recording
In the interview, put the recorder where you can work it and check it easily. Test the equipment before the start of every interview both to make sure it works and to get the best recording levels. Record a minute or so and listen to it play back. Don't be shy about making sure the equipment is doing its job – you are not doing the subject any favours if the interview fails to record.

Outlining the project
Most interviewees will want to know what you are doing and why, and they have a right to know. You should have an information sheet about the project (usually required by a university ethics approval), but also explain it verbally at the start.

Consent
Ethics requirements will usually require you to have signed consent from your participants. Explain the consent requirement and the form, and ensure each informant signs a form at the time of their interview (don't leave this to do for later).

Confidentiality
The information people give you will be confidential to you and them. Reassure your informants about this if necessary. When you write up your project, don't use your informants' real names. Use initials only, or give them pseudonyms, or use some other means of hiding their identity.

Sensitivity

Some informants may be touchy about some of your questions (about age, for example). Ask questions sensitively. Don't contradict your informant if they make a statement or give an opinion you disagree with.

More detail on doing field work can be found in Labov's guide from his own experience (1984), Tagliamonte (2012), and especially Wray and Bloomer (2012), which contains chapters devoted to these tasks, full of practical tips.

Step 5: processing the data

Immediately after an interview:

- Label the questionnaire, forms, recording, file, etc. with the person's name or identity.
- Note down any observations about how the interview went – anything unusual, anything particularly significant, any problems. Was someone else there for part of the interview? Any questions you missed asking?
- Also note your first impressions of the content of the interview – these are often valuable pointers to the findings that will eventually emerge.
- If you have written out answers or information on a questionnaire, go back through and make sure the meaning is clear. Add any points that you remember but didn't write down during the interview.
- As soon as you then can, make copies of everything (files, hard copy, etc.) and store them separately in a safe place.

Non-interview data has the same requirement for orderly cataloguing and archiving, the more so since you can collect a lot of data very easily, for example from the internet, but then have trouble getting it under control. The first rule is not to collect too much – know what you are aiming to do, and get only the minimum you need. The second rule is to be ruthlessly systematic in handling it.

Recorded data will often need transcription before analysis is possible, but don't assume you need to transcribe everything (I did not transcribe my own PhD recordings). Transcription can take at least 5–10 times as long as the actual recording, so it is prohibitively time-consuming if you have a lot of data. Wray and Bloomer (2012) offer extensive guidance on transcription. The transcription manual of Victoria University of Wellington's Language in the Workplace project (headed by Janet Holmes) is available on their website at http://www.victoria.ac.nz/lals/lwp/docs/ops/op5.htm.

7.8 SUMMARY

- Labov's pioneering project on the social stratification of English in New York City is the foundation study of variationist sociolinguistics. His interviews with 122 speakers on the Lower East Side elicited five styles reflecting increasing levels of attention to speech.

- The sociolinguistic variables he analysed included the stable alternation of the ING variable, between *ing* and *in* as in 'walking'. The speech of different social classes was cleanly stratified, and all style-shifted in the same direction from casual to most formal speech. For some variables such as (r) the lower middle class crossed over the upper in their pursuit of prestige.
- Labov's variationist approach became dominant in North America, and has been used with a wide variety of languages around the world. This chapter has covered variation according to class, ethnicity and gender.
- Class was operationalized in Labov's work through indexes of occupation, education, income, etc. Most major sociolinguistic surveys followed this kind of structural-functionalist model, which implies a consensus of all classes agreeing on their evaluation of sociolinguistic differences.
- Opposing vernacular norms also pull speakers towards non-standard forms. This is better explained in the alternative, conflict theory of class associated with Marx. Linguistic and social stratification involve inequality and disadvantage. The conflict approach fitted the structures and conditions in Rickford's study of a sugar-cane village in Guyana.
- Ethnicity involves a group's shared sociocultural characteristics. In ethnolinguistic variation a minority group speaks a distinctive variety of the dominant language because of influence from features of their heritage language. Such differences are usually matters of degree rather than absolutes.
- African American Vernacular English has been the most researched of all language varieties since studies of inner-city youth in the 1960s. Continuing research has detailed the linguistic features and social significance of AAVE, disputed its origins, and contributed to public debate on its relation to educational disadvantage. Ethnic varieties of English have been researched in many countries, including Australia, the United States and New Zealand.
- Gender is a major influence on language choice. Although there are communities where women and men use different varieties or forms, usually gender differences are a matter of degree.
- Labov proposed the generalization that women use more prestige variants of stable sociolinguistic variables. One explanation is that women are more status-conscious than men, but others argue that they are more bound to status because of their lack of power. Gender interacts with other social dimensions like ethnicity, class and age, as in the Cajun English of Louisiana.
- ING has been the most researched linguistic variable around the world over the past 60 years. Its variation patterns by class, style, and especially gender. The non-standard variant *in* reflects and indexes masculinity, physicality and vernacular culture.

7.9   Further Reading

Easiest access to Labov's New York City study is through his 1972(b) collection *Sociolinguistic Patterns*. His thesis, published in 1966 by the Center for Applied Linguistics, was re-issued in 2006 by Cambridge. Labov wrote a new final chapter and 'a series of interventions, in each chapter, where Labov 2006 breaks in with the viewpoint of forty years after … I hope that my junior colleague of 1966 will forgive me for looking over his shoulder with the hindsights gained over the past four decades' (p. xii).

Variationist sociolinguistics has its own handbook – originally Chambers, Trudgill and Schilling-Estes (2002), now in a second edition (Chambers and Schilling 2013). *Language Variation and Change* is the field's journal, while the *Journal of Sociolinguistics* also regularly carries socially oriented variationist work. Kiesling (2011) is a clear and critical introduction. Tagliamonte (2006) is a short manual, and Tagliamonte (2012) a long guidebook to doing variationist research. Websites with a lot of information and resources include Labov's (with a biographical piece 'How I got into linguistics') and John Rickford's.

For lucid coverage of sociological approaches to class, see the latest edition of Giddens's text (2009) – also useful on ethnicity. Guy's long article in the *Cambridge Handbook of Sociolinguistics* (2011) provides a good overview of class in both sociology and sociolinguistics. The Milroys (1992) have offered critiques of and alternatives to the use of functionalist class classifications in sociolinguistics. Lesley Milroy's essay on class and ethnicity (2001) comes in the useful collection on sociolinguistics and social theory edited by Coupland, Sarangi and Candlin (2001). Much of Labov (1966, 1972b) deals with class patterns, as do several chapters in Labov (2001a).

On ethnicity see several of Fishman's books (e.g. Fishman et al. 1985), Harris and Rampton's reader (2003) for a more deconstructive take, and Lesley Milroy (2001) on race and class in the US and UK.

Labov (1972a) is the seminal sociolinguistic work on African American Vernacular English, and the variety continues to figure in his later work (e.g. 2010). Among the vast literature on AAVE, see works by Wolfram, Fasold, Rickford, Winford, Poplack, Schneider and Green. Mufwene et al. (1998) has strong essays by several leading scholars covering some of the field's major issues. Rickford and Rickford's *Spoken Soul* (2000) tells the story of the linguistics and rhetoric of AAVE with humanity and passion. Green (2002) is a student text on all aspects of the dialect.

Research on ethnic or national Englishes appears regularly in the leading journals, including *English World-Wide*. Wolfram and Schilling-Estes (2006) has a useful inventory of 'socially diagnostic features'. For research on recent multiethnic European varieties of other languages, see for example Wiese (2009) on 'Kiezdeutsch' in Germany, Jaspers (2011) on youth appropriation of Antwerp Dutch, and a collection on *Multilingual Urban Scandinavia* edited by Quist and Svendsen (2010).

On gender, Schilling's (2011) essay is an admirable roundup of basics and issues, and Eckert and McConnell-Ginet (2003) is a clear introductory text by two of the field's leaders. Ehrlich's four-volume collection (2008) is an excellent resource of classic and recent articles, as are the handbooks by Holmes and Meyerhoff (2003), and Coates and Pichler (2011). Some general introductory readers have major sections on gender language – Coupland and Jaworski (2009b), Meyerhoff and Schleef (2010). The field has its own journal, *Gender and Language*, published by the International Gender and Language Association, which also runs two-yearly conferences. Leading authors include Bucholtz, Cameron, Coates, Eckert, Ehrlich, Holmes, Lakoff, McConnell-Ginet, Meyerhoff and Tannen.

Wald and Shopen (1981) provide a useful elementary 'researcher's guide' to ING. Labov (2001a, 2006) rounds up findings on ING from other studies as well as New York.

REFERENCES

Bell, Allan, 1997. 'The phonetics of fish and chips in New Zealand: marking national and ethnic identities'. *English World-Wide* 18: 243–70.

Bell, Allan, 2000. 'Māori and Pakeha English: a case study'. In Allan Bell and Koenraad Kuiper (eds), *New Zealand English*. Wellington, New Zealand: Victoria University Press; and Amsterdam: John Benjamins. 221–48.

Bell, Allan and Janet Holmes, 1992. '"H-droppin": Two sociolinguistic variables in New Zealand English'. *Australian Journal of Linguistics* 12: 223–49.

Benor, Sarah Bunin, 2010. 'Ethnolinguistic repertoire: shifting the analytic focus in language and ethnicity'. *Journal of Sociolinguistics* 14: 159–83.

Bradley, John, 2011. 'Yanyuwa: "Men speak one way, women speak another"'. In Jennifer Coates and Pia Pichler (eds), *Language and Gender: A Reader* (2nd edn). Malden, MA: Wiley-Blackwell. 13–19.

Cameron, Deborah, 1992. *Feminism and Linguistic Theory* (2nd edn). Basingstoke, UK: Macmillan.

Chambers, J.K. and Natalie Schilling (eds), 2013. *The Handbook of Language Variation and Change* (2nd edn). Oxford, UK: Wiley-Blackwell.

Chambers, J.K., Peter Trudgill and Natalie Schilling-Estes (eds), 2002. *The Handbook of Language Variation and Change*. Malden, MA: Blackwell Publishing.

Cheshire, Jenny, 2002. 'Sex and gender in variationist research'. In J.K. Chambers, Peter Trudgill and Natalie Schilling-Estes (eds), *The Handbook of Language Variation and Change*. Malden, MA: Blackwell Publishing. 423–43.

Coates, Jennifer and Pia Pichler (eds), 2011. *Language and Gender: A Reader* (2nd edn). Malden, MA: Wiley-Blackwell.

Coupland, Nikolas and Adam Jaworski (eds), 2009b. *The New Sociolinguistics Reader* (2nd edn). Basingstoke, UK: Palgrave Macmillan.

Coupland, Nikolas, Srikant Sarangi and Christopher N. Candlin (eds), 2001. *Sociolinguistics and Social Theory*. Harlow, UK: Longman.

Dannenberg, Clare and Walt Wolfram, 1998. 'Ethnic identity and grammatical restructuring: *be(s)* in Lumbee English'. *American Speech* 73: 139–59.

Dubois, Sylvie and Barbara Horvath, 1999. 'When the music changes, you change too: gender and language change in Cajun English'. *Language Variation and Change* 11: 287–313.

Eckert, Penelope, 1989. 'The whole woman: sex and gender differences in variation'. *Language Variation and Change* 1: 245–67.

Eckert, Penelope and Sally McConnell-Ginet, 2003. *Language and Gender*. New York: Cambridge University Press.

Ehrlich, Susan (ed.), 2008. *Language and Gender* (4 vols). London: Routledge.

Fasold, Ralph W., William Labov, Fay Boyd Vaughn-Cooke, Guy Bailey, Walt Wolfram, Arthur K. Spears and John Rickford, 1987. 'Are Black and White vernaculars diverging? Papers from the NWAVE XIV Panel Discussion'. *American Speech* 62: 3–80.

Fischer, John L., 1958. 'Social influences on the choice of a linguistic variant'. *Word* 14: 47–56.

Fishman, Joshua A., 1985. 'Language, ethnicity and racism'. In Joshua A. Fishman, Michael H. Gertner, Esther G. Lowy and William G. Milán, *The Rise and Fall of the Ethnic Revival: Perspectives on Language and Ethnicity*. Berlin: Mouton Publishers. 3–13.

Fishman, Joshua A., Michael H. Gertner, Esther G. Lowy and William G. Milán, 1985. *The Rise and Fall of the Ethnic Revival: Perspectives on Language and Ethnicity*. Berlin: Mouton Publishers.

Giddens, Anthony, 2009. *Sociology* (6th edn). Cambridge, UK: Polity Press.

Goodwin, Charles. 1993. 'Recording human interaction in natural settings'. *Pragmatics* 3: 181–209.

Green, Lisa J., 2002. *African American English: A Linguistic Introduction*. Cambridge: Cambridge University Press.

Guy, Gregory R., 2011. 'Language, social class, and status'. In Rajend Mesthrie (ed.), *The Cambridge Handbook of Sociolinguistics*. Cambridge: Cambridge University Press. 159–85.

Harris, Roxy and Ben Rampton (eds), 2003. *The Language, Ethnicity and Race Reader*. London: Routledge.

Holmes, Janet, 2005. 'Using Māori English in New Zealand'. *International Journal of the Sociology of Language* 172: 91–115.

Holmes, Janet and Miriam Meyerhoff (eds), 2003. *The Handbook of Language and Gender*. Malden, Massachusetts: Blackwell Publishing.

Horvath, Barbara M., 1985. *Variation in Australian English: The Sociolects of Sydney*. Cambridge: Cambridge University Press.

Jaspers, Jürgen, 2011. 'Strange bedfellows: appropriations of a tainted urban dialect'. *Journal of Sociolinguistics* 15: 493–524.

Kiesling, Scott F., 1998. 'Men's identities and sociolinguistic variation: the case of fraternity men'. *Journal of Sociolinguistics* 2: 69–99.

Kiesling, Scott F., 2011. *Linguistic Variation and Change*. Edinburgh: Edinburgh University Press.

Labov, William, 1966. *The Social Stratification of English in New York City*. Washington, DC: Center for Applied Linguistics.

Labov, William, 1972a. *Language in the Inner City: Studies in the Black English Vernacular*. Philadelphia, PA: University of Pennsylvania Press.

Labov, William, 1972b. *Sociolinguistic Patterns*. Philadelphia, PA: University of Pennsylvania Press.

Labov, William, 1982. 'Objectivity and commitment in linguistic science: the case of the Black English trial in Ann Arbor'. *Language in Society* 11: 165–201.

Labov, William, 1984. 'Field methods of the Project on Linguistic Change and Variation'. In John Baugh and Joel Sherzer (eds), *Language in Use: Readings in Sociolinguistics*. Englewood Cliffs, NJ: Prentice-Hall. 28–53.

Labov, William, 1994. *Principles of Linguistic Change*, vol. 1: *Internal Factors*. Cambridge, MA: Blackwell Publishers.

Labov, William, 2001. *Principles of Linguistic Change*, vol. 2: *Social Factors*. Malden, MA: Blackwell Publishers.

Labov, William, 2006. *The Social Stratification of English in New York City* (2nd edn). Cambridge: Cambridge University Press.

Labov, William, 2010. *Principles of Linguistic Change*, vol. 3: *Cognitive and Cultural Factors*. Malden, MA: Wiley-Blackwell.

Labov, William and Wendell A. Harris, 1986. 'De facto segregation of black and white vernaculars'. In David Sankoff (ed.), *Diversity and Diachrony*. Amsterdam: John Benjamins. 1–24.

Lippi-Green, Rosina, 2012. *English with an Accent: Language, Ideology and Discrimination in the United States* (2nd edn). London: Routledge.

Mather, Patrick-André, 2012. 'The social stratification of /r/ in New York City: Labov's department store study revisited'. *Journal of English Linguistics* 40: 338–56.

Meyerhoff, Miriam and Erik Schleef (eds), 2010. *The Routledge Sociolinguistics Reader*. London: Routledge.

Milroy, Lesley, 2001. 'The social categories of race and class: language ideology and sociolinguistics'. In Nikolas Coupland, Srikant Sarangi and Christopher N. Candlin (eds), *Sociolinguistics and Social Theory*. Harlow, UK: Longman. 235–60.

Milroy, Lesley and James Milroy, 1992. 'Social network and social class: toward an integrated sociolinguistic model'. *Language in Society* 21: 1–26.

Mufwene, Salikoko S., John R. Rickford, Guy Bailey and John Baugh (eds), 1998. *African-American English: Structure, History, and Use*. London: Routledge.

Petyt, K.M., 1985. *Dialect and Accent in Industrial West Yorkshire*. Amsterdam: John Benjamins.

Poplack, Shana (ed.), 2000. *The English History of African American English*. Malden, MA: Blackwell Publishers.

Quist, Pia and Bente A. Svendsen (eds), 2010. *Multilingual Urban Scandinavia: New Linguistic Practices*. Bristol, UK: Multilingual Matters.

Rickford, John R., 1986. 'The need for new approaches to social class analysis in sociolinguistics'. *Language & Communication* 6: 215–21.

Rickford, John R., 1998. 'The creole origins of African-American Vernacular English: evidence from copula absence'. In Salikoko S. Mufwene, John R. Rickford, Guy Bailey and John Baugh (eds), *African-American English: Structure, History, and Use*. London: Routledge. 154–200.

Rickford, John R., 1999. 'The Ebonics controversy in my backyard: a sociolinguist's experiences and reflections'. *Journal of Sociolinguistics* 3: 267–75.

Rickford, John Russell and Russell John Rickford, 2000. *Spoken Soul: The Story of Black English*. New York: John Wiley.

Schilling, Natalie, 2011. 'Language, gender and sexuality'. In Rajend Mesthrie (ed.), *The Cambridge Handbook of Sociolinguistics*. Cambridge: Cambridge University Press. 218–37.

Tagliamonte, Sali A., 2006. *Anaylzing Sociolinguistic Variation*. Cambridge: Cambridge University Press.

Tagliamonte, Sali A., 2012. *Variationist Sociolinguistics: Change, Observation, Interpretation*. Malden, MA: Wiley-Blackwell.

Trudgill, Peter, 1972. 'Sex, covert prestige and linguistic change'. *Language in Society* 1: 179–96.

Trudgill, Peter, 1974. *The Social Differentiation of English in Norwich*. London: Cambridge University Press.

Wald, Benji and Timothy Shopen, 1981. 'A researcher's guide to the sociolinguistic variable (ING)'. In Timothy Shopen and Joseph M. Williams (eds), *Style and Variables in English*. Cambridge, MA: Winthrop. 219–49.

Wiese, Heike, 2009. 'Grammatical innovation in multiethnic urban Europe: new linguistic practices among adolescents'. *Lingua* 119: 782–806.

Wolfram, Walt A., 1969. *A Sociolinguistic Description of Detroit Negro Speech*. Washington, DC: Center for Applied Linguistics.

Wolfram, Walt and Natalie Schilling-Estes, 2006. *American English: Dialects and Variation* (2nd edn). Malden, MA: Blackwell Publishing.

Wray, Alison and Aileen Bloomer, 2012. *Projects in Linguistics and Language Studies* (3rd edn). London: Hodder Education.

Zilles, Ana M.S., 2005. 'The development of a new pronoun: the linguistic and social embedding of *a gente* in Brazilian Portuguese'. *Language Variation and Change* 17: 19–53.

8

LANGUAGE IN TIME

Our coverage of the basics of the variationist approach in Chapter 7 sets the scene for a focus in Chapters 8 and 9 on the sociolinguistics of time and space – twin parameters that are as interconnected in social and linguistic life as they are in theoretical physics. The study of linguistic change was primary in Labov's research from the 1970s, and an interest in the intersection of language and place developed soon after, particularly in Trudgill's work. The emphasis has been on change in the sound systems of language varieties, on how pronunciations shift in response to community-internal factors or as a result of external contact with other communities.

Sociolinguists have concentrated on the language correlates of two of the ways humans experience time: age and change. After introducing the sociolinguistics of age, this chapter covers the study of language change as it is generated inside speech communities, that is innovations that arise spontaneously from among the speakers themselves. Dubois and Horvath (1999) distinguish these from adoptions from outside, and the next chapter deals with how contact with other dialects and languages may introduce changes to a local vernacular. The distinction between internal and externally driven change remains, however, an idealized one, since both kinds of change are often going on at the same time in the same place.

8.1 AGE IN LANGUAGE

Together with gender, age is the most fundamental social factor structuring any study of language variation. Yet Coupland's claim that 'age is sociolinguistics' under-developed social dimension' (2001a: 185) still holds by comparison with class, ethnicity and gender, the other players in the usual quartet of social variables. Like gender

The Guidebook to Sociolinguistics, First Edition. Allan Bell.
© 2014 Allan Bell. Published 2014 by Blackwell Publishing Ltd.

and ethnicity, age cannot be crudely equated with physical/biological characteristics, although sociolinguistics has been slow to reflect this. Chambers, for example, writes: 'Our ages remain fixed … age plays an almost autocratic role in our social lives' (2009: 159). There is no denying the physical dimension, most obvious at the youngest and oldest stages of life, with initial growth from infant to adult and eventual decline from health to death. But age is not controlled by chronological time, it has social and psychological dimensions. It is structured and conceived differently by different cultures and different individuals.

Age interacts with other social characteristics – with gender in several examples in the previous chapter: the use of ING in a college fraternity, African American youth vernacular, the shift from women's to men's language by Yanyuwa boys. There can be strong and specific linguistic opportunities or limitations for particular age × gender groups in a society, for example for young females versus males (Exercise 8.1). Such sociolinguistic expectations usually police young women's usage of non-standard or taboo language.

Exercise 8.1   Youth slang in the United States

Corpus linguistics is an approach on the edge of sociolinguistics which collects and analyses very large samples or 'corpora' (often millions of words) of spoken or written language representing, for example, the state of British English in a given period. The amount of data means that social or contextual information is often limited, and analyses focus on features that can be computer-searched (Biber, Conrad and Reppen 1998).

Barbieri (2008) analysed 400,000 words of transcribed conversations from a 1990s corpus of American English, split between younger (15–25) and older (35–60) speakers. Words which were used very significantly more by younger speakers included *fuck/fucking/fucked*, *cool*, and *man* and *dude* (mainly as address terms):

Who would think it was a pizza without the crust, man?

That would be a bummer, dude.

In a parallel study, Precht (2008) found that such items are also much more frequently used by men than women, showing that younger males are the prime users of slang and taboo words.

Undertake your own study:

1 Gather a corpus of digital language on the internet from genres such as blogs or magazines, some of which target teenage male readers, and some teenage females or adult males.
2 Create a list of slang and swear words. Remember these will be partly dialect-specific: other Englishes will use some different terms from American (not *dude*, for instance).
3 Search for these words in your corpus. Sort the slang uses apart from ordinary use.
4 Compare the magazines targeted at different readerships. Interpret and explain what you find: differences by age and gender, or by type of text.

Age also interacts with ethnicity or class. Very group-specific class × age × ethnicity × gender codes are well known, as shown in Chapter 6's case study of the *gíria* 'slang' spoken by poor young black men in Rio de Janiero.

The sociolinguistic life course

The concept of the lifespan or 'life course' (e.g. Giddens 2009) recognizes that there are identifiable, socially constructed age stages. Childhood as a different stage of life is a relatively modern, western concept, and the teenager was invented in the 1950s. The greying of society has led to a distinction between the 'young old' and the 'old old' and often diverging life chances for the elderly of different social classes. Sociolinguistic behaviour and capability are played out differently across the life course:

- **Childhood**: Studies of the sociolinguistic competence of children show that they learn some linguistic variation by 3 years, and a good deal of social and stylistic competence by 10. The flip side of this is that – as Chambers' (1992) study of children moving from Canada to the UK shows – while children aged 9 can fully learn the dialect of a new region, those over 13 fail to do so. The language of the young merits attention in its own right not just as a precursor to linguistic adulthood (Eckert 1997).
- **Adolescence**: In western societies the teenage years are a time of rich sociolinguistic creativity and innovation, as the case study in section 8.7 shows. Teenagers are also often regarded as the home base of the vernacular. It seems that enduring adult patterns of speech are laid down by the late teens.
- **Adulthood**: We know more about the speech of adults than any other group, and often their language has been treated as the norm against which youth and age are measured. But conversely, adults sometimes appear in the research as the colourless default case, those who are just using language rather than learning or losing it.
- **Old age**: There have been hundreds of studies of youth language, but little focus on linguistic variation in old age. Coupland argues (2001a) that this reflects western phobia against ageing and the aged. Variationist sociolinguistics has tended to utilize older speakers as time capsules of the speech of earlier decades, implying they are out of tune with the mainstream of current culture.

Linguistic change across the lifespan

A central issue of a sociolinguistics of age is whether adults change their language during their life course. If basic sociolinguistic patterns are settled before age 20, do they remain stable? Individual changes across the lifespan would be reflected in age graded patterns in a speech sample of a community. Different age groups would behave differently, but each generation would be repeating the same pattern as the previous one. If we had recorded young people of the last generation as well as young people from the present generation, they would sound the same.

Exercise 8.2   Elderspeak in the UK

Age can make a difference not just to the way we talk but to the way we are talked to. Most obvious is the register of 'babytalk' that some adults use to infants. Sometimes parallelled with this is 'elderspeak', an (over)accommodative style used to older people. Coupland, Coupland and Giles (1991: 36) give this exchange between a trainee optometrist C (female, 22) and a 'functionally competent' eye-test patient P (female, 62):

1	C:	*right* (1.0) let's have a look and see what you can *read* (switches on)
2		OK (.) if you just look there and [er (.)] don't read down the whole chart
3	P:	[yeah]
4	C:	but tell me [one of the lowest ones yeah
5	P:	[no I tell you one of the ((3 sylls.)) yeah (.) well I can
6		see (.) something Z U Y
7	C:	mhm (.) **[that's right at the bottom is it?**
8	P:	[((3 sylls.)) that's right at the bottom yeah
9	C:	mm
10	P:	now then the one [above that
11	C:	**[how about the 1-line above?**
12	P:	yeah (.) now that's (.) R P B Z E P D N (( )) R O N
13	C:	**that's good (.) that's good (.)**

(.)	brief pause
( )	action
(1.0)	1 second pause
(( ))	inaudible
[ ]	overlapping speech

1 **Bolded** above are the sentences the researchers identify as overaccommodative. Do you agree? Then specify what the overaccommodation consist in.
2 Observe and keep notes of how other people talk to older persons you know. Do any of them overaccommodate? Does the overaccommodation seem to help communication? Or hinder it?
3 What appear to be the motivations and social meanings of using this style of speech?
4 In what way do you talk to these older people yourself? Why?
5 What are the similarities and differences between this elderspeak and babytalk? Do they fit the 'inverted U' stereotype of old age as second childhood (Coupland 2001a)?

Such differences between age groups – age grading – have been found, but not often. They tend to follow one of two patterns. In the first, younger people use more non-standard forms but then adopt the standard as they move into adulthood. Macaulay found this in Glasgow (1977), where both working- and middle-class children used the stigmatized glottal stop [ʔ] for /t/, but middle-class children later

shifted to the low-glottal norm of their class. The second pattern is when the youngest and oldest groups both use more non-standard forms, while the middle-aged use
less. Cases are in fact rather rare, but one was found in our work in New Zealand
(Bell and Holmes 1992, see Chapter 7.6, this volume). Pakeha (Anglo) men showed
just this kind of age dip for the ING variable: 56% non-standard *in* for the young,
dropping to 32% for the mid-aged, and back up to 51% for older speakers. Middle-
class women had a similar dip but at a lower frequency (16% to 4% to 24%).
Abstracted, the pattern looks like this:

This U-shape is usually interpreted as a life-course phenomenon. When people are
out and about in the workforce and society during their middle adult years, they
require more standard language than earlier or later in their life when general social
advancement matters less. This is the monolingual equivalent of what can be seen in
bilingual communities, where speakers who have been required to use a majority
language throughout their working lives may revert to their minority language again
when they get older.

Lifespan change has shown up in a series of meticulous studies of Montreal French by
Gillian Sankoff and her colleagues. Using a panel of the same 60 speakers recorded first
in 1971 and again in 1984, they have tracked the alternation between the 'periphrastic'
future (like *going to* in English) and the inflected future:

Elle	**va**	peut-être	**arriver**	bien vite –	on lui	**demandera**.
	PERIPHRASTIC					INFLECTED
She	is going	perhaps	to get here	quite quickly –	we her	will ask

'Maybe she'll get here pretty soon – we'll ask her.'

The researchers anticipated their speakers' usage would be stable across their lifespan
(Wagner and Sankoff 2011). However they found the contrary: in the 13 years between
the two recordings, two-thirds increased their use of the inflected future. And out of the
20 speakers who used no inflected future at all in 1971, 16 had adopted it by 1984. The
change was class-specific. The 'low socioprofessional status' group showed no shift, but
most of the high-status speakers (18/21) used more inflectional futures in 1984
(Figure 8.1). This is a striking lifespan change that is clearly much more dynamic for
speakers than the static label 'age grading' implies. We return to its implications in the
next section.

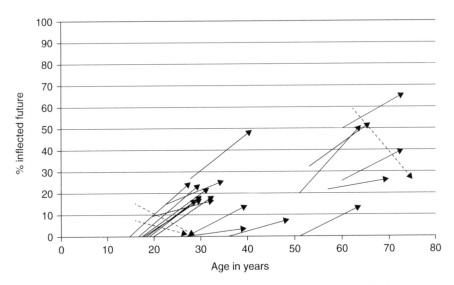

Figure 8.1   Use of inflected future in Montreal French by 21 individuals from the high socioprofessional status group, showing their shift between 1971 and 1984
Source: Wagner and Sankoff (2011), figure 3

Interpret the figure. Estimate percentages by eyeballing the graph. Six of the arrows start
between 15 and 20 years at zero on the horizontal axis:

1   How many speakers have increased their inflectional-future use, and how many have
    decreased (dotted lines)?
2   What is the greatest increase by any one speaker? What is the approximate average
    increase across all the speakers?
3   How many had zero inflectional future in 1971 but show some in 1984?
4   Does any one age cohort show more shift? Why?
5   What would you conclude about life course language change and stability on the
    basis of this data?

8.2   REAL TIME AND APPARENT TIME

In earlier chapters we looked at language change in the sense of shift from the use of
one language to another (Samoan to English, for example). Then, investigating pidgins and creoles (Chapter 4), we saw how social upheaval can create new languages
from old in a century or less. We also know that change in even apparently stable
languages has left modern speakers of English or French or German unable to understand the language of their ancestors of a millennium ago. The variationist study of
change in individual linguistic variables over time is the focus of the rest of this
chapter.

Table 8.1   Real time and apparent time

Generation	Born	State of language in	Recorded	Age group when recorded	
(a) Real time					
G1	1935	1960	1960	25	Young
G2	1960	1985	1985	25	Young
G3	1985	2010	2010	25	Young
(b) Apparent time					
G1	1935	1960	2010	75	Older
G2	1960	1985	2010	50	Mid
G3	1985	2010	2010	25	Young

[handwritten: may not be an accurate representation]

The ruse of apparent time

[handwritten: A B C / Y1 Y1 Y1]

The ideal in studying language change is to catch it as it is happening in real time – that is, to have records of a community's speech in the past as well as the present. Table 8.1a shows how such a study could have looked in 2010: three generations, each recorded as 25-year-old adults, i.e. in 1960, 1985 and 2010. But there is clearly a problem: we are conducting our study in 2010, we have no earlier recordings, and cannot time-travel back half a century. Nor can we afford to just record today's 25-year-olds and then wait until 2060 to compare them with their grandchildren (project funders want rather more immediate results).

Until the 1960s the received wisdom in linguistics was that language change could not be directly observed as it happened. Labov's solution to that is exemplified in Table 8.1b. Column 4 differs from 8.1a in that all the recordings were made in 2010. The older age group are taken to represent the state of the language two generations back, the mid age group represent one generation ago, and the youngest group speak the language of now. The older and mid age groups are therefore treated as linguistic archives for their generations, G1 and G2. This is current time projected back to represent prior times. Labov called it 'apparent time', in which the present is used to explain the past.

But the ruse of apparent time raises two issues:

- It relies wholly on the assumption that people continue to speak similarly throughout their adult lives, that the speech of the middle and older generations has not changed significantly in the intervening 25–50 years since they were themselves 25 years old.
- Secondly: if we depend on age to benchmark change, how do we tell the difference between what is age grading and what is generational change? Both show up as regular increases and/or decreases in use of a feature according to age.

Age grading versus generational change

To take the second issue first. Disambiguating age-stratified findings has been a central interpretive puzzle for every variationist project, and there is only one sure solution to

---

Exercise 8.3   Martha's Vineyard revisited

Labov's 1962 study on the island of Martha's Vineyard off the New England coast was his MA project and the pioneer use of apparent time to research language change. He concluded that the age pattern for increasing centralization of the diphthongs in PRICE and MOUTH probably indicated change in progress. The fishermen who were the most locally identified of the residents were using centralization to mark their distinctiveness from the island's influx of summer visitors (Labov 1972b).

    The study has been replicated twice, also in student projects – in 1997 by Meredith Josey, and in 2002 by Jenny Pope. The two studies produced contradictory findings, one confirming and the other contesting the change Labov had identified.

1 Read the short Pope, Meyerhoff and Ladd (2007) article, which summarizes and compares all three studies. Then check for yourself its representation of both Labov's original (1972b) and Blake and Josey's article (2003).
2 Assess the methodological differences between the two follow-up studies (see Pope et al.) and draw your own conclusions about their effect on the contrasting results.
3 Do you think that the real-time findings confirm or deny Labov's apparent-time interpretation of the 1962 age differences as change in progress?
4 Do you think the real-time findings confirm or deny that diphthong centralization is still an island identity marker?
5 How important to the results are the social and demographic changes on the island over the intervening 40 years, as outlined by the two replication studies?

---

it: calibrate against real-time data. Many of the studies of the 1960s and 70s were in fact conducted in communities where there existed prior descriptions of speech (albeit of varying detail and reliability), often derived from dialect-geographical surveys of a generation or two before – see Chapter 9. This is how Labov benchmarked his findings in New York, as did Trudgill in Norwich. More tellingly, there is now enough time depth to replicate the 1960s and 70s studies and calibrate the apparent-time interpretations the original researchers made then against real-time results. There have been perhaps a score of such studies, and to these we now turn to address the age grade versus change puzzle.

    In generational change, the new generation speaks differently from the last – the language as a whole changes. In age grading, the community's language as a whole does not change. Apparent time interprets age-differentiated data as indicating generational change. How then do apparent-time conclusions fare when tested against later real-time data? Do they show generational change in real time? Sankoff (2006) overviewed 13 studies which claimed to have found change in apparent time and had since been replicated with 'trend' re-studies – that is, with the same population being re-sampled. Covering 10 countries and 7 languages, these confirmed that there had indeed been continuing change. Again, Guy Bailey and his colleagues compared a survey of 13 sociolinguistic variables of Texas English with earlier dialect-geography data. Their apparent-time interpretations of the original data were all confirmed by the later survey as real-time changes (Cukor-Avila and Bailey 2013). Labov's early projects have also been replicated – see Exercise 7.1 for the New York department stores study, and Exercise 8.3 for research on Martha's Vineyard.

Lifespan stability versus change

Such trend studies can confirm in real time that the community's language is changing. But identifying if individuals are changing during their lifespan (our first question earlier) requires a 'panel' of speakers from an original survey who are later re-recorded for comparison with their younger selves. In one study Sankoff and Blondeau (2007) analysed shift in pronunciations of /r/ by their 1971/1984 panel of Montreal speakers. A majority remained stable in their usage across their lifespan, which accords with Sankoff's survey of a dozen other panel studies (2006).

But although stability across the lifespan is the prevailing trend, there is a strong counter-current. Many of these studies also show a minority of speakers who do change across the lifespan. Some of their changes are major, and some of the minorities who change are substantial (a third of the sample). Usually the lifespan changes are in the same direction as any community changes, as Sankoff and Blondeau found for Montreal /r/. That kind of result implies that apparent time underestimates the rate of change. But the lifespan change towards the inflectional future that we saw in Figure 8.1, was going in the **opposite** direction to the general community trend in Montreal, which is towards increased use of the alternative, periphrastic future. In this case, then, lifespan change is retarding the wider community change, meaning that an apparent-time interpretation would have overestimated the rate of the change.

Example 8.1

The Queen's English

In 1952 Queen Elizabeth II delivered the first of her many Christmas broadcasts to the Commonwealth. Australian phoneticians have taken the archive of the Queen's annual messages and compared her speech of the 1950s with the 1980s. Their finding: 'there has been a drift in the Queen's accent towards one that is characteristic of speakers who are younger and/or lower in the social hierarchy' (Harrington, Palethorpe and Watson 2000: 927). Although she remained well behind the trend, most of the Queen's vowels had shifted about halfway towards the younger, Cockney-influenced Received Pronunciation which is sometimes called 'Estuary English'. Her Christmas broadcasts provide a wonderfully customized archive for tracking real-time change in one individual's language: high-quality, annual recordings, with the same theme, setting, genre and audience.

- Queen Elizabeth is arguably the very last speaker of English we would expect to change her speech during her lifespan. What does this mean for our assumptions on age grading and apparent time?

The real-time findings therefore show that many adults can and do shift their speech patterns during their lives, which supports Coupland's contention that even the most conservative of older speakers should not be treated as fossilized (Example 8.1). On the other hand, the fact that a majority of adults do not shift lends to apparent time both qualified legitimation and continued usefulness. And most of the changing minority's shifts go along with community-wide change, confirming that apparent time is a reliably conservative technique for projecting change. But the counter-cases mean that each variable has to be interpreted on its merits. And increasingly it seems that lifespan changes may often ride on an underlying pattern of community change for the same linguistic variable.

8.3   THE LINGUISTICS OF LANGUAGE CHANGE

The empirical foundations for a theory of language change were laid by a long article with that title authored by Uriel Weinreich and his students, Labov and Marvin Herzog in 1968. They stressed that, in contrast to the prevailing theories, language does not have to be homogeneous to be orderly and structured. They identified five problems for a theory of language change:

- Constraints: do changes take some linguistic directions and not others?
- Transition: what intervening stages do changes pass through? How are they transferred between speakers?
- Embedding: where is a change situated in linguistic and social structure?
- Evaluation: how is a change evaluated socially and communicatively?
- Actuation: what triggers and advances a specific change, linguistically and socially? Why did this particular change occur here and now (and not there and then)? – the perhaps unanswerable question.

The empirical illustrations in this 1968 article were largely from Labov's New York City research. His three-volume life's work, *Principles of Linguistic Change* (1994, 2001a, 2010), returns to these original issues throughout. The books incorporate a lot of material from Labov's main publications over several decades, and here I generally reference the book not the original article.

Phonology has been the home base of the variationist study of language change, for some obvious reasons. Most phonological variables occur frequently in speech, sometimes many times per minute, while non-phonological variables can be rare. Also, the traditional definition of a sociolinguistic variable (see Chapter 7) requires a closed set of two or more variants that 'mean the same thing'. This is much more plausible in phonology – *singing* equals *singin'* – than in discourse or syntax (linguistically, discourse is the level of language structure above the sentence, while syntax is structure within the sentence). The constraints on defining variables have meant that most studies of variation and change in discourse and syntax have dealt with quite micro features (such as a single function word) rather than those, for example, involving changes in word order. But this does not prevent us investigating sociolinguistic changes in discourse patterns in a more qualitative way.

Discourse change

Changing communication technologies have always tended to lead to new linguistic patterns, and the language of news has changed markedly in the past hundred years. The adoption of the 'inverted pyramid' structure of news stories in the twentieth century was the most significant of these shifts. The inverted pyramid means that the most important thing is placed first in the story rather than the chronologically first fact (Bell 1995). In a project of my own on news discourse, I took as a case study the reporting of polar expeditions across the twentieth century. In January 1912 Captain Scott and his companions reached the South Pole, only to die on the return journey. The news took over a year to reach the world because the continent was inaccessible until the relief ship got through from New Zealand the following Antarctic summer. The news was published in February 1913 in the *New Zealand Herald*, the country's largest daily, with a 10-deck headline (Figure 8.2) which virtually tells the story. Nearly half a century later when the next overland expedition reached the pole (1958), the news of Sir Edmund Hillary's arrival was broadcast on radio and published in the *Herald* the next morning. In 1999 when Sir Edmund's son Peter arrived at the pole after a three-month trek, he was interviewed live on New Zealand evening television news.

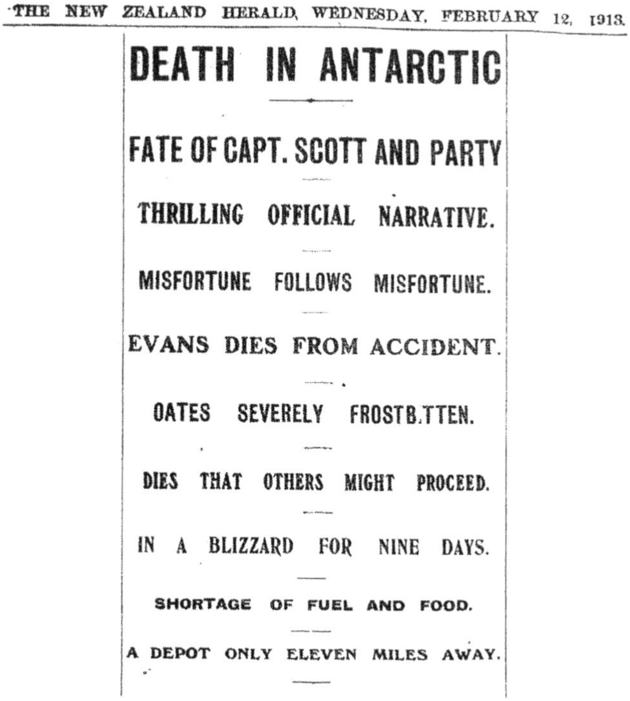

THE NEW ZEALAND HERALD, WEDNESDAY, FEBRUARY 12, 1913.

DEATH IN ANTARCTIC

FATE OF CAPT. SCOTT AND PARTY

THRILLING OFFICIAL NARRATIVE.

MISFORTUNE FOLLOWS MISFORTUNE.

EVANS DIES FROM ACCIDENT.

OATES SEVERELY FROSTB.TTEN.

DIES THAT OTHERS MIGHT PROCEED.

IN A BLIZZARD FOR NINE DAYS.

SHORTAGE OF FUEL AND FOOD.

A DEPOT ONLY ELEVEN MILES AWAY.

Figure 8.2   Captain Scott reaches the South Pole

Exercise 8.4 A century of change in news language

For more detail on this case study, see Bell (2003). This can be an individual or group exercise.

1 Use your knowledge as a reader of contemporary press style to rewrite the head-lines in Figure 8.2 as they would appear in today's newspaper.
2 Then analyse the kinds of linguistic changes you have made: how have you reworked each headline? What have you deleted – or added? What has been reordered? What words have you replaced?
3 Reflect on and explain why you made each of the above changes. What overall trends of change can you see in them?
4 What features of the 1913 headlines just would not appear today? What ideolo-gies do they express that are alien to today's media and society?
5 Based on Figure 8.2, write a single headline for this story in today's newspaper.
6 What do you see as the goals and constraints of news writing? Assess how the changes you made in your rewrite do or do not serve these – that is, how func-tional are they?
7 Consider the changes there have been in communication technologies over the past century. What role may these changes have played in changing news pres-entation and language?
8 How would current media technologies cover an arrival at the South Pole this year? How different to 1999 would the coverage and language be and why?

Changes in communications technology across the century therefore exponentially reduced the time lapse between the event and its reporting and helped trigger changes in news discourse, syntax and lexicon (Exercise 8.4). One issue with such changes is how functional they are – that is, do they make the language more communicatively efficient? This is a question for all language change, with Labov at least being sceptical about the importance of functionalism as a driver of change.

Change in syntax and morphology

Some of the rewrites you have made in Exercise 8.4 will have involved the syntax of the headlines. Variationist sociolinguistics has concentrated its syntactic analysis on easily delimitable features like negatives (e.g. English *never* for *not*, double negatives), relative or demonstrative pronouns, and verb morphology such as marking number (*she were here*), person (*I is coming*) or tense (*he bring it last night*). Often these have been examined as contrasting standard and non-standard alternatives – see the list in the last chapter (Example 7.4) and the inventory of forms in Wolfram and Schilling-Estes (2006).

One example comes from centuries of change in French. While Old French marked negation with *ne* before the verb, in the fourteenth to sixteenth centuries, *pas* was added after the verb, giving the canonical contemporary standard form:

Ils	ne	travaillent	pas	le lundi.
they	NEG	work	NEG	on Monday

'They don't work on Monday.'

Historical research by Martineau and Mougeon (2003) shows that after two centuries of stable use of *ne … pas*, the syntax began changing again in the nineteenth century. The lower social strata led a move to delete the original *ne* marker. By the late twentieth century this shift was well advanced in France, but still socially stratified. A study by Ashby (1981) showed that the working class had far more deletion than the middle classes. Clear age differentiation, with 81 per cent *ne* deletion by the younger cohort compared to 48 per cent for the older, reflected the continuing change and was later confirmed by real-time data. In Québec, *ne* has all but disappeared from spoken French in the twenty-first century and the one-time newcomer *pas* serves as the sole marker. There is also now no social stratification for *ne* deletion in Québec – a typical pattern as a change moves to completion.

8.4 SOUND CHANGE

Sound change has been the central occupation of variationist sociolinguistics. Nearly half the articles in the journal *Language Variation and Change* in the 10 years to 2008 dealt exclusively with phonetic variables (Preston and Niedzielski 2010). Vowel change has been Labov's particular pursuit and dominates his three-volume work, just as his work dominates the field.

Consonants

Change in consonants often involves phonetic weakening or 'lenition'. In Spanish and Portuguese the plural is marked by a word-final /s/, but is often reduced to an [h] or deleted altogether:

las cosas bonitas
la∅ cosa∅ bonita∅
'the beautiful things'

Such deletions often affect the morphology of a language as well as its phonology. It seems communicatively logical that when the plural is marked multiple times (say on article, noun and adjective as in the example), that one or two of these might drop out – after all, only the first is necessary. That would be a functional explanation, but it is not what happens. Rather, marking on one item triggers more marking on subsequent items, and lack of marking triggers more non-marking. This is one of the evidences that leads Labov (1994) to argue that most changes are counter-functional – they do not enhance communication.

In the UK a suite of consonant changes is spreading London pronunciations like /th/ fronting (*fink*), final /l/ vocalization (*milk*) and /t/ glottalization (*butter*). Received Pronunciation has incorporated several of these to produce the Estuary English which we have seen even the Queen accommodating to (Example 8.1). As well as crossing social space from working-class speech into the pan-regional prestige variety RP, these changes are also spreading geographically outwards from London (see Chapter 9).

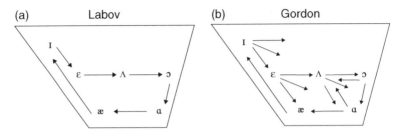

Figure 8.3 Two views of the US Northern Cities Chain Shift
Source: Gordon (2013), figures 9.1 and 9.2

Vowel change

The vowels are the core of what we recognize as an accent, but the phonetics of vowel change is probably the most technically challenging area of linguistics we will touch on in this book, and I will not attempt to go into it in any depth. Most analysis nowadays is carried out instrumentally, feeding the sound signal through a computer program which enables precise measurement of the acoustic formants that characterize vowels. This is followed by normalization to allow for the different vocal tract sizes between females and males. The resulting formant values are then usually plotted on a grid that resembles the traditional vowel chart representing the position of the tongue in the mouth (e.g. Figure 8.3). The phonetic instrumentation has been accompanied by increasing statistical sophistication in both computing and displaying sociolinguistic data. Much of this work is linguistic rather than *socio*linguistic in focus. Sometimes termed **sociophonetics**, it majors on the linguistics of sound variation and change with less attention to its social dimension (e.g. Preston and Niedzielski 2010).

The phonetics of vowel change focuses on two main areas, mergers and chain shifts. **Mergers** occur when two vowel phonemes come to occupy the same phonetic space and so become one, pronounced identically. Mergers routinely move in social and geographical as well as phonetic space. In contemporary American English, the increasing merger between words like *cot* and *caught* – 'the largest single phonological change taking place in American English' (Labov 1994: 316) – is associated with the coal-mining areas of Pennsylvania. Mergers are supposed to be generally not socially salient, although in New Zealand the merger of the *ear* and *air* vowels does give rise to self-aware wordplay in names such as *Hairsay* and *Hair Today* for hairdressing salons. Splits are the opposite of mergers although are much less commonly reported. There is also the phenomenon of **near-mergers**, which I cover in Chapter 10.3.

Chain shifts are the second main focus of research and occur when more than one adjacent vowel moves. If the pronunciation of one vowel begins to encroach on another vowel's space, the second vowel must itself move if it is to remain distinctive, i.e. avoid merger. This sets off a **push chain**. A **drag** or **pull chain** is when a vowel shifts into the space vacated by another vowel. Much of Labov's work has focused on trying to deduce patterns and formulate principles for vowel shifts, and Labov (1994) closes with a dozen such principles for the phonetics of sound change.

The most researched and publicized chain shift is the so-called 'Northern Cities Chain Shift', which has spread throughout an area of the inland northeastern United States largely delimited by the westward extent of nineteenth-century migration flows. Figure 8.3a shows Labov's representation of the general trend of these shifts, with six vowels rotating clockwise. This clean pattern does however involve a high level of abstraction from the actual phonetic data. Matthew Gordon (2001) researched the shift in Michigan: he believes that the much more multidirectional pattern shown in Figure 8.3b gives a truer picture and questions how much this should be construed as a single chain shift. There is some risk of ad-hoc reasoning and overgeneralization in the search for broad principles of sound change. One of the central questions in the study of sound change is whether it spreads regularly across all words or by **lexical diffusion**, that is word by word. We return to this in the next chapter.

8.5   THE SOCIAL LIFE OF LANGUAGE CHANGE

So much for the what of language change, but how and why does change proceed socially? Labov displaces the perhaps unanswerable *why* question onto a search for *who*: who are the leaders of change and what are their social characteristics? Most often they have proven to be located at the intersection of class and gender. Relatively little has been made of the role of ethnicity: major theory-generating projects in Philadelphia, Belfast and Detroit have been mono-ethnic. Labov's work on the Northern Cities Shift set aside consideration of African Americans and Hispanics as being on separate trajectories of change, and found European ethnic differences (Italian, Polish, Jewish) to have relatively little effect. But we know that ethnicity can be a major force in linguistic change, and in contact situations it is crucial (Chapter 9).

Class

A basic distinction is made between 'change from above' and 'change from below' a speech community's level of consciousness. Speakers are aware of some changes but not of others. The classic case of change from above is New York City /r/ which we discussed in the last chapter (Figure 7.2). New Yorkers are very aware of this variable and its social meaning, and this is reflected in the lower middle class crossing over to exceed the upper middle class. Changes from above the level of consciousness are also those that are led 'from above' in society. Such changes appear to be rare and import a prestige form that is external to the community. Otherwise the upper classes do not innovate linguistically – the Queen shows up as a tardy follower of change rather than a leader. Similarly, Labov found in Philadelphia that the upper class 'speak a conservative but distinctively Philadelphian variety of English, and ... follow trends that are set by the upper working class and lower middle class' (2001a: 190).

Most changes, then, are below the level of a community's consciousness, and also come from lower down the social scale. Labov deduces the principle that most change originates in the centre of the social hierarchy. This produces a characteristic 'curvilinear' graph, in which an incoming change is at its peak in these socially central classes, with lower values in the trailing lower and upper classes:

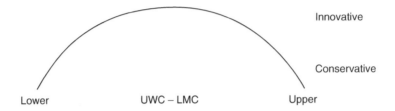

In the 1970s Labov and his colleagues conducted a comprehensive study of the vowel systems of Philadelphia (reported in Labov 2001a). They found changes occurring in many of the vowels, and particularly new and vigorous changes in the diphthongs of words like MOUTH and FACE. These displayed the typical curvilinear shape, with change being led from the upper working class. The same pattern has shown up in widely different languages and locations – the lenition of (ch) from affricate [tʃ] to fricative [ʃ] in words like *muchos* in the Spanish of Panama City, and the palatalization of /t/ and /d/ before front vowels in the Arabic of Cairo.

Change in sign languages

Change affects all languages, and this includes sign languages as well as spoken. Communicatively, sign languages function like any spoken language, and linguistically, their structure and variation can be analysed using similar frameworks. Socially they have borne perhaps even greater discrimination than spoken minority languages. However, they are now publicly recognized in a number of countries, none more so than American Sign Language (ASL), which has been heavily researched over the past 50

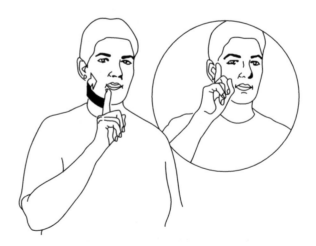

Figure 8.4   Non-standard American Sign Language sign for DEAF

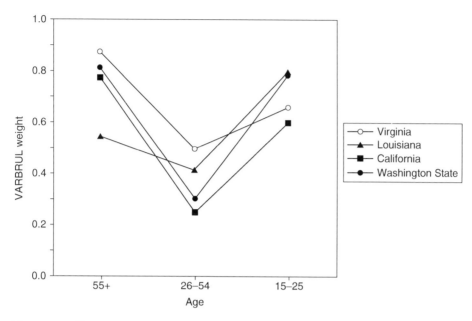

Figure 8.5 Change in American Sign Language sign for DEAF: Varbrul factor values for non-standard forms of the sign by age group and region
Note: Above .5 favours non-standard, below disfavours.
Source: Bayley, Lucas and Rose (2000), figure 3

years especially at Gallaudet University in Washington, DC (e.g. Lucas 2001). Signs can be described linguistically as sequences of hold and movement segments, with each segment consisting of features such as handshape and location. The standard (or 'citation') form of the sign for DEAF in ASL starts with the index finger pointing upwards near the ear, then moving across the cheek to the corner of the mouth. The main non-standard form moves in the opposite direction, from mouth to ear (Figure 8.4).

ASL shows a great deal of variation. A nationwide study found that age and region were the most significant variables affecting the sign DEAF (Bayley, Lucas and Rose 2000). Figure 8.5 shows the Varbrul 'weights' (explained in Chapter 7.6) for DEAF in four of the regional varieties of ASL. The pattern in the graph looks typical of the U-shape that reflects age grading, as shown in section 8.1. That is, younger and older signers use more non-standard forms and the middle-aged use fewer. The researchers, however, advance a different and very specific community-based explanation: this is linguistic change that reflects shifts in deaf education. The oldest signers had their schooling at a time when ASL was suppressed, and they had no contact with a standard form. The middle-aged were schooled when awareness of ASL was heightened and standards prescribed. By the time of the youngest signers, the language's standing was secure enough to no longer be threatened by use of non-standard forms. Therefore, imposed on chronological age we see a very specific social and psychological history of ASL which results in different generations of signers having different experiences and linguistic patterns.

Gender

In the previous chapter, we saw how there are regular differences between women and men in cases of stable linguistic variation. Men prefer the non-standard variant and women the standard, very clearly in the case study of ING. It is no surprise then to find women and men playing different roles in language change. Gender has proved to be arguably the most significant factor affecting change, and Labov has derived principles to explain it:

> In linguistic change from above, women adopt prestige forms at a higher rate than men. (Labov 2001a: 274)

> In linguistic change from below, women use higher frequencies of innovative forms than men do. (Labov 2001a: 292)

These principles mean that women lead in both forms of change, conscious and unconscious, which creates the 'gender paradox' (2001a: 293):

> Women conform more closely than men to sociolinguistic norms that are overtly prescribed, but conform less than men when they are not.

Labov canvasses several explanations for the gender mix of linguistic conformity and nonconformity, but considers them inconclusive. Such generalizations are clearly perilous, particularly in the light of the critiques we saw in Chapter 7.5 of the conceptualization of gender in variationist sociolinguistics, of women's conformity, and of definitions for what is standard and what is prescribed.

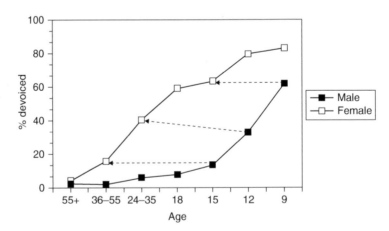

Figure 8.6   Devoicing of /dʒ/ in Buenos Aires Spanish by age and gender
Source: Labov (2001a), figure 8.10, derived from a study by Wolf and Jiménez

- Interpret what the graph means for (1) age and (2) generational differences in /dʒ/ devoicing (see Labov 2001a: 304). The dotted arrows show the relationship between women and men of the same generation. The 30-year-old men and 55-year-old women, although not linked by an arrow, also have about the same devoicing rate (very little).

Profile of a change leader

Labov (2001a) sees the linguistic innovator as the ultimate sociable being, and Celeste S. is his prototype. Celeste (not her real name) is the hub that joins different groups on 'Clark' St in Kensington, Philadelphia. Everybody can name her. She scores at the top of communication indexes, in the wider neighbourhood as well as her own block.

Celeste grew up in Philadelphia during the 1930s/40s. Despite a strict father she would scheme her way out of the house to dances at the local servicemen's canteen during the war. She knows how to look after her own interests. She is verbally adept in negotiation, persuasion, denunciation. She is the person who takes up the collection for flowers for a neighbour's funeral – even for a 'mean old lady' she disliked. She is also the one who chased an enemy down the street with a butcher's knife.

For the two big new changes in the Philadelphia vowel system – the MOUTH and FACE diphthongs – Celeste is leader in her generation, one of a handful of women whose sociolinguistic distinction displays both their history of nonconformity and upward mobility.

However, the lead role of women in change is well evidenced in many studies, several of which we have touched on already for other purposes. Women are leading men in the adoption of /r/ in New York, and in the deletion of *ne* in French negation discussed in section 8.3. In Cajun English (Figure 7.3), women are very far in advance of the men in aspirating stops. In the Spanish of Buenos Aires, the /dʒ/ in words like *llama* is being devoiced to [tʃ]. Figure 8.6 shows that women are a full generation ahead of men in this change. The women's line in the graph reflects what is known as the S-curve, a common pattern of change. That is, the change is relatively slow at the beginning (the line is quite flat at the bottom), speeds up in the middle stages (the line gets generally steeper), and then slows again towards the end (the line flattens near the top).

Labov's quest has been to locate the leaders of linguistic change, the *who* question posed earlier. In Philadelphia he identifies the working-class neighbourhood of Kensington as the crucible of change, and a category of speakers who take the lead role. Their distinguishing characteristic is nonconformity in both general and linguistic behaviour. They are women, and their archetype is Celeste S. – see Example 8.2.

Although Labov's principles of change, particularly on gender and change, may capture a majority tendency, there are significant counter-examples that mean the principles at least need hedging. /t/ glottalization in words like *letter* has been one of the most stigmatized variables in British English, but has been spreading vigorously for some time. And it is women who have been leading the change, according to James Milroy et al. (1994), rather than reacting against it, as Labov would have predicted. The Milroys and their colleagues suggest that women's adoption of the formerly stigmatized feature has

Exercise 8.5 Women and language change

Milroy et al. (1994: 351) propose that:

> females are leading in the spread of the glottal stop in British English, and that its establishment as a middle-class norm ... is contingent on its establishment in the speech of females ... The generalization suggested by such an interpretation is not that females favor prestige forms, as has been previously suggested, but that they create them, in the sense that the forms females favor become prestige forms.

1 Read the Milroy et al. article and assess their line of reasoning. Do you agree that it is women's usage that confers prestige on a change rather than women merely taking on forms that already have prestige (presumably with men)? Do you think the evidence supports their proposal?
2 To what extent, then, does a feature become a middle-class norm through being adopted by women rather than by men?
3 Look back at Exercise 7.6, the debate about the relation between women and standard language forms. Apply Trudgill's three points to language change and to the role of women in change. Debate.

been a condition of its acceptance by the middle class. In this case, then, gender is prior to class. They further argue that the conventional interpretation of women's role in change needs to be turned on its head (Exercise 8.5).

8.6 MARKETS, NETWORKS AND COMMUNITIES

Sociolinguists have long been looking for more nuanced ways of theorizing and operationalizing the social embedding of language variation and change rather than depending on the kind of functionalist class rankings that I critiqued in Chapter 7.2. They have adopted three main alternative approaches from elsewhere in the social sciences:

- the linguistic market
- social networks
- communities of practice.

The second of these has been influential in sociolinguistic research since the 1980s and is the focus of most of this section. The third has been increasingly widespread over the past couple of decades, and will be covered in the next section.

Linguistic market

The first alternative derives from Bourdieu's concept of 'linguistic capital' (1991) – that different language codes serve as commodities which carry different degrees of social

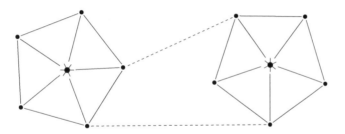

Figure 8.7   Strong and weak network ties (solid lines = strong, dotted lines = weak)

value (more on this in Chapter 10). Language use is central to some jobs, such as teacher or receptionist, and these speakers are expected to use the 'highest-priced' language, that is the standard. This makes for a linguistic market in which speakers are ranked according to how important the standard language is to their occupation.

David Sankoff and Suzanne Laberge (1978) introduced this approach into sociolinguistics, assigning linguistic market scores to speakers in a study of Montreal French. For several syntactic variables, the use of standard forms correlated well with a speaker's location in the linguistic market. In research on Arabic in Cairo, Haeri (1997) found there were two contrasting linguistic markets. One was oriented to Classical Arabic (the language of the Qur'an) as taught in the state school system and required in public-sector jobs, and the other related to Standard Cairene Arabic and education in elite private foreign-language schools.

Social networks

The analysis of social networks maps a person's or group's relationships, with the aim of understanding how these affect their behaviour. Such network ties among people are both structural (who knows who) and interactional (what sorts of relationship). They can be measured on both dimensions:

- Density: that is, the number of people someone has ties with.
- Multiplexity: what kinds of ties these are, such as kin, workmate, or recreation – or all of these strands.

From this information a network strength score can be calculated for every speaker, and the strength of ties within a group or area measured. Ties are categorized as either weak (with an acquaintance) or strong (with friends or relatives). Figure 8.7 shows how individuals' strong and weak ties can be diagrammed. Labov used this kind of mapping in his 1960s research on New York adolescent gangs (1972a), and 1970s neighbourhood studies in Philadelphia (2001a).

Networks and change in Belfast

Social networks have been most fully researched and theorized in sociolinguistics by Lesley and James Milroy, who made this a central concept in their 1970s work in Belfast,

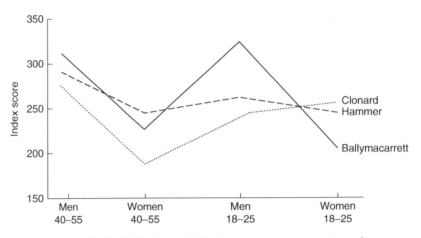

Figure 8.8   Backing of /a/ in Belfast in words like *hat, man, grass*, on 5-point scale
Source: Lesley Milroy (1987), figure 5.4

Northern Ireland (e.g. James Milroy and Lesley Milroy 1985; Lesley Milroy 1987; Lesley Milroy and Llamas 2013). Despite the violent sectarian/ethnic segregation of the city at that time, Lesley Milroy was able to interview 46 speakers on both sides through introductions by a 'friend of a friend' in three inner-city communities:

- Ballymacarrett: East Belfast, Protestant, a stable area, with continuing employment
- Clonard: West Belfast, Catholic, high male unemployment, community intact
- Hammer: West, Protestant, high male unemployment, community being scattered.

On socioeconomic indices everyone in these communities would have rated as from the same – working – class, but the individuals and areas were differentiated by their social networks. For one linguistic variable undergoing change – the backing of the /a/ vowel in words like *hat, man* and *grass* – there was a strikingly high correlation between speakers' pronunciations and their network scores. Ballymacarrett shows a sharp gender differentiation for /a/ backing (Figure 8.8), reflecting the difference between high network scores for the men and low for women in this stable, traditional working-class area. For the disintegrating Hammer community, there is little difference between men and women on their network scores or on /a/ pronunciation. But in the Clonard, young women had unexpectedly high scores for both their networks and /a/ pronunciation. The incoming change to backed /a/ is led, as Figure 8.8 shows, by the men of Protestant Ballymacarrett, but it is being followed by the young women of the Catholic Clonard. How could this happen across the extreme barriers through the then-divided city? It turned out that all the girls were employed in a single central city store that served both communities. They were therefore interacting fleetingly but frequently with backed-/a/ speakers from East Belfast, and carried the pronunciation back to the west.

The Milroys concluded that it is the numerous weak ties between groups (such as service encounters) that spread change across communities. Conversely, we know that in bilingual

Exercise 8.6   Language change and strong/weak ties

1   Labov believes that language change is led by speakers like Celeste S., with strong external network ties, while the Milroys argue it is those with weak ties. What is your stance? Review the evidence presented briefly in the text and Example 8.2, and your knowledge of the workings of social relationships about you. Give the reasons (social and linguistic) for your conclusion.
   • For more detail, see the arguments in Labov (2001a: chapter 10) where he re-analyses the Belfast data), Lesley Milroy (1987: Chapter 7), and James Milroy and Lesley Milroy (1985).

2   The Milroys propose that the reason for their difference from Labov is that the term 'leader' masks more than one role. Drawing on the literature on innovations and their adoption, they distinguish between:
   • the actual **innovators**, who are marginal to a group or even regarded as deviant – the kind of speakers that Labov famously identified as 'lames', and among whom he classed his adolescent self (1972a); and
   • **early adopters**, who are at the core of the group, and who pick up the change from the peripheral innovators and spread it to the rest (e.g. Celeste).

3   Do you agree with the innovator/early-adopter distinction? Does it solve the divergence in views? Try to identify if there are any other reasons for the divergence, for example in differences between the Belfast and Philadelphia communities or the research designs.

4   Who would you identify in your own networks as linguistic leaders? Why do you specify these individuals? Do they fit either of the profiles in question 1? Can you tell what changes they are leading?

communities it is strong ties that help maintain a group's language. Gumperz, for example, differentiated between 'closed' and 'open' networks in his research on German–Slovenian bilingualism (1982a). And in our Chapter 5.6 case study of Oberwart, Gal found that the degree of peasantness of a speaker's network was a very good predictor of their use of Hungarian rather than German. The reason for these findings is that strong ties are conservative. They reinforce group norms, in language as in other behaviours, and therefore support local vernaculars. They form a resistance against language change, whether between or within languages. Weak ties, however, allow difference and divergence to enter because weakly tied peripheral members are less subject to group pressure. You will notice that the Milroys' locating of language change in weak ties is roughly the opposite of Labov's explanation in the previous section: that in Philadelphia the leaders of change were – like Celeste S. in Example 8.2 – those with strong ties outside as well as inside their own group. Exercise 8.6 addresses this debate.

Class and networks are complementary rather than competing approaches to language change, especially if we adopt the kind of conflict model of social class discussed in Chapter 7.2 (Lesley Milroy and James Milroy 1992). The network approach focuses on the individual and small group rather than their place in macro-social structure. But there is also a clear and acknowledged link between networks and classes. Close networks with strong ties tend to occur in the working and upper classes, while looser networks with weak ties are associated with the mobile middle classes. This is broadly consistent with Labov's placing the origins of changes in the central social strata. But researchers have felt that something more was needed beyond the network concept, taking more account of ideology, identity and attitude, and bridging between micro- and macro-social factors. This brings us to the third of the alternatives, **Communities of Practice**, which incorporates aspects of both the linguistic market and network approaches.

8.7 THE CASE OF BELTEN HIGH

Judy wears fringed rawhide boots, tight jeans, dark eye liner – and tense front vowels. She is taut, fierce, independent. Flamboyance is her stock in trade, style is her essence in language as in appearance. She benchmarks social meaning for her cohort, who benchmark it for the school. Judy is a burned-out burnout, a cultural and linguistic icon.

Jocks and **burnouts** are the recognized opposing poles that define the social order in the very American milieu of Belten High School in suburban Detroit. Everyone else – the majority – are 'in-betweens', whether they like it or not. The two groups have conflicting ideologies, norms, practices and trajectories. In the school, jocks dominate and burnouts oppose. For jocks school is their life, they are embedded in the institution and its extracurricular activities. The burnouts are alienated from school and face outwards to the neighbourhood. Jocks are bound for college and corporate America, burnouts for the local workforce. Culturally and linguistically, jocks are on the national market, burnouts the local market. Jocks orient to the standard, burnouts to the vernacular. Jock friendships may serve for advancement, but burnouts stress loyalty and solidarity. Jocks represent the middle class, burnouts working class. While jocks are suburban, burnouts are urban.

The sociolinguistics of jocks and burnouts

Penny Eckert spent two years researching in 'Belten High', and her ethnography is itself an icon of perceptiveness expressed in vivid writing that captures the character of the school's social and linguistic life (Eckert 2000). She studied five vowels affected by the Northern Cities Chain Shift (see Figure 8.3), together with the (ay) diphthong as in PRICE, and one syntactic variable, negative concord (the multiple negative as in *he didn't say nothing about nobody*). Although many of the patterns Eckert found for the shifting vowels are not at all clear cut, the recent changes were more sharply distinguished. The backing of the (ʌ) vowel as in STRUT and (e) as in DRESS are spreading out into the suburbs from the urban centre of Detroit. Eckert could see little relationship between the teenagers' speech and their parents' social class.

Negative concord is the most socially salient and differentiated of the variables. Eckert classified her speakers on an index which rated their level of participation in school

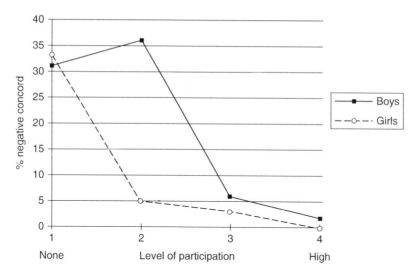

Figure 8.9 Negative concord usage at Belten High according to level of participation in school activities
Source: Eckert (2000), figure 6.91

activities such as sports, performances and student government. Figure 8.9 shows the relationship between school activities and the use of negative concord. Boys who take little or no part in activities (including the burnouts) have 31–36 per cent negative concord. Those with moderate to high participation (including the jocks) have just 2–6 per cent negative concord.

Gender is the other main crosscutting social dimension of Belten High, and this shows up in Figure 8.9. For girls, the boundary between high and low negative concord lies between nil and low activities participation, where for the boys it fell between low and moderate. The difference reflects the strong gendering of activities. Athletic performance is central to male jock accomplishment – these are the 'jock jocks' – but the girls have to content themselves with cheerleading. They must engineer their own popularity. There are different rules for girls and boys in the worlds of jocks and burnouts. Female jocks and burnouts practise mutual avoidance and disdain, while male jocks and burnouts will assert their masculinities against each other in physical competition. For girls 'purity' is central, for boys it is toughness. Therefore girls avoid the urban-associated linguistic variables like the STRUT and DRESS vowels, but it is the other, suburban-oriented variables that boys must be wary of.

The community of practice

Eckert's central tool for analysing this social world is the community of practice (CofP), a construct which she has championed into sociolinguistics. It comes from educational learning theory where it refers to a group whose engagement in a joint enterprise such as apprenticeship leads to a shared repertoire, for example in language. Everyone is involved simultaneously in a number of CofPs – family, choir, research group, sports team. Two aspects of the CofP are crucial:

Exercise 8.7
Researching networks, markets and communities

- Following up the references in these two sections and the further reading at the end of the chapter, summarize and compare the characteristics of social networks, linguistic markets and communities of practice. What are the similarities and differences of the approaches? What are the gaps?
- Apply one or more of the approaches to a group that you are either part of or know well. Different sections of the class could take one of the approaches each and then compare their findings. You could study your sociolinguistics class itself as a network, market or CofP.
- In your research, consider all the modes of communication that people are using. Eckert's fieldwork predated pervasive digital communications. What part do mobile phones and internet affordances play in making for continuous communication among group members now?
- Apply one or more of the three frameworks (markets, networks and communities of practice) to a social media site such as Facebook. How adequate are they in characterizing it, or is something more or different needed for the online situation?
- For all of the frameworks: what are the effects on language? Do different groups show different linguistic usages? Are any groups or individuals leading language changes?
- Re-assess the three frameworks in the light of your application of them. Which did you find the most productive and why? How would you modify or enhance it?

- The CofP focuses on **practice**, what its members do together and how they do it. All the activities, whether athletics or cruising to Detroit, form part of the CofP's defining practice.
- The CofP links the micro and the macro, the individual and social class. Its focus is on individuals and their agency, but ultimately there is a relationship with broader social structures. Categories such as class, Eckert argues, are the product of individuals' practices.

In the west generally, and the US in particular, adolescence marks the peak of social-symbolic activity – in clothing, appearance, adornment, consumption, food, cars, and talk. It is a period of 'flamboyant symbolization' (Eckert 2000: 29), a marketplace defined by the peer group as an alternative to the standard. Eckert diagrams the network ties and clusters among the students, and characterizes them as competing in opposing symbolic markets. Judy and her burned-out burnout cluster form an archetypal CofP. Their makeup and clothes are wilder than the 'ordinary' burnouts'. Their cluster leads all others on most linguistic variables, and Judy and her best friend Joyce lead the leaders. They make 'every single utterance stand out … they are linguistic icons' (p. 211). Their usage concentrates extreme phonetic tokens in focal words, particularly profanities: ultra-raising of the vowel in *damn* and ultra-backing in *fuck*, a blend of form with content. It is their usage that creates social and sociolinguistic meaning for the school (recall the Milroys' statement on women as definers rather than followers of sociolinguistic prestige, Exercise 8.5).

The CofP has now become the framework of choice in much sociolinguistics, especially gender language research. Studies have included Latina gangs (Mendoza-Denton 2008), nerd girls (Bucholtz 1999a) and Beijing yuppies (Zhang 2005). In the process, however, there has been some dilution of the original criteria, particularly of what constitutes a shared enterprise. To serve as a robust and perceptive construct, a CofP should arguably be about something more than just the creation of a group style (Meyerhoff and Strycharz 2013). The style is the outcome but not the goal of a CofP. The approach has much to offer sociolinguistic theory and practice, but is strongest when complemented by macro-level understandings, as it is in Eckert's own study. Its stress on individuals and their agency contrasts with the group correlations of traditional variation research (although note the echoes between Judy and Labov's Celeste S.). Here language is not a reflex but a resource, which the Judys of this world fashion with other symbols into distinctive styles. We return to style, agency and related matters in Chapter 11.

8.8   RESEARCH ACTIVITY
LANGUAGE CHANGE ON THE INTERNET

Conducting research into sound change at the scale and sophistication of most of the research described in this chapter requires time and skills beyond a student project. But there are other kinds of language change and other means to research them. This section suggests some ways to research language change using the internet, which affords access to many real-time print data archives, for example:

- newspapers go back over 200 years, many have been publishing for a century or more, and have digital archives
- other print media, such as magazines and academic journals
- public documents like governmental, educational or legal papers from different periods
- digitalized historical collections, for example of diaries or letters.

The electronic databases available through libraries will provide access to many of these. The limitations will be how much of a publication's archive is digitalized and how readily available it is. However, the greater problem is likely to be an excess of data. Do not collect too much! Limit your sample, e.g. five weekdays of a newspaper, or local news only.

Such materials mean you can investigate real-time change in lexical, morphological, syntactic or discoursal patterns as long as you can specify these adequately and practicably for computer search. Your analysis will involve steps such as:

- Defining precisely the form or structure you are targeting, for example the incidence of certain slang or taboo words in particular magazines, or auxiliary contractions (*it's*, *we've*) in government documents.
- Identifying any qualitative differences between earlier and later periods. Is there a new form? Or an old form that has disappeared? (recall Exercise 8.4 on news headlines).

- Quantifying relative differences between the periods. With forms for which you can specify a small set of alternatives that meet variationist criteria of 'meaning the same thing', you will be able to identify changes in the proportions of different forms used in different periods. With other forms for which this is not possible (like discourse features), you can count and compare the number of occurrences per 1,000 words, for example.

Different members of class could research the same linguistic forms in different text types and compare them, or conversely, different forms in the same text types. Or compare new digital genres with their traditional counterparts, for example print news and online news (see Bell and Smith 2012), or blogs with written diaries. Here are some specific sample projects.

Language change in the press

In the 1980s I researched changes in the language of the British newspaper the *Daily Mirror* through sampling it by the decade since 1920. I focused on the rule for deleting determiners in naming expressions of the form *(the) Prime Minister David Cameron*, which has long been characteristic of American news style but was new to British media. From zero in 1920, determiner deletion eased up to 10% in the *Mirror* by 1940, then rose sharply to 49% in 1960 and 80% by 1980.

- Consult Bell (1988) to see how I defined and analysed this variable, then, using an online archive, yourself extend the sample out to 1990, 2000 and 2010 to see how determiner deletion has progressed in the *Mirror* over recent decades, particularly whether it has gone to completion (100%).
- Analyse determiner deletion in your local newspaper, or any online English-language newspaper anywhere in the world. Or choose another feature, such as use of honorifics (*Ms*, *Mr*, etc.) or first names in referring to people in the news.

Sexist language

The use of the English generic masculine pronoun *he* to represent women as well as men was one of the early battlegrounds for gender-neutral language. But Robin Lakoff (see Chapter 6.7 earlier) doubted that attempting to change this pronoun usage would work, and she herself used a string of generic masculines to discuss it in her founding text of feminist linguistics (1975: 45):

> I think one should force oneself to be realistic: certain aspects of language are available to the native speakers' conscious analysis, and others are too common, too thoroughly mixed throughout the language, for the speaker to be aware each time he [sic] uses them ... My feeling is that this area of pronominal neutralization is both less in need of changing and less open to change.

So, how has this changed over the decades? I am sure that no one would be happier than Lakoff to have been proved wrong (see 2004: 103 for her own comments 30 years later). Pauwels (1998) discusses this and other sexist language issues.

1 Select, say, 1970 and 2010 in any text type (press, government speeches, etc.).
2 Computer search masculine pronouns and identify those that are generic, and/or …
3 search for words like *all, everyone* and *nobody* to see if they are taking a generic masculine pronoun, or what alternatives are being used in the two periods (e.g plural *they*).
4 Compare different text types.
5 If you find a shift, what does it say about the possibilities, limitations and motivations of conscious language change?

Celebrity accents across the lifespan

Recall the shift in the Queen's English described in Example 8.1.

1 Identify someone who was or has been in the public eye and ear for a long time such as a singer, film star or politician (Mick Jagger, Audrey Hepburn, Bill Clinton, …).
2 Locate clips of their speech across time, as far back as you can, and then at 5–10 year intervals, for example through YouTube. For entertainers, try to find spoken interviews rather than acted or sung performances.
3 Identify variables which you expect may have changed in their particular accent – for a British actor, perhaps vowel shifts similar to the Queen's, or salient changing consonants such as /t/ glottalization or /l/ vocalization.
4 Locate these in your subject's speech, code their pronunciations by ear, quantify them.
5 Are there differences across your person's lifespan? Of what kind? What conclusions could you draw about age grading and lifespan linguistic stability?

• Or conduct a similar comparison of successive generations of a celebrity family of actors or politicians or sportspeople – Redgraves, Fondas, Bushes, Kennedys. This makes a real-time study: what language changes can you trace in the generational differences in these families' speech?

8.9   SUMMARY

• Age, together with gender, is the most fundamental social factor structuring any study of language variation. Age is not controlled by chronological time, it has social, cultural and psychological dimensions. The concept of the lifespan recognizes identifiable, socially constructed age stages. In age graded speech, at any one time different age groups behave differently, but each generation repeats the same pattern as the previous one.
• To track language change, we use 'apparent time' – recording older and mid-age speakers as linguistic archives for their generations. But telling the difference with certainty between age grading and generational change requires real-time data.
• 'Trend' re-studies of the same population show that original apparent-time interpretations tend to be confirmed in real time. Apparent time assumes people continue to speak similarly throughout their adult lives. 'Panel' re-studies of the same speakers show that while a majority do remain stable, a large minority may still be changing.

- In the study of language change, phonology has been most researched, while quantitative research in syntax, morphology and discourse has been mainly confined to easily delimitable features. A qualitative case study shows that the language of news has changed markedly in the past century, with technological change helping promote changes in news language.
- Change in consonants often involves phonetic weakening or 'lenition'. The study of vowel change focuses on mergers, when two vowel phonemes come to occupy the same phonetic space, and chain shifts, when more than one adjacent vowel moves. Labov has focused on formulating principles for vowel changes, especially the 'Northern Cities Chain Shift' in the US.
- Speakers are aware of some changes but not others. Change from above the level of consciousness is also led 'from above' in society, but most changes are unconscious and come from the middle of the social hierarchy.
- Gender is the most significant factor in language change. Women lead in both conscious and unconscious changes, creating Labov's 'gender paradox', but the Milroys argue that it is women's usage that confers prestige on a change. Labov identifies the leaders of change as women who combine nonconformity with upward mobility, and have strong networks both in their neighbourhood and beyond.
- The linguistic market sees different language codes as commodities with different social values. Speakers are ranked by how important the standard language is to their occupation.
- The analysis of social networks maps personal or group relationships in order to understand behaviour. The Milroys found three working-class communities in Belfast were differentiated by their networks, which affected their participation in language change.
- Weak network ties carry change between groups, the Milroys conclude, while strong ties reinforce existing norms. Labov's term 'leader' covers two roles: the innovators, who are socially marginalized, and the early adopters, who are central and spread the change.
- Eckert's ethnography of Belten High in Detroit shows jocks and burnouts operating with conflicting ideologies, norms, practices and trajectories. There are different rules for girls ('purity') compared with boys (toughness).
- Jocks and burnouts function as communities of practice, in which members' engagement in a joint enterprise leads to a shared repertoire. The focus on practice – what members do together – links the micro with the macro, the individual and social class. Linguistic change is led by flamboyant style leaders who create sociolinguistic meaning through their extreme usages. The CofP is particularly used in gender language research.

8.10   Further reading

Offering divergent takes on language and age are Chambers (2009) and the Couplands' work, especially on language and the elderly. Eckert (1997) and Coupland (2001a) provide good (though not recent) overviews of language and age. The many studies of adolescent language include Labov (1972a), Eckert (2000) and Mendoza-Denton (2008).

For the concepts of real and apparent time, and studies of language change in real time, see Guy Bailey (especially Cukor-Avila and Bailey 2013) and Gillian Sankoff (especially 2006).

Cheshire (2005, 2007) and Pichler (2010) deal with issues in quantifying change in syntax and discourse. Tagliamonte (2012) majors on change in morphology, syntax and discourse, much of it from the author's own research. Content relevant to linguistic change is scattered through many of the chapters of the *Handbook of Language Variation and Change* (Chambers and Schilling 2013). Matthew Gordon (2013) provides good coverage of mergers and chain shifts, see also Kerswill (2011) more generally on sound change, and chapters in Tagliamonte (2012). Very many articles in *Language Variation and Change* journal present original research on a great range of sound changes.

Labov's three volumes on *Principles of Linguistic Change* (1994, 2001a, 2010) are his magnum opus and the bible of research on linguistic change. They total 1,700 pages, with hundreds of tables and figures, and form a formidable compendium of information, generalization and theorization. They bring together much of his work on American English, plus data from dozens of other studies from many languages. The first volume covers 'internal factors', the second 'social', and the third 'cognitive and cultural factors' (although the division is necessarily not at all clean). Half of volume 1 (1994) focuses on mergers and chain shifts. Volume 2 (2001a) deals largely with the 1970s studies in Philadelphia: the final chapter provides a good roundup of the 'social factors' as a whole.

Cheshire (2002) is an excellent overview of gender and language change, see also Schilling (2011). Labov's take is found especially in his volume 2 (2001a). Classic articles include Trudgill (1972), Eckert (1989), Labov (1990).

For the linguistic market, see Bourdieu (1991), Dodsworth (2011) and Eckert (2000). Networks are the central concept throughout the Milroys' work, see especially Lesley Milroy's book (1987). Also note a (reserved) overview by Vetter (2011).

Eckert and McConnell-Ginet (1992) was the article that introduced the community of practice to sociolinguistics, although Cheshire (1982) pioneered similar methods. As well as Eckert's book (2000), see the 1999 theme issue of *Language in Society* (28/2) edited by Janet Holmes. The *Journal of Sociolinguistics* 9/4 2005 published an exchange between Eckert, Davies and others. Meyerhoff and Strycharz (2013) offer a critical overview. Several articles in the Mesthrie, and Wodak, Johnstone and Kerswill readers (both 2011) deal with the CofP concept from different viewpoints.

On researching media language, see my articles in the references, especially the text *The Language of News Media*: being pre-internet, it is dated in relation to media technologies, but much of the framework and analysis remains useful. Cotter (2010) is the best recent text, also several articles. On internet language, apart from Crystal (2006) and his other publications, the leading sources are several edited collections: Danet and Herring (2007), Thurlow and Mroczek (2011), Baron (2008) and Androutsopoulos (2006).

REFERENCES

Androutsopoulos, Jannis (ed.), 2006. 'Sociolinguistics and computer-mediated communication'. Theme issue of *Journal of Sociolinguistics* 10/4.

Ashby, William J., 1981. 'The loss of the negative particle *ne* in French: a syntactic change in progress'. *Language* 57: 674–87.

Barbieri, Federica, 2008. 'Patterns of age-based linguistic variation in American English'. *Journal of Sociolinguistics* 12: 58–88.

Baron, Naomi S., 2008. *Always On: Language in an Online and Mobile World*. New York: Oxford University Press.

Bayley, Robert, Ceil Lucas and Mary Rose, 2000. 'Variation in American Sign Language: the case of DEAF'. *Journal of Sociolinguistics* 4: 81–107.

Bell, Allan, 1988. 'The British base and the American connection in New Zealand media English'. *American Speech* 63: 326–44.

Bell, Allan, 1995. 'News time'. *Time & Society* 4: 305–28.

Bell, Allan, 2003. 'A century of news discourse'. *International Journal of English Studies* 3: 189–208.

Bell, Allan and Janet Holmes, 1992. '"H-droppin": Two sociolinguistic variables in New Zealand English'. *Australian Journal of Linguistics* 12: 223–49.

Biber, Douglas, Susan Conrad and Randi Reppen, 1998. *Corpus Linguistics: Investigating Language Structure and Use*. Cambridge: Cambridge University Press.

Blake, Renée and Meredith Josey, 2003. 'The /ay/ diphthong in a Martha's Vineyard community: what can we say 40 years after Labov?'. *Language in Society* 32: 451–85.

Bourdieu, Pierre, 1991. *Language and Symbolic Power*. Cambridge, UK: Polity Press.

Bucholtz, Mary, 1999. '"Why be normal?" Language and identity practices in a community of nerd girls'. *Language in Society* 28: 203–23.

Chambers, J.K., 1992. 'Dialect acquisition'. *Language* 68: 673–705.

Chambers, J.K., 2009. *Sociolinguistic Theory: Linguistic Variation and its Social Significance* (revised edn). Malden, MA: Wiley-Blackwell.

Chambers, J.K. and Natalie Schilling (eds), 2013. *The Handbook of Language Variation and Change* (2nd edn). Oxford, UK: Wiley-Blackwell.

Cheshire, Jenny, 1982. *Variation in an English Dialect: A Sociolinguistic Study*. Cambridge: Cambridge University Press.

Cheshire, Jenny, 2002. 'Sex and gender in variationist research'. In J.K. Chambers, Peter Trudgill and Natalie Schilling-Estes (eds), *The Handbook of Language Variation and Change*. Malden, MA: Blackwell Publishing. 423–43.

Cheshire, Jenny, 2005. 'Syntactic variation and beyond: gender and social class variation in the use of discourse-new markers'. *Journal of Sociolinguistics* 9: 479–508.

Cheshire, Jenny, 2007. 'Discourse variation, grammaticalisation and stuff like that'. *Journal of Sociolinguistics* 11: 155–93.

Cotter, Colleen, 2010. *News Talk: Investigating the Language of Journalism*. Cambridge: Cambridge University Press.

Coupland, Nikolas, 2001. 'Age in social and sociolinguistic theory'. In Nikolas Coupland, Srikant Sarangi and Christopher N. Candlin (eds), *Sociolinguistics and Social Theory*. Harlow, UK: Pearson Education. 185–211.

Coupland, Nikolas, Justine Coupland and Howard Giles, 1991. *Language, Society and the Elderly: Discourse, Identity and Ageing*. Oxford: Basil Blackwell.

Crystal, David 2006. *Language and the Internet* (2nd edn). Cambridge: Cambridge University Press.

Cukor-Avila, Patricia and Guy Bailey, 2013. 'Real time and apparent time'. In J.K. Chambers and Natalie Schilling (eds), *The Handbook of Language Variation and Change* (2nd edn). Oxford, UK: Wiley-Blackwell. 239–62.

Danet, Brenda and Susan C. Herring (eds), 2007. *The Multilingual Internet: Language, Culture, and Communication Online*. New York: Oxford University Press.

Dodsworth, Robin, 2011. 'Social class'. In Ruth Wodak, Barbara Johnstone and Paul Kerswill (eds), *The Sage Handbook of Sociolinguistics*. London: Sage. 192–207.

Dubois, Sylvie and Barbara Horvath, 1999. 'When the music changes, you change too: gender and language change in Cajun English'. *Language Variation and Change* 11: 287–313.

Eckert, Penelope, 1989. 'The whole woman: sex and gender differences in variation'. *Language Variation and Change* 1: 245–67.

Eckert, Penelope, 1997. 'Age as a sociolinguistic variable'. In Florian Coulmas (ed.), *The Handbook of Sociolinguistics*. Oxford, UK: Blackwell Publishers. 151–67.

Eckert, Penelope, 2000. *Linguistic Variation as Social Practice: The Linguistic Construction of Identity in Belten High*. Malden, MA: Blackwell Publishers.

Eckert, Penelope and Sally McConnell-Ginet, 1992. 'Think practically and look locally: language and gender as community-based practice'. *Annual Review of Anthropology* 21: 461–90.

Giddens, Anthony, 2009. *Sociology* (6th edn). Cambridge, UK: Polity Press.

Gordon, Matthew J., 2001. *Small-town Values and Big-city Vowels: A Study of the Northern Cities Shift in Michigan*. Durham, NC: American Dialect Society/Duke University Press.

Gordon, Matthew J., 2013. 'Investigating chain shifts and mergers'. In J.K. Chambers and Natalie Schilling (eds), *The Handbook of Language Variation and Change* (2nd edn.). Oxford, UK: Wiley-Blackwell. 203–19.

Gumperz, John J., 1982a. *Discourse Strategies*. Cambridge: Cambridge University Press.

Haeri, Niloofar, 1997. *The Sociolinguistic Market of Cairo: Gender, Class, and Education*. London: Kegan Paul International.

Harrington, Jonathan, Sallyanne Palethorpe and Catherine I. Watson, 2000. 'Does the Queen speak the Queen's English?' *Nature* 408: 927–8.

Holmes, Janet (ed.), 1999. 'Communities of practice in language and gender research'. Theme issue of *Language in Society* 28/2.

Kerswill, Paul, 2011. 'Sociolinguistic approaches to language change: phonology'. In Ruth Wodak, Barbara Johnstone and Paul Kerswill (eds), *The Sage Handbook of Sociolinguistics*. London: Sage. 219–35.

Labov, William, 1972a. *Language in the Inner City: Studies in the Black English Vernacular*. Philadelphia, PA: University of Pennsylvania Press.

Labov, William, 1972b. *Sociolinguistic Patterns*. Philadelphia, PA: University of Pennsylvania Press.

Labov, William, 1990. 'The intersection of sex and social class in the course of linguistic change'. *Language Variation and Change* 2: 205–54.

Labov, William, 1994. *Principles of Linguistic Change*, vol. 1: *Internal Factors*. Cambridge, MA: Blackwell Publishers.

Labov, William, 2001a. *Principles of Linguistic Change*, vol. 2: *Social Factors*. Malden, MA: Blackwell Publishers.

Labov, William, 2010. *Principles of Linguistic Change*, vol. 3: *Cognitive and Cultural Factors*. Malden, MA: Wiley-Blackwell.

Lakoff, Robin, 1975. *Language and Woman's Place*. New York: Harper & Row.

Lakoff, Robin Tolmach, 2004. *Language and Woman's Place: Text and Commentaries* (revised and expanded edn, ed. Mary Bucholtz). Oxford: Oxford University Press.

Lucas, Ceil (ed.), 2001. *The Sociolinguistics of Sign Languages*. Cambridge: Cambridge University Press.

Macaulay, R.K.S., 1977. *Language, Social Class, and Education: A Glasgow Study*. Edinburgh: Edinburgh University Press.

Martineau, France and Raymond Mougeon, 2003. 'A sociolinguistic study of the origins of *ne* deletion in European and Quebec French'. *Language* 79: 118–52.

Mendoza-Denton, Norma, 2008. *Homegirls: Language and Cultural Practice among Latina Youth Gangs*. Malden, MA: Blackwell.

Mesthrie, Rajend (ed.), 2011. *The Cambridge Handbook of Sociolinguistics*. Cambridge: Cambridge University Press.

Meyerhoff, Miriam and Anna Strycharz, 2013. 'Communities of Practice'. In J.K. Chambers and Natalie Schilling (eds), *The Handbook of Language Variation and Change* (2nd edn). Oxford, UK: Wiley-Blackwell. 428–47.

Milroy, James and Lesley Milroy, 1985. 'Linguistic change, social network and speaker innovation'. *Journal of Linguistics* 21: 339–84.

Milroy, James, Lesley Milroy, Sue Hartley and David Walshaw, 1994. 'Glottal stops and Tyneside glottalization: competing patterns of variation and change in British English'. *Language Variation and Change* 6: 327–57.

Milroy, Lesley 1987. *Language and Social Networks* (2nd edn). Oxford, UK: Basil Blackwell.

Milroy, Lesley and Carmen Llamas, 2013. 'Social networks'. In J.K. Chambers and Natalie Schilling (eds), *The Handbook of Language Variation and Change* (2nd edn). Oxford, UK: Wiley-Blackwell. 409–27.

Milroy, Lesley and James Milroy, 1992. 'Social network and social class: toward an integrated socio-linguistic model'. *Language in Society* 21: 1–26.

Pauwels, Anne, 1998. *Women Changing Language*. London: Longman.

Pichler, Heike, 2010. 'Methods in discourse variation analysis: reflections on the way forward'. *Journal of Sociolinguistics* 14: 581–608.

Pope, Jennifer, Miriam Meyerhoff and D. Robert Ladd, 2007. 'Forty years of language change on Martha's Vineyard'. *Language* 83: 615–27.

Precht, Kristen, 2008. 'Sex similarities and differences in stance in informal American conversation'. *Journal of Sociolinguistics* 12: 89–111.

Preston, Dennis R. and Nancy Niedzielski (eds), 2010. *A Reader in Sociophonetics*. New York: De Gruyter Mouton.

Sankoff, David and Suzanne Laberge, 1978. 'The linguistic market and the statistical explanation of variability'. In David Sankoff (ed.), *Linguistic Variation: Models and Methods*. New York: Academic Press. 239–50.

Sankoff, Gillian, 2006. 'Age: apparent time and real time'. In Keith Brown (ed.), *Encyclopedia of Language and Linguistics* (2nd edn), vol. 1. Oxford, UK: Elsevier. 110–16.

Sankoff, Gillian and Hélène Blondeau, 2007. 'Language change across the lifespan: /r/ in Montreal French'. *Language* 83: 560–88.

Tagliamonte, Sali A., 2012. *Variationist Sociolinguistics: Change, Observation, Interpretation*. Malden, MA: Wiley-Blackwell.

Thurlow, Crispin and Kristine Mroczek (eds), 2011. *Digital Discourse: Language in the New Media*. New York: Oxford University Press.

Trudgill, Peter, 1972. 'Sex, covert prestige and linguistic change'. *Language in Society* 1: 179–96.

Vetter, Eva, 2011. 'Social network'. In Ruth Wodak, Barbara Johnstone and Paul Kerswill (eds), *The Sage Handbook of Sociolinguistics*. London: Sage. 208–18.

Wagner, Suzanne Evans and Gillian Sankoff, 2011. 'Age grading in the Montréal French inflected future'. *Language Variation and Change* 23: 275–313.

Weinreich, Uriel, William Labov and Marvin I. Herzog, 1968. 'Empirical foundations for a theory of language change'. In W.P. Lehmann and Yakov Malkiel (eds), *Directions for Historical Linguistics: A Symposium*. Austin, TX: Texas University Press. 95–188.

Wodak, Ruth, Barbara Johnstone and Paul Kerswill (eds), 2011. *The Sage Handbook of Sociolinguistics*. London: Sage.

Wolfram, Walt and Natalie Schilling-Estes, 2006. *American English: Dialects and Variation* (2nd edn). Malden, MA: Blackwell Publishing.

Zhang, Qing, 2005. 'A Chinese yuppie in Beijing: phonological variation and the construction of a new professional identity'. *Language in Society* 34: 431–66.

9

LANGUAGE IN SPACE

In this chapter we look at the relationship between space, place and language, including the role of space in language change. As well as covering the geographical variation of microlinguistic variables, we will touch on the space dimension of macro-level language data, both multilingual and discoursal. Consider first how central 'place' has been to many of the studies presented in earlier chapters, not just as an identifying label but frequently at the heart of the sociolinguistic issues involved:

- the province of Québec and French language maintenance in North America (Chapter 2)
- Māori as the distinctive language of Aotearoa/New Zealand (Chapter 3)
- the geographical and social peripherality of Gaelic in Scotland (Chapter 4)
- the German–Hungarian mix in the border town of Oberwart, Austria (Chapter 5)
- youth Portuguese in the mega-city of Rio de Janiero, Brazil (Chapter 6)
- the Englishes of New York City, Cajun Louisiana and Sydney (Chapter 7)
- the contrasting jock/burnout uses of both urban and vowel space in Detroit, USA (Chapter 8).

9.1   DIALECTOLOGY

The only time a sociolinguist uses the term 'dialect' unreservedly tends to be when referring to geographically defined varieties. Dialect geography was a creation of nineteenth-century Europe and focused on mapping the distinctive forms of traditional rural dialects. The major work began in 1876 when Georg Wenker started to

The Guidebook to Sociolinguistics, First Edition. Allan Bell.
© 2014 Allan Bell. Published 2014 by Blackwell Publishing Ltd.

mail out questionnaires to German schoolmasters, asking them to write down local dialect versions of 40 sample sentences like:

> Der gute alte Mann ist mit dem Pferde durchs Eis gebrochen und in das kalte
> Wasser gefallen.
> 'The good old man broke through the ice with the horse and fell into the cold water.'

Over the next 20 years nearly 50,000 questionnaires were returned from all over Germany to Wenker and his associates, and the results were transcribed onto maps. But the success of the data collection led directly to a broader failure: there was just far too much information to handle and display (2 million sentences!). The initial volume of the *Deutscher Sprachatlas* appeared 50 years after the project started. However, the second founding project, which began in neighbouring France in 1896, used a different method that was much more immediately productive. Jules Gilliéron created a 1,500-item questionnaire and trained a single fieldworker in phonetic transcription. Edmond Edmont then spent the last five years of the nineteenth century cycling round rural France and conducting 700 interviews. Gilliéron's team marshalled their data and completed publication in 13 volumes by 1910.

The French project provided the model for surveys of English. Work began on the *Linguistic Atlas of the United States and Canada* in the 1930s. Publication followed from the 1940s with the linguistic atlas of New England, and other eastern, southern and midwestern regions over the next 50 years. In England, the Survey of English Dialects began in mid-century and published its data in the following decades.

Dialect maps

The outcome of this kind of research is a set of maps displaying lines which show boundaries between areas where alternative forms are used. When several such **isoglosses** fall more or less together, they form a 'bundle' and are taken to mark a dialect boundary. They often but not always reflect geographical barriers (such as rivers or mountains) or social, political or cultural differences.

Figure 9.1 is one of the best-known of dialect maps. It displays the main boundaries within the German–Dutch language continuum, running east–west across northern Europe. These show little coincidence with the borders of nations or of named 'languages': they do not differentiate Flemish and Dutch linguistically from Low German (recall the discussion in Chapter 1 of what makes a dialect or a language). The map distinguishes Low, Middle and High German, and subdivisions of Middle German. Because of the visual appearance of the western dialect boundaries along the river Rhine, this pattern is called the 'Rhenish fan'. As we found for ethnic varieties in Chapter 7, adjacent geographical dialects are usually distinguished by gradient rather than absolute differences.

Time and space are intimately connected in language variation, with geographical difference in language routinely yoked to chronological difference, as we saw in the previous chapter. The geographical–linguistic differences in Figure 9.1 reflect the spread through time of a change in the pronunciation of these consonants that began in the south of the High German region some 1,500 years ago. It spread into the Middle region, with

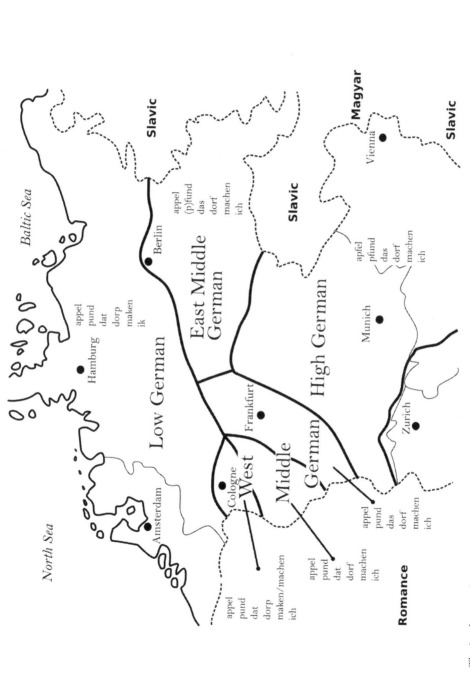

North Sea

Baltic Sea

Slavic

Magyar

Slavic

Hamburg
appel
pund
dat
dorp
maken
ik

Berlin

Vienna

appel
(p)fund
das
dorf
machen
ich

East Middle German

Low German

Amsterdam

appel
pund
dat
dorp
maken/machen
ich

Frankfurt

Cologne

West Middle German

appel
pund
dat
dorf
machen
ich

High German

Slavic

Munich

apfel
pfund
das
dorf
machen
ich

Zurich

appel
pund
das
dorf
machen
ich

Romance

ure 9.1   The isoglosses of Low and High German

ich/machen/dorf/das type pronunciations moving northwards and displacing *ik/maken/ dorp/dat*. The co-existence of different pronunciations in the same dialect area, and the differential change of different words, challenged prevailing theories that sound change worked mechanically and without exceptions. In fact, change is not necessarily uniform, but rather different words may shift at different times. A classic case of such **lexical diffusion** is the split of short /a/ in much American English, so that in Philadelphia the vowel in *bad* is raised but *dad* is not. Labov's conclusion (a quarter of his 1994 book is devoted to the matter) is that both kinds of case occur: change proceeds either regularly or word by word.

A new dialectology

For sociolinguists, dialect surveys have provided valuable real-time benchmarks against which they can judiciously calibrate contemporary findings (for example,

---

Exercise 9.1   Interpreting the Rhenish Fan

Figure 9.1 shows the geographical distribution of different pronunciations of six Germanic words – or rather, the phonological variables exemplified by these words. Each has two kinds of variants:

ik	[k]	ich	[ç]	'I'
maken	[k]	machen	[x]	'make/do'
dorp	[p]	dorf	[f]	'village'
dat	[t]	das	[s]	'that/the'
appel	[p]	apfel	[pf]	'apple'
pund	[p]	(p)fund	[(p)f]	'pound'

The left two columns represent what is now standard Dutch, and the middle columns are standard German.

1 First look at the phonetics of the variables and describe what the main single difference in articulation is between the left and middle columns.
2 Then use this contrast to describe the difference between Low German at the top of the map and High German at the bottom: which and how many of the two articulations do you find in each area?
3 Look at Middle German: list and count the different articulations in the Eastern dialect. Is it more similar to Low or High German?
4 List and count the different articulations in the three branches of West Middle German – the Rhenish Fan. What differs from one dialect to the next? Compare that with Low and High German.
5 Now generalize about the geographical distribution that your findings on 2–4 show, and sum up the pattern across all the dialects.
6 What does the geographical distribution tell us about the historical spread of this sound change?
7 What exactly is the sound change?

Labov in New York and Trudgill in Norwich). But traditional dialectology had considerable problems:

- The amount of data usually outstripped its collectors' ability to handle it. Surveys always sagged under the weight of their own data, and by the mid twentieth century the field had ground to a halt.
- Isoglosses on a map implied clear-cut boundaries between different forms and therefore distinct dialects, but in reality they were often transition zones with a mixture of forms being used (as in parts of Figure 9.1).
- Dialectologists looked for people they regarded as the most authentic speakers of traditional dialects, since dubbed the 'NORMs': Non-mobile Older Rural Males. This kind of sampling did not represent the range of variation across a community.
- There was wide scope for variation and inaccuracy between fieldworkers, who had to make on-the-spot phonetic transcriptions of pronunciations.

In principle, the first and last of these have been solved by technological advances. The advent of portable audio recording technology made fieldworker transcriptions obsolete. And in the late twentieth century, computerization at last overcame the data overload issue and enabled customized analysis and display.

Chambers and Trudgill's textbook *Dialectology* (1998), first published in 1980, laid the foundation for a new approach, informed by the methods and findings of urban sociolinguistics as well as by traditional dialect geography. They re-analysed and re-presented a great deal of existing dialect data, particularly from Europe, including demonstrating the gradience of major traditional boundaries. The dialects of northern and southern England, for example, are divided not by a sharp line but by a wide transition zone across the middle of the country which ends in the east at The Wash on the North Sea (Figure 9.2).

David Britain's research in his native Fens (e.g. 2010, 2013a) shows how the area is a transition zone linguistically – as well as physically, historically, socially and psychologically. What was originally a physical obstacle to east–west communication in this part of England – a near-impassable marshland – remains a functioning barrier to this day. Drainage began in the seventeenth century, but was not completed till the early twentieth century, and the area remains quite sparsely populated. Administratively, it is split across four counties, with one foot on each side of the English north/south cultural divide. Transport links focus the west further west and the east further east, with little mobility between. Students in the transition zone have to travel away from the border in opposite directions to reach their schools. Both sides hold negative stereotypes of people who live on the other side. There is even a blood group distribution boundary running through here.

Unsurprisingly, this is also the site of a cluster of linguistic boundaries and transitions. The map shows one of these: the gradual transition for pronunciation of the STRUT vowel from [ʊ] in the northwest (scored as '5'), via the 'inter-dialect' [ɤ] form (scored 3) to [ʌ] on the east and south (scored 1). In the figure, the actual extremes are 4.5 to 1.5, with intermediate forms 0.5 apart. The linguistic transition zone coincides with and reinforces the other barriers.

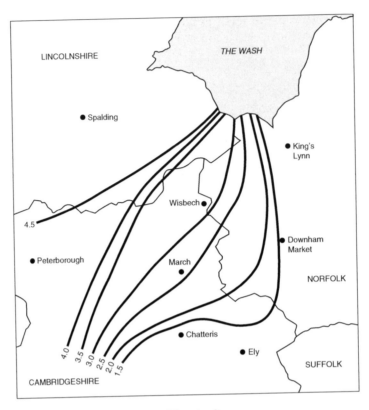

Figure 9.2   Dialect transition in the Fens of East Anglia
Source: Britain (2013a), figure 22.4

9.2   MAKING SPACE

Space is not just a physical thing, it is also social and psychological. Britain identifies three ways in which human geography has looked at space (2010: 72):

- physical, geometric, measurable. How far is it from Paris to Berlin?
- social: space as mediated and manipulated by humans, constructed, organized, institutionalized. A day's driving, or an hour's flying?
- psychological: how we perceive and interpret physical and social spaces. How do we react to the intervening country and cityscapes, and to the difference between France and Germany?

These dimensions configure 'spatiality'. Geographical regions may be boundaried by physical features – oceans, mountains, deserts – but they also reflect the response and imprint of the humans who inhabit them, including linguistically. Spaces are politically organized, divided into nations, which may impose distinguishing labels on linguistically similar entities – Norwegian versus Danish. Space is also constructed perceptually as well as physically and socially. Both inhabitants and outsiders may be aware of what makes an area and its people distinctive. Often these perceptions are called up by geographically based labels – Valley girls, Newfies, Westies – and have a sociolinguistic component or focus.

- As an exercise, google the meaning of the three terms just mentioned – and list other such labels you know.

Routines and interactions

One of the main ways people relate to space is through everyday routines which follow repeated geographical patterns – for the western middle class, perhaps daily commuting to work, weekly trips to the supermarket, monthly visits to the hairdresser, and annual holidays to a sunny place. Such routinization is an essential part of the constitution of individual lives and of society (Giddens 1984). We groove paths through the places that surround us. Bundled across hundreds, thousands or millions of people, such paths define the shape of the regions we live in. They also produce our repeated everyday interactions with workmates, shop assistants or sports club members. Talk is central to these encounters, which provide much of the stuff of what sociolinguists study – both Goffman's interaction order and Gumperz's interactional sociolinguistics (Chapter 6) have a basically spatial aspect. The everyday routinization of life is also a key component of social networks and especially communities of practice (Chapter 8).

Different social groups may have different geographies of the same region (Britain 2010). The ethnic, gender and class differences which we discussed in Chapter 7 often have a spatial reflex. Women may be more restricted in moving through an urban area than men (or vice versa in 1970s Belfast). In highly stratified and segregated inner cities in the United States, people avoid crossing boundaries to where other classes and races live, and this has linguistic repercussions (recall Labov's hypothesis of diverging black/white vernaculars, Chapter 7.4). As Britain reports (2013b), proximity need not equal contact: a housing estate was built alongside a prosperous town in the north of England. The two communities live separate lives cheek by jowl, but their ING productions are polar opposites – under 10% non-standard *in* for the prosperous, over 90% for the estate dwellers. However, at secondary school age, they share the same school, and for just this age cohort, the ING gap diminishes. The prosperous climb to 30% *in*, and the estate dwellers drop to 85%.

Rural and urban

Traditional dialectology was essentially rural, as was Labov's first major study – vowel change on Martha's Vineyard (see Exercise 8.3), using 1930s dialect atlas data as a baseline. Isolation of rural areas by water or mountains often means that a place

Exercise 9.2   The geolinguistics of your area

1   Consider the geographical divides in your country, region or city. To what extent are they physical? – created by natural barriers such as a river.
2   What are the main routines of contact and travel within and between different areas? What sort of interactions do these promote?
3   How do social patterns relate to the physical boundaries? Do they tend to follow them or cut across them? Why? Do different subgroups – ethnicities, classes, ages, genders – have their own different geographies?
4   Do the social differences produce psychological boundaries? Do people view themselves and their area as distinct? And other areas as different?
5   How is this reflected in language? Different words or pronunciations? Different languages, even?
6   And do language differences function actively to construct or reproduce the sociocultural differences?
7   Are there known linguistic stereotypes associated with different areas?

maintains a distinctive dialect, which typically preserves some linguistic forms that are no longer used elsewhere. The dialects of isolated communities in the southeastern United States have been researched since the 1990s by Walt Wolfram and his associates – see Example 9.1. After Labov's New York City work, however, most of the burgeoning research on language variation focused resolutely on cities, and especially urban social change. Immigration from rural areas, and intra-city population movements triggered by development or gentrification, had effects on local urban vernaculars. When Becker (2009) re-studied the Lower East Side of New York four decades after Labov, she found a socially very different area, but long-term locals showed continued and strategic avoidance of postvocalic /r/ to construct their identification with this place.

Linguistic landscape

A linguistically quite different approach to urban language is through the study of the linguistic landscape. This is the language that we see all around as we move through a place – street names, shopfronts, billboards, graffiti. Linguistic landscape research has focused on multilingual urban areas where the choice of language for public display both symbolizes and constructs the relative standing of languages in the local repertoire.

The first study, by Landry and Bourhis (1997), researched the contribution of linguistic landscape to the ethnolinguistic vitality (Chapter 2) of French in Canada. Often there proves to be a difference between public and private signage, with the choices of public authorities reflecting official language policies while shop signs and graffiti use a language that will reach passers-by. Globalization is commonly at issue, especially the presence of English in countries such as Thailand or Japan (Gorter 2006). The language choices are themselves part of the construction of public space, interacting with the visual

Example 9.1

The sociolinguistics of isolation

North Americans find the English of Ocracoke different from anything they have ever heard on the mainland. The island is one of the Outer Banks of North Carolina, a chain of low sandbanks about 20 miles (30 km) out in the Atlantic Ocean from the mainland coast. The *O'cockers* came here in the eighteenth century largely from Ireland and the southwest of England, and until recently had been quite cut off from the rest of the United States.

The iconic feature of the Ocracoke 'brogue' (Wolfram and Schilling-Estes 1995, 1997) is the pronunciation of words like PRICE with a raised and backed diphthong that gives the islanders their nickname of 'Hoi Toiders'. This traditional pronunciation is strongest among a close-knit group of middle-aged men – the 'poker players'. One of them, Rex O'Neal, performs a particular saying to display the dialect:

High tide on the sound side, last night the water fire, tonight the moon shine. No fish. What do you suppose the matter, Uncle Woods?

sound side	on the Pamlico Sound, the western side of the island facing the mainland
water fire	phosphorus shining in the water, making the fishing bad
moon shine	the moon shining on the water
Uncle Woods	probably an ancestor of the narrator

The passage concentrates several tokens of the salient PRICE vowel, as well as other Ocracoke features. Natalie Schilling-Estes' analysis of Rex's performances (1998) shows that he exaggerates his PRICE pronunciation in order to display the dialect at its most distinctive. See section 9.5 for the reason.

appearance of the signs to form what Jaworski and Thurlow call the 'semiotic landscape' (2010). This chapter's research activity (9.7) is a linguistic landscape project.

Before the fall of the Wall in 1990, Prenzlauer Berg was a rundown neighbourhood in East Berlin, home to students, squatters and dissidents. In reunified Berlin the once-bleak area was quickly gentrified, rents soared, and poorer residents were displaced. Within a year of reunification the shopfronts with their plain, descriptive signage such as *Fleischerei* 'Butcher' were giving way to cafes, galleries and boutiques. English appeared, including an eccentrically named women's clothing shop, *No socks, no panties*.

Uta Papen (2012) studied the linguistic landscape of Prenzlauer Berg, photographing signs and graffiti and interviewing shop owners. The area is now dominated by often colourful commercial signage, but graffiti show that the space is contested between old and new residents. *Wir bleiben alle* 'we are all staying' has been on the walls as a slogan of resistance to gentrification for 20 years. Tags such as *Schwabe raus* 'Swabian out' (in Figure 9.3) are directed at a perceived influx of immigrants from southwest Germany.

Figure 9.3   The linguistic landscape of Berlin
Source: Papen (2012), figure 5

It appears (with the tagger's initials) at the entrance to an 'asian deli', whose own signage combines English and French to offer 'Pan Asian cuisine'.

Changes in public space are reflected and embodied in changes in the linguistic landscape. Inner-city gentrification has become a common urban process, although Berlin's destruction, partition and reunification have given it a unique and drastic recent history. The graphic environment of signs, graffiti and street art shape the character of the neighbourhood, and are now advertised as part of Berlin's attraction, commodified for visitors' consumption.

9.3   DIALECT CONTACT

The previous chapter dealt with change as it occurs within speech communities. This section turns to contacts between dialects and examines how linguistic changes result from human movement between communities. This is the geographical dimension of linguistic change or, put conversely, the historical or temporal dimension of language location. Like language contact (Chapter 3), dialect contact is largely the result of mobility. And just as the most radical results of contact between languages are the death of an existing language or birth of a new one (Chapter 4), so the two most extreme outcomes of dialect contact may be the death or birth of a dialect.

Mobility

Both traditional dialectology and variationist methodology chose informants for their immobility, assuming that this represented lack of contamination by outside linguistic influences. Speakers who came into an area after childhood have usually been excluded from sociolinguistic samples. There is evidence behind this: children immigrating to Philadelphia up to the age of 8 may sound like Philadelphians, but only local children whose parents were also locally born and raised proved to have learnt the fine local conditioning for pronunciation of the /æ/ vowel (Payne 1980). But with mobility increasingly the norm rather than the exception, speakers keep on moving from country to town, from city to city, between regions and between nations. Processes such as gentrification and suburbanization change spaces and regions, and the speakers and speech within them. Sociolinguists are now targeting the mobile and their language.

Mobility has also become central to much social theorizing (e.g. Urry 2007), with interaction as its main feature. In the past, mobility often meant a complete break from home, a one-way and permanent movement to a distant place. But the twenty-first-century emigrant may move regularly back and forth between the new and the old country. This is a different kind of mobility, itself routinized into the patterns of life rather than a one-off event – see Thurlow and Jaworski's notion of 'banal globalization' (2010). And it may have different linguistic outcomes.

Extreme mobility and interchange are both an outcome of and a trigger for globalization, that broad stream of developments that have increasingly impacted on all peoples

Exercise 9.3   Dialect mobility in your area

It sometimes seems as if all the world is on the move ... the early retired, international students, terrorists, members of diasporas, holidaymakers, business people, slaves, sports stars, asylum seekers, refugees, backpackers, commuters, young mobile professionals, prostitutes ... The scale of this travelling is immense. (Urry 2007: 3)

1 Who are the mobile? Does mobility affect all nations, regions, and sectors of society equally?
2 Consider the patterns of mobility in and out of your area or country. How much daily commuting occurs? Or other regular movements on longer time cycles such as holidays? Do these movements bring different languages or dialects into contact?
3 Has there been large-scale relocation into or out of the region? What languages or dialects did that bring into contact? With what effects?
4 What non-local or non-native accents of your language do you hear in your area? What sort of people are the speakers? (see for example Urry's list above).
5 Consider one or more of these groups in depth, such as backpackers or business people: do they interact much with locals? In what situations? Does one party ever have difficulty understanding the other?
6 Is one dialect influencing another? For example, are international students with non-native accents adopting local features?
7 Consider the same kinds of issues for outward mobility by locals.

Exercise 9.4   Language and globalization

Look at Coupland (2010) for a wide range of studies and views on language and globalization, covering multilingualism, world languages, global discourses, genres, markets and identities. The internet is one of the core vectors of globalization, and this exercise draws on its affordance of access to widely dispersed language data. Three possible studies are listed here, but you could also devise your own cross-national sample.

- Find online advertisements from different languages or dialects throughout the world for the same or similar products such as cars (e.g. makes like Ford, BMW, Jaguar) or appliances (De'Longhi, Braun, Maytag), or for consumer brands like Nike, Louis Vuitton and Gucci.
- Locate the same or similar news stories as published in online newspapers from different countries, whether in the same or different languages.
- Use online video of television presenters from different regions or nations to compare accents of English or of another world language such as Spanish, Portuguese, French, Arabic or Chinese.

In each case, analyse and compare features of the language and/or discourse in the materials you gather. Identify similarities and differences among them according to product, genre, language, stance, etc. Try to account for the differences – and the similarities. What do these tell you about global and local characteristics of these genres? And about the globalization and localization of language?

since the late twentieth century. The sociolinguistics of globalization has become a major and diverse area of sociolinguistic research which is producing overviews and handbooks of its own (e.g. Blommaert 2010; Coupland 2010). Studies range over the gamut of language phenomena from the worldwide diffusion of specific linguistic features such as the quotative phrase *be like* (e.g. Buchstaller and D'Arcy 2009), to public discourses of globalism (Fairclough 2006), to the international role of English in Korea and its diaspora (Lo and Park 2012). See Exercise 9.4.

Diffusing language change

Mobile speakers spread linguistic changes. **Expansion** diffusion puts individual speakers of one dialect in regular contact with speakers of another, for example through daily commuting. Changes pass from one speaker who has adopted an innovation to another who follows suit. In **relocation** diffusion, groups of speakers shift residence into another dialect area, bringing two dialects into larger confrontation with each other. The most radical version of such relocation occurs when the whole population are immigrants – for example, in the creation of a new town in Britain, or the mass colonization of a new land such as Canada. In between the poles of expansion and relocation are intermediate mobilities, as when one individual relocates to another dialect area.

Sociolinguists have developed two main models to explain expansion diffusion. Both image change as moving like water. The **wave** model (Charles-James Bailey 1973) sees linguistic innovations as spreading out from a central point like ripples from a stone dropped in a pond. This means that there is a direct relationship between the measurable distance from the centre to a place and the time the change takes to reach it. Closer locations are affected by the change before more distant areas. Trudgill's examination (1986) of changes in the STRUT vowel in East Anglia indicated that increasingly fronter pronunciations were spreading out from London in a wave-like movement.

/h/-dropping, however, has diffused from London into the traditional /h/-retaining dialects of East Anglia in **cascade** fashion. This model is more common and sees changes flow through an urban hierarchy – from big city to smaller city to town to village to country. Changes are still seen as spreading out from major centres such as Beijing or Mexico City, but instead of rolling evenly across the intervening distance, they reach larger settlements first, then smaller settlements, then spread into adjacent countryside. Thus, rural areas near the centre will be affected by a change later than urban areas that are further away. The assumption behind this model is that linguistic changes follow the main transport routes which bring people into contact with each other, consistent with the view

---

Example 9.2

Diffusion of changes in Danish

Copenhagen is the traditional centre of linguistic innovation for the Danish language. Changes spread from the lower status dialect of Copenhagen into the city's higher status dialect, and then out into the rest of Denmark. The LANCHART project – 'Language Change in Real Time' – has been tracking shifts in the Danish language since the 1970s (Maegaard et al. 2013). Two of the variables studied are:

- use of second person *du* 'you' as a generic pronoun rather than *man* 'man' or *en* 'one'
- raising of the short /a/ vowel to [ɛ].

The researchers found that both these forms had been spreading out progressively across three settlements west from Copenhagen until *c.* 1970–80, and then began to recede again towards Copenhagen by the 2000s. Both the ebb and the flow of the innovation and its reversal were led from Copenhagen. Unfortunately, the study cannot distinguish whether these were wave or cascade movements. That is, the increasing distance and decreasing settlement size run parallel, so it is impossible to tease their effects apart. Copenhagen's dominance is not surprising: it has 2 million inhabitants, compared to the 3,000–50,000 of the other towns studied.

Unusually, the project also conducted a parallel survey of language attitudes, which support the production findings: evaluations are uniformly positive towards Copenhagen speech and negative to local forms. As a result traditional dialects have almost disappeared from many areas.

that changes are carried by weak social network ties (Chapter 8.6). In Murcia in southeastern Spain, standardized Castilian pronunciations of intervocalic /d/ (as in past participles like *terminado*) have diffused from the capital to progressively smaller and less accessible centres (Hernández-Campoy 2003). In the broader context of globalization, cascade diffusion reflects the power relativities between the centre and the periphery on the world stage (Blommaert 2010).

Both wave and cascade models have been criticized as too mechanistic, insensitive to social factors such as the location of shopping centres or to perceptual factors such as stereotypes about an area. Occasionally also a change may move eccentrically from country to city, against the expected flow – 'upstream', to reprise the water metaphor.

The linguistic outcomes of diffusion are not necessarily predictable. A sound change may itself change as it spreads. The outcome may be linguistically intermediate between the incoming and local pronunciations, or even just phonetically different, not in between.

Exercise 9.5   Media and diffusion of language change

Do the media influence language change? Most sociolinguists have been adamantly opposed to this idea. Trudgill's view is typical (1986: 40):

> The electronic media are not very instrumental in the diffusion of linguistic innovations, in spite of widespread popular notions to the contrary. The point about the TV set is that people, however much they watch and listen to it, do not talk to it (and even if they do, it cannot hear them!).

Even the most sceptical sociolinguist accepts that media may spread specific words or word pronunciations, but also holds that general sound change presupposes face-to-face communication between people. However, the lack of a role for the media has been assumed rather than researched, and media influence is in any case a very difficult thing to investigate. The only major research to directly address the issue is by Jane Stuart-Smith (2011) studying so-called 'Jockney' in Glasgow. She found that the spread of London-based consonant pronunciations such as [f] for /th/– *fing* for *thing* – correlated strongly with a speaker being actively engaged with the TV serial *EastEnders*.

- Identify and evaluate Stuart-Smith's arguments. Are they sufficient to outweigh the established sociolinguistic assumption of no media influence?

- The media are also responsible for circulating discourses and models of language standards – and anti-standards. Coupland and Kristiansen write (2011: 31): 'The mediatization of social life … [is] changing the terms of our engagement with language.' Debate their statement, and assess whether these broader influences may be affecting language change.

- Face-to-face is just one mode of contemporary communication between people. Interactive digital media are increasingly embedded in the flow of our daily life – texting, instant messaging, social media. Do you believe this constitutes a fundamental change in how we communicate with each other? Could such media now be a channel for transmitting language change?

Some speakers may react against an incoming change by adopting an exaggeratedly local form (as did Rex O'Neal of Ocracoke, and the Martha's Vineyard fishermen).

9.4 DIALECT BIRTH

When individuals or groups of migrants move into another dialect area, eventually their descendants fully adopt the local variety, just as immigrants who speak another language shift to the new language around them (see Chapter 7.3 on the formation of ethnic varieties). If Portuguese speakers emigrate from Europe to Brazil, their future children's children will speak like Brazilians not like Continental Portuguese. In the case of mass migration, the consequences can be more drastic.

Multicultural European dialects

Over recent decades large numbers of immigrants have moved into the inner cities of Europe from countries (often ex-colonies) where the host European languages are not natively spoken. Many of these cities have long histories of immigration, none more so than London, where across the centuries immigrants – from elsewhere in Britain as well as abroad – have often outnumbered the locally born. Now, in some neighbourhoods of inner London, first-language speakers of English are in a minority, with the majority consisting of immigrant families who speak a great diversity of languages – and second-language (L2) English.

Such a demography has radical local consequences for the host language. Children of immigrant families shift rapidly away from their parents' first languages and from the first-generation ethnic varieties of English which had been the product of **language** contact. The children pattern their own English on the L2 models around them in a scenario of multiple **dialect** contacts. In this situation it is difficult to describe anything as a 'target variety', since what exists is a set of linguistic features that are variable and transient. The outcome is a 'multiethnolect'.

In researching 'Multicultural London English' (MLE), Cheshire et al. (2011) interviewed 250 people – mainly Anglos (white, British born), Black Caribbean/African, Turkish/Kurdish, and mixed ethnicities. They found that MLE had its beginnings in 1980s London. The diphthongs of current non-Anglo speakers are similar to the inner-London 'patois' of the 1980s, which combined salient Jamaican English features on a London linguistic base. MLE speakers are often heard as 'black' by outsiders, although this is only partly founded in phonetic reality – the authors speculate it also has to do with the salience of black culture. The quite radical contact situation has similarities to the kind of group second language acquisition that produces pidgins and creoles (Chapter 4.2).

One sociolinguistic variable in this study is the alternation of vowel pronunciations in articles preceding nouns that start with a vowel: *the apple*, and *a(n) apple*. In MLE the vowels in the articles receive a schwa pronunciation, plus a bridging glottal stop before the vowel of the noun. This means that *the* is pronounced [ðəʔ] rather than standard [ði] before a vowel, and *a* is [əʔ] rather than the standard [ən] in *an apple*. The schwa variants are dominant for most ethnic groups, for all ages from 4 to 19 years, and for most caregivers.

Table 9.1 Pronunciation of articles before nouns starting with vowels in the Multicultural London English of 16- to 19-year-olds

	[ə] for a		[ðə] for the	
	%	N	%	N
Anglo	11	44	28	119
Black Caribbean	78	37	70	91
Black African	70	10	75	60
Mixed Anglo/Black Caribbean	50	4	75	12
Turkish	79	14	77	44
'Others'	67	6	69	13

Source: From Cheshire et al. (2011), tables 11 and 12

- Interpret the quantitative patterns in the table. What are the main groupings of the ethnicities? What do you observe about intermediate groups?

Table 9.1 shows the researchers' results for the 16 to 19-year-olds. Their overall conclusion is that MLE results from the dominance of L2 speakers in the area, which has led to a 'feature pool' from which learners make their own selections.

Koineization

What happens, however, to dialects where **everyone** is an immigrant? When immigrants who speak quite different languages are thrown together in a new locale, the result is a new language – a pidgin/creole. When different dialects are thrown together in this way, the outcome is a new dialect. Such scenarios will have occurred throughout history, but contemporary research has concentrated on new settlements in two typical situations – the creation of 'new towns' in old countries, and the colonization of new territories which are either un- or under-inhabited. In his foundational book *Dialects in Contact* (1986), Trudgill proposed that several processes are involved in the creation of new dialects:

- **Mixing** is the initial stage when the input dialects of all the immigrants mix freely in the new locale. There then follow:
- **Levelling** – the loss of 'marked' input-dialect features. Mainly this means that minority features (used by fewer speakers) lose out to majority features. But this term has also been applied to features that are marked in the linguistic sense of being less natural. The creation of Fiji Hindi involved three dialects. In most cases whichever form was used in two out of the three input dialects has been maintained, but where two dialects had nasal vowels and the third non-nasal, the non-nasals survived because they are the unmarked option phonologically.
- **Simplification** is the process by which irregularities are ironed out. The resulting output dialect makes fewer distinctions or has fewer exceptions than the inputs.

Gender or case marking may be reduced, or strong verb forms become weak, as in the American English adoption of *burned* not *burnt*. Sometimes the simplification appears to have a direct social trigger: the language of Indian indentured workers in South Africa lost forms indicating respect, presumably because social distinctions were erased and solidarity was important (Mesthrie 1993).

- Lastly, **reallocation** sees more than one form retained but taking on contrasting functions, usually different social or stylistic meanings.

Example 9.3 illustrates these processes in the dialect of Bhojpuri/Hindi spoken in Mauritius. The whole process is known as **koineization** – from 'koine', which was the Greek lingua franca spoken in the eastern Mediterranean 2,000 years ago, and the

Example 9.3

Dialect contact in Mauritius

Mauritius is an island in the Indian Ocean, and most of its population of over a million originated from India and spoke Bhojpuri, a form of Hindi. They were part of a large-scale migration of indentured workers from India to other parts of the British empire, including to Fiji, South Africa and the Caribbean. Bhojpuri has several dialects in India. In Mauritius these all came into contact and have contributed to the local dialect, which demonstrates several of the koineization processes:

- Regional differences in India have in Mauritius been levelled to single forms, for example of possessive pronouns.
- Simplification shows in the loss of distinctions which were made in the Indian input dialects. Some adjectives which marked gender agreement in the Indian dialects show no distinction in Mauritian Bhojpuri.
- There has also been reallocation, illustrated by these alternates (Trudgill 1986: 109):

India			Mauritius		
Eastern	Central	Western	High	Low	Gloss
/bara:/	/baɽa:/		/bara:/	/baɽa:/	'big'
	/mandir/	/mandil/	/mandil/	/mandir/	'temple'
	/ra:hta/	/ra:sta/	/ra:sta/	/ra:hta/	'road'

Both forms of words like these have survived from different dialects, but in Mauritius they have taken on different stylistic meanings, high versus low.

- What generalization would you make based on this last example about the dialect origins of some High and Low forms in Mauritian Bhojpuri?

language in which the New Testament was written. Different linguistic inputs will have different outcomes even in similar situations. A century ago two koines arose in towns established just 5 km apart for the immigrant workforce of smelting works on a Norwegian fjord. The town of Odda was settled mainly from western Norway, while the dominant strand of Tyssedal's immigration was from the east. Residents of Odda still speak an identifiably western dialect, while Tyssedal's is clearly eastern. Both are different from the dialects of the surrounding area (Kerswill 2013). Trudgill's framework proves to be a useful way of approaching this kind of dialect contact, although specific cases often do not quite fit. Only one-third of Tyssedal's immigrants came from the east, but their dialect won out despite being in a minority no larger than the westerners.

Dialect birth in a new settlement has been closely studied by British sociolinguist Paul Kerswill and his colleagues in the 'New Town' of Milton Keynes, 80 km northwest of London. Milton Keynes was populated by migrants from all over the UK. Children growing up there – the first native generation – have quite similar pronunciations of the vowel in GOAT despite the very diverse dialectal pronunciations of their caregivers (Kerswill and Williams 2000). The process has also been called **focusing**, when a very variable mixture of input dialects is honed towards a more unified output.

9.5   DIALECT DEATH

The outcomes of **language** contact include stratification, change, shift, endangerment and language death. **Dialect** contact has the same range of effects. The Ocracoke brogue – Example 9.1 – is changing. The once-isolated island is now popular with tourists, and in summer *dingbatters* (non-islanders) outnumber locals by at least 10:1. Most locals now work in tourist-related jobs, putting them in daily interaction with the ever-growing numbers of mainland American speakers. In this confrontation of dialect on dialect, the distinctives of Ocracoke English are in retreat (Wolfram and Schilling-Estes 1995). Young Ocracokers are losing the brogue, and the dialect is endangered.

In spatial terms, Ocracoke's loss of isolation has had physical, social and psychological dimensions. The advent of coastal highways and regular ferries linking the mainland with the island created the means for outsiders to visit in large numbers. Islanders' routines changed to fit the influx – but not all O'cockers are happy with all the effects. They want to maintain their distinctive identity, and know the brogue is part of that. This resistance is spearheaded culturally and linguistically by the 'poker-players', who were growing up at the time the tourists started to flood in – which is why Rex O'Neal performs the *hoi toide* vowel (Example 9.1).

Part of what attracts tourists to areas such as Ocracoke is an exotic language or dialect that is as much the fruit of isolation as is unspoiled scenery. But the tourists' presence can unwittingly threaten the very things that attracted them, including the dialect or language. While the specific individuals may be on short visits and therefore continually changing, the overall mass presence of tourists continues long term through much of the year (recall Exercise 9.3), and so does their effect on the language.

Exercise 9.6 Tourism and local language

Think of a region of your own country where tourism is a big industry.

1 Does the area have a distinctive dialect or language of its own? Where do you hear or see that? Is it used to tourists? What other languages are used? What is the main language of interaction between tourists and locals?
2 Do locals still speak the local code? Is it being maintained or is it endangered?
3 What languages are used on souvenirs or in printed tourist information? Why? (See Pietikäinen and Kelly-Holmes 2011 for a study of Sámi souvenir labelling in northern Finland.)
4 What languages or dialects appear on the region's tourist websites? How are they used and why?
5 What measures are possible to help maintain a local language or dialect against erosion through dominant codes brought by tourism? Are these being applied in your selected region?
6 The Ocracoke research team worked with locals on steps to preserve the dialect, which included producing a T-shirt that reads 'Save the Brogue' (Wolfram and Schilling-Estes 1995). Debate the economic and linguistic implications.
7 In the islands of the South Pacific, tourism is the main industry, and English usage is increasing at the expense of the indigenous Polynesian languages. Research and evaluate language choices on the tourist websites of nations such as Tonga or the Cook Islands.
8 Read about the once-isolated communities of Ocracoke (Wolfram), Martha's Vineyard (Labov) and East Sutherland (Chapter 4: Dorian). Compare their geographical, economic and social situations, and the outcomes for the languages/dialects.

• Apply the questions in the Research Activity (section 9.7) to the linguistic landscape of your selected tourist region.

9.6   THE CASE OF COLONIAL ENGLISHES

Colonization is the classic case of dialect contact and creation. The most in-depth study of the dialect outcomes of colonization researches the nineteenth-century origins of New Zealand English (NZE), the most recent of the major varieties of colonial English. Based on a unique archive of early recordings, Elizabeth Gordon and her colleagues have studied the English of some of the first native speakers of NZE. These were born from the 1850s onwards but recorded in the 1940s, so the study relies on apparent-time assumptions of their youthful speech (Chapter 8.2).

Various theories of the origins of NZE had been put forward – principally that it came either from London Cockney, or from southeast England generally, or from Australian English. Despite the scale and detail of the project's analyses of both linguistic and social data, its conclusions remained equivocal (Gordon et al. 2004: 256). The Cockney theory was rejected, but the team endorsed what was already the default view on NZE origins – that it is largely a result of southeastern English input, plus Australian influences. Trudgill, however, found evidences for his broader theories of dialect contact and the origins of colonial Englishes and published them separately (2004).

Determinism

Trudgill's theory is boldly deterministic and asocial, with no role for factors such as attitudes, prestige or identity. The character of colonial Englishes in 'tabula rasa' situations (where there was no prior English-speaking settlement) can be explained, he posits, entirely from the linguistic and demographic inputs (2004: 20):

> If you bake cakes, I suggest, from roughly the same ingredients in roughly the same proportions in roughly similar conditions for roughly the same length of time, you will get roughly similar cakes.

The similarities shared by the main southern hemisphere Englishes – New Zealand, Australia, South Africa – arise from their similar linguistic and demographic ingredients. The formation of these new dialects follows a predictable three-stage path which transforms the input dialect mix into a new, focused and predictable dialect by the third generation:

1	adult immigrants	rudimentary levelling, interdialect forms
2	first locally born generation	extreme variability, apparent levelling
3	second and subsequent generations	(final) levelling, reallocation

Dynamism

By contrast, world Englishes specialist Edgar Schneider attributes the formation of colonial Englishes such as NZE centrally to social factors, especially identity. His 'dynamic model' (2007) draws on contact linguistics (Chapters 3 and 4 earlier). It encompasses all kinds of colonial Englishes, not just 'settler' dialects, and later postcolonial development as well as the initial formation period. Schneider's key claim is that 'identity constructions and realignments, and their symbolic linguistic expressions, are ... at the heart of the process of the emergence of Post-Colonial Englishes' (2007: 28).

While Trudgill holds the process of colonial English formation is purely linguistic convergence, for Schneider it is an 'identity-driven process of linguistic convergence' (2007: 30, my emphasis). He identifies five historical phases:

1 Foundation – principally koineization.
2 Exonormative stabilization – the new dialect 'focuses' but still takes its standards from the mother country.
3 Nativization – completion of the focusing process and increasing localization of the language. For NZE, Schneider dates this phase from 1907 (the year New Zealand became a semi-independent 'dominion'), which coincides closely with Trudgill's dating of the stabilization of NZE to the speech of those born c. 1890.

Exercise 9.7 Debating origins

This exercise applies and evaluates Trudgill's (2004) and Schneider's (2007) models. Remember that all models are idealizations that will not necessarily fit the detail of every case, and that Trudgill's was designed to apply to a narrower range of situations. See also Trudgill's brief position article on this (2008) and the responses that follow it.

1 Assess Schneider's application of his model to NZE (2007: 127ff.) and compare it with Trudgill's in his book. Evaluate both.
2 Apply Schneider's model to the development of a postcolonial dialect that you know, such as American English, Brazilian Portuguese, Canadian French, Mexican Spanish.
3 Also apply Trudgill's model to what you can find out about the linguistics of the same dialect's formation phase and its current features.
4 Then evaluate and critique both models: how much insight does each of them yield? Are any aspects of either inadequate or misleading? How would you modify them?
5 Debate the implications for sociolinguistics of a radically asocial interpretation of dialect birth. Overall, do you find Trudgill's linguistic determinism or Schneider's social/identity model more useful or convincing?

4 Endonormative stabilization – the colony moves to or towards full independence, including in its linguistic usage and attitudes.
5 Differentiation – fresh variation begins to evolve, for example through regional or ethnic variability, within what had become a quite uniform dialect.

Each phase includes a causal sequence of four parameters in which the sociopolitical situation leads to identity constructions, which create sociolinguistic conditions, which trigger linguistic effects. Schneider summarizes his model in a useful table (2007: 56). Exercise 9.7 debates these two models.

9.7 RESEARCH ACTIVITY: LINGUISTIC LANDSCAPE

Research the linguistic landscape of your own or another accessible area that has a lot of signage. Don't collect too much, it takes time to process. See the introduction to Gorter (2006) for more detail, and the studies there and in Shohamy, Ben-Rafael and Barni (2010) and Jaworski and Thurlow (2010). The following steps form a sequence, but some can be skipped.

1 Choose a street or block, and photograph or log all the signage you see.
2 What counts as a sign? What do you exclude?
3 Classify signs as either public/official or private/commercial.

4   Identify any unauthorized signs such as graffiti.
5   What languages are used? In which kind of signs? Do some signs have more than one language on them?
6   Describe the visual aspects of the different signs, e.g. placement, standard official lettering and format for street signs, different scripts such as Arabic or Chinese, large and garish letters on some shops, rough and informal signs in some windows. How do you interpret these 'semiotic landscapes'?
7   What do the signs and their language use tell you about these public spaces? How do the signs construct the public space? What would the space be like without any or some signs?
8   What does the linguistic usage on the signs say about the different languages involved and their relationships?
9   Are any surprising languages used? (E.g. Chinese in a non-Chinese-speaking country.)
10 Especially if only one language is used on all the signs you survey: do different signs use different language styles or levels? Describe and explain these.
11 Take your project the next step: talk to the producers of some signs (such as shop owners) about what they have done with their signs and why (see Figure 9.3).
12 And a further step again: talk to passers-by about their understanding of or reaction to the signs.
13 Relate the producer and audience perceptions to each other. Are they different from each other, and from your own interpretations?

9.8   SUMMARY

- Traditional dialect geography mapped the isogloss boundaries between alternative forms in traditional rural dialects, such as between Low and High German across northern Europe. But dialectology encountered problems of overwhelming amounts of data, over-descriptiveness and biased sampling. Isoglosses also implied clear-cut boundaries between forms and dialects, but they proved to be more often gradient.
- Space is not just physical, it is also social and psychological. Routines of movement and interaction groove paths across the space around us. Different social groups may have different geographies of the same region, and proximity need not mean contact between groups.
- Where traditional dialectology was rural, Labov initiated an urban turn which most sociolinguists followed, but Wolfram and associates have researched isolated dialects in the southeastern United States.
- The linguistic landscape is the language that we see on public signs around us. The choice of language for public display symbolizes and constructs the relative standing of the languages in the local repertoire. Processes such as gentrification are embodied in the signs and graffiti of a neighbourhood such as Prenzlauer Berg in Berlin.
- While sociolinguists have traditionally researched nonmobile speakers, mobility is increasingly characteristic of societies and its sociolinguistics is being researched, particularly the phenomenon of globalization.
- Contact leads to diffusion of linguistic forms either through expansion, when individual speakers of different dialects come into contact, or through relocation,

when individuals or groups shift to different dialect areas. Two models of expansion have been proposed – a wave model by which changes diffuse regularly across space, and a cascade model by which they spread from larger to smaller centres.

- Radical relocation of large migrant populations leads to creation of new dialects in places like new towns and inner London, where speakers learn their English through other second-language speakers from many linguistic backgrounds.
- Trudgill has schematized processes of koineization where dialect contact leads to the birth of a new dialect. The mixing of dialects leads to levelling out of minority forms, simplification of irregularities, and reallocation of functions to alternative variants.
- Dialect death now threatens once-isolated varieties in places such as the island of Ocracoke because of constant interaction with an influx of tourists.
- Colonial dialect birth has been researched in New Zealand through an archive of early recordings. From these Trudgill adduced a radically asocial theory, positing that the new dialect's features are predictable from the linguistic and demographic inputs. By contrast, Schneider's 'dynamic model' sees the convergence process as driven by social factors, especially identity.

9.9 FURTHER READING

Chambers and Trudgill's *Dialectology* (1998, 2nd edn) sketches the field's earlier history and reworks the foundations. While the full surveys for the *Linguistic Atlas of the US and Canada* have never been completed, the existing data of the Linguistic Atlas Project has been digitalized at the University of Georgia by William Kretzschmar and is available on line.

Language Variation and Change and *Journal of Sociolinguistics* carry frequent articles on particular regionally defined dialects of different languages, and *English World-Wide* and other journals for English only. There are many books on regional Englishes – for some overviews see Wolfram and Schilling-Estes (2006) on American English, Foulkes and Docherty (1999) on the *Urban Voices* of British and Irish English, Blair and Collins (2001) on Australian English, Bell and Kuiper (2000) on NZ English. The four-volume, 2,500-page world survey of *Varieties of English* edited by Kortmann et al. (2008) is a compendium of information on regional varieties. For dialects of Spanish, see Díaz-Campos (2011).

One of Labov's major productions is the *Atlas of North American English* (Labov, Ash and Boberg 2006), which used a telephone survey to map vowels and vowel shifts across the continent. Variationist work which is geographically focused includes much research by Trudgill and by Britain, and by Wolfram and associates (see website of the North Carolina Language and Life Project).

Johnstone (2011b) is an excellent introduction to language and place: see also her work on phonetics and place in Pittsburgh (e.g. Johnstone and Kiesling 2008). Several of Britain's articles offer good introductions for sociolinguists to relevant geographical thinking (2010, 2013a, 2013b).

Linguistic landscape work is represented in the edited collections of Gorter (2006), Shohamy, Ben-Rafael and Barni (2010), and also Jaworski and Thurlow (2010) – especially their introduction. See also Scollon and Scollon on *Discourses in Place* (2003), and Johnstone (1990) and Modan (2007) on the discourses **of** place. On language and tourism (particularly its discourse), see Jaworski and Pritchard (2005) and Thurlow and Jaworski (2010). And for globalization, Coupland's *Handbook* (2010), and publications by Fairclough, Blommaert and Heller.

On geographical diffusion of change, Trudgill's *Dialects in Contact* (1986) is the original text. See also Labov's major projects, the Danish LANCHART project (online), Britain's research, and also Horvath and Horvath (2002).

For research on contact leading to new-dialect creation in old countries, see the work of Kerswill and his associates over many years (e.g. Kerswill and Williams 2000). Schneider's book (2007) and the major article that preceded it (2003) offer an overview and model for the development of all kinds of colonial Englishes, and a lot of detail on the dialects themselves. Elizabeth Gordon et al. (2004) and Trudgill (2004) are the two divergent books derived from the Origins of NZ English project, along with numerous papers by combinations of the team's authors.

References

Bailey, Charles-James N., 1973. *Variation and Linguistic Theory*. Arlington, VA: Center for Applied Linguistics.

Becker, Kara, 2009. '/r/ and the construction of place identity on New York City's Lower East Side'. *Journal of Sociolinguistics* 13: 634–58.

Bell, Allan, 2000. 'Māori and Pakeha English: a case study'. In Allan Bell and Koenraad Kuiper (eds), *New Zealand English*. Wellington, New Zealand: Victoria University Press; and Amsterdam: John Benjamins. 221–48.

Blair, David and Peter Collins (eds), 2001. *English in Australia*. Amsterdam: John Benjamins.

Blommaert, Jan, 2010. *The Sociolinguistics of Globalization*. Cambridge: Cambridge University Press.

Britain, David, 2010. 'Conceptualizations of geographic space in linguistics'. In Alfred Lameli, Roland Kehrein and Stefan Rabanus (eds), *Language and Space: An International Handbook of Linguistic Variation – Volume 2: Language Mapping*. Berlin: Mouton de Gruyter. 69–97.

Britain, David, 2013a. 'Space, diffusion and mobility'. In J.K. Chambers and Natalie Schilling (eds), *The Handbook of Language Variation and Change* (2nd edn). Oxford, UK: Wiley-Blackwell. 471–500.

Britain, David, 2013b. 'The role of mundane mobility and contact in dialect death and dialect birth'. In Daniel Schreier and Marianne Hundt (eds), *English as a Contact Language*. Cambridge: Cambridge University Press. 165–81.

Buchstaller, Isabelle and Alexandra D'Arcy, 2009. 'Localized globalization: a multi-local, multivariate investigation of quotative *be like*'. *Journal of Sociolinguistics* 13: 291–313.

Chambers, J.K. and Peter Trudgill, 1998. *Dialectology* (2nd edn). Cambridge: Cambridge University Press.

Cheshire, Jenny, Paul Kerswill, Sue Fox and Eivind Torgersen, 2011. 'Contact, the feature pool and the speech community: the emergence of Multicultural London English'. *Journal of Sociolinguistics* 15: 151–96.

Coupland, Nikolas (ed.), 2010. *The Handbook of Language and Globalization*. Malden, MA: Wiley-Blackwell.

Coupland, Nikolas and Tore Kristiansen, 2011. 'SLICE: critical perspectives on language (de)standardization'. In Tore Kristiansen and Nikolas Coupland (eds), *Standard Languages and Language Standards in a Changing Europe*. Oslo: Novus. 11–35.

Díaz-Campos, Manuel (ed.), 2011. *The Handbook of Hispanic Sociolinguistics*. Oxford, UK: Wiley-Blackwell.

Fairclough, Norman, 2006. *Language and Globalization*. London: Routledge.

Foulkes, Paul and Gerard J. Docherty (eds), 1999. *Urban Voices: Accent Studies in the British Isles*. London: Arnold.

Giddens, Anthony, 1984. *The Constitution of Society: Outline of the Theory of Structuration*. Cambridge, UK: Polity Press.

Gordon, Elizabeth, Lyle Campbell, Jennifer Hay, Margaret Maclagan, Andrea Sudbury and Peter Trudgill, 2004. *New Zealand English: Its Origins and Evolution*. Cambridge: Cambridge University Press.

Gorter, Durk (ed.), 2006. *Linguistic Landscape: A New Approach to Multilingualism*. Clevedon, UK: Multilingual Matters.

Hernández-Campoy, Juan Manuel, 2003. 'Exposure to contact and the geographical adoption of standard features: two complementary approaches'. *Language in Society* 32: 227–55.

Horvath, Barbara M. and Ronald J. Horvath, 2002. 'The geolinguistics of /l/ vocalisation in Australia and New Zealand'. *Journal of Sociolinguistics* 6: 319–46.

Jaworski, Adam and Annette Pritchard (eds), 2005. *Discourse, Communication and Tourism*. Clevedon, UK: Channel View Publications.

Jaworski, Adam and Crispin Thurlow (eds), 2010. *Semiotic Landscapes: Language, Image, Space*. London: Continuum.

Johnstone, Barbara, 1990. *Stories, Community, and Place: Narratives from Middle America*. Bloomington, IN: Indiana University Press.

Johnstone, Barbara, 2011b. 'Language and place'. In Rajend Mesthrie (ed.), *The Cambridge Handbook of Sociolinguistics*. Cambridge: Cambridge University Press. 203–17.

Johnstone, Barbara and Scott F. Kiesling, 2008. 'Indexicality and experience: exploring the meanings of /aw/-monophthongization in Pittsburgh'. *Journal of Sociolinguistics* 12: 5–33.

Kerswill, Paul, 2013. 'Koineization'. In J.K. Chambers and Natalie Schilling (eds), *The Handbook of Language Variation and Change* (2nd edn). Oxford, UK: Wiley-Blackwell. 519–36.

Kerswill, Paul and Ann Williams, 2000. 'Creating a New Town koine: children and language change in Milton Keynes'. *Language in Society* 29: 65–115.

Kortmann, Bernd, Clive Upton, Edgar W. Schneider, Kate Burridge and Rajend Mesthrie (eds), 2008. *Varieties of English* (4 vols, various editors). Berlin: Mouton de Gruyter.

Labov, William, 1994. *Principles of Linguistic Change*, vol. 1: *Internal Factors*. Cambridge, MA: Blackwell Publishers.

Labov, William, Sharon Ash and Charles Boberg, 2006. *The Atlas of North American English: Phonetics, Phonology and Sound Change*. Berlin: Mouton de Gruyter.

Landry, Rodrigue and Richard Y. Bourhis, 1997. 'Linguistic landscape and ethnolinguistic vitality: an empirical study'. *Journal of Language and Social Psychology* 16: 23–49.

Lo, Adrienne and Joseph Sung-Yul Park (eds), 2012. 'Globalization, multilingualism and identity in transnational perspective: the case of South Korea'. Theme issue of *Journal of Sociolinguistics* 16/2.

Maegaard, Marie, Torben Jensen, Tore Kristiansen and Jens Jørgensen, 2013. 'Diffusion of language change: accommodation to a moving target'. *Journal of Sociolinguistics* 17: 721–54.

Mesthrie, Rajend, 1993. 'Koineization in the Bhojpuri-Hindi diaspora – with special reference to South Africa'. *International Journal of the Sociology of Language* 99: 25–44.

Modan, Gabriella Gahlia, 2007. *Turf Wars: Discourse, Diversity, and the Politics of Place*. Malden, MA: Blackwell Publishing.

Papen, Uta, 2012. 'Commercial discourses, gentrification and citizens' protest: the linguistic landscape of Prenzlauer Berg, Berlin'. *Journal of Sociolinguistics* 16: 56–80.

Payne, Arvilla C., 1980. 'Factors controlling the acquisition of the Philadelphia dialect by out-of-state children'. In William Labov (ed.), *Locating Language in Time and Space*. New York: Academic Press. 143–78.

Pietikäinen, Sari and Helen Kelly-Holmes, 2011. 'The local political economy of languages in a Sámi tourism destination: authenticity and mobility in the labelling of souvenirs'. *Journal of Sociolinguistics* 15: 323–46.

Schilling-Estes, Natalie. 1998. 'Investigating "self-conscious" speech: the performance register in Ocracoke English'. *Language in Society* 27: 53–83.

Schneider, Edgar W., 2003. 'The dynamics of new Englishes: from identity construction to dialect birth'. *Language* 79: 233–81.

Schneider, Edgar W., 2007. *Postcolonial English: Varieties around the World*. Cambridge: Cambridge University Press.

Scollon, Ron and Suzanne Wong Scollon, 2003. *Discourses in Place: Language in the Material World*. London: Routledge.

Shohamy, Elana, Eliezer Ben-Rafael and Monica Barni (eds), 2010. *Linguistic Landscape in the City*. Bristol, UK: Multilingual Matters.

Stuart-Smith, Jane, 2011. 'The view from the couch: changing perspectives on the role of television in changing language ideologies and use'. In Tore Kristiansen and Nikolas Coupland (eds), *Standard Languages and Language Standards in a Changing Europe*. Oslo, Norway: Novus. 223–39.

Thurlow, Crispin and Adam Jaworski, 2010. *Tourism Discourse: Language and Global Mobility*. Basingstoke, UK: Palgrave Macmillan.

Trudgill, Peter, 1986. *Dialects in Contact*. Oxford, UK: Basil Blackwell.

Trudgill, Peter, 2004. *New-dialect Formation: The Inevitability of Colonial Englishes*. Edinburgh: Edinburgh University Press.

Trudgill, Peter, 2008. 'Colonial dialect contact in the history of European languages: on the irrelevance of identity to new-dialect formation'. *Language in Society* 37: 241–54.

Urry, John, 2007. *Mobilities*. Cambridge, UK: Polity Press.

Wolfram, Walt and Natalie Schilling-Estes, 1995. 'Moribund dialects and the endangerment canon: the case of the Ocracoke Brogue'. *Language* 71: 696–721.

Wolfram, Walt and Natalie Schilling-Estes, 1997. *Hoi Toide on the Outer Banks: The Story of the Ocracoke Brogue*. Chapel Hill, NC: University of North Carolina Press.

Wolfram, Walt and Natalie Schilling-Estes, 2006. *American English: Dialects and Variation* (2nd edn). Malden, MA: Blackwell Publishing.

10

VALUING LANGUAGE

Hungarian speakers in Romania believe their speech is inferior to that spoken in Hungary. In a Disney animation, the villains speak in foreign-accented English. In countless countries children have been punished for speaking their home language at school. All these are the fruits of language ideologies, of the ways in which language is valued. They represent the ideas, beliefs and feelings of people about the varieties and languages involved: that one linguistic form or code sounds more beautiful or more ugly, is superior or inferior, is more or less moral – in short, is on some dimension better or worse than another.

The valuing of language has been an aspect of almost every topic we have covered in this book. Some examples:

- the preference for English over Chichewa in Malawi (Chapter 3)
- widespread denigration of pidgins and creoles (Chapter 4)
- the ideological baggage of a 'descriptive' concept like diglossia (Chapter 5)
- sociopolitically driven shifts in deaf education and language in the US (Chapter 8)
- the dominance of Copenhagen varieties of Danish (Chapter 9).

We now turn to concentrate directly on the valuing of language, which affects all linguistic levels from micro choices to contestation of what even counts as a language. A number of disciplines and methods have approached this field, each in its own way, and I cover these one by one. Work on language ideologies is qualitative and derives from approaches in current anthropology. Language attitudes research comes out of social psychology and has been largely questionnaire based and quantitative. Perceptual dialectology is part of variationist sociolinguistics, using techniques from geography. These are very different traditions with different goals, methods and terminologies. The chapter then turns to examine how individual linguistic variables are evaluated, and the ways in which language standards operate in society.

The Guidebook to Sociolinguistics, First Edition. Allan Bell.
© 2014 Allan Bell. Published 2014 by Blackwell Publishing Ltd.

10.1   IDEOLOGIES OF LANGUAGE

Linguistic ideologies sometimes surface in open debates about language, but more often they remain unspoken and unconscious. While they may have major social and political effects – from individual discrimination through to armed conflict – most of the time people are scarcely aware of their existence. These ideologies are 'naturalized' – they represent commonsense views of language and society that people take for granted. They need no justification, they just describe the way the world is. But while self-presenting as neutral descriptions, ideologies have repercussions which are far from unaligned.

Ideologies become visible when they are brought out in the open by some salient event. I noted in Chapter 8 that sign languages have often been stigmatized. In 1988 Dr Elizabeth Zinser was appointed president of Gallaudet, the Deaf University in Washington, DC. Protests broke out and she was forced to resign – because she knew no American Sign Language, and the Deaf community did not want that. Her ignorance of ASL symbolized her lack of involvement in the American Deaf community. Her later statement that members of the university's board should 'learn a little sign … just a few basic phrases, some warm sentences when they meet people around the school' (quoted in Lucas 2001: 1) indicated awareness of the sociosymbolic value of ASL but did not help her case. For the community, knowledge of ASL was a core value for membership.

Interest in the ideological loading of language goes back to Hymes, but flourished during the 1990s. It was focused in programmatic articles by Woolard (1998) and Irvine and Gal (2000). Woolard identifies several features:

1   Ideologies serve the interests of social groups and are differentiated according to those interests. As Irvine and Gal observe, 'there is no "view from nowhere," no gaze that is not positioned' (2000: 36).
2   Prevalent ideologies serve the interests of the social elite, they legitimate and sustain subordination. Where most approaches can agree on the neutral description of ideology under point 1, not all cross the divide to accept point 2, a 'critical' take that ideologies are about power.
3   Such ideologies disguise the operation of domination from the non-elite groups.

Processes of language ideology

Irvine and Gal (2000) proposed an approach which explicates how people routinely define themselves over against some real or imagined 'Other' through three main processes:

- **Iconization** is the way a linguistic feature – or even a whole variety or language – becomes representative of a particular group. Although the association between the linguistic feature and the group is arbitrary, the feature is treated as somehow having a natural and inherent link with the group. In the Hebrew story of 'shibboleth', this iconization became a matter of life or death (Example 10.1).

Example 10.1

The story of Shibboleth

The Hebrew word 'shibboleth' has been taken into English to mean precisely a language feature which identifies a group – iconization. It derives from an Old Testament story where the inability to pronounce 'sh' as [ʃ] not [s] was fatal. After defeating the tribe of Ephraim in battle, the Gileadites waited for the fleeing Ephraimites at the River Jordan:

Whenever one of the fugitives of Ephraim said, 'Let me go over', the men of Gilead would say to him, 'Are you an Ephraimite?' When he said, 'No', they said to him, 'Then say Shibboleth', and he said, 'Sibboleth', for he could not pronounce it right. Then they seized him and killed him at the fords of the Jordan. (Book of Judges, chapter 12, New Revised Standard Version)

Exercise 10.1   Iconization in your language

Identify a shibboleth in your language variety:

1 Is there one main linguistic feature that people believe especially distinguishes your variety from others? Describe it.
2 Is there one particular other group that this feature distinguishes your group from? What is their variant for the iconic feature?
3 How long has this feature operated as an icon between the two groups? How and why did the difference achieve its status?
4 Are there linguistic reasons why this feature has become so salient? What are the social reasons?
5 What other linguistic differences are being 'erased' through the concentration on this icon?

For an example shibboleth from New Zealand English, especially in contrast with Australian, see my article on 'The phonetics of fish and chips' (Bell 1997b).

- **Recursion** involves the projection of a distinction made at one level onto another level (Irvine and Gal use the precise but opaque geometrical term 'fractal recursivity'). In nineteenth-century southeastern Europe, Macedonia was multiethnic and multilingual to a degree that bewildered western European observers. Still more puzzling, this national-level diversity was often reproduced recursively within families. Each son might be sent to a different school – Bulgarian, Greek, Romanian, Serbian – and emerge adopting its language and nationality.
- **Erasure** is the process by which facts which do not fit the ideology are rendered invisible. They are overlooked or explained away. Even a language that is as highly standardized as French encompasses a large range of variety that is ignored in defining what the standard is. Yet standard French is not regarded as one variety among others – rather, it excludes the idea that variety even exists (Jaffe 1999: 78).

Colonial language ideologies

Colonial situations often make the workings of language ideology more visible because differentials in power are so obvious. No linguistic ideology is more basic than that of defining what does and does not count as 'a language', a process that went on throughout Africa in the late nineteenth century (Irvine and Gal 2000). French military expeditions traversed the territory of Senegal, mapping the boundaries of groups and their languages (iconization). The three main languages were interpreted as having essential characteristics. Fula was seen as a 'delicate' language, and its speakers as intelligent. Wolof was less so, and its speakers were less intelligent. Sereer was held to be a simple language (despite a notably complex morphology), and its speakers primitive. Groups were assumed to be monolingual, but clean boundaries could only be mapped by ignoring the prevailing multilingualism (erasure). The imperial payoff for such idealizations was that territories and their peoples were identified, segmented and ready for governance.

It is, as Irvine and Gal observe, easier to recognize, critique, even ridicule these ideologies at a distance, but similar colonial, postcolonial and quasi-colonial ideologies and their fruits remain alive and well today:

- the requirement to speak fluent English not Swahili to win a national beauty contest in Tanzania (Billings 2009)
- the oppression of the Oroqen language of northeastern China under colonization by the Han Chinese and their language, Mandarin (Li Fengxiang 2005)
- the triumph of Bahasa Indonesia as the national language of Indonesia at the expense of many local languages (Errington 1998).

Exercise 10.2
Language ideologies in Corsica and Singapore

Two of the most researched language-ideological situations are found in the very different and distant islands of Corsica and Singapore.

Corsica is part of France, but has its own language (closer to Italian). Corsican is maintained by a core of language activists against French domination, and is the subject of a finely written ethnography by Jaffe (1999).

Singapore is an independent island-state with a majority of Chinese speakers. The decades-long *Speak Mandarin Campaign* has downgraded the non-Mandarin Chinese 'dialects' to the point where they are now much less spoken (e.g. Bokhorst-Heng 1999; Wee 2006, 2010).

- Use published and internet sources to research one of these situations, and analyse their ideological character following the three-part framework of Woolard, outlined in the text.

10.2   LANGUAGE WITH ATTITUDE

The social psychology of language has a very different take on language evaluation from the ideologies approach. It majors on the role of language in inter-group and inter-personal relations, particularly:

- attitudes
- intergroup relations, especially of different ethnicities and generations
- stereotyping
- accommodation between speakers (see next chapter)
- personality, persuasion, self-disclosure, deception, impression formation
- social problems such as aggression and prejudice.

The research agenda and the methods here – largely experimental and quantitative – have been set by social psychologists rather than linguists, with the exception of a fruitful collaboration between Giles and the Couplands (e.g. Giles, Coupland and Coupland 1991).

Asking about language

The simplest way of doing language attitude research is to simply question people directly about their attitudes. In a study of the language of the Arvanites – ethnic Albanians who live in Greece – the researchers asked bluntly: 'Do you like speaking Arvanitika?' Table 10.1a shows the results broken down by age. Alongside, Table 10.1b

Table 10.1   Attitudes to Arvanitika – percentage of people responding yes/no to two language attitudes questions

Age	(a) Do you like to speak Arvanitika?			(b) Is it necessary to speak Arvanitika to be an Arvanitis?	
	Yes	Indifferent	No	Yes	No
5–9	1	10	89	–	–
10–14	16	17	67	67	33
15–24	17	41	42	42	58
25–34	30	67	3	24	76
35–49	46	53	2	28	72
50–59	67	31	1	33	67
60+	79	21	0	17	83

Source: From Trudgill (1983), tables 7.1 and 7.6

- Interpret the age profile of attitudes towards speaking Arvanitika as shown in the yes/no columns of 10.1a. Note and try to explain any discontinuities.
- The attitudes in 10.1b appear to contradict 10a: specify how and explain why (see Trudgill 1983 for the researchers' interpretation).

Exercise 10.3   Unpacking British language attitudes

Look up Coupland and Bishop's long table 2 (2007). Use their numbers to analyse attitudes to some of the following different groupings of accents. Compare the accents within each group. Interpret and explain the ratings each received:

- Non-UK – Australian, New Zealand, North American, South African, Southern Irish
- Non-native – French, German, Spanish
- Celtic – Belfast, Cardiff, Edinburgh, Glasgow, Northern Irish, Scottish, Southern Irish, Swansea, Welsh
- Cities – Belfast, Birmingham, Bristol, Cardiff, Leeds, Liverpool, Manchester, Newcastle, Norwich, Nottingham
- Ethnic – Afro-Caribbean, Asian
- Regional – Black Country, Cornish, Lancashire, West Country

displays apparently contradictory attitudes to the role of the language in community identity, and the questions below the table ask you to interpret this.

I and my colleagues also researched this identity issue in our surveys of Pasifika languages and their maintenance in New Zealand. We asked our Samoan respondents: 'Do you have to speak Samoan to be a real Samoan?' – 19 out of 30 of them thought so. But when we asked Cook Islanders the parallel question about themselves, only 5 of the 30 agreed. The Cook Islands Maori language is more endangered than Samoan, with far fewer younger people speaking it. Cook Islands Maori is therefore rated as much less crucial to its community's identity than is the Samoan language in that community. Such attitude issues are central to the ethnolinguistic vitality approach we dealt with in Chapters 2 and 3.

Listener attitudes show through even when the stimulus to which they are responding is reduced to just a label. Coupland and Bishop (2007) analysed the results of a BBC online survey of 5,000 British listeners reacting to accent names. 'The Queen's English' and 'Standard English' rated top for prestige, followed by Scottish, with some overseas accents such as New Zealand and North American rated high. The commonly denigrated British urban vernaculars rated bottom, led by Birmingham and followed by ethnically identified accents such as Asian and Afro-Caribbean (see Exercise 10.3). The findings indicate the persistence of entrenched British accent ideologies, the researchers concluded, although younger respondents were less negative about the stigmatized varieties.

Asking about speakers

Rather than direct questioning, attitude researchers usually play recordings to a panel of 'judges' and ask about their attitudes to the **speakers**. This is the kind of thing we do all the time as listeners – most obviously on the phone. After hearing only a few seconds' speech from a stranger we will have come to a number of conclusions about their characteristics – gender, approximate age, probable level of education, possible kind of occupation, their likeability.

In research listener-judges are usually called on to rate speakers' traits on scales from positive to negative, often with a neutral point in the middle. Each point on the scale is

Exercise 10.4   Language attitudes experiment

Play the class short recordings (15–30 seconds each) of two speakers with contrasting accents (YouTube is a source). Have them answer the following abbreviated language attitudes questionnaire for each speaker:

A   Accent identification

Speaker's approximate age (within 10 years)
Ethnic group
What kind of job do you think this speaker
is likely to have?

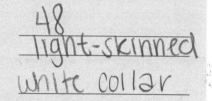

48
light-skinned
white collar

B   Accent evaluation – do you think the speaker is:

	1	2	3	4	5	
educated	✓	: ___	: ___	: ___	: ___	uneducated
intelligent	✓	: ___	: ___	: ___	: ___	not intelligent
ambitious	✓	: ___	: ___	: ___	: ___	unambitious
likeable	✓	: ___	: ___	: ___	: ___	not likeable
reliable	___	: ✓	: ___	: ___	: ___	unreliable
tough	___	: ___	: ✓	: ___	: ___	not tough
pleasant accented	___	: ✓	: ___	: ___	: ___	unpleasant accented

scored and average ratings across a group of listeners calculated. The results tend to form two distinct clusters, one for **status** and one for **solidarity** variables. Status relates to social stratification, e.g. education (see Chapter 7.2 for the use of education to index class). Solidarity involves attributes like reliability and attractiveness. Usually the standard or majority language rates high on status, and often but not always a minority or non-standard code rates well for solidarity. The best way to understand these scales is to take part in an experiment using them – Exercises 10.4 and 10.5. In this questionnaire there is just one question directly about language – accent pleasantness – and the rest ask for judgements about the speakers. But a study of attitudes to regional dialects of Dutch found listeners registered direct responses to the accents as well as to their speakers (Grondelaers, van Hout and Steegs 2010).

The matched guise

Québec has been a leading locale for research on attitudes to different languages in a bilingual situation, pioneered by the social psychologist Wallace Lambert. His interest was piqued by conversations overheard on a bus in Montreal circa 1960. Behind him

Exercise 10.5   Analysing the class's attitudes

- Assemble the class's answers to Section A of the questionnaire in Exercise 10.4.
  1. Have the class interpret their classifications.
  2. Ask members to explain the reasons for the classifications they have made.
  3. Discuss what linguistic markers have cued these classifications.
  4. Consider the range of answers given by the class and why.
  5. Gauge the answers against what you know of the recorded speakers' actual ages, ethnicities and occupations.
  6. Consider discrepancies between perception and actuality.
- Assemble the class's scores for the scales in Section B. For each factor multiply each score (1–5) by the number of students awarding that score, add all these totals together, then divide the grand total score by the total number of students. This yields mean ratings for every factor, e.g. say 2.75 versus 4.15 for your two speakers' reliability levels.
  7. Interpret the class's ratings.
  8. Consider the same issues addressed under 2–4 above.
- Elicit students' feedback on their experience of doing this questionnaire:
  9. What are students' reactions to the stereotyping involved? ('Horrible', said one of mine.) And to the slightness of the stimulus recording?
  10. Discuss the social issues involved in the method and its results.
  11. Evaluate and critique the questionnaire, e.g. the terms used in the scales such as 'ambitious'.
  12. Reflect on the experience of doing this questionnaire and analysis, and the fact that similar experiences were involved during data collection for the published studies. Even behind the clear-cut graphs there has been a process with many shades of grey that ended up appearing as black and white results. What does this mean for our approach to such research findings?

were two women conversing in French. In front two other women were commenting unfavourably in English on the French conversation (which they could not understand) and exchanging stereotypes about French Canadians – 'Well, you can't expect much else from them' (Lambert 1967). Lambert developed the ingenious 'matched guise' technique in which listeners are played both French and English voices but are unaware that the speakers are bilinguals whom they are hearing twice, once in each language. Any difference in a listener's judgement between the same speakers in their 'English guise' versus their 'French guise' represents a bias towards or against English or French.

In Lambert's original experiment, French-speaking and English-speaking students rated voices produced by four bilinguals (Lambert et al. 1960). The English speakers evaluated the English voices more favourably, but so also, to the researchers' surprise, did the French-speaking students. Still more surprisingly, the French group judged French voices less favourably than did the English-speaking group. The researchers concluded that the French speakers had internalized a negative stereotype of their own language. That was more than half a century ago, and a vast amount of sociopolitical change has flowed through Québec in the interim, especially for the status of the French language. Despite this, subsequent replications, including the only recent one that I know of (a short thesis, Boulé 2002), found precisely the same kind of self-denigration, an issue we return to in section 10.5. In attitudes experiments Québecois have also long downgraded their own speech compared with continental French (e.g. d'Anglejan and Tucker 1973) – but this they have had in common with many postcolonial varieties of English and Spanish. Variations on the matched guise continue to be used widely in language attitude research on dozens of languages.

Perceptual dialectology

Championed by American sociolinguist Dennis Preston, perceptual dialectology is the study of what lay people say about language. He and his colleagues have found there is little common ground between folk and linguist beliefs of what language is (Niedzielski and Preston 2000). Linguists may be descriptivists, but everyone else is prescriptivist – a stance that sociolinguists struggle with in their dealings with other people. Correctness dominates folk views. People equate language with the standard language, and everything else is a deviation resulting from speakers' laziness or recalcitrance. Figure 10.1

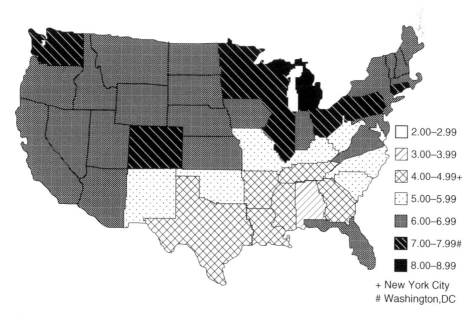

2.00–2.99

3.00–3.99

4.00–4.99+

5.00–5.99

6.00–6.99

7.00–7.99#

8.00–8.99

+ New York City
# Washington, DC

Figure 10.1 Michiganders' ratings of correctness of English in the continental USA on a 10-point scale: higher numbers are better
Source: Preston (1996), figure 13

• Interpret and explain the patterns in the map (see Preston 1996: 310ff. for his interpretation).

shows how a sample of respondents from Michigan rated the states of the US for the correctness of their English.

Much perceptual dialectology research has relied on people mapping dialects and their perceptions of them. One advantage of this method is that people generate their own labels rather than having to fit to the pre-set terms of a questionnaire. The maps are littered with comments such as 'southern hicks', 'hillbilly', 'snobs', 'damn Yankees', 'mid-west drawl'. The most salient dialect areas turn out to be the ones that Americans downgrade for incorrect English, namely the South and New York City. The other main dimension of comment is the pleasantness of accents, and here the denigrated dialects do rather better. The linguistic characteristics of dialects are labelled in terms such as 'nasal', 'twang', 'drawl', and especially 'good/bad'.

10.3   EVALUATING INDIVIDUAL LINGUISTIC VARIABLES

So far we have dealt with the valuing of languages and dialects as if they were 'wholes'. But native listeners do not only – or even primarily – respond to entire linguistic codes, but to the specific forms which make up those codes, that is, the sounds and structures of language.

As in so much else, Labov was the pioneer of the study of listeners' evaluations of individual sociolinguistic variables in his New York City study (1966, 1972b). In addition to recording his informants' language production, he tested their perceptions by playing them recordings of other New York speakers and asking them to rank the speakers for the highest job they were suited to hold. Different sections of the recordings were scripted to concentrate examples of the five phonological variables that Labov was researching (Chapter 7.1). The recordings were matched guises – that is, the listeners heard the same speakers both with and without the target variables in their speech. The differences in how the listeners rated each speaker's job chances between their two different guises indicated their responses to the specific linguistic variables.

The findings were not predictable: the more that informants produced a stigmatized feature in their own speech, the more sensitive they were to hearing it. This involved the lower-middle-class crossover for /r/ discussed in Chapter 7.2. As well as exceeding the upper middle class in *production* of /r/, the lower middle class also surpassed it in the sensitivity of their *perception* of /r/. As an incoming change, the production of /r/ is differentiated between age groups – and so also is its evaluation. All adults under 40 (the group who use it most) register sensitivity to the presence of /r/ in speech, but only half of those over 40. This pattern linking evaluation with use has also shown elsewhere. 'Avant-garde Dutch', which is typified by the lowering of the /ɛi/ diphthong (van Bezooijen and van Heuven 2010), is the variety used by elite young women in the Netherlands. They also turn out to be the ones who rate it favourably in perception tests.

Responding to ING

The most sophisticated recent research on perceptions of linguistic variables brings us back to the subject of our Chapter 7 case study, the variable ING. Kathryn Campbell-Kibler digitally spliced *in/ing* alternates into otherwise identical recordings of the same speakers to create matched guises differing only in their ING realizations. Gathering listener attitudes through group interviews and a web survey, she found that the responses reflected a range of social characteristics, especially region, gender, sexuality and class.

The American South is the one US dialect region where *in* predominates over *ing*. Campbell-Kibler's listeners heard the Southern speakers as being even more Southern when they used *in* rather than *ing*. The listeners associated the Southerners' speech with being 'country' and 'less educated', calling up this set of stereotypes:

Tamika	May be a redneck… Possibly… That's such a bad term.
Abby	No, it's not. Perfectly acceptable to call someone a redneck… But he likes his football and tailgating.
Mary	And whiskey.
Abby	And whiskeyyyy!! Yeah, he's a redneck.

(Campbell-Kibler 2007: 49)

On the other hand, nearly twice as many of the listeners described one speaker as 'gay' when he was using *ing* rather than *in*, and heard him as sounding less 'masculine' and more 'urban'. Recall that *in* had salient gendered associations in the studies by Fischer, Trudgill and especially Kiesling in Chapter 7.6. In perception as well as production, *in* indexes masculinity, physicality and ruralness. By contrast, *ing* is heard as educated and intelligent.

But the picture is by no means so simple, as Campbell-Kibler makes clear elsewhere (2008). Some of her speakers triggered contrasting reactions from their listeners. They agreed with each other on how the speakers sounded, but disagreed on whether those self-presentations rang true or not. The use of *in* by 'Elizabeth' was heard as either compassionate or condescending, depending on what stance the particular listener attributed to her. 'Valerie' in her *ing* guise was heard as intelligent by some, but a quarter of the listeners thought she was unintelligent and trying to impress (Exercise 10.6). If a speaker was heard as trying to do something intentionally – rather than 'naturally' – listeners tended to disallow the claim and give the speaker the opposite grading.

This variability between listeners shows the need to question Labov's assumption that evaluations are shared across a speech community. It recalls Rickford's study of class in Cane Walk, Guyana (Exercise 7.3): language evaluations and attitudes there were contrary rather than consensual, reflexes of the class conflict within the community. Campbell-Kibler (2009) concludes that even a single variable like ING which is the subject of overt comment and has its own recognized label – 'dropping your Gs' – can call up multiple and contrasting social meanings.

Hearing vowel shifts

Sound change presents a challenge to perception and understanding: how do listeners cope with vowels that are shifting, especially if those listeners come from other dialect areas that are not undergoing the changes? Usually local listeners prove – not surprisingly – to be better at hearing local distinctions than are people from elsewhere. The Northern Cities Chain Shift (Chapter 8.4) has been fertile ground for

Exercise 10.6 Evaluating Valerie

In Campbell-Kibler's studies of ING perceptions, some listeners questioned how intelligent one of the speakers really was. This is what Valerie had said in the recording they heard (all five ING tokens were pronounced as *ing*):

> To get a major in history you have to have taken classes from all different time periods, all different areas, every**thing** like that. Um, and that means you're get**ting** breadth. You're basically star**ting** from the begin**ning** every time. You know, you move to a different part of the world you're star**ting** from scratch. (Campbell-Kibler 2007: 59)

Here is what two of the focus groups who listened to that said about her:

Sarah: ... probably not so smart because she's saying the obvious. Or she just, or she may be in a situation where she's not comfortable so she kind of just says whatever comes to mind.

Adam: Yeah, I agree. It sounded like she really didn't know what to say. And just kind of spat something out.

Moderator: Okay.

Jeremy: Yeah, it's definitely, like I get the impression that she's not doing well in history.

Amy: Well I, even if she does have a degree I don't think it was very rigorous ...

Moderator: Anything in particular that gave you that impression?

Amy: Oh it was just that she stammered after she was talking about the different types majors and ... it was just kind of disjointed.

Amelia: Yeah, I don't think she's very smart.

(Campbell-Kibler 2008: 650)

1 Get different class members to read Valerie's transcript out loud to give some sense of how the speech may sound. Also read aloud the discussion transcripts, with class members voicing the speakers in the groups.
2 Analyse the discussants' evaluations and the evidence for them (you cannot hear her actual speech, but most of the comments refer to content).
3 Make your own evaluation of Valerie.
4 Compare the discussants' impressions with your own. Do you agree? Revisit the evidence found in the transcript.
5 What is your view of the study's method? – playing a recording and getting a focus group to discuss it. And the kind of results it has produced? See Campbell-Kibler's articles for detail.

investigating this. Preston (2010) researched perceptions in Michigan and found that listeners whose dialect is most involved in the shift comprehend best and those who are least involved comprehend worst. As the title of Preston's article has it, outsiders would think they heard this nonsense sentence:

Belle's body just caught the fit gnat.

But what the chain-shifting Michigander really said was:

Bill's bawdy jest cut the fat knot.

- Work out the vowel shifts for yourself using Figure 8.3a.

The ability to digitally synthesize vowels very precisely along a phonetic continuum means that sociophoneticians are now able to test perceptions of finely graded pronunciation differences. Listeners from Detroit, which is participating in the chain shift, are sensitive to the shifted vowels, but those who are in northern Michigan remote from the shift are not (Plichta and Rakerd 2010). Frequent exposure to the incoming pronunciations looks to be crucial to perceiving them.

The paradox of near-mergers

The most surprising finding on the perception of linguistic variables is the existence of **near-mergers**. Merger occurs when two vowels come to occupy the same space (Chapter 8.4). It turns out that some pronunciations can be so nearly merged that they are heard as the same even though acoustic measurements show them to be consistently if slightly

---

Exercise 10.7   Coffee or copy?

Academic expertise on mergers does not rescue linguists from misunderstanding other speakers' merged vowels in ordinary conversation. Labov (1994: 326) records these exchanges between sociolinguists which confused *copy* and *coffee* as a result of the low back vowel merger in parts of North America (he wrily notes the tendency of these two words to co-occur in academic discourse).

D. Sankoff: It's time to make the copies.
W. Labov: But I've already had my coffee.

A. Taylor: Do you have the copy key?
D. Ringe: Is there a key to the coffee?

C. Roberts: How did the coffee machine work out?
S. Ash: [Launches into narrative about a copy machine.]

- Take note of differences between your dialect and others which may lead to confusion when the two dialects come into contact.
- Have the class start to note down all instances they hear of such cross-dialectal misunderstandings. As the corpus grows, analyse what phonetic, semantic and lexical issues are involved.
- See Labov (2010: chapter 2) for his group's work on this kind of data.

Example 10.2

The Coach Test

Labov created an ingenious naturalistic experiment (1994) to test Philadelphians' perceptions of the near-merger in words like *ferry* and *furry* while listeners were concentrating away from the actual language. He scripted a narrative about the coach of a high school baseball team, focusing on a boy named Murray and a girl nicknamed Merion. At the crucial stage of the deciding game, the coach has to decide which of them to put in as a substitute fielder. He debates with himself and makes his decision:

A 'I gotta play Merion there.'
B 'I gotta play Murray in there.'

The narrator recorded both phonetic versions, and the denouement of the story was written ambiguously so that it would suit either decision. Subjects hear one of the versions and are asked whether the coach made the right decision. The ensuing conversation shows whether they have interpreted the decision as favouring the boy or the girl, and therefore indicates how they perceived the near-merged vowels.

In a 1988 run of the experiment, 14 out of 15 outsiders gave the correct response on which version they had heard. But 7 out of 21 Philadelphians were wrong, indicating they did not perceive the vowel distinction.

---

different. That is, speakers can produce a difference that they cannot hear. It seems that perception does not always align perfectly with production – although that has always been a tenet of linguistic theory.

Several near-mergers have been found in dialects of both American and British English as well as Swedish (Labov 1994). The most-studied is between pairs like *merry/ Murray* in Philadelphia English. Some Philadelphians show a complete merger, some a clear distinction, but others have a near-merger. Labov devised the 'Coach Test' to study discrimination of these two vowels (Example 10.2).

10.4   THE INDEXICAL CYCLE

The previous section largely begged a foundational question, the answer to which is crucial to our approach in the rest of this book. We have seen how languages and varieties are infused with ideologies (section 10.1), how listeners react to those codes in attitude studies (10.2), and how they respond to individual linguistic forms (10.3). We have covered 'what' but not yet attempted to address the sociolinguistic why and how and who of this. Why do linguistic forms accrue social meaning? How do they do so? And who is responsible?

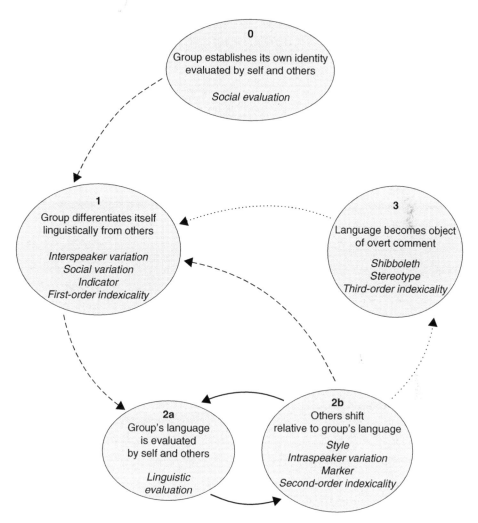

Figure 10.2   The Indexical Cycle: processes of creating social meaning in language
Phases 2a and 2b co-occur. Phases 2–3 constitute the process of enregisterment (Agha 2003).
Source: Derived from Bell (1984), figure 2

The creation of social meaning

The first address to this central issue came not within sociolinguistics nor even in the West, but from the Russian literary theorist Mikhail Bakhtin, whose approach we deal with in the case study in 10.6. Sociolinguistic founders such as Ferguson and Gumperz tackled the issue in the 1950s, and Labov from the 1960s. My own attempt began during doctoral work in the 1970s, and formed the foundation of Audience Design theory (Bell 1984). I proposed a model for understanding how language and linguistic variables take on social meaning, shown in expanded version in Figure 10.2 as the **Indexical Cycle**. Meanwhile the linguistic anthropologist Michael Silverstein was beginning to theorize the process in a more sophisticated fashion in terms of **indexicality**, which he proposed has three 'orders' (2003). An index is a sign that bears a direct connection to what it refers to – thunder is indexical of lightning. In language, a form indexes social values, connecting language form and social meaning (like Irvine and Gal's 'iconization' in section 10.1).

These approaches share a lot in common: in Figure 10.2 I identify five phases which make up the Indexical Cycle and illustrate them through a case we are already familiar with, Eckert's Belten High (Chapter 8.7). The numbering meshes with Silverstein's three orders of indexicality:

0   *A group (or individual) achieves a distinct identity, valued by group members, contrastive with and evaluated by others.*
    - Assume an idealized point of origin for jocks and burnouts in the past: both groups begin to take on their own social practices and characteristics, they are socially differentiated and evaluated.
1   *The group distinguishes aspects of its language from others*, either as part of the founding process or subsequently. This produces 'interspeaker variation', differences between the speech of the group and of others. Labov (1972b) termed this 'social' variation, and labelled linguistic forms which manifested such interspeaker difference as **indicators**. For Silverstein (2003), this is **first-order indexicality**, the initial step in registration of social meaning.
    - Jocks and burnouts differentiate their language from each other, for example using more or less negative concord (Figure 8.9).
2a *Both the group and outsiders put a social value on the group's language and its forms.* The linguistic variables take on social meanings in line with how the user group is evaluated, as we saw in the previous section for ING and postvocalic /r/.
    - For the Belten High community, negative concord attracts the evaluations associated with its user group, the burnouts. The form begins to mean what the group means.
2b *Simultaneously outsiders start to adopt these features to signal would-be affiliation with the group and its values.* This creates 'intraspeaker variation', that is individuals whose speech ranges across both their original repertoire and the newly adopted variants. This is 'style'. Labov termed such linguistic variables **markers**, and Silverstein **second-order indexes**.
    - Belten High 'In-betweens' who want to associate with the burnouts may start to use negative concord. The form has begun to stand for affiliation with the group.
3   *Some linguistic variables may become the object of overt attention and comment.* These are 'shibboleths' (Example 10.1), by which a linguistic form is consciously used to do social work. Labov termed these **stereotypes**, and Silverstein **third-order indexes**.
    - Negative concord is openly identified as a stereotype of burnout speech. It may be performed as an emblem of the group – affiliating or critiquing or satirizing.

Understanding indexicality

My attempt in Figure 10.2 to formalize the making of sociolinguistic meaning is – like any other – inevitably idealized and under-nuanced. It reifies concepts like 'identity' and 'group', chronologically orders phases which are simultaneous or interspersed or recursive, makes the variable discrete and the relative absolute, and implies that all of a group's variables index the same social meaning. Modelling such as the Indexical Cycle is however still worth attempting, and we can draw a number of generalizations from it:

- You cannot read a second-order social meaning off a first-order distribution (Silverstein 2003). The existence of statistical differences between ages or classes does not itself demonstrate that the variable has social meaning (as some variationist work has assumed). You need independent social evidence.
- The stylistic (phase 2b) derives from and mirrors 'social' differentiation (1). You do not get intraspeaker style difference without the pre-existence of interspeaker differences (Bell 1984). First-order indexicality is the prerequisite for second-order.
- Phases 2a and 2b always co-occur. The empirical evidence, for example from Labov's early work, is that once a linguistic variable starts to be evaluated, it necessarily becomes the subject of style shift (e.g. Figure 7.1).
- Most variables are markers, second-order indexicals, evaluated and subject to styling. Few stay arrested at the level of indicators, with the second-order potential only lurking ready to endow social meaning (Silverstein 2003). A few variables proceed to phase 3 to become overtly manipulated shibboleths.
- This model is a way of schematizing how linguistic differences have been created between groups, that is, how styles evolve. It also shows the process by which an individual learns to style. And it can continue to cycle to new variables – note the recursive arrows from 2b/3 back to phase 1.

The most thorough research into indexicality and the enregisterment (Agha 2003) of a dialect that it embodies has been by Barbara Johnstone and her colleagues in Pittsburgh,

---

Exercise 10.8   Researching a linguistic stereotype near you

What are the stereotype features – the third-order indexicals – of your local dialect? Or of a variety you know that is defined socially rather than regionally, such as a youth register? Look at the Pittsburgh research as an example (Johnstone, Andrus and Danielson 2006; Johnstone and Kiesling 2008; Johnstone 2009, 2011a).

1 List as many stereotype linguistic forms as you can for the dialect.
2 What levels of language are they from? – lexical, phonological, even syntactic?
3 For a pronunciation, is it associated with one or more specific lexical items? Why those words? Is a stock phrase used to represent the dialect?
4 Are there dictionaries or web-based word lists of the dialect available, or advice on how to speak it? Choose one and analyse.
5 Choose one or more forms and set about collecting instances of them being deliberately used to represent the variety.
6 What genres (e.g. advertising) or products (e.g. mugs) does the form appear in?
7 How does its representation relate to the social characteristics associated with the dialect?
8 What are attitudes, from both speakers and outsiders, towards the dialect? And to the stereotype forms?

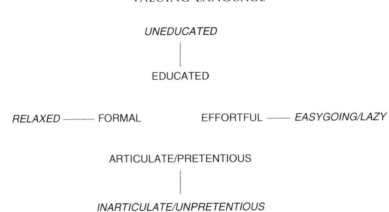

Figure 10.3   The indexical field of the ING variable. Roman type represents the *ing* variant, and italics *in*
Source: Eckert (2008), figure 3

USA. They trace the Pittsburgh dialect through all three indexical orders, from historical differentiation, through evaluation and styling, to stereotyped performance. First labelled in print as 'Pittsburghese' in 1967, it is now commodified on T-shirts, performed in radio skits, and prescribed in a published guide on *How to Speak like a Pittsburgher*. Monophthongization of the diphthong in MOUTH is now well established as a Pittsburgh shibboleth – phase 3 in Figure 10.2. Often such a variant will be displayed in a stock lexical item (perhaps respelt), in this case *dahntahn* for 'downtown'. Recall Rex O'Neal's recitation displaying the Ocracoke *hoi toide* vowel (Example 9.1).

The indexical field

Eckert proposes the **indexical field** as a way of mapping the range of a variable's social meanings, in the belief that a variable need not be tied to a single significance. She takes the variety of associations that ING called up for the subjects in Campbell-Kibler's studies that we looked at earlier, then diagrams them as in Figure 10.3. For individual hearers the two variants *ing* and *in* need not index direct opposites. Johnstone and Kiesling (2008) also found that the MOUTH diphthong had very different meanings for different people, often unpredictable from the person's demographics. In particular, a speaker may have a different social meaning for a variable than the listener takes from it. That said, it is clear from Figure 10.2 that a variable such as ING does carry a core set of social meanings.

10.5   DISCRIMINATING LANGUAGE

Standard language and language standards

The most obvious product of language ideology is the standard language. Although people focus a lot of attention on the forms of the standard language, it is essentially a social rather than a linguistic construct. Standard languages are the outcome of the processes outlined in the first and third sections of this chapter. Recall that the main characteristics of an ideology are that it serves the interests of a social group (Woolard 1998). Standard languages are defined by and serve social elites, legitimizing linguistic domination and concealing it from the dominated.

French is perhaps the world's most standardized language, benchmarked in the seventeenth century by the founding of the Académie Française (Example 10.3). After the French Revolution language unification became more extreme, downgrading all other languages such as Breton and Occitan, and all varieties other than the French of the Île de France (the area round Paris: see Bourhis 1982 for an overview). That history makes it no surprise that French sociologist Pierre Bourdieu should be the one to theorize language standardization. In society there are different kinds and levels of symbolic or cultural

Example 10.3

L'Académie Française

The Académie Française is the world's best-known language standards body. It has 40 seats, each individually numbered and occupied by one of *les immortels* whose average age is over 80. New members are elected for life by the existing members, and on accession must deliver a eulogy to the member they have replaced. Of more than 700 *immortels* over the centuries, six have been women, the first elected in 1980.

The Académie was established in 1635 by Cardinal Richelieu, Louis XIII's powerful chief minister. Its mission is to 'set the French language fast, create rules for it, and make it pure and comprehensible among all'. It gives rulings on standards of correctness, and publishes the official dictionaries of French.

The Académie's main recent concern has been to prevent the perceived creeping anglicization of French. In 2008 it also opposed – vigorously but unsuccessfully – official recognition of over 20 regional languages which had been denied constitutional legitimacy for centuries. The Académie has contested the use of feminine alternates for titles, such as *la ministre* for a woman minister instead of the generic masculine *le ministre*. The feminine is already official practice in other French-speaking nations and widespread in France.

Linguistic purism, then, is prevalent in France. President Nicolas Sarkozy was widely criticized for his language, including dropping the *ne* in negative sentences – which, as we saw in Chapter 8.3, is now the norm for most speakers most of the time.

- Use web resources to research the workings of a prescriptive language institution in your country. This could include an academy, but also educational authorities, dictionary makers, broadcasting organizations.
- Monitor media comment on language usage, especially complaints and prescriptions (what Cameron calls 'verbal hygiene', 1995). What are the patterns in the comments you have collected? What concerns do they represent?

capital, including **linguistic capital**. Language standardization unifies the linguistic market (Chapter 8.6) and necessarily devalues all other codes. Speakers not brought up with 'legitimate language' (Bourdieu 1991) are put at an automatic disadvantage in situations where the standard is expected, such as formal social occasions. If their discourse is to be listened to as well as heard, they must adopt legitimate language – but this they cannot achieve easily. The outcome is a form of symbolic violence which leads to the hypercorrective behaviour of the 'petit bourgeois' discovered by Labov in New York and observed by Bourdieu in France. Labov calculated an 'Index of Linguistic Insecurity' for his New Yorkers, the difference between their own usage and what they thought was correct. The lower middle class were by far the most self-denigrating, leading Labov to characterize New York famously as 'a sink of negative prestige' (1972b: 136).

The processes of standardization

The study of language standardization goes back to the earliest days of sociolinguistics, when language planning was a major activity (see Chapter 3.4). The Norwegian American Einar Haugen (1966) proposed that standardization consisted of four stages:

1   selection of a language or variety to be standard
2   codification of the linguistic characteristics of the standard
3   elaboration – the promotion of the standard across social functions (see Chapter 3.2) and domains (6.1)
4   acceptance – the implementation and diffusion of the standard throughout society.

Haugen's model shares with all descriptivist approaches the tendency to erase the ideological position that it encodes, and therefore meshes with the consensus approach to social structure. In keeping with the conflict model described in Chapter 7.2, the Milroys (2012) regard standardization as an ideology and a process, and the standard as an idea rather than a product.

Received Pronunciation (RP) is the world's best-known standard accent but it is a relatively recent invention, resulting from social processes and partaking in continuing linguistic change (recall Example 8.1). Although the label implies historical authority, until the mid eighteenth century there was no sense of a standard pronunciation for English. But a hundred years later RP had been established as the elite accent of England. It had gone from first- to second-order status on the Indexical Cycle in Figure 10.2. See Agha's study of the enregisterment of RP in Example 10.4.

The main instrument of language standardization is the education system, which routinely promotes monolingualism and monodialectalism. Bourdieu maintains that teachers, grammarians and writers construct legitimate language, which has to be sustained by constant correction. In the UK John Honey conflates standard English with 'educatedness' and social betterment (1997), learning the standard with the ability to gain technological literacy – and regards linguists as among the enemies of the standard. He proposed the establishment of a French-style language academy in Britain. Lippi-Green's work on 'language, ideology and discrimination' in the United States (2012) identifies a range of educational practices that marginalize non-standard English in the classroom.

Example 10.4

The enregisterment of RP

Asif Agha (2003) investigated the process of 'enregisterment' by which a minority accent from southeastern England became the national standard of British English. His term covers phases 2–3 of the Indexical Cycle in Figure 10.2, moving from first- to second- to third-order indexicality.

The prerequisite for enregisterment of RP was for it to be circulated ever more widely in society. This began about 1760 with a proliferation of prescriptivist works on pronunciation, which led on to popular handbooks on correct speech. Nineteenth-century novelists picked up features into their characters' speech. Dickens's Uriah Heep became the icon of (denigrated) h-dropping, a stereotype emblematized in the single repeated word '*umble*. Finally penny weeklies with huge circulations spread the discourse of good speech down the social scale.

RP thus became widely perceived as socially desirable speech, and by the late nineteenth century the English 'public schools' became nurseries for producing its speakers. Increasingly RP was identified with what Agha terms particular 'characterological figures'. Initially public school graduates served as these exemplary speakers, then army officers, and from the mid twentieth century BBC announcers (see Exercise 10.9). Today RP consistently rates high on accent scale evaluations in attitude studies (section 10.2). It is spoken by only a few per cent of the population of the United Kingdom, but it is precisely that scarcity that defines much of its worth: it would be devalued if too many people spoke it.

- Consider a standard language or variety that you know. How did it gain this status?
- Look at the processes for RP in Agha (2003) and consider what are the parallel – or different – processes in your case. How is it circulated, how maintained?
- Who is it associated with, who are its 'characterological figures' (like the Queen for RP)?
- Look at Lynda Mugglestone's fascinating work on the dropping of 'g's and 'h's as icons of not 'talking proper' in English (1995). What are the shibboleths that define the standard you are researching?

Linguistic disadvantage

If speaking the standard is a social advantage, then lacking it must necessarily be a disadvantage. The unavoidable outcome of language standardization is inequity, certainly for some, often for the many. In these last few chapters I have referred blithely and often to 'standard' variants of a linguistic variable, as if that were an unproblematic notion. It is not. The concept has been definitional within variationist sociolinguistics but its ideological freight has been little addressed, with the principal exception of the Milroys (especially 2012). Disadvantage is linguistically encoded. If speakers lack the capital of Bourdieu's 'legitimate language', they *will* be disadvantaged.

Exercise 10.9   Broadcasting as language standard

Newscasters are routinely treated as the 'characterological figures' whose speech embodies the standard. This applies to RP in the UK (Agha 2003), and to 'network English' in the US. Labov endorses this identification through using newscasters as models in evaluation experiments (e.g. Labov et al. 2011).

- What do you think were the reasons that broadcast news adopted the standard language for its own speech from its earliest days? – see Leitner (1980) on early BBC radio.
- Why did broadcast news then come to be identified as the standard by which the standard is itself judged? Identify at least half a dozen reasons.
- Do national radio and television in your country use the standard? If so, what do you assess are their reasons?
- If not, what variety do they use and why? Has it always been this way or has it changed? Is it a case of de- or re-standardization? What are the factors contributing to that?

Resources include Bell (1983, 2011b), Agha (2003), Lippi-Green (2012).

The routine companions of linguistic disadvantage are economic and social disadvantage, whether that be for Moroccans in France, northerners in England, Quechua speakers in Peru, African Americans, or the Estate Class of Cane Walk, Guyana (Chapter 7.2). If the 'best people' speak in a certain way, you will not become one of the best people without their speech, no matter that the actual linguistic indexes are arbitrary – why is /r/-pronouncing prestigious in America and denigrated in England? – and no matter that only a small minority of the population control the standard.

But as the perceptual dialectology research shows, most people accept the standard as natural, normal, commonsense (James Milroy 2001) – see Exercise 10.10. 'Standard' implies, indeed relies on, the consensus view of society that I critiqued in Chapter 7.2, one that elides the often conflictual socioeconomic and sociolinguistic realities. Most sociolinguists have been acutely aware of disadvantage in the communities they studied, and many major projects have been undertaken to address linguistic inequity. But, as we will see in the case study of Bakhtin in 10.6, perhaps something more radical is needed.

Valuing the vernacular

But the standard is not the only story. We saw in the Chapter 7.6 case of ING and Campbell-Kibler's study of perceptions of it (10.3) that there are countervailing forces. These index a range of alternative associations, values and oppositions: working versus middle class, toughness–weakness, masculine–feminine, solidarity–status, local–global, physicality–refinement. Trudgill termed this alternative 'covert prestige', although Labov concluded (2001a: 217) that his evaluation experiments turned up little support for the existence of such norms in Philadelphia.

Exercise 10.10 Verbal hygiene

In his preface to the manual *Rhyming Roadways to Good Speech* (1940), Professor F. Sinclaire of Canterbury University, New Zealand, wrote:

> Debased speech – it cannot too strongly be insisted – is a symptom of general cultural debasement, of growing insensibility to values which lie at the very roots of all culture. Someone has said that people who talk through the nose will think through the nose. It is certain that if we speak badly we shall think badly and feel coarsely. (Quoted in Gordon and Abell 1990: 30)

Many people are language 'mavens' who focus on what Deborah Cameron has called verbal hygiene – 'the urge to meddle in matters of language' (1995: vii). The impetus to cleanse language rests on a firmly held belief in what Labov has labelled – after interviews with thousands of speakers – the Golden Age Principle: 'At some time in the past, language was in a state of perfection' (2001a: 514). All linguistic change, then, must always be for the worse. Complaints (like Sinclaire's) often have a strong moral underlay. But while descriptive linguists may hold that such views are nonsense, sociolinguists need to take them as seriously-held opinions.

- Media publish many such complaints. Computer-search your local newspapers or magazines using clusters of appropriate key words to identify complaint stories and letters. Or locate blogs or other websites devoted to language prescriptivism.
- Analyse and classify the complaints. Compare the views expressed with what linguists believe. Account for differences.
- Take one set of these views, write a statement which focuses them, and hold a two-sided debate on it in class.
- Or debate this statement:
    No accent or dialect is linguistically better than any other: people regard one as better than another on purely social grounds.

- Resources include Bauer and Trudgill's *Language Myths* book (1998), Cameron's *Verbal Hygiene* (1995), Niedzielski and Preston's *Folk Linguistics* (2000), *English with an Accent* (Lippi-Green 2012), and Bex and Watts' *Standard English: The Widening Debate* (1999).

Yet it remains evidently the case that groups such as Eckert's burnouts create and maintain linguistic norms which are defiantly oppositional to the standard. Shared local networks and practices are vernacular maintenance mechanisms with their own powers of persuasion and conformity in the face of institutional propagation of the standard. But by definition, there is no public discourse or discussion around what is covert.

However, we also need to beware of not endorsing unquestioningly the construct of a single standard to non-standard continuum along which all linguistic variation must range. Bourdieu (1991: 95) argues vehemently against such a dualism between standard and 'popular' language, which simply endorses the dominant structuring. Bakhtin makes the same call, as we see in the next section, with his notion of 'heteroglossia'. The vernacular is immensely more variegated than the standard, it is the locus of linguistic innovation and creativity – remember the burned-out burnouts of Chapter 8.7. There is a need to (re)discover diversity, Bourdieu proposes, the alternative markets in which the language of the 'dominated' is valued.

Something of this is now (re)emerging in nations whose linguistic standards were established two or more centuries ago. Processes of de-standardization and re-standardization are evident in Europe and under investigation by the 'SLICE' research consortium – 'Standard Language Ideology in Contemporary Europe' (Kristiansen and Coupland 2011). In restandardization 'the belief that there is, and should be, a "best language" is not abandoned, but the idea of what this "best language" is, or sounds like, changes' (Kristiansen 2009: 2). An example would be the acceptance in California of 'Ebonics' rather than standard English as a medium of instruction.

Much more radical is destandardization, the loss of the notion that a standard even exists, with all the ideological repercussions that involves. Bakhtin's concept of the centrifugal and centripetal forces in language (section 10.6) captures this abolitionist bent. Destandardization involves a scattering away from the standard in all directions, and an accompanying unshackling of language from the idea of the standard. Kristiansen and Coupland's book examines the extent to which de- and restandardization may be operating in contemporary Europe.

10.6   THE CASE OF BAKHTIN

The story of Mikhail Bakhtin comes with a Government Health Warning. Bakhtin was a committed chain smoker – although he lived to nearly 80 – but not all his works lived with him. In the spartan years of the Second World War in the Soviet Union, Bakhtin ran out of cigarette papers. The only suitable paper he could find was one of his own manuscripts, and this he used page by page to roll his cigarettes. However the publisher's copy disappeared in the destruction wreaked by the German invasion – so the book was lost utterly, smoked away by its own author.

That incident exemplifies Bakhtin's rocky road to publication and recognition. His foundational work was done in the 1920s but much of it did not see the light of day even in the Soviet Union until 40 years later. In 1960 he was re/discovered, first within the Soviet Union and then in the West, where his thinking has since been celebrated across a range of disciplines, foreshadowing much in sociolinguistics.

Centrifugal and centripetal language

Bakhtin maintains that in society, language is a site of struggle between the dynamic centrifugal forces which whirl it apart into diversity, and the centripetal forces which strive to standardize and prescribe the way language should be. He acknowledges standardization as a force but celebrates the centrifugal – the divergence, individuality, creativity, even the chaos of language variety:

Circles of English

Bakhtin's concept of the centripetal and centrifugal forces in language – pulling in to a centre or pushing out towards the periphery – is operationalized in some approaches to today's most widespread language ideological issue, the situation of English.

The earliest and still seminal model of international English is Kachru's three concentric circles (1992):

1 Inner Circle: English as a Native Language, 'norm providing' – the long-established first-language nations of the UK, USA, Canada, Australia, New Zealand, South Africa.
2 Outer Circle: English as a Second Language, 'norm developing' – e.g. India, Malaysia.
3 Expanding Circle: English as a Foreign Language, 'norm dependent' – e.g. Korea, Germany.

Kachru intended his framework as a liberating force against the hegemony of the traditional British/American models – witness his 1990s debate with Lord Randolph Quirk on standards in international English. However, his approach has been criticized as cementing rather than challenging the dominant pattern. India, for example, has many millions of native speakers of English.

Another alternative is the centre and periphery model, adopted from postcolonial theory. Canagarajah (1999) sees this as a way of overcoming frequently perceived dichotomies between the western and the indigenous, English and the vernacular, native and non-native. It avoids both the wholesale acceptance or rejection of English, and formulates a 'third way' of the **appropriation** of English into local contexts. Here English is vernacularized and pluralized – a heteroglossic scenario.

- Access the exchange in *English Today* between Quirk (1990) and Kachru (1991). Distill and evaluate their arguments, and draw your own conclusion.
- Compare and assess Kachru's three-circles model (1992) and Canagarajah's centre/periphery approach (1999).
- Pennycook provides a useful table of six approaches to the global role of English (2001: 59). Detail and compare these using information from Pennycook and other sources, and evaluate them as ideologies.

'World Englishes' is a well-established field of research, with three journals (*English World-Wide*, *English Today*, and *World Englishes*), an International Association, annual conferences, its own handbook (Kachru, Kachru and Nelson 2006) and a – very good – six-volume Routledge collection of readings (Bolton and Kachru 2006). See Bolton (2004) for an overview. For critical work see the publications of Canagarajah and Pennycook.

Example 10.5

> Alongside the centripetal forces, the centrifugal forces of language carry on their uninter-
> rupted work; alongside verbal-ideological centralization and unification, the uninterrupted
> processes of decentralization and disunification go forward. (Bakhtin 1981: 272)

The centrifugal and centripetal forces operate at both social and individual levels. Bakhtin saw this struggle as a crusade for the vernacular against the standard. He was not neutral in response to these forces, but celebrated language as kaleidoscope:

> What is involved here is a very important, in fact a radical revolution in the destinies of
> human discourse: the fundamental liberation of cultural-semantic and emotional inten-
> tions from the hegemony of a single and unitary language. (1981: 367)

Sociolinguists are also not neutral in this struggle. As students of language variety, our field aligns us with the centrifugal. We are advocates of variety rather than of homogenization, for example in support for endangered or denigrated languages or dialects.

Heteroglossia

The fruit of the centrifugal forces in language is heteroglossia:

> The internal stratification of any single national language into social dialects, characteristic
> group behavior, professional jargons, generic languages, languages of generations and age
> groups, tendentious languages, languages of the authorities, of various circles and of passing
> fashions, languages that serve the specific sociopolitical purposes of the day, even of the hour
> (each day has its own slogan, its own vocabulary, its own emphases) – this internal stratification
> [is] present in every language at any given moment of its historical existence. (Bakhtin 1981: 262)

To illustrate heteroglossia in action, here are two of the voices of Billy T. James, New Zealand's best comedian, who died in 1991. Example 10.6 is an anecdote about the formidable Māori entertainer, Prince Tui Teka, who pre-deceased Billy. The excerpt is shot through with New Zealand vernacular, more particularly Māori Vernacular English (see Bell 2000):

- an extremely backed DRESS vowel in *fellas*
- raised and fronted KIT vowel where the usual NZ English variant is centralized
- affricated /dh/
- devoiced final /z/, a Māori vernacular marker
- stereotypical Māori tag *eh*
- address form *bro*.

Some of this is undergirded – in line 5, and especially line 19, where Billy is quoting Tui – by the distinctive intonation associated with Māori Vernacular English. Billy T. James was the public icon of this code – a 'characterological figure' in Agha's terms. The visuals fitted the character, with Billy in the guise of a naughty Māori boy, dressed in shorts and a black singlet. This is a vernacular, centrifugal language, locally grounded and interpreted.

Example 10.6

Centrifugal language: Billy T. James narrates Prince Tui and the takeaway bar

1 We drove into this takeaway bar, <u>eh</u>.	
Geez, I was laughing.	
We pulled up.	
Tui wound the window down,	
5 looked up at the girl behind the counter –	
you know, typical Australian,	
smokes Rothmans, chews PK,	
got a fountain pen mark over here, you know,	
where she's been putting it in:	
10 "Yeah, whaddya want?"	
Tui goes:	
"Ah – gi' us – ah – gi' us –	
three double eggburger<u>s</u>	voiceless /z/ [s]
ah – three whole ch<u>i</u>cken<u>s</u>	raised KIT [ɪ] voiceless /z/ [s]
15 and ah – four litre<u>s</u> of diet coke."	voiceless /z/ [s]
And we went:	
"Hah – Tui's shouting <u>the</u> boy<u>s</u>."	affricate /dh/ [dð] voiceless /z/ [s]
And he turned around and said:	
"You f<u>e</u>llas want anyth<u>i</u>ng?"	backed DRESS [ɤ] raised KIT [ɪ]
20 And that's a true story	
and I'll always remember	
<u>that</u> eh about my <u>bro</u> Tui.	affricate /dh/ [dð]

Glosses:
Shout – buy food or drink for someone
Bro – brother or mate

(While this clip could not be located online, YouTube has many of Billy T. James's skits.)

The second excerpt is at the other end of the New Zealand stylistic spectrum, visually as well as dialectally (Example 10.7). In a television variety series called *Radio Times*, Billy plays the host of a fictional 1930s radio show Dexter Fitzgibbons – a saliently stagey, British name. His dress is bow tie and tails. In keeping with stereotypes of the New Zealand broadcast accent of the 1930s, he produces an RP approximation, most noticeably the GOAT vowel, but also KIT. This stylization is separated by 50 years from the era which it targets, and distant in place from the British standard that it is intended to echo. It is, as Bakhtin says of the centripetal, a very obvious example of a frozen form.

As centripetal English this is internationally recognizable and comprehensible, with no glossing required for non-local listeners. The standard looks back in time and away to another place – recall that these are the defining characteristics of diglossia (Chapter 5.3).

Example 10.7

Centripetal language: Billy T. James hosting *Radio Times*

Good evening, good evening, listeners.
And let me assure you
that there is no cause for feeling bad tonight
because everything on Radio Times is looking good.
This is your host Dexter Fitzgibbons
welcoming you to another fun-filled fascinating fifty minutes,
with the Southern Hemisphere's greatest dance band,
the Radio Times Orchestra,
Bunny le Veau, Guy Bosanquet,
Tommy Blackhouse, the High Spots,
and the gentlemen of the Radio Theatre.

1   Locate two audio/video clips (e.g. on YouTube) with contrasting 'centrifugal' and 'centripetal' voices, that is, a standard variety and a vernacular. By the same performer if you can.
2   Analyse the linguistics of the two voices.
3   Interpret the social meanings indexed by the linguistic forms.
4   What generalizations can you make about how the indexicality works?

It is socially charged – an accent that in contemporary New Zealand stands for the outsider and the former. By contrast, Bakhtin calls on heteroglossia to challenge the hegemony of the standard:

> It is necessary that heteroglossia wash over a culture's awareness of itself and its language, penetrate to its core, relativize the primary language system underlying its ideology and literature and deprive it of its naïve absence of conflict … The entire dialectological makeup of a given national language, must have the sense that it is surrounded by an ocean of heteroglossia. (1981: 368)

10.7 RESEARCH ACTIVITY
DOING A PROJECT (3) – RESULTS AND REPORTING

Step 6: coding the data

Because the goals, designs and methods of sociolinguistic projects can be so diverse, it is not possible to provide a single template for coding, analysis and interpretation that would suit all projects. But let us distinguish three broad kinds of project:

1   Qualitative/ethnographic/discourse/observation: the data for analysis are normally texts, whether researcher fieldnotes or recordings/transcripts or print texts.
    • The researcher is looking for themes to be coded, formally or otherwise, for example, mentions of language issues.

2   Linguistic, discoursal: the data are linguistic features and forms in spoken or written language.
    • Language features have to be identified and coded, for example variants of a variable, structures, pragmatic devices or discourse patterns.
3   Survey, quantitative: the data are in the form of answers to a structured questionnaire.
    • The data may be pre-structured by the formal questionnaire (for example a language survey as in Exercise 2.9), and/or may include qualitative comments, which can be coded thematically.

• For linguistic analysis, select features which carry marked social meaning, for example in evoking a particular regional or ethnic variety. For thematic or discourse analysis, target the potentially richest forms.
• Remember to take account not just of language but other aspects of your data that may be relevant, particularly the visuals.
• Eyeball the data as you are coding it to start spotting what patterns are beginning to emerge. Note down what you see. This informal pre-analytical stage is invaluable for identifying what may turn out to be your main findings.

Step 7: data analysis

When done properly, the activity of coding shades across into procedures of analysis. As we code, we start to discern and note patterns in the data. The phases are often recursive – we go back and re-code because of issues that arise during analysis. In analysis we are looking for two main things:

1   patterns of themes or usage
2   the social indexing and significance involved.

If you are, for example, surveying a small sample of bilinguals using a formal questionnaire such as Exercise 2.9, you can enter their answers into a blank questionnaire and begin to systematize them from there. Some tips:

• It is always worth piloting a coding system or analysis procedure on a small sample before applying it to a larger amount of data – re-coding or re-analysing can be a time-consuming and frustrating business.
• If your data are computer-searchable, there are programs that can help you, such as WordSmith.
• If you are working with variable data, Tagliamonte (2012) offers a detailed guide to analysis, including working with Goldvarb or Rbrul.
• If you have structured a sample with certain social characteristics (perhaps 10 young and 10 older people, 10 women and 10 men), you can begin by looking at how each demographic group behaves. Or you can take the behaviour – a certain pronunciation, or a particular answer to a language maintenance question – and analyse which group are saying this.
• Don't try to analyse everything, target what your hunches guide you to.

- Use your early informal observations to guide what to work on in more depth.
- Watch for telling qualitative comments that people make which may vividly capture an important point.
- You will usually have far too much data to do everything. Select and discard text or questions that are not priorities.
- One of the excitements of research is that you are taking a risk. You don't actually know what will come out of your data, your findings may take you by surprise. Be prepared for the unexpected!

Step 8: data interpretation

The analysis is now already shading into interpretation. Again here there is recursion between analysis and interpretation, with new interpretations leading you to revisit and rework earlier analyses. Note down all trends and pointers as you see them, but make sure you complete the hard work of scrupulous analysis to evidence them. Some specifics:

- Use qualitative data to illuminate quantitative.
- Watch for interactions in quantitative work (if you are not doing formal statistics that tell you that), for example in a language maintenance questionnaire, between age and length of residence in the new country.
- Watch for outliers or exceptional informants. They may make illuminating individual cases but could skew overall results.
- Individual case studies or comparisons can be very striking, e.g. of the two most different informants in your data.
- Interpret the patterns you find and their significance. Offer generalizations and explanations not a blow-by-blow account of each detail of raw findings.
- Make it clear how representative your data are of the overall phenomenon you are looking at, for example certain kinds of media texts.
- As you go, note what may provide a good way to display your data – quantitatively, what will make for a telling graph or table, and qualitatively what will be a good excerpt or example to report.
- If you can see no patterns in your data, or it is turning out the opposite of what you expected – don't try to mask this, make the best of describing what you have found. Offer a possible explanation if you can. If not, say that you can't explain it. And take comfort that in my experience only a small minority of student projects are so recalcitrant!
- From the above, decide what your (few) main findings are, what conclusions you can draw, and relate them to the literature you have read.

Step 9: writing up

Focus the whole of your report on presenting your main findings, from setup through to conclusion. Here is an outline for a project report:

1 Abstract (100–200 word summary)

2 Aims and rationale of your project:

  what is the research issue or question that the project addresses?
  what is its point, linguistically and socially?
  why is it interesting?
  why is it worth investigating?

3 Background to the database:

  including social, cultural and dialectal context

4 Literature and research review:

  see Chapter 3.6, step 2

5 Design, method of your study:

  including any ethical and access issues

6 Implementation (getting the data):

  how was the project done?
  how was the data collected, processed and analysed?
  include description of your actual sample and its characteristics
  how does what you did differ from what you had planned?

7 Method of coding and analysis:

  what you have done to produce your findings?

8 Findings and interpretation (majority of report):

  see steps 6–8 above
  think carefully about any displays such as tables or graphs; include the minimum
  information needed to make your point, lay out clearly and spaciously; look at
  examples in journals of good ways to display data

9 Reservations (short):

  any problems or mistakes
  give cautions about any effect these may have had on findings
  what would you do differently next time?

10 Conclusions:

  summarize main findings and their significance
  relate back to aims of project
  generalize and explain, but don't overgeneralize

11 References:

  all references cited should be listed
  ensure these are complete, accurate and done in the prescribed style

12 Appendices – data:

  text or transcript of (excerpts from) your data

Remember to spellcheck and proofread – and number the pages!

Wray and Bloomer (2012) has chapters on analysing different kinds of data, and good guidance on presenting and writing up a project.

10.8 SUMMARY

- Language ideologies are the ways that language is valued, with one linguistic form or code considered better or worse than another. Ideologies usually remain unconscious. They serve the interests of social groups. Prevalent ideologies serve the elite, legitimating domination while disguising it from ordinary people.
- In the processes of ideologies, iconization takes a language, variety or feature as representative of a group. Recursion projects a distinction made at one level on to another level. Erasure renders facts which do not fit the ideology invisible.
- The social psychology of language focuses particularly on language attitudes, sometimes asking directly about language. Most studies involve playing recordings to a panel of judges, who usually rate the standard language high for status, and the non-standard high for solidarity. The 'matched guise' technique was developed in Québec, where listeners heard bilinguals without knowing they were the same speakers in both French and English. French and English listeners both rated English voices more favourably.
- Perceptual dialectology is the study of what lay people say about language. In mapping tasks, it is the salient dialect areas that people downgrade for incorrect English.
- Labov played listeners recordings and compared their ratings of the same speakers using different variants. The more that informants produced a stigmatized feature themselves, the more sensitive they were to hearing it. Campbell-Kibler found Southerners were heard as less educated when using *in*, but *ing* made a man sound more gay. Perceptions of ING differed widely, with contrasting reactions depending whether speakers' self-presentations rang true or not.
- When vowel systems are changing, local listeners are better at hearing distinctions than are people from other dialects. In near-mergers pronunciations are heard as the same even though phonetically they are slightly different.
- The processes by which linguistic forms accrue social meaning have been modelled in five phases and theorized as social indexicality. The Indexical Cycle begins with the social differentiation of a group, which leads to their linguistic differentiation via variables which are indicators or first-order indexicals, then on to social evaluation of the variables and their co-occurrent style variation as markers or second-order indexicals, and sometimes to stereotyping and third-order indexicality.
- The standard language is a product of ideology. For French, standards are benchmarked by the Académie Française. Bourdieu's theory of linguistic capital holds that standardization devalues all other codes, with education as its main instrument. Standardization proceeds in four stages: selection, codification, elaboration and acceptance. Received Pronunciation has been enregistered as the standard accent of Britain, with newscasters as its embodiment.

- Not speaking the standard is a socioeconomic disadvantage, but local vernaculars indexing opposing values are maintained through shared networks and practices. De- and re-standardization are becoming evident in Europe and elsewhere.
- Bakhtin maintained that language is pulled between centrifugal forces which create diversity, and hegemonic centripetal forces which standardize. The centrifugal forces lead to heteroglossia, linguistic variety on all dimensions. These are illustrated in two voices of a New Zealand comedian, first as the icon of Māori Vernacular English, and then producing RP.
- Bakhtin's concepts are reflected in theories of the standing of English. One framework pictures nations on three concentric circles of English use, while in the centre-and-periphery model, English is appropriated into local contexts.

10.9   FURTHER READING

Several collections assemble leading articles from different approaches to the valuing of language. In the Coupland and Jaworski multi-volume collection (2009a), see volume 2: *Subjective and Ideological Processes in Sociolinguistics* and volume 5: *The Sociolinguistics of Culture*.

The foundation collections on language ideologies are the readers *Regimes of Language*, edited by Kroskrity (2000), particularly the opening chapters by Kroskrity and by Irvine and Gal, and *Language Ideologies* (1998), edited by Schieffelin, Woolard and Kroskrity, particularly Woolard's introduction (with a vast bibliography) and Gal's epilogue. The collections edited by Blommaert (1999) and Gal and Woolard (2001) provide good and diverse contributions, as do many chapters in the five-volume *Anthropological Linguistics* collection (Schieffelin and Garrett 2011). The *Journal of Linguistic Anthropology* and *Language in Society* carry many articles on language ideologies, e.g. Strand (2012) on Norwegian dialects, Hachimi on Moroccan Arabic (2012).

The *Journal of Social Psychology* is home base for research on language attitudes. Its 2012 issues carried 30-year retrospectives on developments since the journal's founding. See also the journal *Language Awareness*. There are several early collections edited by Giles and colleagues (e.g. Giles and St Clair 1979). Robinson and Giles (2001) is a handbook covering work to that time. Robinson and Locke (2011) offers a brief history but rather uncertain prospect for the field. On perceptual dialectology, see Dennis Preston's numerous publications, especially the two-volume *Handbook* (1999; volume 2 with Daniel Long, 2002). Garrett (2010) is a comprehensive text covering many of the topics in this chapter.

The majority of research on perception of linguistic variables has been on American English. *Language Variation and Change* publishes frequent articles in the area. Sections of Labov's three volumes major on evaluation: 1994, chapters 12–14; 2001a, chapter 6; 2010, chapters 2–4, 11. Kristiansen (2011) traces and critiques the development of Labov's evaluation thinking. Chapter 6 of Kiesling (2011) offers a good summary of variationist evaluation research. Campbell-Kibler's suite of papers on ING make up a body of sophisticated perception work (2007, 2008, 2009). Many of the contributions to Preston and Niedzielski's sociophonetics reader (2010) focus on perception, including of French, Japanese and Dutch.

Models of the processes of creating social meaning in language were pioneered by Ferguson and Gumperz (1960) and Labov (1972b), and developed in different ways by Bell (1984, 2001a) and Eckert (2000, 2012). Silverstein's theorization of indexicality has become central (1979, 2003) although often couched in impenetrable prose. However Johnstone has produced readable interpretations, see especially her table in Johnstone, Andrus and Danielson (2006). Agha's exploration of RP (2003), and Johnstone and colleagues (2006, 2008, 2009, 2011a) on the Pittsburgh dialect, are the leading studies of the enregisterment of specific varieties. See also theme issue of *American Speech* (2009).

The Milroys have worked extensively on standardization, especially in James Milroy and Lesley Milroy (2012), also James Milroy (2001). Bex and Watts (1999) and Watts and Trudgill (2002) are valuable collections of articles on English, as is Mugglestone's study (1995). Kristiansen and Coupland (2011) brings together chapters on de- and re-standardization, particularly in relation to media, and has a useful general introduction to standardization. Bourdieu (1991) contains English versions of his central work on language, with an excellent introduction. Wolfson and Manes (1985) brings together case studies of *Language and Inequality*, and Harbert et al. (2009) investigate issues of *Language and Poverty*.

Confusion and controversy surround the standing of Bakhtin's publications: his principal work on language was published in a colleague's name (Voloshinov 1973). The two collections (1981, 1986) contain most of the other relevant material in English. Bakhtin's writing is rewarding and influential but difficult to read (apparently also in Russian), with tongue-twisting neologisms such as *multilanguagedness* and *internally dialogized interillumination*. His essay on 'The problem of speech genres' (in Bakhtin 1986) is shortish and relatively accessible. Bell (2007) is designed as a readable introduction to Bakhtin's sociolinguistics.

References

Agha, Asif, 2003. 'The social life of cultural value'. *Language & Communication* 23: 23–73.

Bakhtin, M.M., 1981 [1935]. 'Discourse in the novel'. In M.M. Bakhtin, *The Dialogic Imagination*. Austin, TX: University of Texas Press. 259–422.

Bakhtin, M.M. 1986 [1953]. *Speech Genres and Other Late Essays*. Austin, TX: University of Texas Press.

Bauer, Laurie and Peter Trudgill (eds), 1998. *Language Myths*. Harmondsworth, UK: Penguin.

Bell, Allan, 1983. 'Broadcast news as a language standard'. *International Journal of the Sociology of Language* 40: 29–42.

Bell, Allan, 1984. 'Language style as audience design'. *Language in Society* 13: 145–204.

Bell, Allan, 1997b. 'The phonetics of fish and chips in New Zealand: marking national and ethnic identities'. *English World-Wide* 18: 243–70.

Bell, Allan, 2000. 'Māori and Pakeha English: a case study'. In Allan Bell and Koenraad Kuiper (eds), *New Zealand English*. Wellington, New Zealand: Victoria University Press; and Amsterdam: John Benjamins. 221–48.

Bell, Allan, 2001a. 'Back in style: re-working audience design'. In Penelope Eckert and John R. Rickford (eds), *Style and Sociolinguistic Variation*. New York: Cambridge University Press. 139–69.

Bell, Allan, 2007. 'Style in dialogue: Bakhtin and sociolinguistic theory'. In Robert Bayley and Ceil Lucas (eds), *Sociolinguistic Variation: Theories, Methods and Applications*. New York: Cambridge University Press. 90–109.

Bell, Allan, 2011b. 'Leaving home: de-Europeanization in a post-colonial language variety of broadcast news language'. In Tore Kristiansen and Nikolas Coupland (eds), *Standard Languages and Language Standards in a Changing Europe*. Oslo: Novus. 177–98.

Bex, Tony and Richard J. Watts (eds), 1999. *Standard English: The Widening Debate*. London: Routledge.

Billings, Sabrina, 2009. 'Speaking beauties: linguistic posturing, language inequality, and the construction of a Tanzanian beauty queen'. *Language in Society* 38: 581–606.

Blommaert, Jan (ed.), 1999. *Language Ideological Debates*. Berlin: Mouton de Gruyter.

Bokhorst-Heng, Wendy, 1999. 'Singapore's *Speak Mandarin Campaign*: language ideological debates and the imagining of the nation'. In Jan Blommaert (ed.), *Language Ideological Debates*. Berlin: Mouton de Gruyter. 235–65.

Bolton, Kingsley, 2004. 'World Englishes'. In Alan Davies and Catherine Elder (eds), *The Handbook of Applied Linguistics*. Malden, MA: Blackwell Publishing. 367–96.

Bolton, Kingsley and Braj B. Kachru (eds), 2006. *World Englishes (Critical Concepts in Linguistics)*, 6 vols. London: Routledge.

Boulé, Julie J., 2002. 'Attitudes of young Quebecers towards English and French'. Unpublished MA thesis. Montreal, Canada: Concordia University.

Bourdieu, Pierre, 1991. *Language and Symbolic Power*. Cambridge, UK: Polity Press.

Bourhis, Richard Y, 1982. 'Language policies and language attitudes: le monde de la francophonie'. In Ellen Bouchard Ryan and Howard Giles (eds), *Attitudes towards Language Variation: Social and Applied Contexts*. London: Edward Arnold. 34–62.

Cameron, Deborah, 1995. *Verbal Hygiene*. London: Routledge.

Campbell-Kibler, Kathryn, 2007. 'Accent, (ING), and the social logic of listener perceptions'. *American Speech* 82: 32–64.

Campbell-Kibler, Kathryn, 2008. 'I'll be the judge of that: diversity in social perceptions of (ING)'. *Language in Society* 37: 637–59.

Campbell-Kibler, Kathryn, 2009. 'The nature of sociolinguistic perception'. *Language Variation and Change* 21: 135–54.

Canagarajah, A. Suresh, 1999. *Resisting Linguistic Imperialism in English Teaching*. Oxford: Oxford University Press.

Coupland, Nikolas and Hywel Bishop, 2007. 'Ideologized values for British accents'. *Journal of Sociolinguistics* 11: 74–93.

Coupland, Nikolas and Adam Jaworski (eds), 2009a. *Sociolinguistics (Critical Concepts in Linguistics)*, 6 vols. London: Routledge.

d'Anglejan, Alison and G. Richard Tucker, 1973. 'Sociolinguistic correlates of speech style in Quebec'. In Roger W. Shuy and Ralph Fasold (eds), *Language Attitudes: Current Trends and Prospects*. Washington, DC: Georgetown University Press. 1–27.

Eckert, Penelope, 2000. *Linguistic Variation as Social Practice: The Linguistic Construction of Identity in Belten High*. Malden, MA: Blackwell Publishers.

Eckert, Penelope, 2008. 'Variation and the indexical field'. *Journal of Sociolinguistics* 12: 453–76.

Eckert, Penelope, 2012. 'Three waves of variation study: the emergence of meaning in the study of sociolinguistic variation'. *Annual Review of Anthropology* 41: 87–100.

Errington, Joseph, 1998. 'Indonesian('s) development: on the state of a language of state'. In Bambi B. Schieffelin, Kathryn A. Woolard and Paul V. Kroskrity (eds), *Language Ideologies: Practice and Theory*. New York: Oxford University Press.

Ferguson, Charles A. and John J. Gumperz (eds), 1960. *Linguistic Diversity in South Asia*. Bloomington, IN: Indiana University Press.

Gal, Susan and Kathryn A. Woolard (eds), 2001. *Languages and Publics: The Making of Authority*. Manchester, UK: St Jerome Publishing.

Garrett, Peter, 2010. *Attitudes to Language*. Cambridge: Cambridge University Press.

Giles, Howard, Justine Coupland and Nikolas Coupland (eds), 1991. *Contexts of Accommodation: Developments in Applied Sociolinguistics*. Cambridge: Cambridge University Press.

Giles, Howard and Robert N. St Clair (eds), 1979. *Language and Social Psychology*. Oxford, UK: Basil Blackwell.

Gordon, Elizabeth and Marica Abell, 1990. '"This objectionable colonial dialect": historical and contemporary attitudes to New Zealand speech'. In Allan Bell and Janet Holmes (eds), *New Zealand Ways of Speaking English*. Clevedon, UK: Multilingual Matters; and Wellington, New Zealand: Victoria University Press. 21–48.

Grondelaers, Stefan, Roeland van Hout and Mieke Steegs, 2010. 'Evaluating regional accent variation in Standard Dutch'. *Journal of Language and Social Psychology* 29: 101–16.

Hachimi, Atiqa, 2012. 'The urban and the urbane: identities, language ideologies, and Arabic dialects in Morocco'. *Language in Society* 41: 321–41.

Harbert, Wayne, Sally McConnell-Ginet, Amanda Miller and John Whitman (eds), 2009. *Language and Poverty*. Bristol, UK: Multilingual Matters.

Haugen, Einar, 1966. 'Dialect, language, nation'. *American Anthropologist* 68: 922–35.

Honey, John, 1997. *Language is Power: The Story of Standard English and its Enemies*. London: Faber & Faber.

Irvine, Judith T. and Susan Gal, 2000. 'Language ideology and linguistic differentiation'. In Paul V. Kroskrity (ed.), *Regimes of Language: Ideologies, Polities, and Identities*. Santa Fe, NM: School of American Research Press. 35–83.

Jaffe, Alexandra, 1999. *Ideologies in Action: Language Politics on Corsica*. Berlin: Mouton de Gruyter.

Johnstone, Barbara, Jennifer Andrus and Andrew E. Danielson, 2006. 'Mobility, indexicality, and the enregisterment of "Pittsburghese"'. *Journal of English Linguistics* 34: 77–104.

Johnstone, Barbara and Scott F. Kiesling, 2008. 'Indexicality and experience: exploring the meanings of /aw/-monophthongization in Pittsburgh'. *Journal of Sociolinguistics* 12: 5–33.

Johnstone, Barbara, 2009. 'Pittsburghese shirts: commodification and the enregisterment of an urban dialect'. *American Speech* 84: 157–75.

Johnstone, Barbara, 2011a. 'Dialect enregisterment in performance'. *Journal of Sociolinguistics* 15: 657–79.

Kachru, Braj B., 1991. 'Liberation linguistics and the Quirk concern'. *English Today* 7: 3–13.

Kachru, Braj B., 1992. 'Teaching World Englishes'. In Braj B. Kachru (ed.), *The Other Tongue: English across Cultures* (2nd edn). Urbana, IL: University of Illinois Press. 355–65.

Kachru, Braj B., Yamuna Kachru and Cecil L. Nelson (eds), 2006. *The Handbook of World Englishes*. Malden, MA: Blackwell Publishing.

Kristiansen, Tore, 2009. 'The nature and role of language standardisation and standard languages in late modernity'. Available at http://dgcss.hum.ku.dk/exploratoryworkshops/proposal/ (retrieved 3 March 2010).

Kristiansen, Tore, 2011. 'Attitudes, ideology and awareness'. In Ruth Wodak, Barbara Johnstone and Paul Kerswill (eds), *The Sage Handbook of Sociolinguistics*. London: Sage. 265–78.

Kristiansen, Tore and Nikolas Coupland (eds), 2011. *Standard Languages and Language Standards in a Changing Europe*. Oslo, Norway: Novus.

Kroskrity, Paul V. (ed.), 2000. *Regimes of Language: Ideologies, Polities, and Identities*. Santa Fe, NM: School of American Research Press.

Labov, William, 1966. *The Social Stratification of English in New York City*. Washington, DC: Center for Applied Linguistics.

Labov, William, 1972b. *Sociolinguistic Patterns*. Philadelphia, PA: University of Pennsylvania Press.

Labov, William, 1994. *Principles of Linguistic Change*, vol. 1: *Internal Factors*. Cambridge, MA: Blackwell Publishers.

Labov, William, 2001a. *Principles of Linguistic Change*, vol. 2: *Social Factors*. Malden, MA: Blackwell Publishers.

Labov, William, 2010. *Principles of Linguistic Change*, vol. 3: *Cognitive and Cultural Factors*. Malden, MA: Wiley-Blackwell.

Labov, William, Sharon Ash, Maya Ravindranath, Tracey Weldon, Maciej Baranowski and Naomi Nagy, 2011. 'Properties of the sociolinguistic monitor'. *Journal of Sociolinguistics* 15: 431–63.

Lambert, Wallace E., 1967. 'A social psychology of bilingualism'. *Journal of Social Issues* 23: 91–109.

Lambert, Wallace E., Richard Hodgson, Robert C. Gardner and Samuel Fillenbaum, 1960. 'Evaluational reactions to spoken languages'. *Journal of Abnormal and Social Psychology* 60: 44–51.

Leitner, Gerhard, 1980. '"BBC English" and "Deutsche Rundfunksprache": a comparative and historical analysis of the language on the radio'. *International Journal of the Sociology of Language* 26: 75–100.

Li Fengxiang, 2005. 'Contact, attrition, and structural shift: evidence from Oroqen'. *International Journal of the Sociology of Language* 173: 55–74.

Lippi-Green, Rosina, 2012. *English with an Accent: Language, Ideology and Discrimination in the United States* (2nd edn). London: Routledge.

Long, Daniel and Dennis R. Preston (eds), 2002. *Handbook of Perceptual Dialectology* (vol. 2). Amsterdam: John Benjamins.

Lucas, Ceil (ed.), 2001. *The Sociolinguistics of Sign Languages*. Cambridge: Cambridge University Press.

Milroy, James, 2001. 'Language ideologies and the consequences of standardization'. *Journal of Sociolinguistics* 5: 530–55.

Milroy, James and Lesley Milroy, 2012. *Authority in Language: Investigating Standard English* (4th edn). London: Routledge.

Mugglestone, Lynda, 1995. *'Talking Proper': The Rise of Accent as Social Symbol*. Oxford, UK: Clarendon Press.

Niedzielski, Nancy A. and Dennis R. Preston, 2000. *Folk Linguistics*. Berlin: Mouton de Gruyter.

Pennycook, Alastair, 2001. *Critical Applied Linguistics: A Critical Introduction*. Mahwah, NJ: Lawrence Erlbaum.

Plichta, Bartlomiej and Brad Rakerd, 2010. 'Pereceptions of /a/ fronting across two Michigan dialects'. In Dennis R. Preston and Nancy Niedzielski (eds), *A Reader in Sociophonetics*. New York: De Gruyter Mouton. 223–39.

Preston, Dennis R., 1996. 'Where the worst English is spoken'. In Edgar W. Schneider (ed.), *Varieties of English around the World: Focus on the USA*. Amsterdam: John Benjamins. 297–360.

Preston, Dennis R. (ed.), 1999. *Handbook of Perceptual Dialectology* (vol. 1). Amsterdam: John Benjamins.

Preston, Dennis R., 2010. 'Belle's body just caught the fit gnat: the perception of Northern Cities shifted vowels by local speakers'. In Dennis R. Preston and Nancy Niedzielski (eds), *A Reader in Sociophonetics*. New York: De Gruyter Mouton. 241–52.

Preston, Dennis R. and Nancy Niedzielski (eds), 2010. *A Reader in Sociophonetics*. New York: De Gruyter Mouton.

Quirk, Randolph, 1990. 'Language varieties and standard language'. *English Today* 6: 3–10.

Robinson, W. Peter and Howard Giles (eds), 2001. *The New Handbook of Language and Social Psychology*. Chichester, UK: John Wiley.

Robinson, W. Peter and Abigail Locke, 2011. 'The social psychology of language: a short history'. In Rajend Mesthrie (ed.), *The Cambridge Handbook of Sociolinguistics*. Cambridge: Cambridge University Press. 47–69.

Schieffelin, Bambi B. and Paul B. Garrett (eds), 2011. *Anthropological Linguistics (Critical Concepts in Language Studies)*, 5 vols. London: Routledge.

Schieffelin, Bambi B., Kathryn A. Woolard and Paul V. Kroskrity (eds), 1998. *Language Ideologies: Practice and Theory*. New York: Oxford University Press.

Silverstein, Michael. 1979. 'Language structure and linguistic ideology'. In Paul R. Clyne, William F. Hanks and Carol L. Hofbauer (eds), *The Elements: A Parasession on Linguistic Units and Levels*. Chicago, IL: Chicago Linguistic Society. 193–247.

Silverstein, Michael, 2003. 'Indexical order and the dialectics of sociolinguistic life'. *Language & Communication* 23: 193–229.

Strand, Thea R., 2012. 'Winning the dialect popularity contest: mass-mediated language ideologies and local responses in rural Valdres, Norway'. *Journal of Linguistic Anthropology* 22: 23–43.

Tagliamonte, Sali A., 2012. *Variationist Sociolinguistics: Change, Observation, Interpretation*. Malden, MA: Wiley-Blackwell.

Trudgill, Peter, 1983. *On Dialect: Social and Geographical Perspectives*. Oxford, UK: Basil Blackwell.

van Bezooijen, Renée and Vincent J. van Heuven, 2010. 'Avant-garde Dutch: a perceptual, acoustic, and evaluational study'. In Dennis R. Preston and Nancy Niedzielski (eds), *A Reader in Sociophonetics*. New York: De Gruyter Mouton. 357–78.

Voloshinov, V.N. 1973 [1929]. *Marxism and the Philosophy of Language*. New York: Seminar Press.

Watts, Richard J. and Peter Trudgill (eds), 2002. *Alternative Histories of English*. London: Routledge.

Wee, Lionel, 2006. 'The semiotics of language ideologies in Singapore'. *Journal of Sociolinguistics* 10: 344–61.

Wee, Lionel, 2010. '"Burdens" and "handicaps" in Singapore's language policy: on the limits of language management'. *Language Policy* 9: 97–114.

Wolfson, Nessa and Joan Manes (eds), 1985. *Language of Inequality*. Berlin: Walter de Gruyter.

Woolard, Kathryn A., 1998. 'Introduction: Language ideology as a field of inquiry'. In Bambi B. Schieffelin, Kathryn A. Woolard and Paul V. Kroskrity (eds), *Language Ideologies: Practice and Theory*. New York: Oxford University Press. 3–47.

Wray, Alison and Aileen Bloomer, 2012. *Projects in Linguistics and Language Studies* (3rd edn). London: Hodder Education.

11

STYLING LANGUAGE
AND IDENTITIES

On 11 March 2011 the following news story was broadcast on 91ZM, a youth music radio station in Auckland, New Zealand:

> Police in Napier are *pretty stoked* with the *haul* of *pot* they've *grabbed*. Over forty people arrested after a *sting* targeting cannabis growers seizing *around* twelve thousand plants worth *around* forty *mill*.

The content is routine news, but the way it is told is not. The string of *colloquial* lexical items sets this apart. It contrasts radically with our expectations of news style, and therefore draws attention to itself. This distinctiveness cohabits with other features – the brevity of the story, the musical beat playing underneath the newscaster's voice, the colloquial morphosyntax (Exercise 11.1). This way of telling news is different from the mainstream, and in that distinctiveness lies its style.

This chapter is about language styles and their meanings. An advance word about the nature of the chapter: because style has been central to my own work for several decades, and reciprocally my work has been central to the sociolinguistics of style, my take in this chapter differs from that in the rest of the book. It majors on my own approach to the topic (although in dialogue with other leading approaches), and a good deal of the data it presents come from my own work. I hope this will function as a plus rather than a minus.

11.1 TWO TAKES ON STYLE

Style is what speakers do with language. The basis of style is that people have choices. The sociolinguist's core question about style is this:

Why did **this speaker** say it **this way** on **this occasion**?

The Guidebook to Sociolinguistics, First Edition. Allan Bell.
© 2014 Allan Bell. Published 2014 by Blackwell Publishing Ltd.

Exercise 11.1   News distinctives

1   In the example at the start of the chapter identify the three non-lexical style features (two are deletions).
2   Rewrite the story for broadcast on a regular news station. Do an analysis of the changes you have made.
3   What kind of audience does this style imply? What relationship between broadcaster and audience? What social meanings does the style index?

4   Locate two contrasting news media either in your local area or online from anywhere, one with a standard style and the other with a distinctive style. The British national daily newspapers, for example, exhibit wide differences, e.g. between *The Sun* and *The Daily Telegraph*.
5   Identify linguistic differences in these two sets of news, and seek to interpret their social meanings. Why have these choices been made, and not the alternatives?
6   Also attend to other aspects of the news in your chosen medium, for example the visuals if you choose television or press. How do they interact with the language?

The question implies an alternative – a **that** way that could have been chosen instead of the **this** way. It locates style in **distinction**: the ways in which people differentiate themselves from each other. Our question also implies that the sociolinguist's main interest is not just in describing style but in explaining: **why**.

This chapter relates closely to some of what we have covered in earlier chapters, especially 5 and 6. In Chapter 5.1 I introduced the notion of speaker repertoire – the range of linguistic codes they have at their disposal. That range may include different languages, or different varieties of the same language – there is no principled difference between the different kinds of codes. All can index social meaning, generated through the Indexical Cycle we discussed in the last chapter. Linguistic style is the monolingual counterpart of the bilingual's choice between languages, which we saw throughout Chapter 5. The same social meaning-making accomplished by an English monolingual's *in/ing* alternation could, for the bilingual, be indexed by code switching. My Chapter 6 discussion of situations, and speaker and audience formats, indicates that these are all strongly implicated in style, and I concentrate on the role of the audience in section 11.2. In Chapter 7.1 we encountered Labov's approach to style in New York City, which I return to (critically) here. Finally, Chapter 10's coverage of the valuing of language, of ideologies and standardization, is essential background to – and interwoven with – the nature of style.

Style as linguistic range

We can identify two main approaches to style in sociolinguistics, one macro and the other micro. The first encompasses the full range of linguistic levels, from micro-variables of pronunciation through to broad discourse or genre patterns – the many ways individual speakers may express themselves differently. It also embraces a great diversity of social factors – such as the many situational components in Hymes's SPEAKING taxonomy (Chapter 6.2) – a range on which speakers browse for choices.

In accord with this tradition, the linguistic anthropologist Judith Irvine (2001) stresses style as difference, drawing on Bourdieu's work on distinction (1984). Ben Rampton captures nicely the fact of the 'indelible relationality of styles, of the central part that contrast and difference play in defining a style's symbolic significance' (2006: 379). Here language is seen as one semiotic resource among others – dress, music, even posture – by which persons and groups set themselves apart. Eckert's jocks and burnouts (2000) and Mendoza-Denton's Latina gang study (2008) show amply how a cluster of such practices compose an ideologically charged style – nicely encapsulated in a title of Eckert's, 'Vowels and nail polish' (2010). Similarly in the last chapter we saw how Billy T. James's vernacular and standard voices meshed with parallel contrasts in dress: singlet and shorts versus bow tie and tails. While sociolinguists may mainly focus on the language dimension of such style-making, they will also be wise to take account of the wider resources and practices. This is a 'maximalist' approach to style both linguistically and socially, wide-ranging and eclectic.

Style shift as linguistic variation

The other approach is contrastingly minimalist, that is, Labov's variationist methodology introduced in Chapter 7. This takes micro linguistic features and defines them very tightly as 'variables' with alternating variants occurring in highly specified linguistic environments. And as we have seen, variationism has tended to also constrain the social side of the equation, aiming for statistical correlations with 'objective' social factors such as class or age. Labov's conception of style shift fits into this tightly delimited approach. In Chapter 7.1 we saw how a series of tasks were designed to focus more and more of the speaker's attention on speech, with the outcomes classed as a range of styles from 'casual speech' through to word lists and minimal pairs.

Figure 11.1 is a set of social × style graphs (from Bell 1984) which show in idealized form the two main quantitative patterns found in early variationist studies, together with two infrequent and deviant patterns. Figure 11.1a shows an indicator variable, Silverstein's first-order indexical (as mapped in the Indexical Cycle in Figure 10.2). There is social differentiation here but no style shift (as Trudgill 1974 found for several variables). Figure 11.1b has regular stratification between the social classes and regular shift across styles (as in Figure 7.1 for ING). This is the typical pattern for most variables, these are the markers/second-order indexicals.

Figure 11.1c displays an exception to regular structure: the lower-middle-class (LMC) hypercorrection pattern of the kind shown in Figure 7.2 for New York /r/ (although here graphed in the opposite direction). Its social and stylistic deviance is visible in the cross-over structure of the graph. Lastly, Figure 11.1d is also a deviant pattern, one that in fact almost never occurs (see Bell 1984 for detail). It involves steep style shift with little social difference.

- Looking back to the Indexical Cycle I presented earlier in Figure 10.2, consider why the Figure 11.1d pattern is so rare – more on this later.

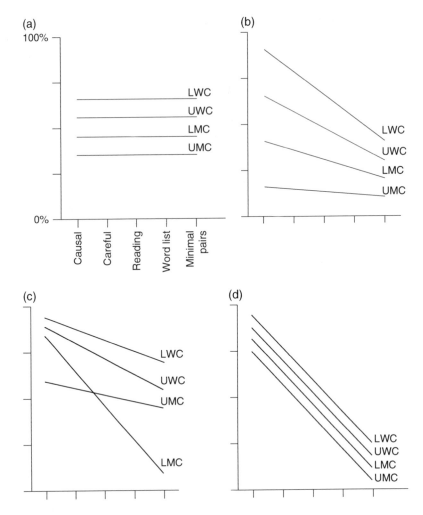

Figure 11.1   Quantitative relations of style and social variation
LWC = lower working class; UWC = upper working class; LMC = lower middle class; UMC = upper middle class
a   Class × style stratification of an indicator/first-order index
b   Marker/second-order index
c   Lower-middle-class crossover
d   Deviant hyper-style variable
Source: Bell (1984), figure 3

Critique and development

Labov's techniques for eliciting 'styles' within a recorded interview have been highly productive, utilized in countless studies, languages and countries, often finding similar patterns. Many of these techniques focus on eliciting casual speech by reducing the 'Observer's Paradox' – that we want to observe how speakers talk when they are not being observed. They are however best regarded as methodological ploys for simulating a range of speech levels rather than themselves representing styles. Their relationship to speech beyond the interview remains questionable – people do not often speak in minimal pairs. Labov's attribution of graded levels of attention paid to speech as the operative factor has been widely challenged since (e.g. Bell 1984). Attention can be directed at producing all levels of linguistic alternatives not just the more prestigious – recall Kiesling's fraternity members who positioned themselves with *in* as well as with *ing* (Chapter 7.6). My Audience Design approach, to which we turn next, was developed partly in reaction to what I regarded as the mechanistic attribution of style to attention. I believed that style centred on persons not mechanisms.

Although I have distinguished two broad approaches to style in this section, in the past decade or more there has been an increasing and fruitful crossover between the two. Variationist analysis has been extended to a wide range of stylistic material, and richer social concepts have been applied to all kinds of language. When I began research on style in the 1970s, I could justifiably label it 'the neglected dimension'. Now style is at the centre of sociolinguistic theorization and method, and we turn to explore what this means.

11.2   AUDIENCE DESIGN

Genesis

Audience Design has been the central model of sociolinguistic style since being proposed in Bell (1984). In search of an explanation of the style differences I was finding in my doctoral research on the language of radio news in Auckland, I turned up a situation which proved to be tailored to spotlighting style differences. Two of the radio stations originated in the same public-broadcasting organization, using the same newscasters, in the same studios. It was in effect a natural matched guise situation – different audiences listening to the same newscaster who was switching between stations.

Working in variationist fashion, I examined a number of linguistic variables, including intervocalic /t/ voicing – the flap that makes words like *writer* sound like *rider*. In New Zealand this is a variable feature, and in the broadcast context it indexes informality and Americanness (since it is semi-categorical in American English). Figure 11.2 shows the percentage of intervocalic /t/ voicing for four newscasters that I recorded on the two stations. YA is New Zealand's 'National Radio', which has a higher status audience than the local community station ZB (see Bell 1991a for detail on the study). The graph shows that each newscaster shifts considerably and consistently between the two stations. To return to the question which opened the chapter: *Why do these speakers say it in these different ways on these occasions?* There is after all just one individual producing two divergent styles. The institution, the genre, the topic mix of the news, the studio setting and the amount of attention paid to speech are held constant in each 'guise'. Only the audience differences appear to be a plausible explanation.

Looking beyond my study, I began to see that the same regularities which were writ large in my media-originated data were also operating in face-to-face communication. Later I discovered that outside sociolinguistics this idea was not quite new when I encountered Speech Accommodation Theory – see later in section 11.2.

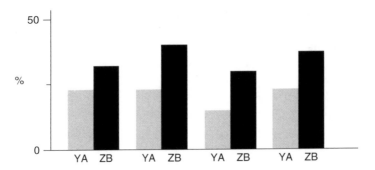

Figure 11.2   Percentage of intervocalic /t/ voicing by four newscasters on two New Zealand radio stations
Source: Bell (1984), figure 9

The model

In Bell (1997a) I summarized the Audience Design model under nine points, revised and expanded somewhat here in the light of subsequent developments:

1 *Style is what an individual speaker does with a language in relation to self and others.* The premise of Audience Design is that style focuses on people, it is essentially a social thing. Style is interactive and contrastive, marking personal identification and interpersonal relations.

2 *Style derives its meaning from the association of linguistic features with particular social groups.* As developed in the Indexical Cycle (Figure 10.2), the social evaluation of a group is projected onto the linguistic features associated with that group. Style therefore has a normative basis. That is, a particular style carries with it the flavour of its associations. Bakhtin puts it this way:

> All words have the 'taste' of a profession, a genre, a tendency, a party, a particular work, a particular person, a generation, an age group, the day and hour. (1981: 293)

3 *Speakers design their style primarily for and in response to their audience.* This is the heart of Audience Design. I regard response to the audience as the primary mode of style shift – but it is an active responsiveness not passivity. Bakhtin again: 'Discourse ... is oriented toward an understanding that is "responsive" ... Responsive understanding is ... an *active* understanding' (1981: 280). There is nothing, he writes, more terrible than a lack of response. The audience is as crucial in interaction as the speaker (Exercise 11.2). To illustrate: Coupland (1984) recorded a travel agent in conversation with a wide social range of clients, and analysed the level of /t/ voicing in the speech of both her and her clients. The agent converged towards more /t/ voicing with lower-class clients, who were themselves using more voicing, and she used less voicing when talking to higher-class clients, who used less voicing (Figure 11.3).

4 *Audience Design applies to all codes and levels of a language repertoire.* As we saw in Chapters 5 and 6, bilinguals' language choices largely depend on who their

Exercise 11.2 Bakhtin on response

He writes:

The person to whom I respond is my addressee, from whom I, in turn expect a response (or in any case an active responsive understanding) ... After all, the utterance of the person to whom I am responding (I agree, I object, I execute, I take under advisement, and so forth) is already at hand, but his response (or responsive understanding) is still forthcoming. When constructing my utterance, I try actively to determine this response. Moreover, I try to act in accordance with the response I anticipate, so this anticipated response, in turn, exerts an active influence on my utterance (I parry objections that I foresee, I make all kinds of provisos, and so forth). When speaking I always take into account the apperceptive background of the addressee's perception of my speech ... These considerations also determine my choice of a genre for my utterance, my choice of compositional devices, and, finally, my choice of language vehicles, that is, the *style* of my utterance. (1986: 95)

- Unpack the specifics of the to-and-fro process Bakhtin describes for how speakers conduct conversations. How does this work? How conscious do you think it is?
- What implications does it have for our language style choices?
- Do you agree that this is how we operate in conversation?

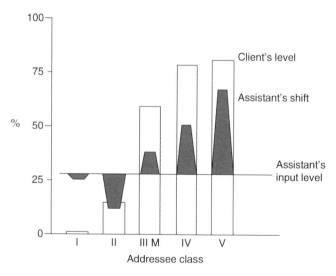

Figure 11.3 Convergence by Cardiff travel agent on intervocalic /t/ voicing to five occupational classes of clients (Class I highest, Class V lowest)
Source: Bell (1984), figure 8, derived from Coupland (1984), figure 4

audience is. The same process underlies monolingual style shifting, as argued earlier in this chapter. In addition, Audience Design applies to all levels of language not just variationist style shift. Some early sociolinguistic work took account of interlocutors. In Brown and Gilman's study (1960) of the T/V pronouns in European languages (such as French *tu* and *vous*), the focus on the second person form necessarily prioritizes the addressee.

    5 *A speaker's range of styles generally derives from and echoes the range that exists among speakers in the community.* As speakers we mainly draw on the linguistic range we hear about us as the resource for our own range of variety. While all speakers are creative, most of their creativity lies in novel use of the existing variety in their speech community rather than in creating new forms. Most of us are not innovators like Labov's Celeste and Eckert's Judy (Chapter 8). This follows directly from the Indexical Cycle, the processes by which language generates social meaning: it is the common pool of linguistic variety that speakers draw on in their styling. And that is the reason why graphs of the shape of Figure 11.1d do not (generally) occur, because they would pre-suppose the existence of extreme styling alongside little social variation. They imply that you can have second-order indexing without first-order, counter to the cycle shown in Figure 10.2. On the other hand, as we have seen, it is completely possible to have variables where there is difference between speakers but no style movement – those are the indicators, the first-order indexes. And as in Figure 11.1b, quantitative style shifts are normally less than the differences between social groups (what Labov 2001b: 86 terms 'Bell's principle') reinforcing the sense of the stylistic echoing the social.

    6 *Speakers show a fine-grained ability to design their style for a range of different address-ees, and to a lessening degree for other audience members.* In Chapter 6.4 I presented the concept of layered audience roles – the direct addressee, the unaddressed auditor, and the unratified overhearer (Table 6.4). We saw how the different audience members can affect bilinguals' language choices. By the same token monolingual speakers can subtly adjust their style to audience changes, for example when a stranger joins a group. A study by Bickerton showed a Hawaiian creole speaker shifting markedly towards standard English variants to address the researcher, but only half as much when the researcher was present just as an auditor but not being directly addressed (Bell 1984: 173).

    7 *Styling according to topic or setting derives its meaning and direction from the underlying association of topics or settings with typical audience members.* This kind of association among audience, topic and setting is the foundation of Fishman's domains concept (Chapter 6.1). It is, however, one of the more tentative proposals of the Audience Design model, and there is evidence for and against it.

    8 *As well as the 'Responsive' dimension of style, there is the 'Initiative' dimension where a shift in style itself initiates a change in the situation rather than resulting from such a change.*

    9 *Such initiative style shifts are in essence 'Referee Design', by which the linguistic features associated with a group can be used to express affiliation with that group.*

These last two briefly-put points constitute a major dimension of style, and will be the focus of much of the rest of the chapter. Research on style necessarily investigates in depth, and therefore usually takes few speakers – often just one. In a study of style shifting by an African American teenager, Rickford and McNair-Knox explicitly set out to test some of the 'bold hypotheses and predictions' (1994: 241) of Audience Design as outlined earlier. They found a high degree of influence by audience and by topic on their informant's style. Exercise 11.3 invites you to assess and critique the theory for yourself.

Exercise 11.3   Critiquing Audience Design

Like all models, Audience Design has been challenged for its inadequacies. One of the most detailed comes in Coupland's *Style*, the best book on the subject (2007). Coupland devotes a chapter to Audience Design, and I see eight main challenges being raised:

1 Argument by elimination is unsatisfactory, for example in setting aside factors other than audience in the radio station data exemplified by Figure 11.2.
2 Style is treated as a linear scale (as in earlier variationist work), linked to a framework of static social categories such as class.
3 The quantification of 'social' and 'style' categories, particularly in relation to each other, is founded on questionable assumptions about community linguistic ranges.
4 Stylistic frequencies are assumed to be socially meaningful without theorizing how that happens, for example through indexicality.
5 The nature of the audience is inadequately theorized, for example the formulations of styling as both 'for and in response to' an audience conflates two different things.
6 The significance of 'design' needs to be unpacked, particularly in relation to what precisely 'responsiveness' means.
7 Audience Design over-stresses the audience aspect of verbal interaction and underplays the role of the speaker.
8 The approach over-stresses the constraints on speakers' styling, without adequate account of speakers' creative freedom.

Decades on, I agree with some among these criticisms, and in my exposition of the framework here have re-formulated certain things accordingly (in the early 1980s I had not come across Bakhtin, for example). Here are some ways to assess the theory and challenges to it:

9 Class members could take up one or more challenges from the eight above and research them.
10 Read Bell (1984) or (1997a) on Audience Design, and evaluate the model. See also Rickford and McNair-Knox's article (1994) which builds on it.
11 Read especially chapter 3 of Coupland (2007). Consider Coupland's challenges and evaluate them.
12 Draw your own conclusions about the different arguments. See also the chapters in Eckert and Rickford (2001) for a range of theory and data on style, including by Labov, Coupland, Giles and Bell.

Accommodation theory

While I was beginning to work up Audience Design in New Zealand, the Welsh social psychologist Howard Giles and his associates were much further advanced in devising a parallel approach, accommodation theory (Giles and Powesland 1975). Accommodation means adjusting your speech to the people you are interacting with. Initially titled Speech Accommodation Theory (SAT), it was broadened in the 1980s to encompass wider aspects of interaction as 'Communication Accommodation

Theory' (CAT). The theory goes beyond description to give social-psychological content to the processes I have described.

Accommodation commonly shows in a speaker shifting her style to be more like that of the person she is talking to – **convergence**. The convergence may be upwards or downwards depending on the relative social status of the interlocutors, symmetrical or asymmetrical depending whether the shift is unilateral or mutual. Alternatively, instead of converging, speakers may diverge from their addressee. Divergence is regarded as a tactic for differentiating oneself from others. Research examined issues like the motivations for accommodation (such as seeking approval) and how it is evaluated (Giles and Ogay 2007).

The theory became increasingly complex as it tried to cope with findings which did not sit easily with simple convergence or divergence. For example, Giles and Smith (1979) found that speakers can converge too much, causing addressees to react unfavourably to what they may feel is patronizing or ingratiating behaviour (recall the listeners' reactions to 'Valerie' in Campbell-Kibler's ING experiment, Exercise 10.6). Riders to the theory proliferated in the 1980s, and while research activity has continued apace, the theory has not advanced greatly, perhaps partly because the models had already become quite unwieldy.

To linguists, early accommodation theory's chief deficiency was its linguistic naivety, dealing largely in parameters such as speech rate or ratings of whole 'accents'. By the 1980s, some sociolinguists came to accommodation theory in search of an explanation of the patterns they were finding in their study of specific linguistic features. As well as Coupland and myself, this included Trudgill, who re-visited his Norwich interviews in order to investigate accommodation there, by comparing his own speech as interviewer with his informants'. The result for the variable of glottalization of /t/ in words like *butter* is shown in Figure 11.4. Trudgill is clearly in his own production tracking the /t/ levels of the informants, who are ordered by social class.

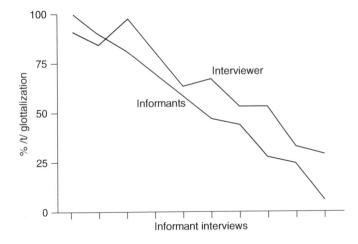

Figure 11.4   An interviewer's accommodation to 10 informants on /t/ glottalization in Norwich
Source: Bell (1984), figure 7, after Trudgill

11.3 REFEREE DESIGN

Frames for stylization

Rex O'Neal stands on a dock on the island of Ocracoke, North Carolina, performing his *hoi toide* vowels. An upper-middle-class teenager from New York uses features from African American Vernacular English. A white adolescent Londoner breaks into a phrase of Panjabi. Moroccan teenagers in Belgium take on the local Antwerp dialect usually associated with anti-immigrant racists.

These are stylizations, roughly what I have called earlier **Referee Design**. The previous section dealt with the 'responsive' dimension of style, and we now turn to the 'initiative' dimension (points 8 and 9 in the Audience Design model) where speakers intentionally stylize linguistic features in order to call up associations with particular groups or identities. There have been a series of attempts in sociolinguistics to capture how this works, listed in Table 11.1. This smorgasbord of frameworks and labellings covers socially similar phenomena with a range of linguistic outcomes, from a bilingual's switching to a monolingual's manipulation of dialects.

Here language makes reference to a group – often an outgroup, but it may also be the speaker's own group – through intentional use of its linguistic code. That is, in line with the Indexical Cycle, the language associated with a group can be used to evoke that group. These references are by their nature usually short-term, but in some circumstances, outgroup referee design can be long-term. Silverstein notes (1979) that a form may go from being 'creative' in his terms to being 'presupposing' – that is, it becomes established as a norm, taking on a new cycle of indexicality. This may even be the case for a whole linguistic code. In diglossia (Chapter 5.3) part of a speech community's repertoire is a code from a different place or time. Usually we would class this as an initiative or referee situation, but here it is normalized as part of the baseline.

The approaches in Table 11.1 differ in terminology and emphasis, but the commonalities between them are more striking than their differences. All of them assume that linguistic form has social meaning and that it is imbued and moulded by the multitude of past usages. They propose that those meanings can be intentionally applied and manipulated in speakers' performances. And they accept that there is a dialectical movement back-and-forth between the responsive and initiative dimensions, by which meanings are adapted in the very acts of being adopted.

Taking the initiative

In these frameworks, a responsive shift results from a change in the situation, and an initiative shift itself **initiates** such a change. This is the 'situational' and 'metaphorical' switching that Blom and Gumperz (1972) found in the Norwegian community they researched. In responsive style there tends to be a regular association between language and social situation, which initiative style trades on, infusing the flavour of one setting into a different context. To quote Bakhtin again:

Table 11.1 Approaches to stylization

Responsive	Initiative	Source
Style	Stylization	Bakhtin (1981) [1934/5]
Situational	Metaphorical	Blom and Gumperz (1972)
Presupposing	Creating	Silverstein (1979)
Audience Design	Referee Design	Bell (1984, 2001a)
–	Crossing	Rampton (1995)
Relational	Identity	Coupland (2001a, 2007)

- Different class members/groups can each research one of these approaches (omit Bakhtin).
- Summarize and present the framework to the class, including some of the data to which it has been applied. Assess each framework and how well it explains the example data.
- Compare the frameworks. Can you suggest an overarching approach which incorporates the best aspects of them all? What terms would you adopt?

As a result of the work done by all these stratifying forces in language, there are no 'neutral' words and forms – words and forms that can belong to 'no one'; language has been completely taken over, shot through with intentions and accents ... Each word tastes of the context and contexts in which it has lived its socially charged life. (1981: 293)

Bakhtin's own term 'stylization' is the simplest and perhaps clearest, with its implication of the intentional re-configuring of the style resource of a community. Stylization often involves a re-orientation by speakers of their own identity in relation to their audience, hence my term Referee Design – the linguistic features associated with a group are used to refer to that group. Sometimes that will focus on an absent reference group – for example by adopting another accent – rather than the present addressee. Referee Design can involve a speaker shifting to identify more strongly with their own ingroup, or to an outgroup with which they wish to associate. It can even involve simultaneous identification with two groups at once: Yaeger-Dror (1993) found that Israeli singers could co-articulate two variants of /r/ simultaneously, thus aiming at two targets at the same time.

The force of stylization

If a particular style can be used to create a situation, the question is how does it get to carry the meaning that makes it usable for that purpose? It gets the force that can be put to work in initiative style from its routine use in response to certain kinds of situation – the Indexical Cycle. The notion that we can stylize another group's speech presupposes that their variety has some distinguishable and relatively stable linguistic features. For me to be able to 'sound American' or 'sound RP' requires that there are some forms, or clusters of forms, or frequencies of forms which are distinctive to those varieties. If analysts wishes to cut loose from all such categorization, they must provide an explanation for the pervasive if partial regularities which we find in speakers' style choices – just as those who wish to establish generalizations must make allowance for that significant chunk of style which even their best theories refuse to account for.

The question arises then of what 'referring' to the language of a group means. Speakers' Referee Design may run the full gamut of degrees of association with the referred-to group, from simple evocation of the other's voice, through to whole-hearted identification with the group to which the code belongs. At the maximal end of association lies the possibility of **appropriation**, whereby an outgroup takes possession of another group's code. Cases where an outgroup speaker adopts African American Vernacular forms could be construed in this way, at least by African Americans themselves. In contrast, the kind of 'crossing' to Stylized Asian English that Rampton researched (1995), although relatively frequent, does not appear to be attempting appropriation or to carry the pejorative implication of that label (Example 11.1). It evokes rather than appropriates.

Critiques

The preceding section is my own account of stylization – but others would disagree. To my mind the main challenge for any theory of style, including Audience Design, is to take account of the dynamics of stylization while achieving a worthwhile level of generalization about the patterns that we can discern in style. The basic criticism of frameworks that attempt to systematize style is that they are reductionist: they minimize or discount the complexity of speakers' moment-by-moment, self-expressive use of language – of the kind Eckert's burned-out burnouts display. This is indeed an issue for Audience Design, but it is equally one that **any** style model will face, because any attempt to discern patterns or regularities in people's style will be open to the same challenge.

There is force to the challenges made by scholars such as Eckert (2000), Schilling-Estes (2004) and Coupland (2007). I think the basis of a dynamic view of style is present in my concept of Referee Design; however as originally presented in Bell (1984) it had the character of an add-on. I treated Referee Design as a secondary dimension, which could kick in when Audience Design failed. At very least, this left the problem of knowing what was the boundary between the two dimensions: where did Audience Design end, and Referee Design begin? When did speakers shift from responsive to initiative mode?

More recently I have tended to the view (Bell 2001a) that we have to acknowledge Referee Design as an ever-present part of individuals' use of language. We are always proactively positioning ourselves in relation to our own ingroup, other groups and our interlocutors. These are complementary and co-existent dimensions of style, which operate simultaneously in all speech events. Yes, we are designing our talk for our audience. But we are also concurrently designing it in relation to other factors and referee groups. The intractable fact nevertheless remains that the initiative dimension does derive from the responsive. As the Indexical Cycle shows, stylization only works because it leverages off a style with known social associations.

The responsive and initiative dimensions of style are part of a dilemma that has a long history in social theory – the relationship between **structure** and **agency**. Structure is the social scaffolding that shapes and constrains the way we live, and agency is our ability as humans to take our own actions, follow our own practices, make our own way. The social sciences have a long tradition of oscillating between the two dimensions.

Exercise 11.4   Stylizing ethnicity

Natalie Schilling-Estes (2004) analysed a single conversation between an African American and a Lumbee Indian. She found considerable evidence that these two speakers were adjusting their speech styles to accommodate each other at different stages of the conversation, sometimes converging and sometimes diverging. The speakers used the linguistic resources at their disposal to actively adopt different stances and personas, and to take the initiative in framing the encounter, their relationship and their positioning towards what they were discussing. Schilling-Estes mixed both quantitative and qualitative analysis to present a much more complete account of this interaction than has often been achieved.

- Record a conversation between two people you know who speak different ethnic varieties. Ask them to talk about ethnic relations in your country.
- Analyse their linguistic self-presentation, both across the whole interview and as the interview develops from topic to topic and the two participants position themselves in relation to each other. For example studies, see Schilling-Estes (2004) and Bell (2001a – next section).

In sociolinguistics the pendulum has currently swung very much towards agency rather than structure. This has major repercussions for our approach to style. I take the view that the swing to agency has unbalanced our view of language style. Approaches which treat speakers as untrammelled agents do not take enough account of the role of structure in interaction and life, just as approaches which treat speakers as sociodemographic correlates did not take adequate account of individual agency. I return to the social theory underlying the responsive/initiative dilemma in the next, concluding chapter.

11.4   PERFORMING SOCIOLINGUISTIC IDENTITIES

What I have called stylization or Referee Design involves speakers performing language. Now, there is a sense in which all language is performed – very obviously by speakers like Eckert's burned-out burnouts, who appear to be always 'on stage'. More commonly language performance occurs when a speaker breaks out briefly from conversation into an overt performance mode. Here a speaker puts language on display, most obviously when quoting or reporting speech. In the flow of an otherwise everyday interaction, a speaker takes on – spontaneously and fleetingly – a performing role. What differentiates this 'mundane' performance (Coupland 2007) from staged performance is that it is informal, transient, unscheduled, uninstitutionalized.

Such everyday language performance is close bound with notions of identity, as my exposition of Referee Design will have indicated. 'Identity' is one of the most used and least specified terms in sociolinguistic studies, and there is a case for avoiding it – but the notion is not easily avoidable. I take identity to include both structured and agentive dimensions. It is partly a product, a given – you cannot choose where you were born, either socially or geographically, nor usually where or how you are brought up. But identity is also part process, something constructed over time – you can make choices as you grow up and mould what you become both overall and in specific situations.

The role of language in identities formation and presentation has been a prime interest of sociolinguists at least since Labov studied the local meaning of a single vowel on Martha's Vineyard. An ever-increasing strand of research focuses on how speakers claim sociolinguistic identities on parameters such as gender or ethnicity, whether that identity appears 'natural' to them – males emphasizing their masculinity, as did Kiesling's fraternity members – or an apparently other identity which they are claiming: a White imitating African American vernacular. Now, performed language is arguably the most innovative, productive and intriguing sector of sociolinguistics.

Doing gender

We saw in Chapter 7 how gender has been increasingly regarded as a constructed or performed matter rather than defined by biological sex. Speakers use variables such as ING to index social meaning, in the process performing an identity such as male or female. Elinor Ochs pioneered research in linguistic indexing of social meaning, exploring gender in a comparative study of the language of Samoan and American mothering (1992). Where American mothers accommodated their speech to their children (especially through 'baby talk'), the Samoan mothers expected their children to accommodate to them. This contributes to very different positioning of women as mothers in the different cultures. The many ways in which people index gender have been researched in a wide range of situations such as:

- how accent and language choice index a range of masculinities in Barcelona (Pujolar i Cos 1997)
- how senior managers 'do femininity' in workplaces in New Zealand (Holmes 2006)
- how young American men construct heterosexual masculinity by their discourse about gays (Cameron 1997)
- how Latina, jock and burnout girls perform gender in their respective communities of practice (Mendoza-Denton 2008, Eckert 2000).

Much of the gendering of language in these studies is quite responsive in kind, although some of it breaks out into overt performance. But performed gender is most obvious when language initiates a claim to either a heightened or an alternative gender identity. Researchers such as Hall have investigated how language operates as part of cross-gender identification, for example by trans-gendered Hindi-speaking *hijras* (1997).

Pitch range is one feature often associated with gay speech. Heath is an openly gay American, recorded by Podesva (2007) in a range of social situations. In one of these – a barbecue with close friends – his frequent use of a falsetto voice stands out as higher and wider than elsewhere. Podesva argues that the falsetto indexes expressiveness and is used for surprise, evaluation, narration and quotation. More specifically it evokes a 'diva' persona and links to a gay identity – 'bitch' is a frequent description by his friends. Exercise 11.5 examines a short conversation Heath had at the barbecue.

Exercise 11.5   Performing the diva

Bold italics mark falsetto voice. The discussion is about a 'vent' feature in Eliza's clothing.

1	Heath	Do you want me to do anything, dear?
2	Eliza	No, just to stay and be pretty.
3	Heath	<laughter>You know that's my job.
4		**Ooh, ooh**, a little **vent** thing!
5	Eliza	Yeah.
6	Heath	**Oh cool**. I **like** it!
7		I'm so ex*cit*ed about your little **vent** [thing.
8	Eliza	[I know.
9		Isn't it awesome? It's such a cute little [outfit.
10	Heath	[It **is**,
11		I really, I like it.

(Podesva 2007: 493)

1   As well as the falsetto, identify the other features that index 'diva' or 'gay' in this exchange. How do these features work together to construct the persona?
2   How do Eliza's turns contribute to constructing Heath as diva? How do the two of them jointly collaborate in the enterprise?
3   How does the topic of the conversation relate to the persona?
4   Re-script the exchange using lexicon and features that index a neutral persona. Analyse the changes you have made and their linguistic form, and interpret their social meanings.

Doing ethnicity

In stylization a single salient linguistic token can be enough to evoke social meaning, and researching it calls for several kinds of linguistic analysis. Overall quantifying of speakers' performance on particular linguistic variables may not be possible or productive, depending on the number of tokens. But the individual uses of each feature can be identified and tracked, and its relation to other features. This blending of quantitative, qualitative and co-occurrence analysis (Bell 2001a) represents a powerful combination of tools for understanding sociolinguistic style.

In a project of my own specifically designed to test several of the Audience Design hypotheses (Bell and Johnson 1997; Bell 2001a), a set of 4 informants were interviewed in succession by 4 interviewers, a total of 12 interviews (one set of interviews was dropped). The demographics of the informant and interviewer samples were matched by gender and ethnicity, so that each contained a Māori woman, Māori man, Pakeha (Anglo) woman and Pakeha man. We concentrate on the occurrence of

Table 11.2 Index of *eh* usage in interviews between cross-ethnic/ gender-matched sample of interviewers and informants (tokens per 10,000 words), New Zealand

	To Interviewers			
	MM	*MF*	*PM*	*PF*
By Informants				
MM	46	26	19	–
MF	2	4	–	0
PM	0	–	0	1
PF	–	0	0	0

MM   Māori Male
MF   Māori Female
PM   Pakeha Male
PF   Pakeha Female
Source: Bell (2001a), table 9.2

the discourse particle *eh*, which is a stereotype, third-order index of Māori English (recall Example 10.6 from Billy T. James).

Quantitatively Duncan, the Māori man, uses most of the tokens of *eh* that occur in the recordings, many more than the other three informants (Table 11.2). And he uses most *eh* to the Māori male interviewer, and least to the Pakeha male – clearly an audience-designed style. Qualitatively, it is noticeable that even with the other Māori man, he uses only three tokens of *eh* in the first 20 minutes. This increases once he has settled in to the interaction, and tokens tend to cluster together when he is talking about 'Māori' topics – family, his grandmother's *tangi* (funeral), Māori language and culture. When he is talking to the Pakeha man, Duncan uses few *eh* but a lot of other pragmatic markers such as *y'know*. It seems clear that *eh* is functioning to index shared Māoriness between Duncan and the other Māori man and in the topics of their talk.

As well as affirming one's ingroup ethnic identity, language can be used to voice an ethnicity to which a speaker does not naturally belong. Rampton's research on such 'crossing' among London teenagers is the benchmark study (1995). He found that his speakers would switch from their normal vernacular to an ethnic minority code, mainly 'Stylized Asian English', which often served to sanction someone for an offence by imputing diminished cultural competence to them (Example 11.1). In the US Bucholtz has investigated the ways in which European Americans reference African American Vernacular. She found a white boy using features of what she terms CRAAVE – Cross-Racial African American Vernacular English (1999b). The move laid claim to heightened masculinity by its association with stereotypical African American male culture. She found this same linguistic and social indexing in film characters played by Steve Martin and Warren Beattie (Bucholtz and Lopez 2011): such staged performances of identities form a rich field for linguistic, social and semiotic analysis which we now turn to.

Example 11.1

Stylized Asian English

The boys are queuing to go in for dinner when they notice a pupil of Bangladeshi descent trying to push in (Rampton 1995: 143). Stylized Asian English in **BOLD CAPS**; ( )=pause.

7	Rich:	OI EH EH WHERE YOU GOING (.) GET BACK OI
8		( )
9	Rich:	EH GET BACK (1.0) HEY WHAT **A RAAS**
		((= *approximation to Creole*)) (.)
10	Ian :	EH ( ) EH MISS (.) WHERE THEY GOING (.)
11	Rich:	MISS THEY'VE PUSHED IN
12	Ian :	OI (.) LOOK Baker ((*a 6th former*)) THESE LOT
		PUSHED IN
13		(.) THEY JUST (OUR DINNER) THEY (BOUGHT) (.)
14		GET BACK TO THE BACK
15	Rich:	GED OU'
16	Anon A:	*((in exaggerated Asian English::))* **OUT**:
17	Rich:	GED OU'
18	Anon A [M]:	((*slowly in stylised Asian English*:)) **GE:T OU:T**
19	Anon B [M]:	((*slow*:)): **OUT BOY OUT**
20	Anon A	((*slow*:)): **GE:T OU:T**
21	Rich:	(those others) pushed in

- What do you make of this usage of Stylized Asian English – its setting and social meaning, its positioning of the participants, its effect on the interaction?

11.5   THE CASE OF MARLENE DIETRICH

If she had nothing more than her voice she could break your heart with it. (Ernest Hemingway, *Life* magazine, 1952)

It is July 1930. A steamer is approaching the coast of Morocco through fog. As a woman crosses the crowded deck to the rail, her suitcase falls open. An urbane fellow-passenger picks up the contents for her and offers further assistance. 'I won't need any help', she replies.

At least, that is what Marlene Dietrich is scripted to say. But what has come out is a non-native disyllable, an epenthetic vowel creating 'hellubh', as director Josef von Sternberg will transcribe it later (1966: 249). What is to be done? He believes that much more than a single word is at stake for his leading lady in her first American film,

Morocco. A stage parody of Germanic English will negate the charm and mystique of her appearance. But take follows unsuccessful take, until von Sternberg eventually suggests: pronounce *help* as if all four letters were German. She immediately gets it, and nearly 50 attempts later, the director has his usable footage.

The incident was pivotal in the making of Dietrich as a star. The film's final soundtrack reveals that Dietrich has produced an accent that is enigmatic because listeners hear something different but cannot specify quite what it is or means. It sets the pattern for Dietrich's future performed English and the mysterious edge of linguistic otherness which will be part of her persona. Her star has risen with language as a core component.

The non-native performer

The spread of English has produced a century of performers who are not native speakers, but whose performances are mainly enacted and recorded in English – Greta Garbo, Maurice Chevalier, Arnold Schwarzenegger, ABBA, Björk. Marlene Dietrich was arguably the most stellar and iconic of these. Her career spanned 50 years and made her a cult figure. This case study analyses the linguistic character of Dietrich's English, mainly in repeat performances of 'Falling in love again'. It examines the nature of Dietrich's celebrity and persona, and the role that her voice quality and non-native English played in this. And it uses the case of Marlene to address wider issues of the place of language in staged and mediated performance, particularly in the creation, establishment and iconization of a celebrity performer. It draws on my detailed study in Bell (2011a).

'Falling in love again': 1930

Dietrich came to stardom in the 1930 film, *The Blue Angel*, after being 'discovered' on the Berlin stage by von Sternberg and cast as the seductive cabaret singer, Lola Lola. The film was shot simultaneously in German and English and provided her career-long signature tune, 'Ich bin von Kopf bis Fuß/Falling in love again'. The music and German lyrics were by Friedrich Holländer, a leading Berlin composer and musician, although in English the chorus 'falling in love again' conveys more or less the opposite sense to the German original (Example 11.2). Holländer and Dietrich are both said to have detested the sweetened English version.

The film is set in the Blue Angel, a raucous, chaotic beer hall. Lola wears a top hat, sits on a beer barrel, leans back with her legs crooked, lifts and grasps one knee and sings directly and seductively to the repressed schoolmaster Emmanuel Rath: the pose will become a classic (see still photograph at http://www.imdb.com/media/rm407214080/tt0020697). Rath preens himself, hopelessly enraptured. As a performance Dietrich's deserves the iconic status it will achieve (URL http://www.youtube.com/watch?v=HaZDiKRT1is).

At the start of filming *The Blue Angel* in Berlin, Dietrich could scarcely be described as a speaker of English, and analysis of her pronunciation in the film shows her accent as markedly non-native. Table 11.3 presents the features that I hear as non-native – consonantal,

'Falling in love again' lyrics

Example 11.2

English version	German original	Translation of German
Falling in love again	Ich bin von Kopf bis Fuß	From head to foot
Never wanted to	Auf Liebe eingestellt,	I am set for love
What's a girl to do?*	Denn das ist meine Welt	For that is my world
Can't help it.	Und sonst gar nichts.	And nothing else besides.
Love's always been my game	Das ist, was soll ich machen,	What am I to do –
Play it how I may	Meine Natur,	That is my nature,
I was made that way	Ich kann halt lieben nur	All I can do is love
Can't help it.	Und sonst gar nichts.	And nothing else besides.

* In later performances:
'What am I to do?'

- Undertake your own project comparing for example other performances of 'Falling in love again' by Dietrich, or performances by any of the many other singers who have recorded it, or other recordings by Dietrich. Or other non-native performers. Access the material through YouTube.

Table 11.3 Count of non-nativisms in Marlene Dietrich's performance of 'Falling in love again' in *The Blue Angel*, 1930 (tokens in parentheses are intermediate)

	Feature	Example	N
Vowels	Full vowel for schwa	to, wanted	10
	Monophthongization of /ʊu/, /ei/	do, to, always, flame	12
	Vowel shortening	been, moth	2
	Unrounding/lowering to [a]	burn	3
Consonants	Mis-aspiration	to, wanted	5
	Fortis /d/	around	1
	Affrication	their	1
	/w/ unrounded/labiodental	what, wanted	3 (+1)
	Hyper-clear postvocalic /l/	help	(+2)
Prosody	Over-even rhythm	I just can't help it	4
TOTAL			41 (44)

vocalic and prosodic – most of which are L1 transfer effects. Most prevalent are issues with the vowels. Diphthongs are monophthongized in words like 'way' and 'do'. Some unstressed vowels retain full value rather than being reduced to schwa, triggered by a non-native prosody. The overall result is that Dietrich produces a pronunciation of this song which is hearably marked as non-native for the English-speaking listener.

Referee Design

Dietrich's performance can be theorized as Referee Design:

- **Ingroup/outgroup**. Performing in a language (English) other than her own (German) represents a self-evident instance of outgroup referee design.
- **Short/long term**. Dietrich's initial performance of English was short term – produced in Germany for a film made in English. But when she subsequently moved to and was based in the US, the dynamic became longer term.
- **Accurate versus inaccurate**. Her 'inaccurate' non-nativeness was hearable to English audiences, but they could understand her and evaluated it as positive.
- **Successful versus unsuccessful**. Dietrich is strictly unsuccessful in the linguistics of her referee design – that is, her lifelong pronunciation remains identifiably non-native. But her accent, according to Lawrence (2007: 84), 'functions as a marker of difference, a guarantee of her "otherness"'. It was a linguistic resource on which she drew to highlight her difference, rather than a failure to sound native.

From 1930 Dietrich made six films with von Sternberg in Hollywood, the first of them *Morocco*. In these he crafted her persona as the femme fatale (Hanson and O'Rawe 2010), enregistering her non-native accent and baritone quality as the first voice of the femme fatale in sound films. That voice had to be Other, exotic, non-native. Dietrich established and carried forward the femme fatale image through the 1930s, and then on into her stage acts during the Second World War. She was both the original and the enduring voice of the femme fatale, a 'characterological figure' in Agha's terms (2003) – an icon.

'Falling in love again': 1964

For three decades from the 1940s Dietrich toured a live show renowned for her stunning costumes (photo at http://www.imdb.com/media/rm1699059712/nm0000017). A triumphant London season in 1964 produced a recording on its closing night (URL: http://www.youtube.com/watch?v=SYI5GaSKZcw). Comparison reveals her English as much more native than 35 years earlier but still retaining a hearably different accent, which is now valorized as her distinctive voice. Table 11.4 displays the non-nativisms in Dietrich's performance of 'Falling in love again' during this 1964 show. Several non-native features present in 1930 have disappeared altogether. The features that still show in 1964 are at much lower levels than 35 years before, and are much less phonetically extreme or obvious. By now Marlene has lived and worked in an English-speaking milieu for decades. She is still distinctive – but not too distinctive.

Table 11.4　Count of non-nativisms in Dietrich's performance of 'Falling in love again', Queen's Theatre, London, 1964 (tokens in parentheses are intermediate)

	Feature	Example	N
Vowels	Full vowel for schwa	falling, wanted	2 (+1)
	Monophthongization of /ei/ (no /ʊu/)	blame, flame	(3)
	Vowel shortening	not	1
	Unrounding/lowering to [a]	–	0
Consonants	Mis-aspiration	can't help	(2)
	Fortis /d/	–	0
	Th affrication	–	0
	/w/ unrounded/labiodental	–	0
	Hyper-clear postvocalic /l/	help	(2)
Prosody	Over-even rhythm	–	0
TOTAL			3 (11)

Iconization and enregisterment

As a celebrity of the past, but one whose iconicity remains in active circulation and cultural dialogue with the present, the case of Marlene Dietrich offers an enlightening perspective on the sociolinguistics of contemporary performance. Dietrich's decades of repeated performances established her as an icon, and her appearance and pronunciation were widely circulated, referenced, imitated, and occasionally parodied. The engine of enregisterment as one of Agha's 'characterological figures' is repetition of salient features through a succession of cognate performances. Such repetition is the requirement and the bane of the successful live performer. In addition the icon must be refracted and circulated in the referencing it receives in the wider culture. Dietrich's appearance (especially dress) was constantly referenced and imitated, sometimes parodied. As well as non-native, Dietrich's voice was distinctively low register. From the thirties it trended towards increasingly baritone quality: the low register became a trademark.

Living the femme fatale persona in her own life, and cultivating her image with extreme reflexivity, Marlene Dietrich achieved the ultimate ingroup identification. She devoted immense attention and labour to maintaining her established persona on all fronts. This may be interpreted as a particular and extreme case of ingroup referee design in which a speaker's target becomes a heightened version of her own individual linguistic production. From the 1930s to the end of her career 40 years later, we may say that Marlene Dietrich's referee was, in fact, **herself**.

11.6　RESEARCH ACTIVITY
A PERFORMANCE LANGUAGE PROJECT

This research activity offers the opportunity to conduct a project on language performance. The staged performance of language which has burgeoned as an area of interest in recent sociolinguistics covers frequently fascinating, multi-layered data where stylization of linguistic resources is rife. It invites us to theorize about the nature of language in society on the basis of analytically challenging and rewarding 'texts' which open up some of the most significant contemporary social issues such as globalization.

Staged performance

First, a definition: staged performance is the overt, scheduled identification and elevation (usually literally) of one or more people to perform, typically on a stage, or in a stage-like area such as the space in front of a camera or microphone. It normally involves a clearly demarcated distinction between performer and audience. Prototypically, staged performance occurs through genres such as a play, concert or religious service, and in venues dedicated to such presentations – a theatre, concert hall or place of worship. Here it also includes performances disseminated through the media or internet.

Several factors are central to staged performance and its sociolinguistics (Bell and Gibson 2011):

- Identities – performance is commonly focused on the projection of identities, and involves referencing target groups at a range of levels from evocation to appropriation.
- Reflexivity – performance self-consciously displays language forms for delight and critique.
- Audience – as Coupland notes (2007), performances are not just **to** audiences but **for** them, and audience response moulds the performance itself. The audience is also layered (as in my framework of roles, Chapter 6.4).
- Authenticity – there are differential expectations. In folk music, audiences will expect an 'authentic' self to be projected, but drag involves strategic inauthenticity (Coupland 2011b).
- Genre – the particular manner and import of a performance is specific to the genre, for example differences between jazz and rock performances.
- Modalities – non-language dimensions can be crucial. As we saw with Dietrich, the visuals of appearance, movement and stage/film setting cue a reading of the language. And when singing is involved, the music is as central as the words.

The sociolinguistics of performance

Performance assumes the operation of agentive action, of intentional representation of language in the service of social meaning. But it also assumes a backdrop of existing meanings and forms against which the performance is enacted and from which it draws meanings. In performance, there is a tension between a genre's tradition and the individual talent. Performers are both innovating originals and bearers of traditions – often simultaneously.

Staged performances tend to be linguistically stylized, pushing the limits of language creativity, rehearsed, self-aware, stagey, and at times hyperbolic (Coupland 2007). The phonology of performance is selective in the features it realizes. It mis-realizes some, on occasions undershooting the target (as in Dietrich's non-native English), at other times overshooting it – for example, in renditions of African American Vernacular (Bucholtz and Lopez 2011).

Example 11.3

Sample performance projects

By way of example, the following studies were conducted as part of a *Hauptseminar* (graduate-level course) I taught at a German university on Performing Englishes. The students each created and designed their own project. Most students are apprehensive about their ability to do this, but almost all succeed, sometimes brilliantly.

- Subversive gender performance in the film *The Rocky Horror Picture Show*
- Analysis of the song 'We belong dead' by the death metal band Impaled
- Comparison of the British and American versions of the television comedy *The Office*
- Comparison of the 1938 and 1964 films of *Pygmalion/My Fair Lady*
- Cockney Rhyming Slang in *The Bible in Cockney*
- Ewan McGregor's film performances in Scottish English – or not
- Vicky Pollard's 'chavspeak' in the television comedy *Little Britain*
- The linguistic personas of Sacha Baron Cohen
- Social and linguistic differences in obituaries
- New York dialect as social marker in the sitcom *The King of Queens*.

Finally, media performances have the potential to trigger wider sociolinguistic effects. They circulate novel forms and may contribute to language change. They associate linguistic resources with characterological figures, such as Catherine Tate and 'chav' in the UK, focused in her catchline 'Am I bovvered?'. Performance 'packages up stylistic and socio-semantic complexes and makes them transportable' (Coupland 2007: 155).

Doing a performance project

Such a project follows the nine steps outlined in Chapters 3, 7 and 10. Your data can come from any of the many genres accessible through media or live performance. Example 11.3 shows the kind of projects that can be done. YouTube and other websites offer a vast array of material which has originated in other media such as music videos, newspaper text, DVDs.

For analysis, locate a specific stretch of language that you believe contains interesting linguistic features, casts light on the language or variety that is being performed or referred to, and carries social meanings for you to interpret. Select a relatively short 'text' – in some cases, e.g. a television commercial, it could be as short as 1 minute long. In other cases, e.g. a film or video excerpt, perhaps as much as 10 minutes. For written material, up to 2 pages long. Don't try to cover too much.

Look for linguistic features of all kinds and at all levels of language – phonology, morphology, syntax, discourse. Concentrate especially on those features which carry marked social meaning, for example in evoking particular regional, ethnic or age identities. Take account of other, multimodal aspects of your data such as visuals and music.

Interpret the social meaning of the linguistic features of your chosen data excerpt. To do this, you must background the social situation, cultural genre, etc. from which the data comes (e.g. the singer, television comedy, magazine, musical genre, etc.) and the language situations that it comes from or refers to (region, ethnic group, etc.). Exercise 11.6 outlines a way of approaching sociolinguistic performance analysis.

Exercise 11.6   Analysing performance language

These are some pointers to analysis of performed language under six main headings (which I call the 'Sociolinguistics of Voice'):

Physicality
- What is the physicality of the medium, technology – and its reception?
- And of the text (e.g. the set, layout)?

Locality
- What is the locality?
- Is the content only – or differently – locally interpretable?
- Is there a global reflex of the local?

Variety
- Where is this situated among language or variety choices?
- Are there evidences of centrifugal or centripetal linguistic pressures?
- Are there contrasting voices?
- Is there a transposition between cultures?

Performativity
- How intentional or knowing is the performance?
- What are the sociocultural resonances?
- What language resources does the performance draw on?
- Are there reference groups for this performance?
- Is the performance 'natural' to this audience?
- What is the keying of the performance? How does it relate to authenticity?
- What skill or expertise is involved? Has there been rehearsal?

Dialogicality
- Are there evidences here of the dialogical nature of language? – is there collaboration, or exchange, or competition?
- What kind of audience or audience layers are likely for this performance? How would the audience engage with the performance (laughter, silence, etc.)?

Identity
- What voices are there in the performance? Whose voices are they?
- What is their social meaning?
- Is there 'othering'? Is there appropriation?

11.7 SUMMARY

- Style is what individual speakers do with language. Sociolinguists ask why a speaker made specific style choices and not their alternatives, thus locating style in distinction. The first main approach to style in sociolinguistics is maximalist, encompassing a full range of linguistic levels and a diversity of social factors.
- The second, variationist approach is contrastingly minimalist. It tightly delimits linguistic variables and correlates them with styles defined by interview tasks through which Labov aimed to focus increasing amounts of a speaker's attention on speech. However, his attribution of attention as the operative factor in style has been widely challenged.
- Audience Design was proposed as a model by Bell (1984) in which speakers design their style primarily in response to their audience. In my research on radio news language, only audience differences plausibly explained style differences. The same processes appear to operate in face-to-face communication. Audience Design has been distilled under nine headings, summarized and italicized in section 11.2.
- Giles's accommodation approach is a social psychological theory parallel to Audience Design. It asks why speakers adjust their speech to the people they are interacting with, especially by converging to them.
- Several approaches have attempted to capture the relation of response and initiative – style and stylization. A responsive shift results from a change in the situation, and an initiative shift triggers such a change. In terms of Referee Design, this means that speakers are re-orienting their own identity in relation to their audience, either focusing on a reference outgroup or enhancing identification with their ingroup.
- The responsive and initiative dimensions of style reflect social theory's oscillation between the roles of structure and of agency in society. However the swing to agency in sociolinguistics has unbalanced our view of language style. We need to regain the sense that structure is what provides the resource speakers draw on in their styling.
- Referee Design involves speakers performing language, breaking out briefly from everyday conversational mode into overt performance. Such performance is close bound to identity, which includes both structured and agentive dimensions, part product, part process.
- Speakers can use language to claim identities that may not appear 'natural' to them. Gender is increasingly regarded as a constructed or performed matter rather than defined by biological sex. Language can be used to initiate a claim to a heightened or alternative gender identity, for example as part of cross-gender identification.
- Style research calls for a blend of quantitative, qualitative and co-occurrence analysis. In a project focusing on styling of ethnic and gender identities, I found that a Māori man used many more tokens of the ethnic marker *eh* to a Māori interviewer than to a Pakeha, and *eh* clustered when the topic was on Māori matters.
- Marlene Dietrich came to stardom in the 1930 German-made film, *The Blue Angel*, which provided her career-long signature tune 'Falling in love again'. Her pronunciation was markedly non-native, which can be theorized as Referee Design. Her subsequent Hollywood films enregistered her non-native accent as the first and lasting voice of the femme fatale.

- Comparison with a 1964 stage performance of 'Falling in love again' reveals Dietrich's English had become much more native after 35 years but retained an accent that was now valorized as her distinctive voice. After decades of repeated performances, circulation of her vocal style and appearance, and living out the femme fatale persona, Dietrich had become her own referee.

11.8 FURTHER READING

On language style overall Coupland (2011a) offers an excellent summary and overview. His *Style* (2007) is the best book to date, including an exposition and critique of Audience Design. There is a clutch of chapters in Coupland and Jaworski's one-volume reader (2009b). Eckert and Rickford's comprehensive collection (2001) came from a symposium which brought together many of the leading scholars and the main theoretical alternatives. It includes response pieces.

Several chapters of Labov (1972a) major on style. For critiques of Labov's approach, especially attention to speech, see Bell (1984) and a chapter in Coupland (2007). Labov (2001b) mainly reaffirms his earlier positions.

My original long paper in *Language in Society* (1984) laid out Audience Design and remains foundational reading on sociolinguistic style. The condensed version (1997a, republished several times) distils that into nine main points more fully than has been presented here. Bell (2001a) 'Back in style' revised and extended the model. Rickford and McNair-Knox is a major article testing some of Audience Design's hypotheses (1994).

Bell (1984) offers detail on Referee Design and its parameters, expanded in Bell (1999, 2001a). See Table 11.1 for reading on the other parallel frameworks. For Rampton's Crossing construct, see his 1995 book, also his more recent work on 'posh' versus Cockney (2006).

Giles and Powesland (1975) is the foundation text of accommodation theory, followed by many articles and collections co-authored or edited by Giles. Giles, Coupland and Coupland (1991) was the last of the major developments of the theory. Trudgill (1981) was sociolinguistics' first encounter with accommodation. Meyerhoff (1998) applies and evaluates its relevance for our field. Shepard, Giles and Le Poire (2001) and Giles and Ogay (2007) review more recent work. The *Journal of Language and Social Psychology* published much of the work in the 1980s/90s.

Elinor Ochs pioneered research on linguistic indexing of gender (1992). For work on the doing of masculinity and femininity, see publications by Holmes, Cameron, Kiesling and Pujolar. On gay and cross-gender languaging, Kulick, Levon, Cameron, Podesva and Barrett. For ethnicity, Schilling-Estes, Rampton, Rickford, Bucholtz, Bell and many others. There are numerous publications in the two main journals, plus the *Journal of Linguistic Anthropology* and *Gender and Language*.

On Marlene Dietrich, see the paper from which this case study is drawn (Bell 2011a) and the references it contains, especially Gemünden and Desjardins (2007) on *Dietrich Icon*. My other work on style in staged performance covers television advertisements (1992), 'styling the other' in a Māori song (1999), nationalistic New Zealand commercials (2001b), and the Pasifika animated comedy *bro'town* (Gibson and Bell 2010). Bell and Gibson (2011) and Gibson and Bell (2012) contain the most recent theoretical developments.

For 'the sociolinguistics of performance', consult the 2011 theme issue of the *Journal of Sociolinguistics*, edited by Bell and Gibson, especially the Introduction for its theorization and overview. Also a theme issue of the *Journal of English Linguistics* (2009) edited by Ruth King. Hernández-Campoy and Cutillas-Espinosa (2012) is an excellent collection on stylization in the media. Beyond these, see many articles by Coupland, Bauman, Johnstone, Bucholtz, Hernández-Campoy and Joanna Thornborrow.

REFERENCES

Agha, Asif, 2003. 'The social life of cultural value'. *Language & Communication* 23: 23–73.

Bakhtin, M.M., 1981 [1935]. 'Discourse in the novel'. In M.M. Bakhtin, *The Dialogic Imagination*. Austin, TX: University of Texas Press. 259–422.

Bakhtin, M.M. 1986 [1953]. *Speech Genres and Other Late Essays*. Austin, TX: University of Texas Press.

Bell, Allan, 1984. 'Language style as audience design'. *Language in Society* 13: 145–204.

Bell, Allan, 1991a. 'Audience accommodation in the mass media'. In Howard Giles, Nikolas Coupland and Justine Coupland (eds), *Contexts of Accommodation: Developments in Applied Sociolinguistics*. Cambridge: Cambridge University Press. 69–102.

Bell, Allan, 1992. 'Hit and miss: referee design in the dialects of New Zealand television advertisements'. *Language & Communication* 12: 1–14.

Bell, Allan, 1997a. 'Style as audience design'. In Nikolas Coupland and Adam Jaworski (eds), *Sociolinguistics: A Reader and Coursebook*. London: Macmillan. 240–50.

Bell, Allan, 1999. 'Styling the other to define the self: a study in New Zealand identity making'. *Journal of Sociolinguistics* 3: 523–41.

Bell, Allan, 2001a. 'Back in style: re-working audience design'. In Penelope Eckert and John R. Rickford (eds), *Style and Sociolinguistic Variation*. New York: Cambridge University Press. 139–69.

Bell, Allan, 2001b. '"Bugger!" Media language, identity and post-modernity in Aotearoa/New Zealand'. *New Zealand Sociology* 16: 128–50.

Bell, Allan, 2011a. 'Falling in love again and again: Marlene Dietrich and the iconization of non-native English'. *Journal of Sociolinguistics* 15: 627–56.

Bell, Allan and Andy Gibson, 2011. 'Staging language: an introduction to the sociolinguistics of performance'. *Journal of Sociolinguistics* 15: 555–72.

Bell, Allan and Gary Johnson, 1997. 'Towards a sociolinguistics of style'. *University of Pennsylvania Working Papers in Linguistics* 4: 1–21.

Blom, Jan-Petter and John J. Gumperz, 1972. 'Social meaning in linguistic structure: code-switching in Norway'. In John J. Gumperz and Dell Hymes (eds), *Directions in Sociolinguistics*. New York: Holt, Rinehart & Winston. 407–34.

Bourdieu, Pierre, 1984. *Distinction: A Social Critique of the Judgement of Taste*. Cambridge, MA: Harvard University Press.

Brown, Roger and Albert Gilman, 1960. 'The pronouns of power and solidarity'. In Thomas A. Sebeok (ed.), *Style in Language*. Cambridge, MA: MIT Press. 253–76.

Bucholtz, Mary, 1999. 'You da man: narrating the racial other in the production of white masculinity'. *Journal of Sociolinguistics* 3: 443–60.

Bucholtz, Mary and Qiuana Lopez, 2011. 'Performing blackness, forming whiteness: linguistic minstrelsy in Hollywood film'. *Journal of Sociolinguistics* 15: 680–706.

Cameron, Deborah, 1997. 'Performing gender identity: young men's talk and the construction of heterosexual masculinity'. In Sally Johnson and Ulrike Hanna Meinhof (eds), *Language and Masculinity*. Oxford, UK: Blackwell Publishers. 47–64.

Coupland, Nikolas, 1984. 'Accommodation at work: some phonological data and their implications'. *International Journal of the Sociology of Language* 46: 49–70.

Coupland, Nikolas, 2001a. 'Age in social and sociolinguistic theory'. In Nikolas Coupland, Srikant Sarangi and Christopher N. Candlin (eds), *Sociolinguistics and Social Theory*. Harlow, UK: Pearson Education. 185–211.

Coupland, Nikolas, 2007. *Style: Language Variation and Identity*. Cambridge: Cambridge University Press.

Coupland, Nikolas, 2011a. 'The sociolinguistics of style'. In Rajend Mesthrie (ed.), *The Cambridge Handbook of Sociolinguistics*. Cambridge: Cambridge University Press. 138–56.

Coupland, Nikolas, 2011b. 'Voice, place and genre in popular song performance'. *Journal of Sociolinguistics* 15: 573–602.

Coupland, Nikolas and Adam Jaworski (eds), 2009a. *The New Sociolinguistics Reader* (2nd edn). Basingstoke, UK: Palgrave Macmillan.

Eckert, Penelope, 2000. *Linguistic Variation as Social Practice: The Linguistic Construction of Identity in Belten High*. Malden, MA: Blackwell Publishers.

Eckert, Penelope, 2010. 'Vowels and nail polish: the emergence of linguistic style in the preadolescent heterosexual marketplace'. In Miriam Meyerhoff and Erik Schleef (eds), *The Routledge Sociolinguistics Reader*. London: Routledge. 441–7.

Eckert, Penelope and John R. Rickford (eds), 2001. *Style and Sociolinguistic Variation*. New York: Cambridge University Press.

Gemünden, Gerd and Mary R. Desjardins (eds), 2007. *Dietrich Icon*. Durham, NC: Duke University Press.

Gibson, Andy and Allan Bell, 2010. 'Performing Pasifika English in New Zealand: the case of bro'Town'. *English World-Wide* 31: 231–51.

Gibson, Andy and Allan Bell, 2012. 'Popular music singing as referee design'. In Juan Manuel Hernández-Campoy and Juan Antonio Cutillas-Espinosa (eds), *Style-shifting in Public: New Perspectives on Stylistic Variation*. Amsterdam: John Benjamins. 139–64.

Giles, Howard, Justine Coupland and Nikolas Coupland (eds), 1991. *Contexts of Accommodation: Developments in Applied Sociolinguistics*. Cambridge: Cambridge University Press.

Giles, Howard and Tania Ogay, 2007. 'Communication Accommodation Theory'. In Bryan B. Whaley and Wendy Samter (eds), *Explaining Communication: Contemporary Theories and Exemplars*. Mahwah, NJ: Lawrence Erlbaum. 293–310.

Giles, Howard and Peter F. Powesland, 1975. *Speech Style and Social Evaluation*. London: Academic Press.

Giles, Howard and Philip Smith, 1979. 'Accommodation theory: optimal levels of convergence'. In Howard Giles and Robert N. St Clair (eds), *Language and Social Psychology*. Oxford, UK: Basil Blackwell. 45–65.

Hall, Kira, 1997. '"Go suck your husband's sugarcane!": Hijras and the use of sexual insult'. In Anna Livia and Kira Hall (eds), *Queerly Phrased: Language, Gender, and Sexuality*. New York: Oxford University Press. 430–60.

Hanson, Helen and Catherine O'Rawe (eds), 2010. *The Femme Fatale: Images, Histories, Contexts*. Basingstoke, UK: Palgrave Macmillan.

Hernández-Campoy, Juan Manuel and Juan Antonio Cutillas-Espinosa (eds), 2012. *Style-shifting in Public: New Perspectives on Stylistic Variation*. Amsterdam: John Benjamins.

Holmes, Janet, 2006. *Gendered Talk at Work: Constructing Gender Identity through Workplace Discourse*. Malden, MA: Blackwell Publishing.

Irvine, Judith T., 2001. '"Style" as distinctiveness: the culture and ideology of linguistic differentiation'. In Penelope Eckert and John R. Rickford (eds), *Style and Sociolinguistic Variation*. New York: Cambridge University Press. 21–43.

Labov, William, 1972a. *Language in the Inner City: Studies in the Black English Vernacular.* Philadelphia, PA: University of Pennsylvania Press.

Labov, William, 2001b. 'The anatomy of style-shifting'. In Penelope Eckert and John R. Rickford (eds), *Style and Sociolinguistic Variation.* New York: Cambridge University Press. 85–108.

Lawrence, Amy, 2007. 'The voice as mask'. In Gerd Gemünden and Mary R. Desjardins (eds), *Dietrich Icon.* Durham, NC: Duke University Press. 79–99.

Mendoza-Denton, Norma, 2008. *Homegirls: Language and Cultural Practice among Latina Youth Gangs.* Malden, MA: Blackwell.

Meyerhoff, Miriam, 1998. 'Accommodating your data: the use and misuse of accommodation theory in sociolinguistics'. *Language & Communication* 18: 205–25.

Ochs, Elinor, 1992. 'Indexing gender'. In Alessandro Duranti and Charles Goodwin (eds), *Rethinking Context: Language as an Interactive Phenomenon.* Cambridge: Cambridge University Press. 335–58.

Podesva, Robert J., 2007. 'Phonation type as a stylistic variable: the use of falsetto in constructing a persona'. *Journal of Sociolinguistics* 11: 478–504.

Pujolar i Cos, Joan, 1997. 'Masculinities in a multilingual setting'. In Sally Johnson and Ulrike Hanna Meinhof (eds), *Language and Masculinity.* Oxford, UK: Blackwell Publishers. 86–106.

Rampton, Ben, 2006. *Language in Late Modernity: Interaction in an Urban School.* Cambridge: Cambridge University Press.

Rickford, John R. and Faye McNair-Knox, 1994. 'Addressee- and topic-influenced style shift: a quantitative sociolinguistic study'. In Douglas Biber and Edward Finegan (eds), *Sociolinguistic Perspectives on Register.* New York: Oxford University Press. 235–76.

Rampton, Ben, 1995. *Crossing: Language and Ethnicity among Adolescents.* London: Longman.

Rampton, Ben, 2006. *Language in Late Modernity: Interaction in an Urban School.* Cambridge: Cambridge University Press.

Schilling-Estes, Natalie, 2004. 'Constructing ethnicity in interaction'. *Journal of Sociolinguistics* 8: 163–95.

Shepard, Carolyn A., Howard Giles and Beth A. Le Poire, 2001. 'Communication Accommodation Theory'. In W. Peter Robinson and Howard Giles (eds), *The New Handbook of Language and Social Psychology.* Chichester, UK: Wiley. 33–56.

Silverstein, Michael. 1979. 'Language structure and linguistic ideology'. In Paul R. Clyne, William F. Hanks and Carol L. Hofbauer (eds), *The Elements: A Parasession on Linguistic Units and Levels.* Chicago, IL: Chicago Linguistic Society. 193–247.

Trudgill, Peter, 1974. *The Social Differentiation of English in Norwich.* London: Cambridge University Press.

Trudgill, Peter, 1981. 'Linguistic accommodation: sociolinguistic observations on a sociopsychological theory'. In C.S. Masek, R.A. Hendrick and M.F. Miller (eds), *Papers from the Parasession on Language and Behavior.* Chicago, IL: Chicago Linguistic Society. 218–37.

von Sternberg, Josef, 1966. *Fun in a Chinese Laundry.* London: Secker & Warburg.

Yaeger-Dror, Malcah, 1993. 'Linguistic analysis of dialect "correction" and its interaction with cognitive salience'. *Language Variation and Change* 5: 189–224.

12

THEORY AND ENGAGEMENT

This final, short chapter rounds off the matter of this book. It confronts directly some core issues of sociolinguistic theory which we have only circled around earlier. Then I will turn briefly to the application of sociolinguistics to real-world problems, and finally consider the shape of the socially constituted discipline that I introduced in the opening chapter. That will enable us to reflect back on the path that we have taken through socio-linguistics in the course of this book, especially in the light of the aims I laid out in Chapter 1. These included a grasp of the shape of sociolinguistics, understanding of its research and hands-on experience of doing it, together with two further goals:

- to present you with the opportunity to reflect on your own sociolinguistic situation – the profusion of languages and voices which are part of your life
- to offer you the chance to engage with how language affects and constitutes society, in particular where that produces inequity.

The core chapters of the book have threaded through areas such as multilingualisms, code switching, language change and styles, and have invited consideration of your own experience of these. In the process they have raised broad questions about the role of language in society, and its political and ideological positioning, which press for our engagement and which we consider briefly in this chapter.

12.1 THE PLACE OF THE SOCIAL IN SOCIOLINGUISTICS

In opening this book I asked 'What is language?', noting that this question is not raised often enough by sociolinguists. But I did not put the parallel question that our field's name invites: 'What is society?' That we have asked even less frequently. Because most of us are

The Guidebook to Sociolinguistics, First Edition. Allan Bell.
© 2014 Allan Bell. Published 2014 by Blackwell Publishing Ltd.

Exercise 12.1 Sociolinguistics and social theory

Woolard writes in an early essay (1985: 738):

> In developing descriptions of and explanations for variation in speech, sociolinguists have often borrowed sociological concepts in an ad hoc and unreflecting fashion, not usually considering critically the implicit theoretical frameworks that are imported wholesale along with such convenient constructs as three-, four-, or nine-sector scalings of socioeconomic status. In other cases those of us interested in sociolinguistic variation have invented or at least elaborated our own favorite explanatory concepts, developing through these what amount to partial social theories to account for our immediate empirical data. In either case, the enterprise often amounts to a reliance on implicit rather than explicit social theory, with little consideration given to how sociolinguistic findings might be modified by the adoption of a different theoretical frame of investigation, or in turn might validate or modify grander theories of how society works.

- In the light of the many studies you have become acquainted with in the foregoing chapters, consider and debate Woolard's view. Do you agree with her diagnosis, and if so, what practical moves could be made to deal with it?

linguists by background rather than sociologists, sociolinguists have not been strong on meshing our work with social theory. We have preferred to cobble up our own bric-a-brac answers to questions that have long been addressed in sociology, or to adopt second-hand socio-scientific solutions as givens, without due consideration for where they came from or where they are going to. Exercise 12.1 invites you to reflect on this issue.

The relation of the social and linguistic has seen two contrary trends in recent sociolinguistics. The main impetus has been to engage much more directly with social theories and incorporate them critically into the discipline. The other has downplayed the role of the social and positioned some sociolinguistic behaviours as mechanistic rather than socially driven.

Taking the social out

It is a curious twist that two of the founding and leading figures of variationist sociolinguistics have in the twenty-first century markedly reduced the role of the social in language variation and change, heading away from rather than towards an encounter between sociolinguistics and social theory. Social psychological drivers have been sidelined in favour of more mechanical factors.

In his early work Labov (1972b) made language evaluation and style central issues on the sociolinguistic agenda – while simultaneously resisting the label 'sociolinguistics' in his introduction to what was one of the first books with the term in its title. More recently, however, he has set aside the role of evaluation and attitudes as forces in

Exercise 12.2   An a-social sociolinguistics?

The principle of density implicitly asserts that we do not have to search for a motivating force behind the diffusion of linguistic change. The effect is a mechanical and inevitable one; the implicit assumption is that social evaluation and attitudes play a minor role. (Labov 2001a: 20)

Read pp. 18–20 in Labov (2001a), and Trudgill's short article in *Language in Society* on this question (2008), and the half-dozen responses published with it (recall Exercise 9.7).

1   Use these writings as a basis to understand and evaluate the case for and against motivational and identity factors in language variation, change and contact.

2   Debate the issue in class.

3   Both Labov and Trudgill rightly point out that sociolinguists have too often proposed identity as an explanation of variation or change without data other than the variation itself to support it. Revisit one of the case studies in earlier chapters – e.g. slang in Rio de Janiero (Chapter 6), an American fraternity's use of ING (Chapter 7), the jocks and burnouts of Belten High (Chapter 8), Marlene Dietrich's non-native English (Chapter 11). Assess the role of evaluation, motivation, attitudes and identity in the interpretations that the researchers offered for their findings. To what extent are these social-psychological constructs appropriate or even necessary to explain the sociolinguistic behaviours?

linguistic change. Instead he has adopted a mechanical 'principle of density', which says that people influence each other's language merely through encountering and talking to each other. What matters is not their social psychological motivations and responses but the simple fact that they have interacted (Labov 2001a: 19). Gauging sociolinguistic influence then becomes a matter of mathematically calculating interaction patterns in the manner of traffic flows.

Trudgill had introduced the social psychological theory of accommodation (Chapter 11.2) into sociolinguistics in 1981. His later work on New Zealand English speculated that the front vowel shift in that dialect derived from identity motivations: New Zealanders did not want to sound like Australians, therefore they differentiated their vowels (Trudgill, Gordon and Lewis 1998). But as we saw in Chapter 9.6, Trudgill (2004) has since taken the view that the process of colonial dialect formation in such situations is linguistically mechanistic and inevitable, and identity characteristics play no part in it (although they may follow as a consequence). The accommodation that takes place is an automatic process of behavioural coordination between speakers and not at all motivationally driven.

Labov and Trudgill have been two of the scholars whose work I have drawn on most in this text, and their position needs close consideration. Exercise 12.2 addresses questions raised by the stances they have taken.

Putting the social into sociolinguistics

In his introduction to the 2001 Coupland, Sarangi and Candlin volume on socio-linguistics and social theory, Nikolas Coupland outlines three positions he sees sociolinguistics taking on theory:

A   Sociolinguistic theory is proper linguistic theory. That is, sociolinguistics does linguistics the way linguistics should be done.
B   Sociolinguistics is an accumulation of socially relevant mini-theories. It has theories but no theory.
C   Sociolinguistic theory is (or should be) social theory. That is, sociolinguistics necessarily involves social-theoretical content.

The last point is a starting place. In sociolinguistics whether we like it or not, we are working with social theory merely by plying our trade. We will be adopting a theory even if we are not aware what it is. Arguably it is better to do so consciously and selectively than by default.

Labov and Trudgill surely have it right that linguistic and mechanistic factors must be considered in the causal mix as well as social psychological drivers. But for my part I would not want to see that lead to the social being sidelined in sociolinguistics. It seems to me to be the unique contribution of our field that we treat seriously and skil-fully the analysis and theorization of society and language **together**, and that we not endorse that they are separate or separable entities. The push should be to theorize both society and language in an ever more well-founded and integrated way. That brings us to consider briefly one central issue in social theory and its place in sociolinguistic thought.

12.2   STRUCTURE AND AGENCY

The increased foregrounding of style in sociolinguistics that I pointed to in the previous chapter is one aspect of a 'turn to the social' in our field. There has been much said in the past couple of decades of the 'turn to language' in the social sciences, and the reciprocal turn in sociolinguistics comes not before time. We now recur to the social-theoretical issue that assumed importance in the last chapter – the interplay in social life between agency and structure, between the initiative and the responsive. This proves to be a central matter for sociolinguistic theory and practice.

On the one hand, social structure constrains how we live. We do not start with a blank slate in life but with what we inherit (linguistically as well as socially). On the other side, agency is our freedom to live as we choose. Even in the most regimented milieu such as a prison, there is room for human agency to create something new. We saw in Chapter 9 that our relationship with space is constrained by how other humans and their social structures have already shaped the space we inherit – but we in turn re-shape that and create new spaces from old. Humans and society are therefore simultaneously both free and fettered.

In the mid twentieth century, when sociolinguistics arose, structure ruled in the functionalist paradigms of the social sciences at the time. In the twenty-first century, agency rules and constructivist approaches prevail. Different strands of sociolinguistics have been heirs to opposite sides in this dualism. Variationist sociolinguistics and the sociology of language come clearly out of an empiricist social science tradition which sits squarely on the structure side, as we saw in Chapter 7.2. By contrast, the more anthropological strands of the discipline have always leaned towards the agentive. Constructivism has become increasingly dominant in sociolinguistics as in all the social sciences over the past couple of decades.

This has major repercussions for the shape and conduct of the discipline, beginning with how we view language and languages (Chapters 1 and 10) and the use of language (Chapters 6, 7). Eckert approvingly captures the nature of the shift since the 1960s:

> The entire view of the relation between language and society has been reversed. The emphasis on stylistic practice ... places speakers not as passive and stable carriers of dialect, but as stylistic agents ... It has become clear that patterns of variation do not simply unfold from the speaker's structural position in a system of production, but are part of the active – stylistic – production of social differentiation. (Eckert 2012: 97)

This is neatly summarized – but also partially. Speakers are not the untrammelled agents that the quotation may imply, any more than they were the social automatons of mid-twentieth-century social theory. Eckert has re-interpreted the history of variationist sociolinguistics from an agentive standpoint, proposing that we are now in a 'third wave' of its development. Clearly, as I outlined in Chapter 1, there has been increasing and welcome melding of the different strands of sociolinguistics, especially ethnographic and interactional approaches intertwining with multilingual and variationist research. Exercise 12.3 invites you to reflect on Eckert's take on the shape of sociolinguistics and to consider alternatives.

Many social thinkers have devoted themselves to seeking a way through the structure/agency duality. Giddens's theory of 'structuration' is one such attempt (see Chapter 9), treating structures as the ongoing creation of human agency. The approach I have found most conducive is 'realist' sociology, particularly as brought to sociolinguistics by Carter and Sealey (2000) in a remarkably clear short article, followed by a full-length book (Sealey and Carter 2004). They treat both structure and agency as present and necessary. Social structure is at once prior to action and modified as a result of action. But structure is also more than just the sum of individual actions: its shape becomes independent of the individuals who contributed to it:

> Too great an emphasis on structures denies actors any power and fails to account for human beings making a difference. Too great an emphasis on agency overlooks the ... very real constraints acting on us in time and space. (Carter and Sealey 2000: 11)

Exercise 12.3   Interrogating the third wave

Putting forward a thesis that has been influential for some time, although not published till 2012, Penelope Eckert interpreted variationist sociolinguistics as developing in three waves:

1   The first was based on survey methodology and establishing correlations between linguistic variation and sociodemographic categories, from Labov's New York study onwards.
2   Then came the use of ethnographic methods to identify local categories that affect variation. This began with the Milroys' Belfast studies, and included Eckert's Belten High project.
3   In the third wave, variation itself constructs social meaning, and styles are the focus. This includes Eckert's more recent research, and work by Kiesling, Campbell-Kibler and many others. It has increasingly become the current orthodoxy.

Read Eckert's short article (2012). Now that you are near the end of this book and of your course, reflect on what you know of the strands of sociolinguistics.

- Do you agree with Eckert's description of the history of variationist sociolinguistics? For example, are there indeed three waves? Or are there alternative waves? Specify any disagreements you have.
- Do you agree with her interpretation of the development? Give your reasons.
- If you disagree, what is your alternative interpretation? Justify in detail.
- The class could debate the issues, one side for and the other against Eckert's proposal.
- Consider what you now know of the history and shape of other strands of sociolinguistics, such as multilingualism or code switching. What do you see as the stages of their development?

What lies at the base of these debates is our view of the nature of personhood. Such views of course are not a provable hypothesis of sociolinguistics or any other academic discipline. They are a premise, a prime based on our own belief system. My belief is that a person is indeed more than a static bundle of sociological categories – although to say that someone is male, or anglo, or middle class does tell us something about that person. A part of our behaviour is a reflection of the social characteristics of groups we are associated with.

But a person is also more than an ever-shifting kaleidoscope of personas created in and by different situations, with no stable core – although to say that we appear as child to our parents, employee to our boss, partner to our partner does tell us something about the person. We do not recreate ourselves moment by moment out of nothing. To the present we bring the shapings of our past, of our relationships, of our environment. Yet we are more than the sum of those things. We creatively mould our language – together with other meaningful signs – to re-present ourselves in ever-changing guises as we move through our days, their people and their happenings.

12.3   TOWARDS A SOCIALLY CONSTITUTED SOCIOLINGUISTICS

At the beginning of Chapter 1, I quoted Hymes distinguishing three different imaginable relations between sociolinguistics and society:

- the social as well as the linguistic
- socially realistic linguistics
- socially constituted linguistics.

The first of these involves addressing social issues which have a language component. Sociolinguists of all kinds have always done this – applied their knowledge to the benefit of those they are researching. Often such social intervention has been itself a motivation for conducting the research. Most chapters of this book have referred to such outworkings, and they are the focus of several of the dozen related subfields that I illustrated in Chapter 1. Although it has been beyond our scope in this book to go into them in specific detail, applied sociolinguistics offers many possibilities:

- **Language maintenance**. The many sociolinguists who have studied threatened languages have usually turned their expertise to the benefit of the community and its language, although linguistic expertise does not guarantee a positive sociopolitical outcome.
- **Language in education**. Sociolinguists have been leading advocates for the validity of the languages and dialects of disadvantaged minority speakers in education.
- **Language policy and planning**. Here academic knowledge meets political demands. Sometimes this leads to a fruitful outcome, as in the Australian national language policy of the 1980s. By contrast, New Zealand's excellent proposed language policy of a few years later came to nothing, and the country still has no language policy.

Such commitments were often the prime drivers that motivated our field's founders, and have continued to spur my own and successive generations of sociolinguists. They are a necessary outworking of the engagement to research for and with communities (recall Exercise 3.11). However, Dell Hymes envisaged – and I would endorse – something more fundamental and comprehensive. We seek not only amelioration of people's linguistic conditions, but – with Bakhtin – we need to challenge the foundations of linguistic discrimination and inequity (Chapter 10.6). There is a critical function in sociolinguistics just as there is in discourse analysis. Support for one dimension of such rethinking comes from a perhaps surprising source.

Babel revisited

The belief that multilingualism is a curse and monolingualism is natural (Chapter 2) is deeply embedded in western consciousness. The leading image and narrative of this in

Exercise 12.4   Reconstructing Babel

1 Read the story of Babel (available on line). What is your interpretation of it?
2 Compare this with the interpretation that I offer in Bell (2011c: 548ff.). Assess the evidence I put forward, make your own analysis, and draw your own conclusions.
3 Research and debate the relationship between monolingualism, power and empire. Use internet and library resources to find out about the sociolinguistic practices of one of these empires and their long-term effects, or compare two or more of them. Ostler (2005) is a good place to start:

Persian, Greek, Roman, Chinese, Spanish, French, British, American.

the cultural memory of the West is the Jewish/Christian story of Babel. This is understood as a condemnation of language diversity, and is still enormously influential and productive in twenty-first-century culture. But there is an alternative reading available for the story: that the judgment of Babel promoted the spread of humankind and the rich diversification of its languages. In Bell (2011c) I argue that Babel is a blessing rather than a curse. It is a charter for linguistic variety, a manifesto for multilingualism rather than a lament for lost monolingualism. See Exercise 12.4 to reconsider the story of Babel.

We can note that Babel is in part a story about linguistic power, about the social and political meanings of monolingualism and multilingualism. As discussed in Chapter 1, the European nation-state was created with the assumption that a nation should have its own single language. Such monolingualism is routinely coercive against other languages. Stories of children being punished at school for speaking the minority language of their home are sociolinguistic universals. The monolingual impetus of empire was for centuries most evident in France, but more recently the English-only movement in the United States has striven to ban other languages from public life, especially Spanish. But Babel stands as a monument to the ultimate futility of the drive to enforce monolingualism.

There is a close link between this reading of Babel and Bakhtin's subversive take on language diversity – the centripetal and centrifugal forces in language. The stabilizing, centralizing impetus of linguistic standard and convention seeks to define and name languages. It is always in tension with the decentralizing, momentary, creative use of language. Bakhtin has often been regarded as a herald of constructivist, agentive approaches, but he is equally adamant about language's simultaneous and inseparable normativity (1981: 272). The centrifugal forces always whirl language apart into diversity, spinning new words, new dialects, new languages, new voices, regardless of all efforts to the contrary by academies, educators, politicians or pedants.

A sociolinguistics of voice

It is at this point that the book's overarching themes of language profusion and equity join together. Language is social – dialogical – profuse – ideological, I wrote in Chapter 1. And

I quoted Dell Hymes asking what voices a society would privilege and what that would say about the society. I see it as the role of such a sociolinguistics to 'give voice'. This includes giving voice to ourselves, but saliently it also stresses the need to enable the voices of others. Such responsiveness is part of a sociolinguistics of voice. To accept someone's voice is to accept them; to reject someone's voice, rejects them.

If we can give voice, we can also take voice away. We can disable the voices of others through not listening to them or by drowning them out. I know that my country has a particular responsibility to Māori and Pasifika voices. Other nations will have their own parallel situations. Part of the reflection and hands-on research that this book has invited its readers to undertake focuses on identifying and engaging with such issues in their own situations.

For this we need a politics of voice. I see this as a direction for the future of the field, which I hope this text will contribute to shaping: a sociolinguistics which celebrates the profusion of voices that is its subject matter, and which is committed to an equitable hearing for all those voices.

REFERENCES

Bakhtin, M.M., 1981 [1935]. 'Discourse in the novel'. In M.M. Bakhtin, *The Dialogic Imagination*. Austin, TX: University of Texas Press. 259–422.

Bell, Allan, 2011c. 'Re-constructing Babel: discourse analysis, hermeneutics and the Interpretive Arc'. *Discourse Studies* 13: 519–68.

Carter, Bob and Alison Sealey, 2000. 'Language, structure and agency: what can realist social theory offer to sociolinguistics?' *Journal of Sociolinguistics* 4: 3–20.

Coupland, Nikolas, Srikant Sarangi and Christopher N. Candlin (eds), 2001. *Sociolinguistics and Social Theory*. Harlow, UK: Longman.

Eckert, Penelope, 2012. 'Three waves of variation study: the emergence of meaning in the study of sociolinguistic variation'. *Annual Review of Anthropology* 41: 87–100.

Labov, William, 1972b. *Sociolinguistic Patterns*. Philadelphia, PA: University of Pennsylvania Press.

Labov, William, 2001a. *Principles of Linguistic Change*, vol. 2: *Social Factors*. Malden, MA: Blackwell Publishers.

Ostler, Nicholas, 2005. *Empires of the Word: A Language History of the World*. London: HarperCollins Publishers.

Sealey, Alison and Bob Carter, 2004. *Applied Linguistics as Social Science*. London: Continuum.

Trudgill, Peter, 2004. *New-dialect Formation: The Inevitability of Colonial Englishes*. Edinburgh: Edinburgh University Press.

Trudgill, Peter, 2008. 'Colonial dialect contact in the history of European languages: on the irrelevance of identity to new-dialect formation'. *Language in Society* 37: 241–54.

Trudgill, Peter, Elizabeth Gordon and Gillian Lewis, 1998. 'New-dialect formation and Southern Hemisphere English: the New Zealand short front vowels'. *Journal of Sociolinguistics* 2: 35–51.

Woolard, Kathryn A., 1985. 'Language variation and cultural hegemony: toward an integration of sociolinguistic and social theory'. *American Ethnologist* 12: 738–48.

REFERENCES

Adamson, Lilian and Norval Smith, 1995. 'Sranan'. In Jacques Arends, Pieter Muysken and Norval Smith (eds), *Pidgins and Creoles: An Introduction*. Amsterdam: John Benjamins. 219–32.

Agha, Asif, 2003. 'The social life of cultural value'. *Language & Communication* 23: 23–73.

Aitchison, John and Harold Carter, 2004. *Spreading the Word: The Welsh Language 2001*. Talybont, UK: Y Lolfa.

Allan, Keith and Kasia M. Jaszczolt (eds), 2012. *The Cambridge Handbook of Pragmatics*. Cambridge: Cambridge University Press.

Allard, Réal and Rodrigue Landry, 1986. 'Subjective ethnolinguistic vitality viewed as a belief system'. *Journal of Multilingual and Multicultural Development* 7: 1–12.

Alleyne, Mervyn C., 1980. *Comparative Afro-American: An Historical-Comparative Study of English-Based Afro-American Dialects of the New World*. Ann Arbor, MI: Karoma Publishers.

Androutsopoulos, Jannis (ed.), 2006. 'Sociolinguistics and computer-mediated communication'. Theme issue of *Journal of Sociolinguistics* 10/4.

Arends, Jacques, Pieter Muysken and Norval Smith (eds), 1995. *Pidgins and Creoles: An Introduction*. Amsterdam: John Benjamins.

Arzoz, Xabier (ed.), 2008. *Respecting Linguistic Diversity in the European Union*. Amsterdam: John Benjamins.

Ashby, William J., 1981. 'The loss of the negative particle *ne* in French: a syntactic change in progress'. *Language* 57: 674–87.

Auer, Peter, 1988. 'A conversation analytic approach to code-switching and transfer'. In Monica Heller (ed.), *Codeswitching: Anthropological and Sociological Perspectives*. Berlin: Mouton de Gruyter. 187–213.

Auer, Peter (ed.), 1998. *Code-switching in Conversation: Language, Interaction and Identity*. London: Routledge.

Auer, Peter, 2007. 'The monolingual bias in bilingualism research, or: why bilingual talk is (still) a challenge for linguistics'. In Monica Heller (ed.), *Bilingualism: A Social Approach*. Basingstoke, UK: Palgrave Macmillan. 319–39.

Auer, Peter and Li Wei (eds), 2007a. *Handbook of Multilingualism and Multilingual Communication*. Berlin: Mouton de Gruyter.

Auer, Peter and Li Wei, 2007b. 'Introduction: multilingualism as a problem? Monolingualism as a problem?' In Peter Auer and Li Wei (eds), *Handbook of Multilingualism and Multilingual Communication*. Berlin: Mouton de Gruyter. 1–12.

Austin, J.L., 1962. *How to Do Things with Words*. Cambridge, MA: Harvard University Press.

Austin, Peter K. and Julia Sallabank (eds), 2011. *The Cambridge Handbook of Endangered Languages*. Cambridge, UK: Cambridge University Press.

Bailey, Charles-James N., 1973. *Variation and Linguistic Theory*. Arlington, VA: Center for Applied Linguistics.

Bakhtin, M.M., 1981 [1935]. 'Discourse in the novel'. In M.M. Bakhtin, *The Dialogic Imagination*. Austin, TX: University of Texas Press. 259–422.

Bakhtin, M.M. 1986 [1953]. *Speech Genres and Other Late Essays*. Austin, TX: University of Texas Press.

Barbieri, Federica, 2008. 'Patterns of age-based linguistic variation in American English'. *Journal of Sociolinguistics* 12: 58–88.

Baron, Naomi S., 2008. *Always On: Language in an Online and Mobile World*. New York: Oxford University Press.

Bauer, Laurie and Peter Trudgill (eds), 1998. *Language Myths*. Harmondsworth, UK: Penguin.

Bauer, Winifred, 2008. 'Is the health of te reo Māori improving?' *Te Reo* 51: 33–73.

Bayley, Robert, Richard Cameron and Ceil Lucas (eds), 2013. *The Oxford Handbook of Sociolinguistics*. New York: Oxford.

Bayley, Robert, Ceil Lucas and Mary Rose, 2000. 'Variation in American Sign Language: the case of DEAF'. *Journal of Sociolinguistics* 4: 81–107.

Becker, Kara, 2009. '/r/ and the construction of place identity on New York City's Lower East Side'. *Journal of Sociolinguistics* 13: 634–58.

Bell, Allan, 1983. 'Broadcast news as a language standard'. *International Journal of the Sociology of Language* 40: 29–42.

Bell, Allan, 1984. 'Language style as audience design'. *Language in Society* 13: 145–204.

Bell, Allan, 1988. 'The British base and the American connection in New Zealand media English'. *American Speech* 63: 326–44.

Bell, Allan, 1991a. 'Audience accommodation in the mass media'. In Howard Giles, Nikolas Coupland and Justine Coupland (eds), *Contexts of Accommodation: Developments in Applied Sociolinguistics*. Cambridge: Cambridge University Press. 69–102.

Bell, Allan, 1991b. *The Language of News Media*. Oxford, UK: Basil Blackwell.

Bell, Allan, 1991c. 'The politics of English in New Zealand'. In Mark Williams and Graham McGregor (eds), *Dirty Silence: Aspects of Language and Literature in New Zealand*. Auckland, New Zealand: Oxford University Press. 65–75.

Bell, Allan, 1992. 'Hit and miss: referee design in the dialects of New Zealand television advertisements'. *Language & Communication* 12: 1–14.

Bell, Allan, 1995. 'News time'. *Time & Society* 4: 305–28.

Bell, Allan, 1997a. 'Style as audience design'. In Nikolas Coupland and Adam Jaworski (eds), *Sociolinguistics: A Reader and Coursebook*. London: Macmillan. 240–50.

Bell, Allan, 1997b. 'The phonetics of fish and chips in New Zealand: marking national and ethnic identities'. *English World-Wide* 18: 243–70.

Bell, Allan, 1999. 'Styling the other to define the self: a study in New Zealand identity making'. *Journal of Sociolinguistics* 3: 523–41.

Bell, Allan, 2000. 'Māori and Pakeha English: a case study'. In Allan Bell and Koenraad Kuiper (eds), *New Zealand English*. Wellington, New Zealand: Victoria University Press; and Amsterdam: John Benjamins. 221–48.

Bell, Allan, 2001a. 'Back in style: re-working audience design'. In Penelope Eckert and John R. Rickford (eds), *Style and Sociolinguistic Variation*. New York: Cambridge University Press. 139–69.

Bell, Allan, 2001b. '"Bugger!" Media language, identity and post-modernity in Aotearoa/New Zealand'. *New Zealand Sociology* 16: 128–50.

Bell, Allan, 2003. 'A century of news discourse'. *International Journal of English Studies* 3: 189–208.

Bell, Allan, 2007. 'Style in dialogue: Bakhtin and sociolinguistic theory'. In Robert Bayley and Ceil Lucas (eds), *Sociolinguistic Variation: Theories, Methods and Applications*. New York: Cambridge University Press. 90–109.

Bell, Allan, 2010. 'Advocating for a threatened language: the case for Māori on television in Aotearoa/New Zealand'. *Te Reo* 53: 3–25.

Bell, Allan, 2011a. 'Falling in love again and again: Marlene Dietrich and the iconization of non-native English'. *Journal of Sociolinguistics* 15: 627–56.

Bell, Allan, 2011b. 'Leaving home: de-Europeanization in a post-colonial language variety of broadcast news language'. In Tore Kristiansen and Nikolas Coupland (eds), *Standard Languages and Language Standards in a Changing Europe*. Oslo: Novus. 177–98.

Bell, Allan, 2011c. 'Re-constructing Babel: discourse analysis, hermeneutics and the Interpretive Arc'. *Discourse Studies* 13: 519–68.

Bell, Allan and Andy Gibson, 2011. 'Staging language: an introduction to the sociolinguistics of performance'. *Journal of Sociolinguistics* 15: 555–72.

Bell, Allan and Janet Holmes, 1992. '"H-droppin": Two sociolinguistic variables in New Zealand English'. *Australian Journal of Linguistics* 12: 223–49.

Bell, Allan and Gary Johnson, 1997. 'Towards a sociolinguistics of style'. *University of Pennsylvania Working Papers in Linguistics* 4: 1–21.

Bell, Allan and Koenraad Kuiper (eds), 2000. *New Zealand English*. Wellington, New Zealand: Victoria University Press; and Amsterdam: John Benjamins.

Bell, Allan and Philippa Smith, 2012. 'News discourse. In Carol A. Chapelle (ed.), *The Encyclopedia of Applied Linguistics* (1st edn). Oxford, UK and Malden, MA: Wiley-Blackwell (online at http://onlinelibrary.wiley.com/book/10.1002/9781405198431; retrieved 1 February 2013).

Bennett, Joe, 2012. '"And what comes out may be a kind of screeching": the stylisation of *chavspeak* in contemporary Britain'. *Journal of Sociolinguistics* 16: 5–27.

Benor, Sarah Bunin, 2010. 'Ethnolinguistic repertoire: shifting the analytic focus in language and ethnicity'. *Journal of Sociolinguistics* 14: 159–83.

Benton, Richard A., 1983. *The NZCER Māori Language Survey*. Wellington, New Zealand: NZ Council for Educational Research.

Bex, Tony and Richard J. Watts (eds), 1999. *Standard English: The Widening Debate*. London: Routledge.

Bhatia, Tej K. and William C. Ritchie (eds), 2004. *The Handbook of Bilingualism*. Malden, MA: Blackwell Publishing.

Biber, Douglas, Susan Conrad and Randi Reppen, 1998. *Corpus Linguistics: Investigating Language Structure and Use*. Cambridge: Cambridge University Press.

Bickerton, Derek, 1981. *Roots of Language*. Ann Arbor, MI: Karoma Publishers.

Billings, Sabrina, 2009. 'Speaking beauties: linguistic posturing, language inequality, and the construction of a Tanzanian beauty queen'. *Language in Society* 38: 581–606.

Blair, David and Peter Collins (eds), 2001. *English in Australia*. Amsterdam: John Benjamins.

Blake, Renée and Meredith Josey, 2003. 'The /ay/ diphthong in a Martha's Vineyard community: what can we say 40 years after Labov?'. *Language in Society* 32: 451–85.

Blom, Jan-Petter and John J. Gumperz, 1972. 'Social meaning in linguistic structure: code-switching in Norway'. In John J. Gumperz and Dell Hymes (eds), *Directions in Sociolinguistics*. New York: Holt, Rinehart & Winston. 407–34.

Blommaert, Jan (ed.), 1999. *Language Ideological Debates*. Berlin: Mouton de Gruyter.

Blommaert, Jan, 2010. *The Sociolinguistics of Globalization*. Cambridge: Cambridge University Press.

Bloomfield, Leonard, 1933. *Language*. New York: Henry Holt & Co.

Bokhorst-Heng, Wendy, 1999. 'Singapore's *Speak Mandarin Campaign*: language ideological debates and the imagining of the nation'. In Jan Blommaert (ed.), *Language Ideological Debates*. Berlin: Mouton de Gruyter. 235–65.

Bolinger, Dwight, 1975. *Aspects of Language* (2nd edn). New York: Harcourt Brace Jovanovich.

Bolton, Kingsley, 2004. 'World Englishes'. In Alan Davies and Catherine Elder (eds), *The Handbook of Applied Linguistics*. Malden, MA: Blackwell Publishing. 367–96.

Bolton, Kingsley and Braj B. Kachru (eds), 2006. *World Englishes (Critical Concepts in Linguistics)*, 6 vols. London: Routledge.

Boulé, Julie J., 2002. 'Attitudes of young Quebecers towards English and French'. Unpublished MA thesis. Montreal, Canada: Concordia University.

Bourdieu, Pierre, 1984. *Distinction: A Social Critique of the Judgement of Taste*. Cambridge, MA: Harvard University Press.

Bourdieu, Pierre, 1991. *Language and Symbolic Power*. Cambridge, UK: Polity Press.

Bourhis, Richard Y, 1982. 'Language policies and language attitudes: le monde de la francophonie'. In Ellen Bouchard Ryan and Howard Giles (eds), *Attitudes towards Language Variation: Social and Applied Contexts*. London: Edward Arnold. 34–62.

Bourhis, Richard Y., Howard Giles and Doreen Rosenthal, 1981. 'Notes on the construction of a "Subjective Vitality Questionnaire" for ethnolinguistic groups'. *Journal of Multilingual and Multicultural Development* 2: 145–55.

Bradley, David, 2005. 'Introduction: language policy and language endangerment in China'. *International Journal of the Sociology of Language* 173: 1–21.

Bradley, John, 2011. 'Yanyuwa: "Men speak one way, women speak another"'. In Jennifer Coates and Pia Pichler (eds), *Language and Gender: A Reader* (2nd edn). Malden, MA: Wiley-Blackwell. 13–19.

Brenzinger, Matthias (ed.), 1992. *Language Death: Factual and Theoretical Explorations with Special Reference to East Africa*. Berlin and New York: Mouton de Gruyter.

Britain, David, 2010. 'Conceptualizations of geographic space in linguistics'. In Alfred Lameli, Roland Kehrein and Stefan Rabanus (eds), *Language and Space: An International Handbook of Linguistic Variation – Volume 2: Language Mapping*. Berlin: Mouton de Gruyter. 69–97.

Britain, David, 2013a. 'Space, diffusion and mobility'. In J.K. Chambers and Natalie Schilling (eds), *The Handbook of Language Variation and Change* (2nd edn). Oxford, UK: Wiley-Blackwell. 471–500.

Britain, David, 2013b. 'The role of mundane mobility and contact in dialect death and dialect birth'. In Daniel Schreier and Marianne Hundt (eds), *English as a Contact Language*. Cambridge: Cambridge University Press. 165–81.

Broch, Ingvild and Ernst Håkon Jahr, 1984. 'Russenorsk: a new look at the Russo-Norwegian pidgin in northern Norway'. In P. Sture Ureland and Iain Clarkson (eds), *Scandinavian Language Contacts*. Cambridge: Cambridge University Press. 21–65.

Brown, Penelope and Stephen C. Levinson, 1987. *Politeness: Some Universals in Language Usage*. Cambridge: Cambridge University Press.

Brown, Roger and Marguerite Ford, 1964. 'Address in American English'. In Dell Hymes (ed.), *Language in Culture and Society*. New York: Harper & Row. 234–44.

Brown, Roger and Albert Gilman, 1960. 'The pronouns of power and solidarity'. In Thomas A. Sebeok (ed.), *Style in Language*. Cambridge, MA: MIT Press. 253–76.

Bucholtz, Mary, 1999a. '"Why be normal?" Language and identity practices in a community of nerd girls'. *Language in Society* 28: 203–23.

Bucholtz, Mary, 1999b. 'You da man: narrating the racial other in the production of white masculinity'. *Journal of Sociolinguistics* 3: 443–60.

Bucholtz, Mary and Qiuana Lopez, 2011. 'Performing blackness, forming whiteness: linguistic minstrelsy in Hollywood film'. *Journal of Sociolinguistics* 15: 680–706.

Buchstaller, Isabelle and Alexandra D'Arcy, 2009. 'Localized globalization: a multi-local, multivariate investigation of quotative *be like*'. *Journal of Sociolinguistics* 13: 291–313.

Bullock, Barbara E. and Almeida Jacqueline Toribio (eds), 2009. *The Cambridge Handbook of Linguistic Code-switching*. Cambridge: Cambridge University Press.

Busch, Brigitta, 2012. 'The linguistic repertoire revisited'. *Applied Linguistics* 33: 503–23.

Cameron, Deborah, 1992. *Feminism and Linguistic Theory* (2nd edn). Basingstoke, UK: Macmillan.

Cameron, Deborah, 1995. *Verbal Hygiene*. London: Routledge.

Cameron, Deborah, 1997. 'Performing gender identity: young men's talk and the construction of heterosexual masculinity'. In Sally Johnson and Ulrike Hanna Meinhof (eds), *Language and Masculinity*. Oxford, UK: Blackwell Publishers. 47–64.

Cameron, Deborah, Elizabeth Frazer, Penelope Harvey, M.B.H. Rampton and Kay Richardson, 1992. *Researching Language: Issues of Power and Method*. London: Longman.

Campbell, Lyle and Verónica Grondona, 2010. 'Who speaks what to whom? Multilingualism and language choice in Misión La Paz'. *Language in Society* 39: 617–46.

Campbell, Lyle and Martha C. Muntzel, 1989. 'The structural consequences of language death'. In Nancy C. Dorian (ed.), *Investigating Obsolescence: Studies in Language Contraction and Death*. Cambridge: Cambridge University Press. 181–96.

Campbell-Kibler, Kathryn, 2007. 'Accent, (ING), and the social logic of listener perceptions'. *American Speech* 82: 32–64.

Campbell-Kibler, Kathryn, 2008. 'I'll be the judge of that: diversity in social perceptions of (ING)'. *Language in Society* 37: 637–59.

Campbell-Kibler, Kathryn, 2009. 'The nature of sociolinguistic perception'. *Language Variation and Change* 21: 135–54.

Canagarajah, A. Suresh, 1999. *Resisting Linguistic Imperialism in English Teaching*. Oxford, UK: Oxford University Press.

Canagarajah, A. Suresh, 2008. 'Language shift and the family: questions from the Sri Lankan Tamil diaspora'. *Journal of Sociolinguistics* 12: 143–76.

Carter, Bob and Alison Sealey, 2000. 'Language, structure and agency: what can realist social theory offer to sociolinguistics?' *Journal of Sociolinguistics* 4: 3–20.

Chambers, J.K., 1992. 'Dialect acquisition'. *Language* 68: 673–705.

Chambers, J.K., 2009. *Sociolinguistic Theory: Linguistic Variation and its Social Significance* (revised edn). Malden, MA: Wiley-Blackwell.

Chambers, J.K. and Natalie Schilling (eds), 2013. *The Handbook of Language Variation and Change* (2nd edn). Oxford, UK: Wiley-Blackwell.

Chambers, J.K. and Peter Trudgill, 1998. *Dialectology* (2nd edn). Cambridge: Cambridge University Press.

Chambers, J.K., Peter Trudgill and Natalie Schilling-Estes (eds), 2002. *The Handbook of Language Variation and Change*. Malden, MA: Blackwell Publishing.

Chand, Vineeta, 2011. 'Elite positionings towards Hindi: language policies, political stances and language competence in India'. *Journal of Sociolinguistics* 15: 6–35.

Chaudenson, Robert, 2001 (revised in collaboration with Salikoko S. Mufwene). *Creolization of Language and Culture*. London: Routledge.

Cheshire, Jenny, 1982. *Variation in an English Dialect: A Sociolinguistic Study*. Cambridge: Cambridge University Press.

Cheshire, Jenny, 2002. 'Sex and gender in variationist research'. In J.K. Chambers, Peter Trudgill and Natalie Schilling-Estes (eds), *The Handbook of Language Variation and Change*. Malden, MA: Blackwell Publishing. 423–43.

Cheshire, Jenny, 2005. 'Syntactic variation and beyond: gender and social class variation in the use of discourse-new markers'. *Journal of Sociolinguistics* 9: 479–508.

Cheshire, Jenny, 2007. 'Discourse variation, grammaticalisation and stuff like that'. *Journal of Sociolinguistics* 11: 155–93.

Cheshire, Jenny, Paul Kerswill, Sue Fox and Eivind Torgersen, 2011. 'Contact, the feature pool and the speech community: the emergence of Multicultural London English'. *Journal of Sociolinguistics* 15: 151–96.

Chomsky, Noam, 1965. *Aspects of the Theory of Syntax*. Cambridge, MA: MIT Press.

Chrisp, Steven, 2005. 'Māori intergenerational language transmission'. *International Journal of the Sociology of Language* 172: 149–81.

Clyne, Michael and Sandra Kipp, 2006. 'Australia's community languages'. *International Journal of the Sociology of Language* 180: 7–21.

Coates, Jennifer and Pia Pichler (eds), 2011. *Language and Gender: A Reader* (2nd edn). Malden, MA: Wiley-Blackwell.

Corbeil, Jean-Pierre and Christine Blaser, 2007. *The Evolving Linguistic Portrait, 2006 Census*. Ottawa: Statistics Canada (http://www12.statcan.gc.ca/census-recensement/2006/rt-td/lng-eng.cfm; retrieved 6 April 2011).

Cotter, Colleen, 2010. *News Talk: Investigating the Language of Journalism*. Cambridge: Cambridge University Press.

Coupland, Nikolas, 1984. 'Accommodation at work: some phonological data and their implications'. *International Journal of the Sociology of Language* 46: 49–70.

Coupland, Nikolas, 2001a. 'Age in social and sociolinguistic theory'. In Nikolas Coupland, Srikant Sarangi and Christopher N. Candlin (eds), *Sociolinguistics and Social Theory*. Harlow, UK: Pearson Education. 185–211.

Coupland, Nikolas, 2001b. 'Language, situation, and the relational self: theorizing dialect-style in sociolinguistics'. In Penelope Eckert and John R. Rickford (eds), *Style and Sociolinguistic Variation*. New York: Cambridge University Press. 185–210.

Coupland, Nikolas, 2007. *Style: Language Variation and Identity*. Cambridge: Cambridge University Press.

Coupland, Nikolas (ed.), 2010. *The Handbook of Language and Globalization*. Malden, MA: Wiley-Blackwell.

Coupland, Nikolas, 2011a. 'The sociolinguistics of style'. In Rajend Mesthrie (ed.), *The Cambridge Handbook of Sociolinguistics*. Cambridge: Cambridge University Press. 138–56.

Coupland, Nikolas, 2011b. 'Voice, place and genre in popular song performance'. *Journal of Sociolinguistics* 15: 573–602.

Coupland, Nikolas and Michelle Aldridge, 2009. 'Introduction: a critical approach to the revitalisation of Welsh'. *International Journal of the Sociology of Language* 195: 5–13.

Coupland, Nikolas and Hywel Bishop, 2007. 'Ideologized values for British accents'. *Journal of Sociolinguistics* 11: 74–93.

Coupland, Nikolas, Justine Coupland and Howard Giles, 1991. *Language, Society and the Elderly: Discourse, Identity and Ageing*. Oxford, UK: Basil Blackwell.

Coupland, Nikolas and Adam Jaworski (eds), 2009a. *Sociolinguistics (Critical Concepts in Linguistics)*, 6 vols. London: Routledge.

Coupland, Nikolas and Adam Jaworski (eds), 2009b. *The New Sociolinguistics Reader* (2nd edn). Basingstoke, UK: Palgrave Macmillan.

Coupland, Nikolas and Tore Kristiansen, 2011. 'SLICE: critical perspectives on language (de) standardization'. In Tore Kristiansen and Nikolas Coupland (eds), *Standard Languages and Language Standards in a Changing Europe*. Oslo: Novus. 11–35.

Coupland, Nikolas, Srikant Sarangi and Christopher N. Candlin (eds), 2001. *Sociolinguistics and Social Theory*. Harlow, UK: Longman.

Crystal, David, 2006. *Language and the Internet* (2nd edn). Cambridge: Cambridge University Press.

Crystal, David, 2008. *A Dictionary of Linguistics and Phonetics* (6th edn). Malden, MA: Blackwell Publishing.

Cukor-Avila, Patricia and Guy Bailey, 2013. 'Real time and apparent time'. In J.K. Chambers and Natalie Schilling (eds), *The Handbook of Language Variation and Change* (2nd edn). Oxford, UK: Wiley-Blackwell. 239–62.

Danet, Brenda and Susan C. Herring (eds), 2007. *The Multilingual Internet: Language, Culture, and Communication Online*. New York: Oxford University Press.

d'Anglejan, Alison and G. Richard Tucker, 1973. 'Sociolinguistic correlates of speech style in Quebec'. In Roger W. Shuy and Ralph Fasold (eds), *Language Attitudes: Current Trends and Prospects*. Washington, DC: Georgetown University Press. 1–27.

Dannenberg, Clare and Walt Wolfram, 1998. 'Ethnic identity and grammatical restructuring: *be(s)* in Lumbee English'. *American Speech* 73: 139–59.

De Fina, Anna, 1997. 'An analysis of Spanish *bien* as a marker of classroom management in teacher–student interactions'. *Journal of Pragmatics* 28: 337–54.

De Fina, Anna, 2007. 'Code-switching and the construction of ethnic identity in a community of practice'. *Language in Society* 36: 371–92.

Díaz-Campos, Manuel (ed.), 2011. *The Handbook of Hispanic Sociolinguistics*. Oxford, UK: Wiley-Blackwell.

Dimmendaal, Gerrit J., 1992. 'Reduction in Kore reconsidered'. In Matthias Brenzinger (ed.), *Language Death: Factual and Theoretical Explorations with Special Reference to East Africa*. Berlin: Mouton de Gruyter. 117–35.

Dixon, R.M.W., 1972. *The Dyirbal Language of North Queensland*. London: Cambridge University Press.

Dixon, R.M.W., 1983. *Searching for Aboriginal Languages: Memoirs of a Field Worker*. St Lucia, Queensland: University of Queensland Press.

Dodsworth, Robin, 2011. 'Social class'. In Ruth Wodak, Barbara Johnstone and Paul Kerswill (eds), *The Sage Handbook of Sociolinguistics*. London: Sage. 192–207.

Dorian, Nancy C., 1981. *Language Death: The Life Cycle of a Scottish Gaelic Dialect*. Philadelphia, PA: University of Pennsylvania Press.

Dorian, Nancy C. (ed.), 1989. *Investigating Obsolescence: Studies in Language Contraction and Death*. Cambridge: Cambridge University Press.

Dorian, Nancy, 1998. 'Western language ideologies and small-language prospects'. In Lenore A. Grenoble and Lindsay J. Whaley (eds), *Endangered Languages: Language Loss and Community Response*. Cambridge: Cambridge University Press. 3–21.

Dorian, Nancy C., 2002. 'Diglossia and the simplification of linguistic space'. *International Journal of the Sociology of Language* 157: 63–9.

Dubois, Sylvie and Barbara Horvath, 1999. 'When the music changes, you change too: gender and language change in Cajun English'. *Language Variation and Change* 11: 287–313.

Duchêne, Alexandre and Monica Heller (eds), 2007. *Discourses of Endangerment: Ideology and Interest in the Defence of Languages*. London: Continuum.

Duranti, Alessandro, 1997. *Linguistic Anthropology*. Cambridge: Cambridge University Press.

Duranti, Alessandro (ed.), 2004. *A Companion to Linguistic Anthropology*. Malden, MA: Blackwell.

Duranti, Alessandro (ed.), 2009. *Linguistic Anthropology: A Reader* (2nd edn). Malden, MA: Wiley-Blackwell.

Duranti, Alessandro Duranti and Charles Goodwin (eds), 1992. *Rethinking Context: Language as an Interactive Phenomenon*. Cambridge: Cambridge University Press.

Dutton, Tom and Peter Mühlhäusler, 1984. 'Queensland Kanaka English'. *English World-Wide* 4: 231–63.

Eckert, Penelope, 1989. 'The whole woman: sex and gender differences in variation'. *Language Variation and Change* 1: 245–67.

Eckert, Penelope, 1997. 'Age as a sociolinguistic variable'. In Florian Coulmas (ed.), *The Handbook of Sociolinguistics*. Oxford, UK: Blackwell Publishers. 151–67.

Eckert, Penelope, 2000. *Linguistic Variation as Social Practice: The Linguistic Construction of Identity in Belten High*. Malden, MA: Blackwell Publishers.

Eckert, Penelope, 2008. 'Variation and the indexical field'. *Journal of Sociolinguistics* 12: 453–76.

Eckert, Penelope, 2010. 'Vowels and nail polish: the emergence of linguistic style in the preadolescent heterosexual marketplace'. In Miriam Meyerhoff and Erik Schleef (eds), *The Routledge Sociolinguistics Reader*. London: Routledge. 441–7.

Eckert, Penelope, 2012. 'Three waves of variation study: the emergence of meaning in the study of sociolinguistic variation'. *Annual Review of Anthropology* 41: 87–100.

Eckert, Penelope and Sally McConnell-Ginet, 1992. 'Think practically and look locally: language and gender as community-based practice'. *Annual Review of Anthropology* 21: 461–90.

Eckert, Penelope and Sally McConnell-Ginet, 2003. *Language and Gender*. New York: Cambridge University Press.

Eckert, Penelope and John R. Rickford (eds), 2001. *Style and Sociolinguistic Variation*. New York: Cambridge University Press.

Edwards, John V., 2004. 'Foundations of bilingualism'. In Tej K. Bhatia and William C. Ritchie (eds), *The Handbook of Bilingualism*. Malden, MA: Blackwell Publishing. 7–31.

Edwards, John, 2007. 'Societal multilingualism: reality, recognition and response'. In Peter Auer and Li Wei (eds), *Handbook of Multilingualism and Multilingual Communication*. Berlin: Mouton de Gruyter. 447–67.

Eerdmans, Susan L., Carlo L. Prevignano and Paul J. Thibault (eds), 2002. *Language and Interaction: Discussions with John J. Gumperz*. Amsterdam: John Benjamins.

Ehala, Martin and Kutlay Yagmur (eds), 2011. *Ethnolinguistic Vitality*. Special issue of the *Journal of Multilingual and Multicultural Development* 32: 101–200.

Ehrlich, Susan (ed.), 2008. *Language and Gender* (4 vols). London: Routledge.

England, Nora C., 1992. 'Doing Mayan linguistics in Guatemala'. *Language* 68: 29–35.

Errington, Joseph, 1998. 'Indonesian('s) development: on the state of a language of state'. In Bambi B. Schieffelin, Kathryn A. Woolard and Paul V. Kroskrity (eds), *Language Ideologies: Practice and Theory*. New York: Oxford University Press.

Ervin-Tripp, Susan M., 1972. 'On sociolinguistic rules: alternation and co-occurrence'. In John J. Gumperz and Dell Hymes (eds), *Directions in Sociolinguistics*. New York: Holt, Rinehart & Winston. 213–50.

Fairclough, Norman, 2006. *Language and Globalization*. London: Routledge.

Fasold, Ralph, 1984. *The Sociolinguistics of Society*. Oxford, UK: Basil Blackwell.

Fasold, Ralph W., William Labov, Fay Boyd Vaughn-Cooke, Guy Bailey, Walt Wolfram, Arthur K. Spears and John Rickford, 1987. 'Are Black and White vernaculars diverging? Papers from the NWAVE XIV Panel Discussion'. *American Speech* 62: 3–80.

Ferguson, Charles A., 1959. 'Diglossia'. *Word* 15: 325–40.

Ferguson, Charles A. and John J. Gumperz (eds), 1960. *Linguistic Diversity in South Asia*. Bloomington, IN: Indiana University Press.

Fernández, Mauro, 1993. *Diglossia: A Comprehensive Bibliography, 1960–1990*. Amsterdam: John Benjamins.

Fischer, John L., 1958. 'Social influences on the choice of a linguistic variant'. *Word* 14: 47–56.

Fishman, Joshua A., 1965. 'Who speaks what language to whom and when'. *La Linguistique* 2: 67–88.

Fishman, Joshua A., 1967. 'Bilingualism with and without diglossia; diglossia with and without bilingualism'. *Journal of Social Issues* 23: 29–38.

Fishman, Joshua A. (ed.), 1968. *Readings in the Sociology of Language*. The Hague: Mouton.

Fishman, Joshua A. (ed.), 1971. *Advances in the Sociology of Language*, vol. 1: *Basic Concepts, Theorys and Problems – Alternative Approaches*. The Hague: Mouton.

Fishman, Joshua A. (ed.), 1972. *Advances in the Sociology of Language*, vol. 2: *Selected Studies and Applications*. The Hague: Mouton.

Fishman, Joshua A. (ed.), 1978. *Advances in the Study of Societal Multilingualism*. The Hague: Mouton.

Fishman, Joshua A., 1985. 'Language, ethnicity and racism'. In Joshua A. Fishman, Michael H. Gertner, Esther G. Lowy and William G. Milán, *The Rise and Fall of the Ethnic Revival: Perspectives on Language and Ethnicity*. Berlin: Mouton Publishers. 3–13.

Fishman, Joshua A., 1991. *Reversing Language Shift: Theoretical and Empirical Foundations of Assistance to Threatened Languages*. Clevedon, UK: Multilingual Matters.

Fishman, Joshua A., 1996. *In Praise of the Beloved Language: A Comparative View of Positive Ethnolinguistic Consciousness*. Berlin: Mouton de Gruyter.

Fishman, Joshua A. (ed.), 2001. *Can Threatened Languages be Saved? Reversing Language Shift, Revisited: A 21st Century Perspective*. Clevedon, UK: Multilingual Matters.

Fishman, Joshua A., Michael H. Gertner, Esther G. Lowy and William G. Milán, 1985. *The Rise and Fall of the Ethnic Revival: Perspectives on Language and Ethnicity*. Berlin: Mouton Publishers.

Fishman, Pamela M., 1978. 'Interaction: the work women do'. *Social Problems* 25: 397–406.

Foley, William, 1997. *Anthropological Linguistics: An Introduction*. Malden, MA: Blackwell.

Foulkes, Paul and Gerard J. Docherty (eds), 1999. *Urban Voices: Accent Studies in the British Isles*. London: Arnold.

Frangoudaki, Anna, 2002. 'Greek societal bilingualism of more than a century'. *International Journal of the Sociology of Language* 157: 101–7.

Gafaranga, Joseph, 2007. *Talk in Two Languages*. Basingstoke, UK: Palgrave Macmillan.

Gal, Susan, 1978. 'Peasant men can't get wives: language change and sex roles in a bilingual community'. *Language in Society* 7: 1–16.

Gal, Susan, 1979. *Language Shift: Social Determinants of Linguistic Change in Bilingual Austria*. New York: Academic Press.

Gal, Susan, 2006. 'Migration, minorities and multilingualism: language ideologies in Europe'. In Clare Mar-Molinero and Patrick Stevenson (eds), *Language Ideologies, Policies and Practices: Language and the Future of Europe*. Basingstoke, UK: Palgrave Macmillan. 13–27.

Gal, Susan and Judith T. Irvine, 1995. 'The boundaries of languages and disciplines: how ideologies construct difference'. *Social Research* 62: 967–1001.

Gal, Susan and Kathryn A. Woolard (eds), 2001. *Languages and Publics: The Making of Authority*. Manchester, UK: St Jerome Publishing.

Gardner-Chloros, Penelope, 2009. *Code-switching*. Cambridge: Cambridge University Press.

Garrett, Peter, 2010. *Attitudes to Language*. Cambridge: Cambridge University Press.

Gemünden, Gerd and Mary R. Desjardins (eds), 2007. *Dietrich Icon*. Durham, NC: Duke University Press.

Gibson, Andy and Allan Bell, 2010. 'Performing Pasifika English in New Zealand: the case of bro'Town'. *English World-Wide* 31: 231–51.

Gibson, Andy and Allan Bell, 2012. 'Popular music singing as referee design'. In Juan Manuel Hernández-Campoy and Juan Antonio Cutillas-Espinosa (eds), *Style-shifting in Public: New Perspectives on Stylistic Variation*. Amsterdam: John Benjamins. 139–64.

Giddens, Anthony, 1984. *The Constitution of Society: Outline of the Theory of Structuration*. Cambridge, UK: Polity Press.

Giddens, Anthony, 2009. *Sociology* (6th edn). Cambridge, UK: Polity Press.

Giles, Howard (ed.), 1977. *Language, Ethnicity and Intergroup Relations*. London: Academic Press.

Giles, Howard, Richard Y. Bourhis and Donald M. Taylor, 1977. 'Towards a theory of language in ethnic group relations'. In Howard Giles (ed.), *Language, Ethnicity and Intergroup Relations*. London: Academic Press. 307–48.

Giles, Howard, Justine Coupland and Nikolas Coupland (eds), 1991. *Contexts of Accommodation: Developments in Applied Sociolinguistics*. Cambridge: Cambridge University Press.

Giles, Howard and Tania Ogay, 2007. 'Communication Accommodation Theory'. In Bryan B. Whaley and Wendy Samter (eds), *Explaining Communication: Contemporary Theories and Exemplars*. Mahwah, NJ: Lawrence Erlbaum. 293–310.

Giles, Howard and Peter F. Powesland, 1975. *Speech Style and Social Evaluation*. London: Academic Press.

Giles, Howard and Philip Smith, 1979. 'Accommodation theory: optimal levels of convergence'. In Howard Giles and Robert N. St Clair (eds), *Language and Social Psychology*. Oxford, UK: Basil Blackwell. 45–65.

Giles, Howard and Robert N. St Clair (eds), 1979. *Language and Social Psychology*. Oxford, UK: Basil Blackwell.

Goffman, Erving, 1964. 'The neglected situation'. *American Anthropologist* 66/6, part 2: 133–6.

Goffman, Erving, 1981. *Forms of Talk*. Philadelphia, PA: University of Pennsylvania Press.

Goodwin, Charles, 1993. 'Recording human interaction in natural settings'. *Pragmatics* 3: 181–209.

Goodwin, Charles and Alessandro Duranti, 1992. 'Rethinking context: an introduction'. In Alessandro Duranti and Charles Goodwin (eds), *Rethinking Context: Language as an Interactive Phenomenon*. Cambridge: Cambridge University Press. 1–42.

Gordon, Elizabeth and Marica Abell, 1990. '"This objectionable colonial dialect": historical and contemporary attitudes to New Zealand speech'. In Allan Bell and Janet Holmes (eds), *New Zealand Ways of Speaking English*. Clevedon, UK: Multilingual Matters; and Wellington, New Zealand: Victoria University Press. 21–48.

Gordon, Elizabeth, Lyle Campbell, Jennifer Hay, Margaret Maclagan, Andrea Sudbury and Peter Trudgill, 2004. *New Zealand English: Its Origins and Evolution*. Cambridge: Cambridge University Press.

Gordon, Matthew J., 2001. *Small-town Values and Big-city Vowels: A Study of the Northern Cities Shift in Michigan*. Durham, NC: American Dialect Society/Duke University Press.

Gordon, Matthew J., 2013. 'Investigating chain shifts and mergers'. In J.K. Chambers and Natalie Schilling (eds), *The Handbook of Language Variation and Change* (2nd edn). Oxford, UK: Wiley-Blackwell. 203–19.

Gorter, Durk (ed.), 2006. *Linguistic Landscape: A New Approach to Multilingualism*. Clevedon, UK: Multilingual Matters.

Green, Lisa J., 2002. *African American English: A Linguistic Introduction*. Cambridge: Cambridge University Press.

Grenoble, Lenore A. and Lindsay J. Whaley (eds), 1998. *Endangered Languages: Language Loss and Community Response*. Cambridge: Cambridge University Press.

Grice, H.P., 1975. 'Logic and conversation'. In Peter Cole and Jerry L. Morgan (eds), *Speech Acts*. New York: Academic Press. 41–58.

Grimes, Barbara F. (ed.), 1988. *Ethnologue: Languages of the World* (11th edn). Dallas, TX: Summer Institute of Linguistics.

Grondelaers, Stefan, Roeland van Hout and Mieke Steegs, 2010. 'Evaluating regional accent variation in Standard Dutch'. *Journal of Language and Social Psychology* 29: 101–16.

Gumperz, John J., 1962. 'Types of linguistic communities'. *Anthropological Linguistics* 4: 28–40.

Gumperz, John J., 1968. 'The speech community'. In David L. Sills (ed.), *International Encyclopedia of the Social Sciences*. New York: Macmillan and Free Press. 381–6.

Gumperz, John J., 1982a. *Discourse Strategies*. Cambridge: Cambridge University Press.

Gumperz, John J. (ed.), 1982b. *Language and Social Identity*. Cambridge: Cambridge University Press.

Gumperz, John J., 2001. 'Interactional sociolinguistics: a personal perspective'. In Deborah Schiffrin, Deborah Tannen and Heidi E. Hamilton (eds), *The Handbook of Discourse Analysis*. Malden, MA: Blackwell. 215–28.

Gumperz, John J. and Dell Hymes (eds), 1972. *Directions in Sociolinguistics*. New York: Holt, Rinehart & Winston.

Guy, Gregory R., 2011. 'Language, social class, and status'. In Rajend Mesthrie (ed.), *The Cambridge Handbook of Sociolinguistics*. Cambridge: Cambridge University Press. 159–85.

Hachimi, Atiqa, 2012. 'The urban and the urbane: identities, language ideologies, and Arabic dialects in Morocco'. *Language in Society* 41: 321–41.

Haeri, Niloofar, 1997. *The Sociolinguistic Market of Cairo: Gender, Class, and Education*. London: Kegan Paul International.

Haiman, John, 1979. 'Hua: a Papuan language of New Guinea'. In Timothy Shopen (ed.), *Languages and their Status*. Cambridge, MA: Winthrop Publishers. 35–89.

Hale, Ken, 1998. 'On endangered languages and the importance of linguistic diversity'. In Lenore A. Grenoble and Lindsay J. Whaley (eds), *Endangered Languages: Language Loss and Community Response*. Cambridge: Cambridge University Press. 192–216.

Hale, Ken, Michael Krauss, Lucille J. Watahomigie, Akira Y. Yamamoto, Colette Craig, LaVerne Masayesva Jeanne and Nora C. England, 1992. 'Endangered languages'. *Language* 68: 1–42.

Hall, Kira, 1997. '"Go suck your husband's sugarcane!": Hijras and the use of sexual insult'. In Anna Livia and Kira Hall (eds), *Queerly Phrased: Language, Gender, and Sexuality*. New York: Oxford University Press. 430–60.

Hamp, Eric P., 1989. 'On signs of health and death'. In Nancy C. Dorian (ed.), *Investigating Obsolescence: Studies in Language Contraction and Death*. Cambridge: Cambridge University Press. 197–210.

Hanson, Helen and Catherine O'Rawe (eds), 2010. *The Femme Fatale: Images, Histories, Contexts*. Basingstoke, UK: Palgrave Macmillan.

Harbert, Wayne, Sally McConnell-Ginet, Amanda Miller and John Whitman (eds), 2009. *Language and Poverty*. Bristol, UK: Multilingual Matters.

Harrington, Jonathan, Sallyanne Palethorpe and Catherine I. Watson, 2000. 'Does the Queen speak the Queen's English?' *Nature* 408: 927–8.

Harris, Roxy and Ben Rampton (eds), 2003. *The Language, Ethnicity and Race Reader*. London: Routledge.

Haugen, Einar, 1966. 'Dialect, language, nation'. *American Anthropologist* 68: 922–35.

Haugen, Einar, 1972. *The Ecology of Language (Essays by Einar Haugen, Selected and Introduced by Anwar S. Dil)*. Stanford, CA: Stanford University Press.

Heller, Monica (ed.), 1988. *Codeswitching: Anthropological and Sociological Perspectives*. Berlin: Mouton de Gruyter.

Heller, Monica (ed.), 2007a. *Bilingualism: A Social Approach*. Basingstoke, UK: Palgrave Macmillan.

Heller, Monica, 2007b. 'Bilingualism as ideology and practice'. In Monica Heller (ed.), *Bilingualism: A Social Approach*. Basingstoke, UK: Palgrave Macmillan. 1–22.

Heller, Monica, 2011. *Paths to Post-nationalism: A Critical Ethnography of Language and Identity*. New York: Oxford University Press.

Heller, Monica and Alexandre Duchêne, 2007. 'Discourses of endangerment: sociolinguistics, globalization and social order'. In Alexandre Duchêne and Monica Heller (eds), *Discourses of Endangerment: Ideology and Interest in the Defence of Languages*. London: Continuum. 1–13.

Hernández-Campoy, Juan Manuel, 2003. 'Exposure to contact and the geographical adoption of standard features: two complementary approaches'. *Language in Society* 32: 227–55.

Hernández-Campoy, Juan Manuel and Juan Antonio Cutillas-Espinosa (eds), 2012. *Style-shifting in Public: New Perspectives on Stylistic Variation*. Amsterdam: John Benjamins.

Hill, Jane H., 2002. '"Expert rhetorics" in advocacy for endangered languages: who is listening, and what do they hear?' *Journal of Linguistic Anthropology* 12: 119–33.

Hinton, Leanne and Ken Hale, 2001. *The Green Book of Language Revitalization in Practice*. San Diego, CA: Academic Press.

Hollings, Mike, 2005. 'Māori language broadcasting: panacea or pipedream'. In Allan Bell, Ray Harlow and Donna Starks (eds), *Languages of New Zealand*. Wellington, New Zealand: Victoria University Press. 111–30.

Holm, John A., 1988. *Pidgins and Creoles*, vol. 1: *Theory and Structure*. Cambridge: Cambridge University Press.

Holm, John, 1989. *Pidgins and Creoles*, vol. 2: *Reference Survey*. Cambridge: Cambridge University Press.

Holm, John, 2000. *An Introduction to Pidgins and Creoles*. Cambridge: Cambridge University Press.

Holm, John and Susanne Michaelis (eds), 2009. *Contact Languages (Critical Concepts in Language Studies)*, 5 vols. London: Routledge.

Holmes, Janet, 1988. 'Paying compliments: a sex-preferential politeness strategy'. *Journal of Pragmatics* 12: 445–65.

Holmes, Janet, 1995. *Women, Men and Politeness*. London: Longman.

Holmes, Janet (ed.), 1999. 'Communities of practice in language and gender research'. Theme issue of *Language in Society* 28/2.

Holmes, Janet, 2005. 'Using Māori English in New Zealand'. *International Journal of the Sociology of Language* 172: 91–115.

Holmes, Janet, 2006. *Gendered Talk at Work: Constructing Gender Identity through Workplace Discourse*. Malden, MA: Blackwell Publishing.

Holmes, Janet, Meredith Marra and Bernadette Vine, 2011. *Leadership, Discourse and Ethnicity*. New York: Oxford University Press.

Holmes, Janet and Miriam Meyerhoff (eds), 2003. *The Handbook of Language and Gender*. Malden, Massachusetts: Blackwell Publishing.

Holmes, Janet and Maria Stubbe, 2003. *Power and Politeness in the Workplace: A Sociolinguistic Analysis of Talk at Work*. London: Longman.

Honey, John, 1997. *Language is Power: The Story of Standard English and its Enemies*. London: Faber & Faber.

Horvath, Barbara M., 1985. *Variation in Australian English: The Sociolects of Sydney*. Cambridge: Cambridge University Press.

Horvath, Barbara M. and Ronald J. Horvath, 2002. 'The geolinguistics of /l/ vocalisation in Australia and New Zealand'. *Journal of Sociolinguistics* 6: 319–46.

Hudson, Alan, 1992. 'Diglossia: a bibliographic review'. *Language in Society* 21: 611–74.

Hudson, Alan, 2002. 'Outline of a theory of diglossia'. *International Journal of the Sociology of Language* 157: 1–48.

Hymes, Dell H., 1962. 'The ethnography of speaking'. In Thomas Gladwin and William C. Sturtevant (eds), *Anthropology and Human Behavior*. Washington, DC: Anthropological Society of Washington. 13–53.

Hymes, Dell (ed.), 1964. *Language in Culture and Society: A Reader in Linguistics and Anthropology*. New York: Harper & Row.

Hymes, Dell (ed.), 1971. *Pidginization and Creolization of Languages*. Cambridge: Cambridge University Press.

Hymes, Dell, 1972. 'Models of the interaction of language and social life'. In John J. Gumperz and Dell Hymes (eds), *Directions in Sociolinguistics*. New York: Holt, Rinehart & Winston. 35–71.

Hymes, Dell, 1974. *Foundations in Sociolinguistics: An Ethnographic Approach*. Philadelphia, PA: University of Pennsylvania Press.

Hymes, Dell, 1996. *Ethnography, Linguistics, Narrative Inequality: Toward an Understanding of Voice*. London: Taylor & Francis.

Igboanusi, Herbert and Peter Lothar, 2004. 'Oppressing the oppressed: the threats of Hausa and English to Nigeria's minority languages'. *International Journal of the Sociology of Language* 170: 131–40.

Irvine, Judith T., 2001. '"Style" as distinctiveness: the culture and ideology of linguistic differentiation'. In Penelope Eckert and John R. Rickford (eds), *Style and Sociolinguistic Variation*. New York: Cambridge University Press. 21–43.

Irvine, Judith T. and Susan Gal, 2000. 'Language ideology and linguistic differentiation'. In Paul V. Kroskrity (ed.), *Regimes of Language: Ideologies, Polities, and Identities*. Santa Fe, NM: School of American Research Press. 35–83.

Jaffe, Alexandra, 1999. *Ideologies in Action: Language Politics on Corsica*. Berlin: Mouton de Gruyter.

Jaffe, Alexandra, 2007a. 'Discourses of endangerment: contexts and consequences of essentializing discourses'. In Alexandre Duchêne and Monica Heller (eds), *Discourses of Endangerment: Ideology and Interest in the Defence of Languages*. London: Continuum. 57–75.

Jaffe, Alexandra, 2007b. 'Minority language movements'. In Monica Heller (ed.), *Bilingualism: A Social Approach*. Basingstoke, UK: Palgrave Macmillan. 50–70.

Jaspers, Jürgen, 2011. 'Strange bedfellows: appropriations of a tainted urban dialect'. *Journal of Sociolinguistics* 15: 493–524.

Jaworski, Adam and Annette Pritchard (eds), 2005. *Discourse, Communication and Tourism*. Clevedon, UK: Channel View Publications.

Jaworski, Adam and Crispin Thurlow (eds), 2010. *Semiotic Landscapes: Language, Image, Space*. London: Continuum.

Johnson, Ian, 2010. 'Tourism, transnationality and ethnolinguistic vitality: the Welsh in the Chubut Province, Argentina'. *Journal of Multilingual and Multicultural Development* 31: 553–68.

Johnson-Weiner, Karen M., 1998. 'Community identity and language change in North American Anabaptist communities'. *Journal of Sociolinguistics* 2: 375–94.

Johnstone, Barbara, 1990. *Stories, Community, and Place: Narratives from Middle America*. Bloomington, IN: Indiana University Press.

Johnstone, Barbara, 2009. 'Pittsburghese shirts: commodification and the enregisterment of an urban dialect'. *American Speech* 84: 157–75.

Johnstone, Barbara, 2011a. 'Dialect enregisterment in performance'. *Journal of Sociolinguistics* 15: 657–79.

Johnstone, Barbara, 2011b. 'Language and place'. In Rajend Mesthrie (ed.), *The Cambridge Handbook of Sociolinguistics*. Cambridge: Cambridge University Press. 203–17.

Johnstone, Barbara, Jennifer Andrus and Andrew E. Danielson, 2006. 'Mobility, indexicality, and the enregisterment of "Pittsburghese"'. *Journal of English Linguistics* 34: 77–104.

Johnstone, Barbara and Scott F. Kiesling, 2008. 'Indexicality and experience: exploring the meanings of /aw/-monophthongization in Pittsburgh'. *Journal of Sociolinguistics* 12: 5–33.

Kachru, Braj B., 1991. 'Liberation linguistics and the Quirk concern'. *English Today* 7: 3–13.

Kachru, Braj B., 1992. 'Teaching World Englishes'. In Braj B. Kachru (ed.), *The Other Tongue: English across Cultures* (2nd edn). Urbana, IL: University of Illinois Press. 355–65.

Kachru, Braj B., 2001. 'Speech community'. In Rajend Mesthrie (ed.), *Concise Encyclopedia of Sociolinguistics*. Oxford, UK: Elsevier. 105–7.

Kachru, Braj B., Yamuna Kachru and Cecil L. Nelson (eds), 2006. *The Handbook of World Englishes*. Malden, MA: Blackwell Publishing.

Kamwendo, Gregory and Theophilus Mooko, 2006. 'Language planning in Botswana and Malawi: a comparative study'. *International Journal of the Sociology of Language* 182: 117–33.

Kasher, Asa (ed.), 1998. *Pragmatics: Critical Concepts* (6 vols). London: Routledge.

Kaye, Alan S., 1972. 'Remarks on diglossia in Arabic: well-defined vs. ill-defined'. *Linguistics* 81: 32–48.

Keenan, Elinor, 1989. 'Norm-makers, norm-breakers: uses of speech by men and women in a Malagasy community'. In Richard Bauman and Joel Sherzer (eds), *Explorations in the Ethnography of Speaking* (2nd edn). London: Cambridge University Press. 125–43.

Kelly-Holmes, Helen, 2010. 'Rethinking the macro–micro relationship: some insights from the marketing domain'. *International Journal of the Sociology of Language* 202: 25–39.

Kerswill, Paul, 2011. 'Sociolinguistic approaches to language change: phonology'. In Ruth Wodak, Barbara Johnstone and Paul Kerswill (eds), *The Sage Handbook of Sociolinguistics*. London: Sage. 219–35.

Kerswill, Paul, 2013. 'Koineization'. In J.K. Chambers and Natalie Schilling (eds), *The Handbook of Language Variation and Change* (2nd edn). Oxford, UK: Wiley-Blackwell. 519–36.

Kerswill, Paul and Ann Williams, 2000. 'Creating a New Town koine: children and language change in Milton Keynes'. *Language in Society* 29: 65–115.

Kiesling, Scott F., 1998. 'Men's identities and sociolinguistic variation: the case of fraternity men'. *Journal of Sociolinguistics* 2: 69–99.

Kiesling, Scott F., 2004. 'Dude'. *American Speech* 79: 281–305.

Kiesling, Scott F., 2011. *Linguistic Variation and Change*. Edinburgh: Edinburgh University Press.

Klatter-Folmer, Jetske and Sjaale Kroon (eds), 1997. *Dutch Overseas: Studies in Maintenance and Loss of Dutch as an Immigrant Language*. Tilburg, the Netherlands: Tilburg University Press.

Kortmann, Bernd, Clive Upton, Edgar W. Schneider, Kate Burridge and Rajend Mesthrie (eds), 2008. *Varieties of English* (4 vols, various editors). Berlin: Mouton de Gruyter.

Kouwenberg, Silvia and John Victor Singler (eds), 2008. *The Handbook of Pidgin and Creole Studies*. Oxford, UK: Wiley-Blackwell.

Koven, Michele, 2007. *Selves in Two Languages: Bilinguals' Verbal Enactments of Identity in French and Portuguese*. Amsterdam: John Benjamins.

Krauss, Michael, 1992. 'The world's languages in crisis'. *Language* 68: 4–10.

Kristiansen, Tore, 2009. 'The nature and role of language standardisation and standard languages in late modernity'. Available at http://dgcss.hum.ku.dk/exploratoryworkshops/proposal/ (retrieved 3 March 2010).

Kristiansen, Tore, 2011. 'Attitudes, ideology and awareness'. In Ruth Wodak, Barbara Johnstone and Paul Kerswill (eds), *The Sage Handbook of Sociolinguistics*. London: Sage. 265–78.

Kristiansen, Tore and Nikolas Coupland (eds), 2011. *Standard Languages and Language Standards in a Changing Europe*. Oslo, Norway: Novus.

Kroskrity, Paul V., 1993. *Language, History, and Identity: Ethnolinguistic Studies of the Arizona Tewa*. Tucson, AZ: University of Arizona Press.

Kroskrity, Paul V. (ed.), 2000. *Regimes of Language: Ideologies, Polities, and Identities*. Santa Fe, NM: School of American Research Press.

Labov, William, 1966. *The Social Stratification of English in New York City*. Washington, DC: Center for Applied Linguistics.

Labov, William, 1972a. *Language in the Inner City: Studies in the Black English Vernacular.* Philadelphia, PA: University of Pennsylvania Press.

Labov, William, 1972b. *Sociolinguistic Patterns.* Philadelphia, PA: University of Pennsylvania Press.

Labov, William, 1982. 'Objectivity and commitment in linguistic science: the case of the Black English trial in Ann Arbor'. *Language in Society* 11: 165–201.

Labov, William, 1984. 'Field methods of the Project on Linguistic Change and Variation'. In John Baugh and Joel Sherzer (eds), *Language in Use: Readings in Sociolinguistics.* Englewood Cliffs, NJ: Prentice-Hall. 28–53.

Labov, William, 1990. 'The intersection of sex and social class in the course of linguistic change'. *Language Variation and Change* 2: 205–54.

Labov, William, 1994. *Principles of Linguistic Change*, vol. 1: *Internal Factors.* Cambridge, MA: Blackwell Publishers.

Labov, William, 2001a. *Principles of Linguistic Change,* vol. 2: *Social Factors.* Malden, MA: Blackwell Publishers.

Labov, William, 2001b. 'The anatomy of style-shifting'. In Penelope Eckert and John R. Rickford (eds), *Style and Sociolinguistic Variation.* New York: Cambridge University Press. 85–108.

Labov, William, 2006. *The Social Stratification of English in New York City* (2nd edn). Cambridge: Cambridge University Press.

Labov, William, 2010. *Principles of Linguistic Change*, vol. 3: *Cognitive and Cultural Factors.* Malden, MA: Wiley-Blackwell.

Labov, William, Sharon Ash and Charles Boberg, 2006. *The Atlas of North American English: Phonetics, Phonology and Sound Change.* Berlin: Mouton de Gruyter.

Labov, William, Sharon Ash, Maya Ravindranath, Tracey Weldon, Maciej Baranowski and Naomi Nagy, 2011. 'Properties of the sociolinguistic monitor'. *Journal of Sociolinguistics* 15: 431–63.

Labov, William and Wendell A. Harris, 1986. 'De facto segregation of black and white vernaculars'. In David Sankoff (ed.), *Diversity and Diachrony.* Amsterdam: John Benjamins. 1–24.

Laforest, Marty, 2009. 'Complaining in front of a witness: aspects of blaming others for their behaviour in multi-party family interactions'. *Journal of Pragmatics* 41: 2452–64.

Lakoff, George, 1987. *Women, Fire and Dangerous Things: What Categories Reveal about the Mind.* Chicago, IL: University of Chicago Press.

Lakoff, Robin, 1973. 'Language and woman's place'. *Language in Society* 2: 45–80.

Lakoff, Robin, 1975. *Language and Woman's Place.* New York: Harper & Row.

Lakoff, Robin Tolmach, 2004. *Language and Woman's Place: Text and Commentaries* (revised and expanded edn, ed. Mary Bucholtz). Oxford: Oxford University Press.

Lambert, Wallace E., 1967. 'A social psychology of bilingualism'. *Journal of Social Issues* 23: 91–109.

Lambert, Wallace E., Richard Hodgson, Robert C. Gardner and Samuel Fillenbaum, 1960. 'Evaluational reactions to spoken languages'. *Journal of Abnormal and Social Psychology* 60: 44–51.

Landry, Rodrigue and Réal Allard, 1994. Diglossia, ethnolinguistic vitality, and language behavior. *International Journal of the Sociology of Language* 108: 15–42.

Landry, Rodrigue and Richard Y. Bourhis, 1997. 'Linguistic landscape and ethnolinguistic vitality: an empirical study'. *Journal of Language and Social Psychology* 16: 23–49.

Lawrence, Amy, 2007. 'The voice as mask'. In Gerd Gemünden and Mary R. Desjardins (eds), *Dietrich Icon.* Durham, NC: Duke University Press. 79–99.

Lefebvre, Claire, 1998. *Creole Genesis and the Acquisition of Grammar: The Case of Haitian Creole.* Cambridge: Cambridge University Press.

Lefebvre, Claire, Lydia White and Christine Jourdan (eds), 2006. *L2 Acquisition and Creole Genesis.* Amsterdam: John Benjamins.

Leitner, Gerhard, 1980. '"BBC English" and "Deutsche Rundfunksprache": a comparative and historical analysis of the language on the radio'. *International Journal of the Sociology of Language* 26: 75–100.

Lempert, Michael, 2009. 'On "flip-flopping": branded stance-taking in U.S. electoral politics'. *Journal of Sociolinguistics* 13: 223–48.

Lewis, M. Paul (ed.), 2009. *Ethnologue: Languages of the World* (16th edn). Dallas, TX: SIL International (online version: http://www.ethnologue.com; retrieved 6 April 2011).

Li Fengxiang, 2005. 'Contact, attrition, and structural shift: evidence from Oroqen'. *International Journal of the Sociology of Language* 173: 55–74.

Li Wei (ed.), 2000. *The Bilingualism Reader*. London: Routledge.

Li Wei (ed.), 2010. *Bilingualism and Multilingualism: Critical Concepts in Linguistics* (4 vols). London: Routledge.

Lieberson, Stanley, 1972. 'Bilingualism in Montreal: a demographic analysis'. In Joshua A. Fishman (ed.), *Advances in the Sociology of Language* (vol. 2). The Hague: Mouton. 231–54.

Lin, Chia-Yen 2010. '. . . that's *actually sort of you know* trying to get consultants in . . .': functions and multifunctionality of modifiers in academic lectures'. *Journal of Pragmatics* 42: 1173–83.

Lippi-Green, Rosina, 2012. *English with an Accent: Language, Ideology and Discrimination in the United States* (2nd edn). London: Routledge.

Lo, Adrienne and Joseph Sung-Yul Park (eds), 2012. 'Globalization, multilingualism and identity in transnational perspective: the case of South Korea'. Theme issue of *Journal of Sociolinguistics* 16/2.

Long, Daniel and Dennis R. Preston (eds), 2002. *Handbook of Perceptual Dialectology* (vol. 2). Amsterdam: John Benjamins.

Lucas, Ceil (ed.), 2001. *The Sociolinguistics of Sign Languages*. Cambridge: Cambridge University Press.

Macaulay, R.K.S., 1977. *Language, Social Class, and Education: A Glasgow Study*. Edinburgh: Edinburgh University Press.

Maegaard, Marie, Torben Jensen, Tore Kristiansen and Jens Jørgensen, 2013. 'Diffusion of language change: accommodation to a moving target'. *Journal of Sociolinguistics* 17: 721–54.

Makihara, Miki, 2005. 'Rapa Nui ways of speaking Spanish: language shift and socialization on Easter Island'. *Language in Society* 34: 727–62.

Maltz, Daniel N. and Ruth A. Borker, 1982. 'A cultural approach to male–female miscommunication'. In John J. Gumperz (ed.), *Language and Social Identity*. Cambridge: Cambridge University Press. 196–216.

Martin-Jones, Marilyn, Adrian Blackledge and Angela Creese (eds), 2012. *The Routledge Handbook of Multilingualism*. London: Routledge.

Martineau, France and Raymond Mougeon, 2003. 'A sociolinguistic study of the origins of *ne* deletion in European and Quebec French'. *Language* 79: 118–52.

Mather, Patrick-André, 2012. 'The social stratification of /r/ in New York City: Labov's department store study revisited'. *Journal of English Linguistics* 40: 338–56.

May, Stephen (ed.), 2005. 'Debating Language Rights'. Theme issue of *Journal of Sociolinguistics* 9/3.

McNeill, Laurie, 2009. 'Diary 2.0? A genre moves from page to screen'. In Charley Rowe and Eva L. Wyss (eds), *Language and New Media: Linguistic, Cultural and Technological Evolutions*. Cresskill, NJ: Hampton Press. 313–25.

Mendoza-Denton, Norma, 2008. *Homegirls: Language and Cultural Practice among Latina Youth Gangs*. Malden, MA: Blackwell.

Mesthrie, Rajend, 1993. 'Koineization in the Bhojpuri-Hindi diaspora – with special reference to South Africa'. *International Journal of the Sociology of Language* 99: 25–44.

Mesthrie, Rajend (ed.), 2011. *The Cambridge Handbook of Sociolinguistics*. Cambridge: Cambridge University Press.

Meyerhoff, Miriam, 1998. 'Accommodating your data: the use and misuse of accommodation theory in sociolinguistics'. *Language & Communication* 18: 205–25.

Meyerhoff, Miriam and Erik Schleef (eds), 2010. *The Routledge Sociolinguistics Reader*. London: Routledge.

Meyerhoff, Miriam and Anna Strycharz, 2013. 'Communities of Practice'. In J.K. Chambers and Natalie Schilling (eds), *The Handbook of Language Variation and Change* (2nd edn). Oxford, UK: Wiley-Blackwell. 428–47.

Migge, Bettina, 2007. 'Code-switching and social identities in the Eastern Maroon community of Suriname and French Guiana'. *Journal of Sociolinguistics* 11: 53–73.

Migge, Bettina and Norval Smith, 2007. 'Introduction: substrate influence in creole formation'. *Journal of Pidgin and Creole Languages* 22: 1–15.

Milroy, James, 2001. 'Language ideologies and the consequences of standardization'. *Journal of Sociolinguistics* 5: 530–55.

Milroy, James and Lesley Milroy, 1985. 'Linguistic change, social network and speaker innovation'. *Journal of Linguistics* 21: 339–84.

Milroy, James and Lesley Milroy, 2012. *Authority in Language: Investigating Standard English* (4th edn). London: Routledge.

Milroy, James, Lesley Milroy, Sue Hartley and David Walshaw, 1994. 'Glottal stops and Tyneside glottalization: competing patterns of variation and change in British English'. *Language Variation and Change* 6: 327–57.

Milroy, Lesley, 1987. *Language and Social Networks* (2nd edn). Oxford, UK: Basil Blackwell.

Milroy, Lesley, 2001. 'The social categories of race and class: language ideology and sociolinguistics'. In Nikolas Coupland, Srikant Sarangi and Christopher N. Candlin (eds), *Sociolinguistics and Social Theory*. Harlow, UK: Longman. 235–60.

Milroy, Lesley and Carmen Llamas, 2013. 'Social networks'. In J.K. Chambers and Natalie Schilling (eds), *The Handbook of Language Variation and Change* (2nd edn). Oxford, UK: Wiley-Blackwell. 409–27.

Milroy, Lesley and James Milroy, 1992. 'Social network and social class: toward an integrated sociolinguistic model'. *Language in Society* 21: 1–26.

Milroy, Lesley and Pieter Muysken (eds), 1995. *One Speaker, Two Languages: Cross-disciplinary Perspectives on Code-switching*. Cambridge: Cambridge University Press.

Mitchell, D. Roy, IV, 2005. 'Tlingit language immersion retreats: creating new language habitat for the twenty-first century'. *International Journal of the Sociology of Language* 172: 187–95.

Modan, Gabriella Gahlia, 2007. *Turf Wars: Discourse, Diversity, and the Politics of Place*. Malden, MA: Blackwell Publishing.

Muehlmann, Shaylih, 2007. 'Defending diversity: staking out a common global interest?' In Alexandre Duchêne and Monica Heller (eds), *Discourses of Endangerment: Ideology and Interest in the Defence of Languages*. London: Continuum. 14–34.

Mufwene, Salikoko S., 2001. *The Ecology of Language Evolution*. Cambridge: Cambridge University Press.

Mufwene, Salikoko S., John R. Rickford, Guy Bailey and John Baugh (eds), 1998. *African-American English: Structure, History, and Use*. London: Routledge.

Mugglestone, Lynda, 1995. *'Talking Proper': The Rise of Accent as Social Symbol*. Oxford, UK: Clarendon Press.

Murray, K.M. Elisabeth, 1977. *Caught in the Web of Words: James A. H. Murray and the Oxford English Dictionary*. New Haven, CN: Yale University Press.

Muysken, Pieter and Norval Smith, 1995. 'The study of pidgin and creole languages'. In Jacques Arends, Pieter Muysken and Norval Smith (eds), *Pidgins and Creoles: An Introduction*. Amsterdam: John Benjamins. 3–14.

Myers Scotton, Carol, 1988. 'Code-switching as indexical of social negotiations'. In Monica Heller (ed.), *Codeswitching: Anthropological and Sociological Perspectives*. Berlin: Mouton de Gruyter. 151–86.

Myers-Scotton, Carol, 1993a. *Duelling Languages: Grammatical Structure in Codeswitching*. Oxford: Oxford University Press.

Myers-Scotton, Carol, 1993b. *Social Motivations for Codeswitching: Evidence from Africa*. Oxford: Oxford University Press.

Myers-Scotton, Carol and Janice Jake, 2009. 'A universal model of code-switching and bilingual language processing and production'. In Barbara E. Bullock and Almeida Jacqueline Toribio (eds), *The Cambridge Handbook of Linguistic Code-switching*. Cambridge: Cambridge University Press. 336–57.

Nettle, Daniel and Suzanne Romaine, 2000. *Vanishing Voices: The Extinction of the World's Languages*. Oxford: Oxford University Press.

Niedzielski, Nancy A. and Dennis R. Preston, 2000. *Folk Linguistics*. Berlin: Mouton de Gruyter.

O'Barr, William M. and Bowman K. Atkins, 1980. '"Women's language" or "powerless language"?' In Sally McConnell-Ginet, Ruth Borker and Nelly Furman (eds), *Women and Language in Literature and Society*. New York: Praeger. 93–110.

Ochs, Elinor, 1992. 'Indexing gender'. In Alessandro Duranti and Charles Goodwin (eds), *Rethinking Context: Language as an Interactive Phenomenon*. Cambridge: Cambridge University Press. 335–58.

Ojwang, Benson Oduor, Peter Maina Matu and Emily Atieno Ogutu, 2010. 'Face attack and patients' response strategies in a Kenyan hospital'. *Journal of Sociolinguistics* 14: 501–23.

Omoniyi, Tope, 2004. *The Sociolinguistics of Borderlands: Two Nations, One Community*. Trenton, NJ and Asmara, Eritrea: Africa World Press.

Ostler, Nicholas, 2005. *Empires of the Word: A Language History of the World*. London: HarperCollins Publishers.

Papen, Uta, 2012. 'Commercial discourses, gentrification and citizens' protest: the linguistic landscape of Prenzlauer Berg, Berlin'. *Journal of Sociolinguistics* 16: 56–80.

Patrick, Donna, 2005. 'Language rights in indigenous communities: the case of the Inuit of Arctic Quebec'. *Journal of Sociolinguistics* 9: 369–89.

Patrick, Donna, 2007. 'Language endangerment, language rights and indigeneity'. In Monica Heller (ed.), *Bilingualism: A Social Approach*. Basingstoke, UK: Palgrave Macmillan. 111–34.

Patrick, Peter L., 2002. 'The speech community'. In J.K. Chambers, Peter Trudgill and Natalie Schilling-Estes (eds), *The Handbook of Language Variation and Change*. Malden, MA: Blackwell Publishing. 573–97.

Patrick, Peter L., 2008. 'Pidgins, creoles, and variation'. In Silvia Kouwenberg and John Victor Singler (eds), *The Handbook of Pidgin and Creole Studies*. Oxford, UK: Wiley-Blackwell. 461–87.

Pauwels, Anne, 1998. *Women Changing Language*. London: Longman.

Pavlenko, Aneta, 2006. 'Bilingual selves'. In Aneta Pavlenko (ed.), *Bilingual Minds: Emotional Experience, Expression and Representation*. Clevedon, UK: Multilingual Matters. 1–33.

Pavlenko, Aneta (ed.), 2008. *Multilingualism in Post-Soviet Countries*. Bristol, UK: Multilingual Matters.

Pavlidou, Theodossia-Soula, 2011. 'Gender and interaction'. In Ruth Wodak, Barbara Johnstone and Paul Kerswill (eds), *The Sage Handbook of Sociolinguistics*. London: Sage. 412–27.

Payne, Arvilla C., 1980. 'Factors controlling the acquisition of the Philadelphia dialect by out-of-state children'. In William Labov (ed.), *Locating Language in Time and Space*. New York: Academic Press. 143–78.

Peal, E. and W.E. Lambert, 1962. 'The relation of bilingualism to intelligence'. *Psychological Monographs* 76, no. 27: 1–23.

Pennycook, Alastair, 2001. *Critical Applied Linguistics: A Critical Introduction*. Mahwah, NJ: Lawrence Erlbaum.

Pensalfini, Rob, 2004. 'Eulogizing a language: the Ngarnka experience'. *International Journal of the Sociology of Language* 168: 141–56.

Petyt, K.M., 1985. *Dialect and Accent in Industrial West Yorkshire*. Amsterdam: John Benjamins.

Pichler, Heike, 2010. 'Methods in discourse variation analysis: reflections on the way forward'. *Journal of Sociolinguistics* 14: 581–608.

Pietikäinen, Sari and Helen Kelly-Holmes, 2011. 'The local political economy of languages in a Sámi tourism destination: authenticity and mobility in the labelling of souvenirs'. *Journal of Sociolinguistics* 15: 323–46.

Plichta, Bartlomiej and Brad Rakerd, 2010. 'Pereceptions of /a/ fronting across two Michigan dialects'. In Dennis R. Preston and Nancy Niedzielski (eds), *A Reader in Sociophonetics*. New York: De Gruyter Mouton. 223–39.

Podesva, Robert J., 2007. 'Phonation type as a stylistic variable: the use of falsetto in constructing a persona'. *Journal of Sociolinguistics* 11: 478–504.

Pope, Jennifer, Miriam Meyerhoff and D. Robert Ladd, 2007. 'Forty years of language change on Martha's Vineyard'. *Language* 83: 615–27.

Poplack, Shana, 1980. 'Sometimes I'll start a sentence in Spanish Y TERMINO EN ESPAÑOL: toward a typology of code-switching'. *Linguistics* 18: 581–618.

Poplack, Shana (ed.), 2000. *The English History of African American English*. Malden, MA: Blackwell Publishers.

Porcel, Jorgen, 2006. 'The paradox of Spanish among Miami Cubans'. *Journal of Sociolinguistics* 10: 93–110.

Precht, Kristen, 2008. 'Sex similarities and differences in stance in informal American conversation'. *Journal of Sociolinguistics* 12: 89–111.

Preston, Dennis R., 1996. 'Where the worst English is spoken'. In Edgar W. Schneider (ed.), *Varieties of English around the World: Focus on the USA*. Amsterdam: John Benjamins. 297–360.

Preston, Dennis R. (ed.), 1999. *Handbook of Perceptual Dialectology* (vol. 1). Amsterdam: John Benjamins.

Preston, Dennis R., 2010. 'Belle's body just caught the fit gnat: the perception of Northern Cities shifted vowels by local speakers'. In Dennis R. Preston and Nancy Niedzielski (eds), *A Reader in Sociophonetics*. New York: De Gruyter Mouton. 241–52.

Preston, Dennis R. and Nancy Niedzielski (eds), 2010. *A Reader in Sociophonetics*. New York: De Gruyter Mouton.

Pujolar i Cos, Joan, 1997. 'Masculinities in a multilingual setting'. In Sally Johnson and Ulrike Hanna Meinhof (eds), *Language and Masculinity*. Oxford, UK: Blackwell Publishers. 86–106.

Quirk, Randolph, 1990. 'Language varieties and standard language'. *English Today* 6: 3–10.

Quist, Pia and Bente A. Svendsen (eds), 2010. *Multilingual Urban Scandinavia: New Linguistic Practices*. Bristol, UK: Multilingual Matters.

Rampton, Ben, 1995. *Crossing: Language and Ethnicity among Adolescents*. London: Longman.

Rampton, Ben, 2006. *Language in Late Modernity: Interaction in an Urban School*. Cambridge: Cambridge University Press.

Rampton, Ben, 2009. 'Speech community and beyond'. In Nikolas Coupland and Adam Jaworski (eds), *The New Sociolinguistics Reader*. Basingstoke, UK: Palgrave Macmillan. 694–713.

Rees-Miller, Janie, 2011. 'Compliments revisited: contemporary compliments and gender'. *Journal of Pragmatics* 43: 2673–88.

Reyes, Angela, 2005. 'Appropriation of African American slang by Asian American youth'. Journal of Sociolinguistics 9: 509–32.

Ricento, Thomas (ed.), 2006. *An Introduction to Language Policy: Theory and Method*. Malden, MA: Blackwell Publishing.

Rickford, John R., 1986. 'The need for new approaches to social class analysis in sociolinguistics'. *Language & Communication* 6: 215–21.

Rickford, John R., 1998. 'The creole origins of African-American Vernacular English: evidence from copula absence'. In Salikoko S. Mufwene, John R. Rickford, Guy Bailey and John Baugh (eds), *African-American English: Structure, History, and Use*. London: Routledge. 154–200.

Rickford, John R., 1999. 'The Ebonics controversy in my backyard: a sociolinguist's experiences and reflections'. *Journal of Sociolinguistics* 3: 267–75.

Rickford, John R. and Faye McNair-Knox, 1994. 'Addressee- and topic-influenced style shift: a quantitative sociolinguistic study'. In Douglas Biber and Edward Finegan (eds), *Sociolinguistic Perspectives on Register*. New York: Oxford University Press. 235–76.

Rickford, John Russell and Russell John Rickford, 2000. *Spoken Soul: The Story of Black English*. New York: John Wiley.

Ricoeur, Paul, 1981. *Paul Ricoeur: Hermeneutics and the Human Sciences – Essays on Language, Action and Interpretation* (ed. and trans. John B. Thompson). Cambridge: Cambridge University Press; and Paris, France: Éditions de la Maison des Sciences de l'Homme.

Rindstedt, Camilla and Karin Aronsson, 2002. 'Growing up monolingual in a bilingual community: the Quichua revitalization paradox'. *Language in Society* 31: 721–42.

Robinson, W. Peter and Howard Giles (eds), 2001. *The New Handbook of Language and Social Psychology*. Chichester, UK: John Wiley.

Robinson, W. Peter and Abigail Locke, 2011. 'The social psychology of language: a short history'. In Rajend Mesthrie (ed.), *The Cambridge Handbook of Sociolinguistics*. Cambridge: Cambridge University Press. 47–69.

Romaine, Suzanne, 1995. *Bilingualism* (2nd edn). Oxford, UK: Blackwell Publishers.

Romaine, Suzanne, 2004. 'The bilingual and multilingual community'. In Tej K. Bhatia and William C. Ritchie (eds), *The Handbook of Bilingualism*. Malden, MA: Blackwell Publishing. 385–405.

Roth-Gordon, Jennifer, 2007. 'Youth, slang, and pragmatic expressions: examples from Brazilian Portuguese'. *Journal of Sociolinguistics* 11: 322–45.

Rowe, Charley and Eva L. Wyss (eds), 2009. *Language and New Media: Linguistic, Cultural and Technological Evolutions*. Cresskill, NJ: Hampton Press.

Rubin, Joan, 1968. 'Bilingual usage in Paraguay'. In Joshua A. Fishman (ed.), *Readings in the Sociology of Language*. The Hague: Mouton. 512–30.

Salisbury, R.F., 1962. 'Notes on bilingualism and linguistic change in New Guinea'. *Anthropological Linguistics* 4/7: 1–13.

Sankoff, David and Suzanne Laberge, 1978. 'The linguistic market and the statistical explanation of variability'. In David Sankoff (ed.), *Linguistic Variation: Models and Methods*. New York: Academic Press. 239–50.

Sankoff, Gillian, 2006. 'Age: apparent time and real time'. In Keith Brown (ed.), *Encyclopedia of Language and Linguistics* (2nd edn), vol. 1. Oxford, UK: Elsevier. 110–16.

Sankoff, Gillian and Hélène Blondeau, 2007. 'Language change across the lifespan: /r/ in Montreal French'. *Language* 83: 560–88.

Sankoff, Gillian and Suzanne Laberge, 1980. 'On the acquisition of native speakers by a language'. In Gillian Sankoff (ed.), *The Social Life of Language*. Philadelphia, PA: University of Pennsylvania Press. 195–209.

Saville-Troike, Muriel, 2003. *The Ethnography of Communication: An Introduction* (3rd edn). Malden, MA: Blackwell.

Schieffelin, Bambi B. and Paul B. Garrett (eds), 2011. *Anthropological Linguistics (Critical Concepts in Language Studies)*, 5 vols. London: Routledge.

Schieffelin, Bambi B., Kathryn A. Woolard and Paul V. Kroskrity (eds), 1998. *Language Ideologies: Practice and Theory*. New York: Oxford University Press.

Schiffrin, Deborah, 1987. *Discourse Markers*. Cambridge: Cambridge University Press.

Schilling, Natalie, 2011. 'Language, gender and sexuality'. In Rajend Mesthrie (ed.), *The Cambridge Handbook of Sociolinguistics*. Cambridge: Cambridge University Press. 218–37.

Schilling-Estes, Natalie. 1998. 'Investigating "self-conscious" speech: the performance register in Ocracoke English'. *Language in Society* 27: 53–83.

Schilling-Estes, Natalie, 2004. 'Constructing ethnicity in interaction'. *Journal of Sociolinguistics* 8: 163–95.

Schmid, Monika S. and Kees de Bot, 2004. 'Language attrition'. In Alan Davies and Catherine Elder (eds), *The Handbook of Applied Linguistics*. Malden, MA: Blackwell Publishing. 210–34.

Schmidt, Annette, 1985. *Young People's Dyirbal: An Example of Language Death from Australia*. Cambridge: Cambridge University Press.

Schneider, Edgar W., 2003. 'The dynamics of new Englishes: from identity construction to dialect birth'. *Language* 79: 233–81.

Schneider, Edgar W., 2007. *Postcolonial English: Varieties around the World*. Cambridge: Cambridge University Press.

Scollon, Ron and Suzanne Scollon, 1981. *Narrative, Literacy and Face in Interethnic Communication*. Norwood, NJ: Ablex.

Scollon, Ron and Suzanne Wong Scollon, 2001. *Intercultural Communication: A Discourse Approach* (2nd edn). Malden, MA: Blackwell Publishers.

Scollon, Ron and Suzanne Wong Scollon, 2003. *Discourses in Place: Language in the Material World*. London: Routledge.

Sealey, Alison and Bob Carter, 2004. *Applied Linguistics as Social Science*. London: Continuum.

Searle, John R., 1969. *Speech Acts: An Essay in the Philosophy of Language*. Cambridge: Cambridge University Press.

Searle, John R., 1976. 'A classification of illocutionary acts'. *Language in Society* 5: 1–23.

Shepard, Carolyn A., Howard Giles and Beth A. Le Poire, 2001. 'Communication Accommodation Theory'. In W. Peter Robinson and Howard Giles (eds), *The New Handbook of Language and Social Psychology*. Chichester, UK: Wiley. 33–56.

Shohamy, Elana, Eliezer Ben-Rafael and Monica Barni (eds), 2010. *Linguistic Landscape in the City*. Bristol, UK: Multilingual Matters.

Shuy, Roger W., Walt Wolfram and William K. Riley, 1968. *A Study of Social Dialects in Detroit*. Washington, DC: Educational Resources Information Center.

Siegel, Jeff, 2008. *The Emergence of Pidgin and Creole Languages*. Oxford: Oxford University Press.

Silverstein, Michael, 1979. 'Language structure and linguistic ideology'. In Paul R. Clyne, William F. Hanks and Carol L. Hofbauer (eds), *The Elements: A Parasession on Linguistic Units and Levels*. Chicago, IL: Chicago Linguistic Society. 193–247.

Silverstein, Michael, 2003. 'Indexical order and the dialectics of sociolinguistic life'. *Language & Communication* 23: 193–229.

Singler, John Victor, 1996. 'Theories of creole genesis, sociohistorical considerations, and the evaluation of evidence: the case of Haitian Creole and the Relexification Hypothesis'. *Journal of Pidgin and Creole Languages* 11: 185–230.

Skutnabb-Kangas, Tove and Sertaç Bucak, 1994. 'Killing a mother tongue – how the Kurds are deprived of linguistic human rights'. In Tove Skutnabb-Kangas, Robert Phillipson and Mart Rannut (eds), *Linguistic Human Rights: Overcoming Linguistic Discrimination*. Berlin: Mouton de Gruyter. 347–70.

Skutnabb-Kangas, Tove and Robert Phillipson (eds), 1994. *Linguistic Human Rights: Overcoming Linguistic Discrimination*. Berlin: Mouton de Gruyter.

Snow, Don, 2010. 'Hong Kong and modern diglossia'. *International Journal of the Sociology of Language* 206: 155–79.

Spolsky, Bernard, 2003. 'Reassessing Māori regeneration'. *Language in Society* 32: 553–78.

Spolsky, Bernard, 2004. *Language Policy*. Cambridge: Cambridge University Press.

Spolsky, Bernard (ed.), 2012. *The Cambridge Handbook of Language Policy*. Cambridge: Cambridge University Press.

Starks, Donna, Ray Harlow and Allan Bell, 2005. 'Who speaks what language in New Zealand'. In Allan Bell, Ray Harlow and Donna Starks (eds), *Languages of New Zealand*. Wellington, New Zealand: Victoria University Press. 13–29.

Strand, Thea R., 2012. 'Winning the dialect popularity contest: mass-mediated language ideologies and local responses in rural Valdres, Norway'. *Journal of Linguistic Anthropology* 22: 23–43.

Stuart-Smith, Jane, 2011. 'The view from the couch: changing perspectives on the role of television in changing language ideologies and use'. In Tore Kristiansen and Nikolas Coupland (eds), *Standard Languages and Language Standards in a Changing Europe*. Oslo, Norway: Novus. 223–39.

Tagliamonte, Sali A., 2006. *Analyzing Sociolinguistic Variation*. Cambridge: Cambridge University Press.

Tagliamonte, Sali A., 2012. *Variationist Sociolinguistics: Change, Observation, Interpretation*. Malden, MA: Wiley-Blackwell.

Tannen, Deborah, 1984. *Conversational Style: Analyzing Talk among Friends*. Norwood, NJ: Ablex.

Tannen, Deborah, 1986. 'Introducing constructed dialogue in Greek and American conversational and literary narrative'. In Florian Coulmas (ed.), *Direct and Indirect Speech*. Berlin: Mouton de Gruyter. 311–32.

Tannen, Deborah, 1990. *You Just Don't Understand: Women and Men in Conversation*. New York: William Morrow.

Tannen, Deborah, 1994. *Talking from 9 to 5: Women and Men at Work – Language, Sex and Power*. New York: William Morrow.

Taumoefolau, Melenaite, Donna Starks, Karen Davis and Allan Bell, 2002. 'Linguists and language maintenance: Pasifika languages in Manukau, New Zealand'. *Oceanic Linguistics* 41: 15–27.

Te Puni Kōkiri, 2008a. *Te Oranga o te Reo Māori 2006/The Health of the Māori Language in 2006*. Wellington, New Zealand: Te Puni Kōkiri.

Te Puni Kōkiri, 2008b. *Te Oranga o te Reo Māori i te Rāngai Pāpāho 2006/The Health of the Māori Language in the Broadcasting Sector 2006*. Wellington, New Zealand: Te Puni Kōkiri.

Thomason, Sarah G., 2001. *Language Contact: An Introduction*. Edinburgh: Edinburgh University Press.

Thomason, Sarah G. and Terrence Kaufman, 1988. *Language Contact, Creolization, and Genetic Linguistics*. Berkeley, CA: University of California Press.

Thurlow, Crispin and Adam Jaworski, 2010. *Tourism Discourse: Language and Global Mobility*. Basingstoke, UK: Palgrave Macmillan.

Thurlow, Crispin and Kristine Mroczek (eds), 2011. *Digital Discourse: Language in the New Media*. New York: Oxford University Press.

Tosco, Mauro, 2008. 'Introduction: *Ausbau* is everywhere!' *International Journal of the Sociology of Language* 191: 1–16.

Trudgill, Peter, 1972. 'Sex, covert prestige and linguistic change'. *Language in Society* 1: 179–96.

Trudgill, Peter, 1974. *The Social Differentiation of English in Norwich*. London: Cambridge University Press.

Trudgill, Peter, 1981. 'Linguistic accommodation: sociolinguistic observations on a sociopsychological theory'. In C.S. Masek, R.A. Hendrick and M.F. Miller (eds), *Papers from the Parasession on Language and Behavior*. Chicago, IL: Chicago Linguistic Society. 218–37.

Trudgill, Peter, 1983. *On Dialect: Social and Geographical Perspectives*. Oxford, UK: Basil Blackwell.

Trudgill, Peter, 1986. *Dialects in Contact*. Oxford, UK: Basil Blackwell.

Trudgill, Peter, 2004. *New-dialect Formation: The Inevitability of Colonial Englishes*. Edinburgh: Edinburgh University Press.

Trudgill, Peter, 2008. 'Colonial dialect contact in the history of European languages: on the irrelevance of identity to new-dialect formation'. *Language in Society* 37: 241–54.

Trudgill, Peter, Elizabeth Gordon and Gillian Lewis, 1998. 'New-dialect formation and Southern Hemisphere English: the New Zealand short front vowels'. *Journal of Sociolinguistics* 2: 35–51.

Tryon, Darrell T. and Jean-Michel Charpentier, 2004. *Pacific Pidgins and Creoles: Origins, Growth and Development*. Berlin: Mouton de Gruyter.

Urry, John, 2007. *Mobilities*. Cambridge, UK: Polity Press.

van Bezooijen, Renée and Vincent J. van Heuven, 2010. 'Avant-garde Dutch: a perceptual, acoustic, and evaluational study'. In Dennis R. Preston and Nancy Niedzielski (eds), *A Reader in Sociophonetics*. New York: De Gruyter Mouton. 357–78.

van Dijk, Teun A., 2009. *Society and Discourse: How Social Contexts Influence Text and Talk*. Cambridge: Cambridge University Press.

Veenstra, Tonjes, 2008. 'Creole genesis: the impact of the Language Bioprogram Hypothesis'. In Siliva Kouwenberg and John Victor Singler (eds), *The Handbook of Pidgin and Creole Studies*. Oxford, UK: Wiley-Blackwell. 219–41.

Vetter, Eva, 2011. 'Social network'. In Ruth Wodak, Barbara Johnstone and Paul Kerswill (eds), *The Sage Handbook of Sociolinguistics*. London: Sage. 208–18.

Vigouroux, Cécile B., 2010. 'Double-mouthed discourse: interpreting, framing and participant roles'. *Journal of Sociolinguistics* 14: 341–69.

Voloshinov, V.N. 1973 [1929]. *Marxism and the Philosophy of Language*. New York: Seminar Press.

von Sternberg, Josef, 1966. *Fun in a Chinese Laundry*. London: Secker & Warburg.

Wagner, Suzanne Evans and Gillian Sankoff, 2011. 'Age grading in the Montréal French inflected future'. *Language Variation and Change* 23: 275–313.

Wald, Benji and Timothy Shopen, 1981. 'A researcher's guide to the sociolinguistic variable (ING)'. In Timothy Shopen and Joseph M. Williams (eds), *Style and Variables in English*. Cambridge, MA: Winthrop. 219–49.

Watts, Richard J., 2003. *Politeness*. Cambridge: Cambridge University Press.

Watts, Richard J. and Peter Trudgill (eds), 2002. *Alternative Histories of English*. London: Routledge.

Wee, Lionel, 2006. 'The semiotics of language ideologies in Singapore'. *Journal of Sociolinguistics* 10: 344–61.

Wee, Lionel, 2010. '"Burdens" and "handicaps" in Singapore's language policy: on the limits of language management'. *Language Policy* 9: 97–114.

Weinreich, Uriel, 1953. *Languages in Contact: Findings and Problems*. The Hague: Mouton.

Weinreich, Uriel, William Labov and Marvin I. Herzog, 1968. 'Empirical foundations for a theory of language change'. In W.P. Lehmann and Yakov Malkiel (eds), *Directions for Historical Linguistics: A Symposium*. Austin, TX: Texas University Press. 95–188.

Wells, J.C., 1982. *Accents of English I: An Introduction*. Cambridge: Cambridge University Press.

West, Candace, and Don H. Zimmerman, 1983. 'Small insults: a study of interruptions in cross-sex conversations between unacquainted persons'. In Barrie Thorne, Cheris Kramarae and Nancy Henley (eds), *Language, Gender and Society*. Rowley, MA: Newbury House. 102–17.

Wiese, Heike, 2009. 'Grammatical innovation in multiethnic urban Europe: new linguistic practices among adolescents'. *Lingua* 119: 782–806.

Williams, Glyn, 1992. *Sociolinguistics: A Sociological Critique*. London: Routledge.

Winford, Donald, 2003. *An Introduction to Contact Linguistics*. Malden, MA: Blackwell Publishing.

Wodak, Ruth, Barbara Johnstone and Paul Kerswill (eds), 2011. *The Sage Handbook of Sociolinguistics*. London: Sage.

Wolfram, Walt A., 1969. *A Sociolinguistic Description of Detroit Negro Speech*. Washington, DC: Center for Applied Linguistics.

Wolfram, Walt, 1998. 'Scrutinizing linguistic gratuity: issues from the field'. *Journal of Sociolinguistics* 2: 271–9.

Wolfram, Walt and Natalie Schilling-Estes, 1995. 'Moribund dialects and the endangerment canon: the case of the Ocracoke Brogue'. *Language* 71: 696–721.

Wolfram, Walt and Natalie Schilling-Estes, 1997. *Hoi Toide on the Outer Banks: The Story of the Ocracoke Brogue*. Chapel Hill, NC: University of North Carolina Press.

Wolfram, Walt and Natalie Schilling-Estes, 2006. *American English: Dialects and Variation* (2nd edn). Malden, MA: Blackwell Publishing.

Wolfson, Nessa and Joan Manes (eds), 1985. *Language of Inequality*. Berlin: Walter de Gruyter.

Woolard, Kathryn A., 1985. 'Language variation and cultural hegemony: toward an integration of sociolinguistic and social theory'. *American Ethnologist* 12: 738–48.

Woolard, Kathryn A., 1998. 'Introduction: Language ideology as a field of inquiry'. In Bambi B. Schieffelin, Kathryn A. Woolard and Paul V. Kroskrity (eds), *Language Ideologies: Practice and Theory*. New York: Oxford University Press. 3–47.

Woolard, Kathryn A., 1999. 'Simultaneity and bivalency as strategies in bilingualism'. *Journal of Linguistic Anthropology* 8: 3–29.

Woolard, Kathryn A. and E. Nicholas Genovese, 2007. 'Strategic bivalency in Latin and Spanish in early modern Spain'. *Language in Society* 36: 487–509.

Wray, Alison and Aileen Bloomer, 2012. *Projects in Linguistics and Language Studies* (3rd edn). London: Hodder Education.

Yaeger-Dror, Malcah, 1993. 'Linguistic analysis of dialect "correction" and its interaction with cognitive salience'. *Language Variation and Change* 5: 189–224.

Yagmur, Kutlay and Martin Ehala, 2011. 'Tradition and innovation in the Ethnolinguistic Vitality theory'. *Journal of Multilingual and Multicultural Development* 32: 101–10.

Zhang, Qing, 2005. 'A Chinese yuppie in Beijing: phonological variation and the construction of a new professional identity'. *Language in Society* 34: 431–66.

Zilles, Ana M.S., 2005. 'The development of a new pronoun: the linguistic and social embedding of *a gente* in Brazilian Portuguese'. *Language Variation and Change* 17: 19–53.

INDEX

AAVE *see* African American Vernacular
    English
accents of English 203, 208, 223, 260, 281
    ethnic 178, 260
    evaluation of 260–261
    non-native 1, 239, 259, 311–314
    prestige/standard 207, 274–275
    stigmatized 179, 264
    see also Received Pronunciation
accommodation 198, 207, 301–302, 307, 325
acrolect 83
address systems 133
addressee 133, 135, 136, 140–142, 144,
    154–155
    see also audience
addressee-oriented tags 152–153
addressor 135, 136, 139
adstrate 175, 179
advertisements 69, 140, 240
Africa 23, 52, 77, 260, 279
African American Vernacular English 50, 84,
    172, 175, 176–178, 190, 191, 300
    features of 152, 169
    styling of 300, 303, 305–307, 309, 315
African languages 79, 81, 89, 105, 109
Afrikaans 4, 103
age 195–200
age grading of language 56, 197–199,
    201–203, 211, 223

agency 219–221
    see also structure
Agha, A. 269, 274–276, 313–314
Alaska 59, 85
alternation and co-occurrence 133
American English 51, 133, 196, 208, 230, 232,
    236–237, 245, 251, 287, 297
American Sign Language (ASL) 210–211,
    256
Amish people 47
Anglo-Romani 91
animator 138–139, 155
anthropological linguistics *see* linguistic
    anthropology
anthropology 7, 9–10, 131, 255, 327
    social 32, 134
Aotearoa 62, 229
    see also New Zealand
apparent time 200–204, 223, 224
applied linguistics 6, 12, 26, 329
appropriation of language 305, 315, 317
Arabic 5, 26, 77, 109–111, 215, 240, 250
    Classical 49, 109, 215
Argentina 105, 179
Arvanitika 259
Athabaskans 137
Atlantic Ocean 77, 95, 237
atlas, linguistic 99, 230, 235, 251
attention to speech 270, 295, 297, 318

The Guidebook to Sociolinguistics, First Edition. Allan Bell.
© 2014 Allan Bell. Published 2014 by Blackwell Publishing Ltd.

Made in the USA
Lexington, KY
24 August 2019